Yuchi Ceremonial Life

Studies in the Anthropology of
North American Indians

JASON BAIRD JACKSON

Yucchi Ceremonial Life

Performance, Meaning, and Tradition in a Contemporary American Indian Community

With an afterword by the author

University of Nebraska Press
Lincoln and London

In cooperation with the
American Indian Studies
Research Institute, Indiana
University, Bloomington

A version of chapter 5 appeared in volume 57 of *Southern Folklore* (2000). It is used here with permission.

Manufactured in the United States of America
∞
First Nebraska paperback printing: 2005
Library of Congress Cataloging-in-Publication Data
Jackson, Jason Baird, 1969– Yuchi Ceremonial life: performance, meaning, and tradition in a contemporary American Indian community / Jason Baird Jackson. – 1st Nebraska pbk. print.
p. cm. – (Studies in the anthropology of North American Indians)
Originally published in 2003. With new afterword.
Includes bibliographical references and index.
ISBN-13: 978-0-8032-7628-4 (pbk.: alk. paper)
ISBN-10: 0-8032-7628-1 (pbk.: alk. paper)
1. Yuchi Indians – Rites and ceremonies.
2. Yuchi dance.
3. Speeches, addresses, etc., Yuchi.
I. Title. II. Series.
E99.Y9J33 2005
299.7'89 – dc22
2005011393

This work is dedicated to the memory of Chief Felix Brown, Sr., Chief James Brown, Sr., and Ceremonial Ground Speaker Jimmie Skeeter.

Proceeds from the sale of this book will be given to the Yuchi chiefs and their officers to support the ongoing activities of the Yuchi ceremonial grounds.

CONTENTS

ILLUSTRATIONS

MAPS

TABLES

Yuchi/Euchee

A Note on Usage

Outsiders have known the Tsoyaha ("Descendants of the Sun") by a great many names. Over the last few centuries, the name Yuchi has become the most common of those, but this term has been spelled in a wide variety of ways (Uchee, Uchi, Euchee, Yutci, etc.). Today two spellings are in active use in the community. Many people prefer the form "Euchee," which gained widespread use in Oklahoma because it was the spelling associated with the now defunct Euchee Mission Boarding School in the town of Sapulpa. A significant number of Yuchi people attended this school during its years of operation. The spelling "Yuchi" was established by anthropologist Albert S. Gatschet, who used it in an 1893 publication. This version of the name has become the standard spelling in American Indian scholarship, but it is also used in the community itself (see "Yuchi Tribal Organization," chapter 2). The Euchee (Yuchi) Tribe of Indians, with whom I have collaborated extensively, has recognized this diversity of use in the name that they chose for their organization. The convention of placing an alternative tribal name or spelling parenthetically within an official tribal name is found among other Native groups in Oklahoma, most significantly in the name of the Muscogee (Creek) Nation.

In working with me as well as with other outsiders, the Yuchi people have sought to achieve the very practical goal of obtaining greater recognition of their little-known community and its distinct culture and history. To facilitate this, I have retained the spelling "Yuchi." My purpose in this is to avoid the creation of new confusion within the academic literature. My broader goal is to make clear that the Yuchi of today and the Yuchi communities studied by scholars in centuries past are the same people. Through changing times, the Yuchi of today keep alive the same cultural practices, social norms, and historical traditions studied by my own predecessors.

A Note on Transcription

For my studies of Yuchi culture and society, a primary source of insight is public oratories delivered at the Yuchi ceremonial grounds. For this reason, texts of such performances play a prominent role in this work. As practiced today, the Yuchi oratory genre is marked by short phrases separated by breath pauses, similar to what Wallace Chafe, discussing Seneca oratory, has called "intonation units" (1993). This more staccato-like prosody differentiates oratory from conversational styles and, for Yuchi listeners, lends it a poetic quality. In transcribing such speeches, I have followed ethnopoetic convention and treated such breath-marked units as lines (Tedlock 1983, 1992). In most of the texts presented in this work, sentences extending over more than one line are grouped and indented after the initial line. As readers will discern, sentence boundaries are approximate. Increased volume is indicated with the use of capital letters. Emphatic lengthening is marked with spaces between letters. Hesitations and truncated words are marked with a dash. Native language words appear in italics. Syllabic pronunciation is indicated by dashes between the syllables. Double parentheses enclose a best guess of an only partially audible word or passage. Square brackets contain implied information or editorial comments. Double angled brackets contain extralinguistic features such as laughter.

This same system of presentation is adapted to varying degrees in my transcriptions of other forms of Yuchi spoken discourse. The format chosen for texts differs depending on their relationship to the surrounding argument in this work, on the basis of its length and degree of formality, and in response to the goal of clarity in presentation. This variation means that some spoken material is presented in block quotation, while other texts are presented in variations of the ethnopoetic format used for oratory.

Orthography

The small amount of Yuchi language material presented in this work is given in the orthography developed by Mary Linn in consultation with present-day Yuchi speakers. For more information on the Yuchi language, readers are directed to Linn's grammar of Yuchi together with various published essays (1996, 1997, 2001). Yuchi has both oral and nasal vowels. Except for text 12, which follows the convention used in Jackson and Linn (2000), nasalized vowels are marked with a tilde. An apostrophe indicates a glottal stop.

Acknowledgments

The Yuchi, like many North American Indian communities, are elder-centric. In North American popular culture, the term *elder* itself seems to be defined by reference to images of American Indian community and family life. In small communities governed by consensus, deference to elders, among its various functions, helps younger people save face and avoid public embarrassment. All of the Yuchi people whom I have met deserve my deepest thanks for allowing me to enter into, and participate in, the life of a community that is not my own. Any attempt on my part to name all of the people who have touched this work and my life would end in embarrassment better avoided. Such a listing is impossible. Instead, I single out here those community elders who have made my experiences in Oklahoma possible. Each should be seen, the way Yuchi people do, as representatives of extended families and community institutions. In thanking them publicly, I am also thanking their families and constituencies.

As officers of the Euchee (Yuchi) Tribe of Indians, Chiefs Felix Brown, Sr. (Duck Creek), James Brown, Sr. (Polecat), and Wade Bucktrot, Jr. (Sand Creek), together with then Assistant Chief (now Chief) Simon Harry (Duck Creek) and Speakers Jimmie Skeeter (Duck Creek) and Newman Littlebear (Polecat), first gave approval for me to conduct work among the Yuchi ceremonial ground people. As the primary ritual leaders of their people, all of these men also served as my teachers in the realm of Yuchi ceremonial ground customs and beliefs. As will be evident throughout this work, Newman Littlebear has played a crucial role as the formal speaker for the current Yuchi chiefs. This importance is reflected in this book, and I am especially grateful for the many hours that he and I have spent together on the back roads of eastern Oklahoma.

This work is admittedly biased toward male experiences and understandings of Yuchi ritual life, yet many Yuchi women have extended me every kindness. Mary Watashe, the head woman dancer at the Polecat ground, has been generous in opening her family circle to me. Her counterpart at the Duck Creek ground, Ester Littlebear, has always had a kind word for me and has regularly been brave enough to "shake shells" for me in the sleepy hours before sunrise. Among the many other elders who have helped me understand something of Yuchi life are Josephine Bigler, John D. Brown, Mose Cahwee, William Cahwee, Caroline Harry, Nancy Jo Harry, Virgil Harry, Dorothy Lee, Josephine Madewell, Viola Thomas, Mae Tulsa, Dimmie Washburn, and Henry Washburn. I am grateful to them and to their families.

I owe a particular debt to the families of Jimmie Skeeter and James Brown, Sr. Both families have generously incorporated my wife and me into the life of their ceremonial ground camps. Inclusion in camp life, as the primary expression of family among Yuchi ceremonialists, was a priceless gift that continues to enrich us immeasurably.

Since 1993, I have had the good fortune to regularly attend dances and other celebrations in approximately thirty different Oklahoma Indian communities. Everywhere that I have traveled in Indian Country, I have been accorded boundless hospitality and kindness, for which I am very thankful. I especially appreciate the many friends and acquaintances whom I have made among Oklahoma ceremonial ground people. I especially ask their forgiveness if I have misunderstood something that they have shared with me or if I have erred in my use of published sources dealing with their communities.

In developing permanent personal ties and scholarly relationships with Yuchi people, I was fortunate to be the beneficiary of various forms of financial support. From 1995 to 1997, generous aid for aspects of this work was provided by The Wenner-Gren Foundation, The Jacobs Fund of the Whatcom Museum Society, The Phillips Fund for Native American Research of the American Philosophical Society, The Central States Anthropological Society, and the Graduate School and College of Arts and Sciences at Indiana University. A Summer Fieldwork Grant from the David C. Skomp Fund of the Department of Anthropology at Indiana University supported a preliminary visit to Oklahoma in 1993. A 1997 exhibition development grant awarded jointly to The Thomas Gilcrease Museum Association and Euchees United Cultural, Historical, and Educational Efforts (E.U.C.H.E.E.) by The Fund For Folk Culture, with funds provided by the Lila Wallace-Reader's Digest Community Folklife Program, enabled me to continue collaborative work documenting traditional Yuchi culture, while inquiring with my collaborators into what labels such as traditional or "folk culture" might mean. Study of Yuchi music, undertaken with Victoria Levine during 1998 and 1999, with support from the Gerald and Corrine Parsons Fund of the Library of Congress, has further enriched the store of experiences that I draw upon in this work. All of these agencies have given me the opportunity to remain active in Yuchi community life for an extended period, expanding my understanding of both the content and responsibilities of Yuchi tradition.

Just as the content of my notebooks and interview tapes is a pale reflection of the full richness of the cultural and social life that Yuchi people have shared with me, my experiences as a student in the Department of Anthropology and the Folklore Institute at Indiana University have a value for me beyond words. One of the most fortunate occurrences in my life was Raymond DeMallie allowing me to become an apprentice in his vital and crowded workshop. For this, and for his continued friendship, guidance, and encouragement, I am most grateful. The amount of time and energy that he expends in the service of his students and colleagues is remarkable. Also at Indiana University, Professors Richard Bauman, Geoffrey Conrad, David Dinwoodie, Henry Glassie, Carol Greenhouse, Douglas Parks, and Christopher Peebles all provided intellectual encouragement and personal courtesy beyond the expectations of even a naive graduate student. For their investment in my development, and their interest in my projects, I am thankful. I am equally appreciative of my circle of classmates at Indiana. From these fellow students turned colleagues, I have learned much.

One of the great gifts that my teachers at Indiana gave to me was an introduction into a larger community of scholars who have had a deep impact on my development as a scholar and as a person. Among these many colleagues, I especially must thank those who have taken a specific interest in assisting me with this project: Karen Blu, Erika Brady, Raymond Bucko, Gary Dunham, Raymond D. Fogelson, Morris Foster, Pam Innes, Victoria Levine, Ann McMullen, Jack Martin, Jay Miller, William Sturtevant, Joan Thomas, Jim Rementer, Gloria Young, and James VanStone. None among this gifted group are responsible for the particular uses that I made of their own field materials or advice.

My friend Daniel Swan, Senior Curator at the Gilcrease Museum, deserves my gratitude both for providing me an institutional home and for serving as my primary source of professional encouragement in Tulsa. Our discussions of Indian country and anthropology, together with our collaborations at the museum, have been a high point of my professional life in Oklahoma.

Work among the Yuchi has also brought me into contact with other scholars who have collaborated with them on various projects. Linguist W. L. Ballard generously provided me with materials from his files. Mary Linn and Pamela Wallace were both fellow doctoral students working with the Yuchi during the 1990s. They have come to define for me the spirit of collaboration. Both have shared many experiences with me and both have been generous in sharing their own ideas and findings. Mary's work on documenting the Yuchi language, and Pam's studies of genealogy and political history, complement this study, and, like me, they have sought to make their work useful to the Yuchi.

I owe a well-deserved expression of thanks to my family for their personal support and their encouragement of my work as a folklorist and anthropologist. In particular, my wife, Amy, has shared in my adventures and has been a constant source of support during the long years preceding this milepost. Her own relationships with our Yuchi friends are rich and meaningful, and it has been the blessing of my life to share so many wonderful experiences with her. Nothing that I have accomplished in my adult life could have been achieved without her partnership. My parents and brother have always been interested in my work and good-humored about the complexities of academic life. They shaped my anthropological sensibility before I knew what anthropology was.

In an earlier, less self-conscious day, the career histories of anthropology easily could be mapped out atop a culture-area map. In professional shorthand, an anthropologist might speak possessively of "my" people, referring to the tribe, band, or community that provided the focus for his or her ethnographic work. Times, or at least usages, have changed. In my own case, I feel privileged that the Yuchi have been willing to claim me as one of "their" anthropologists. I hope that my Yuchi friends accept this work as a token of my respect for them and for the beliefs and cultural commitments that they hold so dear.

Yuchi Ceremonial Life

Mr. Newman Littlebear (standing left) and Chief Simon Harry (standing right), together with Assistant Chief Felix Brown, Jr. (standing between the first and second row of women) confer with the women of the Duck Creek Ceremonial Ground prior to the performance of the Ribbon Dance during their Green Corn Ceremonial, 20 June 1997. Mr. Littlebear and Chief Harry, together with their deceased colleagues, Chief Felix Brown, Sr., Chief James Brown, Sr. and Mr. Jimmie Skeeter, served as my primary teachers regarding the form and significance of Yuchi ceremonial ground life.

1 Introduction

"To keep history moving . . ."

In this study I am concerned with two obligations that many Yuchi people feel guide the life of their community today. The first of these is longstanding. Each year Yuchi people reenact a complex series of community ceremonies. These ritual occasions embody a range of meanings and, as collective action, they serve to perpetuate the social order that both holds Yuchi people together as a community and links them in wider relationships with other American Indian peoples. This study describes some of the expressive forms, cultural meanings, and social patterns that make up this annual ceremonial progression.

While the obligation to renew these ceremonies each year is a responsibility that Yuchis have felt since the time of their creation as a people, this study relates secondarily to a newer, but growing, concern in Yuchi community life. In the time that I have known them, the Yuchi people have demonstrated an expanding, passionate interest in documenting their own culture and history. Emblematic of this concern is the emergence of the focus group and other research-focused gatherings as institutions in Yuchi community life. Drawing on one such meeting held during the summer of 1997, I present certain remarks made by Newman Littlebear, a Yuchi ceremonial ground orator, a friend, and a principal consultant for the work reported here. Mr. Littlebear's observations were delivered to a group of approximately forty Yuchis assembled during the week separating the two major Yuchi calendrical rituals at the Polecat Ceremonial Ground. Not only were these comments directed to the assembled participants, but a video recording of the proceedings was also made by tribal leaders to archive the discussion. The ceremonial site itself provided the backdrop for Mr. Littlebear's comments.

TEXT 1

Excerpt from comments on Yuchi history and religion delivered by Newman Littlebear as an introduction to a Yuchi community discussion group meeting held at the Polecat Ceremonial Ground, 16 July 1997.

What history we know about . . .
about Yuchi people
it came from the non-Indian
like writing
by interviews and stuff.

So.

That has been helpful
years ago
by them doing that
just as things that are taking place today
like Jason
and Pam [anthropologist Pamela Wallace]
and different ones
in this modern time.

See we're in the modern time
and it's history also.

It is going to come a time when
this day is going to be history
when we may all be gone
just like those elders are gone before us.

And.

We are trying to keep history moving
and have an account of it.

And.

Perhaps what we have
in these works that we're doing
there may be able to come a time when our . . .

  the younger generation
  can refer back
  to something that is useful
  when it comes to this . . .
  this ceremony.

Now if you think . . .
  if you think
  what . . .

Today
  what has the Yuchi got that pertains
  such as this? [*gesturing toward the ceremonial ground*]

Is there anything besides this that
  that our Yuchis have?

I think
  if we just really think, there really isn't . . .
  there isn't nothing.

There isn't nothing [else] that our o l d elders had.

This is what they, we believe, that they first had.

And we're still trying to . . .
  trying to
  go by it
  and continue on
  with what we've learned in our lifetimes.

That's the way it is and that's the way
  it is supposed to be.

Mr. Littlebear's comments link clearly the two obligations that I am describing – to perpetuate Yuchi ceremonies and create a useful record of their form, meaning, and history. This linkage also combines those themes in a way that Yuchi people feel is very important. For those Yuchi involved in ceremonial ground ritual, those practices are the primary warrant for their assertion of a distinct Yuchi identity.

Although anthropologists and others familiar with Yuchi culture and history have noted and recorded their distinct existence for over one hundred years, the Yuchi constantly face denials of their status as a people. Despite the preservation of their unique language and social order, Yuchi people have been externally constituted as *Creek* for over two hundred years. At the time of removal from the Southeast to Indian Territory in the 1830s, the Yuchi were in political alliance with the towns of the Muskogee (Creek) confederacy, in the area of the present-day states of Georgia and Alabama. Since this period, the governments of the Muscogee (Creek) Nation have politically subsumed the Yuchi. In the eyes of United States federal Indian policy, the Yuchi do not exist. They are Creeks. Added to this lack of federal recognition is unwillingness on the part of the Creek national government to accord any special recognition to the contemporary Yuchi community.

This lack of recognition may seem to relate only to problems of identity, but it has far-reaching practical consequences. As a politically disadvantaged minority within the Creek Nation, the Yuchi do not have access to mechanisms of sovereign government that afford other American Indian groups a minimal ability to protect their interests within the larger national political arena. Federal repatriation law provides one example of that issue. As the federally recognized tribal government delivering services to Yuchi people, the Creek national government is responsible for consulting with federal agencies and other repositories possessing Yuchi archaeological materials covered under the 1990 Native American Graves Protection and Repatriation Act. Despite the fact that the Yuchi have been affiliated with the Creek for only the last two centuries of a much longer history, the Creek possess the right to speak on behalf of Yuchi people in repatriation deliberations. As of 2000, the Creek Nation has not extended any invitations to Yuchi religious leaders or other Yuchi people to participate in these discussions. Under federal law, as an unrecognized tribe, the Yuchi must rely on the courtesy of museums and other institutions to insist on their inclusion in discussions related to repatriation. Without recourse to any formalized tribal government, the Yuchi are not well positioned to foster such independent collaboration. As the Yuchi do not appear on any list of tribal entities prepared by the Bureau of Indian Affairs, museums and other institutions have no way of knowing that there are Yuchi people interested in learning about existing museum collections. The same frustrating story is narrated by Yuchi people in other domains where the lack of standing as a federally recognized tribal government blocks their efforts at community institution building and cultural preservation.

As Mr. Littlebear's observation makes clear, ceremonial ground ritual life is a prominent factor in the maintenance of a distinct Yuchi community. This explains, in part, the focus of this work. I first met Yuchi people in 1993 during a period in which community members were actively discussing the possibility of obtaining separate federal recognition from the Bureau of Indian Affairs. Such recognition was, and is, theoretically possible because of recognition legislation that was developed and implemented in the late 1970s to enable unrecognized Native communities to establish standing as recognized tribes. This recognition process, which has been widely discussed in connection with the petition efforts of the Lumbee (Blu 1980), Poarch Creek (Paredes 1992), and other groups (Brown 1993), requires petitioning groups to prove their identity as Indians on the basis of three criteria – genealogical descent from members of a previously acknowledged Indian community, continuity in distinct community institutions persisting through time, and indications that the petitioning community retains these measures of sociocultural distinctness in the present. While the essentialism of such legal criteria warrants extended treatment (see Clifford 1988; Silverstein 1996), the Yuchi community quite easily meets these standards of proof.

In order to prepare for such a recognition effort, Yuchi community leaders began seeking outside research assistance during the early 1990s. Following what amounted to a job interview with the ceremonial ground chiefs and officers in the spring of 1993, I was given permission to begin research among the Yuchi in the summer of that year. My explicit task was to begin documenting community oral history. In the process I began learning a great deal more, about both the broader contexts that inform Yuchi community life and the present-day institutions that Yuchi people use to organize their social world.

When I returned to Oklahoma in 1995, activity related to seeking federal acknowledgment had subsided. By this time a petition for recognition had been submitted to the BIA by the Yuchi Tribal Organization, a group with whom I had not had any contact. I had been involved in preparing a research report presenting evidence in support of recognition (Foster et al. 1995), but those issues were not explored, as this petition was eventually rejected on procedural grounds. The ceremonial ground leaders with whom I had established relationships had not been in support of this particular request for recognition because they felt that not enough evidence of community support or documentary materials had been assembled. One of the reasons that those leaders have continued to offer support for my ongoing ethnographic work is the hope that someday, once an adequate amount of documentary evidence (as well as community support and infrastructure) is in place, the recognition effort can be resumed on more solid footing.

In the meantime, since returning to Oklahoma in 1995, I have undertaken further fieldwork exploring the forms and meanings of Yuchi community life, while simultaneously becoming deeply involved in a range of Yuchi community initiatives. Formal projects to which I have sought to contribute include language revitalization programs, children's Yuchi language classes and summer camps, the now annual Euchee Heritage Days festival, and grant writing for these as well as additional projects. While I have sought to make my presence useful in those and other less formal settings, the Yuchi people have generously incorporated me into the everyday life of their community. I have participated in most Yuchi community gatherings since the spring of 1995, including fourteen Green Corn Ceremonies and most other Yuchi ceremonial ground events. During this period (1993; 1995–2000), I also accompanied Yuchi ceremonial ground delegations on their visits to the ceremonies of other Oklahoma Native communities, including events among the Cherokee, Creek, Shawnee, Seminole, Delaware, Miami, and Ottawa. In addition to ceremonial ground activities, I have participated, to varying degrees, in political meetings, workshops, symposia, garage sales, picnics, powwows, festivals, rodeos, Native American Church meetings, sweatlodge ceremonies, Methodist Church events, and other activities that have involved Yuchi people as organizers or participants. In many cases, organizers recruited me to photograph or videotape the activities. It was in this way that my external identity as ethnographer and my community identity as a non-Yuchi participant began to merge into a relatively natural way of engaging in Yuchi cultural life. The richness of my personal relationships with Yuchi people, and my experience of participating in Yuchi life, are in no way adequately expressed in this work or in anything that I have yet written. Some experiences that Yuchi friends have shared with me remain such powerful and personal memories that they will forever remain unarticulated.

The experience of reciprocal involvement – sometimes formal and practical, sometimes academic, sometimes intimate and personal – has been personally rewarding and has enriched my understandings of contemporary Yuchi life. This pattern is characteristic of much ethnographically framed anthropological and linguistic research in Native North American communities today, but it is also a very Yuchi way of organizing the flow of social life (see Wax 1982). That the Yuchi have been successful in their experiment of taming the personalities and channeling the enthusiasms of the young scholars who have presented themselves to the community in recent years is testimony to their ability and confidence as a people.[1]

Through this varied involvement with Yuchi people, I have been exposed to the full breadth of Yuchi life and belief in all its diversity, although this exposure has, of necessity, been uneven. Full participation in Yuchi ceremonial ground life precluded my active involvement in other settings, such as the two

Yuchi Methodist congregations. Perhaps it is needless to say that, in focusing on contemporary ceremonial ground ritual, this work is not a general ethnography of Yuchi society. There are Yuchi people who know little or nothing about ceremonial ground life. There are Yuchi people for whom participation in the Methodist Church is just as traditional a Yuchi activity as is going to a stomp dance. There are Yuchi people who will disagree with much that I say in this work. This is the nature of social life, Yuchi or otherwise. I have no desire to create a prescriptive account of Yuchi tradition or culture. Among the Yuchi people whom I know, language revitalization, funerals, powwows, politics, Christian worship and service, informal networks of friendship and kinship, and for a few, even social drinking, can all provide social space in which Yuchi identity and culture are organized and expressed. In making this disclaimer, I most importantly want to express my view that such activities are not inherently less traditional than ceremonial ground ritual. As I suggest below, tradition is, in part, a feeling that people form and articulate about the significance of their cultural practices. All of these activities have the capacity to make Yuchi life meaningful and to connect Yuchi people to a significant past.

TRADITION

Like many basic concepts in the working lexicon of social science discourse, notions of *tradition* have begun multiplying just as the idea has entered a period of critical reflection and refinement. Some scholars have focused on the ways in which *invented traditions*, such as the ritual surrounding the modern British monarchy, have been used to further the imperial or nationalist aspirations of large, stratified "imagined communities" (Hobsbawm and Ranger 1983; Cannadine 1983; Anderson 1991). Others have focused on the problems that unreflective use of a notion of tradition derived from western cultural experience has posed for the work of anthropology and related fields (Handler and Linnekin 1984). Foremost among these failures is the static image of changelessness that the label "traditional society" evokes. This is a particular problem when such a vision of tradition is coupled with a dichotomous – before and after – view of contact between western and non-western societies, as if history, movement, and change begin with the entrance of Europeans into local social worlds (Sahlins 1993:5). Related has been the use of tradition as a conceptual ideal-type paired with modernity, as if the experience of modernity precluded any connection to a sense of tradition (Abramson 1997; Comaroff and Comaroff 1992).

An inverse reaction to the dilemmas of these "traditional" uses of tradition is found in a varied body of scholarship that has considered the ways in which understandings of tradition are produced in local communities as cultural practices are reified into expressions of identity in the experience of cultural contact. Describing the experience of missionization among the Heiltsuks and other peoples, Michael Harkin writes: "As missionaries present a 'package' of their own culture, in explicit contradistinction to the natives' culture, so the natives begin to think consciously about their own culture and, later, construct a concept of tradition. As culture reaches the higher echelons of consciousness, it becomes both a symbol and an arena for meaningful action" (1997:100–101). This view is compelling and I do think that process of this sort accompany missionization, but I am concerned that here the varieties of modern colonialism are framed as unique culture-contact situations within the context of world history. As Marshall Sahlins notes, "Western peoples have no monopoly on practices of cultural encompassment, nor are they playing with amateurs in the game of 'constructing the other.' Every society known to history is a global society, every culture a cosmological order" (1993:5). If this is so, then self-consciousness of culture, conceptualized as tradition, is not inherently the unique by-product of European imperialism. We have no direct way of knowing if the ancient Yuchi articulated a strong sense of their culture as a tradition, but their presence in the complicated, multiethnic, Mississippian world described by prehistoric archaeologists suggests that this is not an unreasonable hypothesis. Differences in culture and social organization observed archaeologically and ethnohistorically suggest that the mutual "othering" of Creek and Yuchi people has precolonial roots. The grammatical segregation of Yuchi and non-Yuchi persons in the Yuchi language provides even clearer evidence of this othering (Linn 1997).

In this work, I postpone a direct focus on the construction of a general, theoretical definition of tradition and instead begin ethnographically by seeking to learn what modern Yuchi people refer to when they talk about Yuchi culture and Yuchi tradition. To do this, I have looked especially at the ways in which tradition is publicly evoked and explicated by Yuchi community leaders in ongoing community life. Particularly helpful in this task has been the notion of *traditionalization* as developed in Richard Bauman's (1992) work connecting folklore, linguistic anthropology, and related fields. This approach points first to the specific means by which tradition is actualized in public discourse as a context into which particular beliefs and practices are situated. In uncovering the *how* of tradition as a way of talking about culture, a focus on traditionalization provides insights into the nature of authority, cultural reproduction, and the ways in which social life is made meaningful. This ethnographic approach to understanding tradition is especially useful in Native North American contexts. While their cultural and historical circumstances are unique, Yuchi experience resonates with understandings evident in other American Indian communities where tradition provides a key symbol around which the social work of interpreting the past, present, and future is organized (DeMallie 1988).

If an ethnographic approach to tradition and traditionalization requires a general mandate, then such can be found in Henry Glassie's (1995) essay "Tradition." Not wishing to box in a dynamic and interesting concept, Glassie surveys the meaning of tradition, or its local analogs, in a range of cultural settings. This ongoing enterprise leads him to observe that tradition encompasses a range of concerns in varied proportions in different settings. Focusing on individual creativity, it is both the "means for deriving the future from the past" and "volitional, temporal action" (1995:409). Capturing the concerns of those who focus on colonial experience as the midwife of tradition without reducing the world's peoples to the West and the rest, Glassie notes that "tradition is the result of differences among cultures" (1995:409). As a cultural form itself, "tradition can be identified with the products, whether casual or canonical, of historical action, or as the historical axis within creative acts, or as a style of historical construction peculiar to a culture" (1995:409). Glassie frames tradition both as a kind of symbolic resource and as a social process.[2]

The range of inflections that can be attached to local uses of tradition was also the focus of a widely read essay on tradition by Richard Handler and Jocelyn Linnekin (1984). They explore how their own "ethnographic materials offer a range of representations of tradition, from the most self-conscious to the apparently unconscious, from the obviously reconstructive to those that seem to be naively inherited" (1984:276). Such a processual view provides insight into where to look ethnographically to learn what tradition means in the social life of particular communities. Building on Clifford Geertz's understanding of interpretive anthropology as the search for other people's answers to life's serious questions, the search for the meaning of tradition properly becomes an anthropological project when it is pluralized as the search for meaningful *understandings* of tradition, thereby enlarging the "consultable record of what man has said" (Geertz 1973:30).

ANTHROPOLOGICAL CONTEXTS

In its approach to anthropology, this work is a modest contribution to a growing body of work that seeks to combine interpretive methods with a discourse-centered approach to culture. The object in this effort is a balance between two descriptive goals. The first centers on nuanced generalizations about local contexts based on the cumulative experience of the ethnographer who has struggled in a search for meaning in the social life of a particular community (see

Geertz 1973). The second is a detailed examination of the artful ways in which particular moments in this social life – unique encounters and dances, disagreements and feasts – are organized in locally specific ways. This balance has been modeled in the writings of a range of anthropologists, including Ellen Basso (1990:3), Keith Basso (1990), Dell Hymes (1968), Joel Sherzer (1983:15), and others whose work I draw upon directly elsewhere in this study. The integration of these two facets of culture – interactional and subjective – has long been an anthropological concern. Edward Sapir, an intellectual forebear of both interpretive cultural anthropologists and discourse-centered linguistic anthropologists, wrote: "The true locus of culture is in the interactions of specific individuals and, on the subjective side, in the world of meanings which each of these individuals may unconsciously abstract for himself from his participation in these interactions" (1985:515).

Although this study is an ethnography of present-day Yuchi ritual and not an ethnohistory of Yuchi community life, an ethnohistorical approach has informed my work. Ethnohistory has become an ever-broadening area of interdisciplinary inquiry, but several concerns at the center of current work in the field are reflected here. Central to my work with Yuchi elders is an interest in the ways in which they narrate their own community and personal histories in public settings. Such a view treats oral history not only as a source for information about the past, but as an important kind of social action in which individuals articulate understandings of culture and identity as well. In this sense, ethnohistory becomes not only the study of history in local settings, but the study of history as a cultural system organized in particular ways like other aspects of culture. The works of Raymond DeMallie (1993), Raymond Fogelson (1989), Ellen Basso (1995), and others provide valuable insight into the forms that such study can take.

Another historical aspect of this work is my attempt to consider Yuchi ritual forms and social processes in light of their past, as understood both by Yuchi people and by previous outside observers. From fragmentary observations of the Yuchi past, such a point of view reveals continuities in Yuchi culture and society observable more clearly in the present. One example, to reappear at various points in my account, concerns the close ties of culture and affinity that bind the Yuchi with their Shawnee neighbors. In light of their history of close association, one that predates Yuchi involvement with the peoples who came to be known as the Creek, the affiliation of Yuchi and Shawnee people in the present can be more richly understood. In this concern with culture through time, I ally myself with the general movement in cultural anthropology to appreciate more fully the historical dimensions of the social and cultural life encountered by ethnographers in the field.

Finally, this study can be seen within its own context of cultural continuity. In many respects it represents an extension of earlier investigations of American Indian social and cultural life generally, and of Yuchi culture and society specifically. More than any of my anthropological predecessors among the Yuchi, I have had the opportunity to experience and participate in the full round of Yuchi community life and to engage in extended discussion and reflection on its meaning with Yuchi ritual leaders. These advantages have enabled me to present a more detailed account of Yuchi practices and beliefs discussed by earlier researchers, while describing aspects of community life that they were unable to witness or investigate. While deviating in this way, I explore here many of the same interests that Frank Speck, Günter Wagner, and W. L. Ballard brought with them to their fieldwork with the Yuchi.

In particular, this study can be seen as an extension of Speck's work among the Native peoples of the Eastern Woodlands. Like Speck, I have tried to combine a sensitivity to the local details of ceremonial life with an interest in comparison, not only in the interest of understanding regional patterns and sociocultural contacts, but as a resource for ethnography itself. Just as Speck's consultants seemed to cherish the opportunity to work out ethnographic descriptions and ethnological comparisons in dialogue with their collaborator, so too have my Yuchi teachers enjoyed exploring the form and meaning of their own ceremonies in contrast with those of their neighbors. To this dialogue I have brought the cumulative ethnographic record on Woodland ceremonialism, while they have brought not only their experiences of Yuchi ritual life, but their oftentimes-rich knowledge of their present-day neighbors, as well. To learn from Speck (1995), via me, that Indian football (see chapter 5) is played, but played differently, among the Iroquois in Canada is perhaps a fact of greater interest to my Yuchi friends than to contemporary anthropology. As for Speck, such a dialogue on cultural variation is not only a productive way of doing ethnography (see Blankenship 1991), but also a great deal of fun when one's collaborators share an ethnological enthusiasm for it. Playing audiotapes of Iroquois songs or video recordings of Eastern Cherokee dances for Yuchi ritualists has never failed to generate interesting observations. These experiences exploring Yuchi appreciation for cultural difference and commonality resonate with James Boon's idea of cultures as systems of meaningful contrasts whose "ideals and actualities neither simply confirm each other nor revolutionarily conflict with each other; rather, each stands in meaningful contrast to another, consistently" (1982:52).

The interest that contemporary Yuchi people show in the ethnographic record of both their own community and that of other peoples echoes Karl Kroeber's interesting observations on the place of such writings in contemporary

American Indian life. He argues that, in part, the oeuvre of early North American anthropology provided "grounding for the later resurgence of Indian self-awareness and self-assertiveness," at the same time that the circumstances of its production entailed understandable ambivalence or frustration for some younger Native peoples (1992:14–15). If, at times, my account of Yuchi ritual practices reads like a new work executed in the antique style of Speck and other of Franz Boas's students, this is only partially an artifact of my own predilections. Literate, curious, and committed to cultural documentation, the classic works on American Indian anthropology, most of all Speck's own dissertation, *Ethnology of the Yuchi Indians* (1909), have shaped a Yuchi ideal of what ethnography can usefully be.

If Yuchis have a complaint about Speck's *Ethnology* it is that his synthesis cannot easily be deconstructed so that they can learn which of their ancestors told Speck what particular fact about Yuchi life (cf. Feld 1990:251–53). They would most of all like to be able to reconstruct the genealogies of knowledge that shaped what Speck came to learn about the Yuchi during the summers of 1904 and 1905. Not yet having fully blossomed as an ethnographer, Speck did not yet give full credit to his Yuchi collaborators, as he did in his later works (Fenton 1995:viii), nor did he describe the processes that underlay his work. Through study of Speck's literary remains, I have been able to reconstitute, for those Yuchis who have been interested, some sense of Speck's experience. More than curiosity, Yuchi interest in the identity of those who acted as Speck's consultants derives from a general concern with establishing and recording the provenance of the cultural information and interpretations that he recorded.

Such a concern emerges in the descriptions of oratory and storytelling given below, but it also has implications for how I construct this work. Referring in his comments to earlier works by outsiders, particularly Speck's *Ethnology*, Mr. Littlebear can only refer to the "old people" who gave interviews and facilitated the work. To be maximally useful to Yuchi people today, ethnographic work should be, in part, an archive of what older people have to say on important subjects.

For these reasons, and in keeping with what I think of as the more humane traditions of American folklore scholarship, I have not disguised (in anthropological fashion) the identities of the Yuchi elders who have worked with me and whose interpretations of Yuchi culture are reflected here. I view the Yuchi elders whom I know as talented, knowledgeable people who go about the business of recreating Yuchi cultural life with seriousness and commitment (see Glassie 1982:xv). Yuchi ritual, oratory, storytelling, and cultural exegesis have artistic qualities, and I respect Yuchi people for their concern that these activities be done well. They deserve proper recognition for their efforts. As the preceding discussion reveals, the attribution of texts and commentary to real people furthers the Yuchi ideal of ethnography as a consultable documentary record. Yuchis disinterested in (or in disagreement with) what I have to say, as an outsider, about the subjects of this book can at least have recourse to the texts that I have transcribed and presented here.[3] As the Yuchi community is small, all interested Yuchi people today know exactly who worked with me, particularly since much of this "work" took place in public contexts. Pseudonyms would do little good in this local context. Fully connected to the rest of modern North America, obfuscation on my part does not seem to have much value, as there is no way that I can hide the Yuchi. Being hidden is exactly what Yuchi leaders are at present trying to undo.

THE STRUCTURE OF THIS STUDY

This study is composed of two linked parts. Chapters 2–4 present background information on the Yuchi and their ritual tradition. After these introductions, the remainder of this work takes its structure from the seasonal progression of the Yuchi ceremonial cycle.

Chapter 2 provides a general orientation to Yuchi culture and history. An introduction to those Yuchi cultural practices and beliefs that are specific to the ceremonial ground context is given in chapter 3. From these initial orientations, chapter 4 forms a bridge to the remainder of the work by presenting an ethnography of Yuchi ritual oratory. In the remaining chapters, such oratory performances provide an important window on the events of the Yuchi ritual calendar.

Yuchi football, the focus of the first ceremonial ground event of the year, is examined in chapter 5. Chapter 6 examines the stomp dance both from the perspective of social interaction within event performances and from the broader point of view of long-term corporate community interactions.

Three specific ceremonial events form the climax and conclusion of the Yuchi ritual calendar. Chapter 7 describes and interprets the first of these, the Arbor Dance. In this event, the Yuchi communities renew their ceremonial ground sites in preparation for the year's major event, the annual Green Corn Ceremony. The activities undertaken during Arbor Dance express broader themes of renewal that permeate Yuchi ceremonialism more generally.

The best-known Yuchi ritual is the Green Corn Ceremony that forms the highlight of the ceremonial ground year. Rather than examining this event from the point of view of ritual action, as has been undertaken by W. L. Ballard (1978), chapter 8 examines the sacred narrative traditions that interpret and give meaning to this ceremony.

The Soup Dance, which concludes the modern Yuchi ceremonial cycle, highlights themes of cultural continuity, spirituality, and reciprocity that are important concepts in Yuchi life. The form and meanings of this ceremony are explored in chapter 9. Chapter 10 links these specific events in a concluding consideration of culture, meaning, and tradition in Yuchi ceremonial ground life.

2 "This has been going on all the way through."

Yuchi History, Culture, and Society

This chapter provides ethnographic and historical contexts for the more detailed cultural descriptions and interpretations presented in the chapters that follow. In the first section I situate Yuchi social and cultural patterns, viewed ahistorically, within the broader Woodland culture area. Within this context, the Yuchi appear to bridge cultural patterns that are found in the Northeastern and Southeastern Woodlands. The role of the Yuchi in mediating various cultural practices within the Woodlands is reexamined ethnographically throughout the chapters that follow, but it is initially understandable in terms of Yuchi historical experience. In the second section, I present a brief account of Yuchi history, as presently understood on the basis of archaeology and ethnohistory, together with contemporary Yuchi perspectives on contact and colonial history. I also reflect on ways that Yuchi history echoes contemporary social patterns. In the final section, I outline the position of Yuchi society today, as an enclave within Oklahoma and the United States. Consideration of Yuchi social life, past and present, particularly contacts with other Native communities, foreshadows a general concern with social interaction addressed in the chapters that follow. In sketching these contexts, I seek to provide a minimal background for understanding present-day Yuchi social interactions and cultural forms. These contextual summaries are based primarily on secondary accounts and Euro-American sources. In the chapters that follow, I seek to balance this bias by more directly presenting Yuchi narratives, practices, and social patterns.

CULTURAL AREAL CONTEXT

Anthropologists have customarily viewed the Yuchi as sharing the generalized regional patterns common to the Southeastern culture area. Although culture areas are imperfect models, lacking sensitivity to changes in time and hampered by the fuzziness of areal boundaries, they remain useful heuristic devices for organizing cultural information on the basis of regional similarities derived from common adjustments to environment and common interactional histories (Driver 1961; Howard 1975). In Native North America, the Northeastern and Southeastern Woodland areas pose a particular problem, as no clear set of linguistic or cultural patterns divide the two. The division between them is based more on geography than on cultural patterns. During the historic era, cultural patterns in eastern North America varied gradually along north-south and east-west gradients. Rather than attempting to resolve the ambiguities inherent in the culture area classification of the East, in this study I discuss Yuchi cultural patterns by switching between more general references to the *Woodlands* and more specific ones to the *Southeast*. By documenting the intermediary cultural position of the Yuchi with respect to their neighbors, I hope to illustrate the nature of the social interactions that underlie areal patterns of cultural similarity and variation.

With their neighbors in the Southeast, the Yuchi shared and still share a core list of cultural patterns. Many of the central features of this Southeastern way of life were areal universals through the nineteenth century and most persist vigorously into the present. Significant features of the areal pattern include an economy based on corn horticulture (Swanton 1928a), the existence of the village or town as the dominant social unit beyond the family (Gearing 1962), frequent multilingualism (Booker, Hudson, and Rankin 1992; Haas 1974), participation in a regional ritual pattern of "Green Corn Ceremonialism" (Witthoft 1949), shared antiphonal music and line dance forms (Nettl 1954), common understandings of cosmology (Fogelson 1977), roughly standard medical practices and ethnobotany (Taylor 1940; W. Walker 1981), socially distinct and cosmologically marked gender roles (Bell 1990; Fogelson 1990), familiar folk narratives, featuring Rabbit as trickster (Speck 1905, Lankford 1987), and mild (during the historic period, much greater during the late prehistoric period) social stratification expressed in such forms as hereditary chiefs (Smith and Hally 1992). Many of these features hold equally well for the Northeastern Woodlands, showing how the Southeast is better viewed as a sub-area within the Woodlands of eastern North America.[1]

Since virtually all knowledge of the Yuchi postdates their political alliance with the Creek Confederacy, the small published literature concerned with them has, with the exception of linguistic studies, downplayed their cultural and social differentiation from the Creek communities. Yuchi society and culture have been treated as variants of Creek patterns. In turn, the Creek, comparatively well documented through John Swanton's extensive research, have been treated as representative of a common regional pattern. Recently Greg Urban (1994) has advocated the reassessment of this canonical, Creek-inspired view of the Southeastern culture area as culturally and socially monolithic.[2] Through a controlled comparison of Southeastern social organizations, he has found evidence supporting a "multiparadigm model of the Southeast" that recognizes greater social diversity in the area (1994:173). In particular, he found that social organization types closely align with language family groupings, and while the speakers of Muskogean languages and the Cherokee share the classic social patterns described by Swanton (matrilineal clans, Crow-type kinship systems, and matrilocal residence rules), societies outside this core group, including the Yuchi, exhibit surprising organizational diversity. Urban's effort at reassessment is, at present, hampered by a lack of new ethnographic information on social organization among Southeastern groups. The next chapter, which outlines some aspects of contemporary Yuchi social organization, will, I hope, contribute to furthering the interpretation of Woodland social systems.

Although Swanton is regarded as the main architect of the synthesized view of the Southeast, he did acknowledge that social differentiation before the historic era was probably greater in the region and that, for many groups, he lacked adequate data to assess local differences. Regarding the Yuchi, he was in a position to note:

> Our information regarding the Yuchi renders it quite certain that not long before white contact they must have had a distinctive culture corresponding with their distinctive language, but we know little about them anterior to the time when they were adopted into the Creek confederacy and not enough peculiar features are on record regarding them to enable us to give them an independent status. The most characteristic features of their culture, aside from their speech, were their tradition of a solar origin, and the solar cult that went with it, the division of the tribe into two societies perpetuated patrilineally, and perhaps the extensive use of the bull snake motive in their art. [1928a:712]

Unfortunately for Creek and Yuchi studies, ethnographic work comparable to that initiated among the Iroquois by William Fenton (1951), aimed at uncovering and documenting local diversity within a social system previously treated as analytically homogenous, is only beginning across the Creek social universe.[3]

Further study of some of the features identified as distinctly Yuchi by Swanton strengthens the view not only that the Yuchi were, and are, culturally distinct from the Creek and other Muskogean peoples but that they are positioned as a cultural bridge between more distinctly Northeastern and Southeastern cultural groups. In their protohistoric Tennessee homeland, the Yuchi were well located to sustain extended contact with northern peoples. In addition, during their wanderings in the historic period, the Yuchi were the frequent companions and allies of various Shawnee bands. In present-day Oklahoma, the Yuchi have sustained patterns of contact with groups, particularly the Shawnee and Sauk, that are notably different from the interaction patterns of Creek communities. Later in this study, I explore the Yuchi-Shawnee relationship from the perspective of contemporary stomp dance events. Further work documenting Yuchi relations with the Sauk and other Algonkian peoples in Oklahoma remains to be done. Today, sweat lodge ceremonies and Native American Church meetings provide the major venues for sustaining Yuchi-Sauk contacts. There is evidence that a number of Yuchi families received initial instruction in the Native American Church from Sauk peyotists (Wagner 1932:85). Prior to widespread adoption of English, Shawnee and Sauk were prominent languages in the Yuchi multilingual repertoire.

Recent work has connected the patrilineal men's societies of the Yuchi – so unusual in contrast with the matrilineal, clan-focused Muskogean tribes – to dual divisions and other social institutions found among the Shawnee, Sauk, Kickapoo, and other Central Algonkian tribes of the Midwest and Great Lakes (Callender 1994; Jackson 1996a). As among those peoples, the Yuchi men's societies govern the assignment of political and ritual offices, and structure institutionalized competition and joking – functions served by clans among the Creek.

Fred Eggan, focusing on changes in Southeastern social organization occurring after removal to Oklahoma, posited that the Yuchi had switched from a matrilineal (Crow-type) to a patrilineal (Omaha-type) kinship system under the influence of both their Algonkian neighbors and the dominant American society (Eggan 1937, 1966; Jackson 1996a). As Urban (1994) has argued, though, Eggan's view that the Yuchi once possessed a Crow-type kinship system rests primarily on the assumption that the Yuchi shared a common Southeastern heritage that dictated a common matrilineal, Crow kinship system. Urban suggests that there is countervailing evidence supporting the view that the Yuchi kinship system was unambiguously of the patrilineal Omaha type throughout their known history. The nature of Yuchi kinship and its relationship to other social institutions remains to be thoroughly studied, but both Eggan's suggestion of recent Algonkian influence and Urban's alternative view emphasizing long-standing Yuchi similarity to Algonkian patterns support the view that Yuchi social organization provides a bridge from the core Southeastern societies best represented by the Creek to non-Southeastern peoples.

Similarly, the solar mythology noted by Swanton as distinctively Yuchi becomes even more significant when examined in the present. Several versions of a common sacred narrative explaining Yuchi understandings of creation and their origin as a people have been collected by ethnographers.[4] Yuchi accounts of the creation of the earth are similar to earth-diver stories common in North America, but the creation of the Yuchi people and the provision of their sacred ceremonies through the agency of the sun is unique in the Southeast and the Woodlands generally. This narrative, which is familiar to many Yuchi elders today, is in striking contrast to creation accounts of Creek and other Muskogean peoples. In their myths, the Muskogeans emerged as peoples into this world from previous subterranean worlds (Swanton 1929). The belief that the Yuchi are the "Children of the Sun," as their ethnonym *Tsoyaha* translates, is widespread among contemporary Yuchi people. Yuchi people who are oriented toward Christianity and those focused on ceremonial grounds both reconcile this mythic history with Christian theology by viewing the sun as one manifestation of the Creator.[5]

In the chapters that follow, I seek to highlight some additional cultural and social differences that separate the Yuchi from their neighbors, while exploring the patterns of social interaction that sustain Yuchi identity and continue to link the Yuchi to other Woodland peoples. I will also indicate some of the ways in which each of the Yuchi communities, particularly the ritual groups within them, possess their own social histories and exhibit patterns of cultural variation.

HISTORICAL CONTEXT

The Yuchi presence in modern Oklahoma and their political incorporation within the United States and the Creek Nation are the direct outcome of more than four centuries of colonial contact with European peoples. Much of this history is poorly documented and the standard works on Southeastern Indian peoples during the colonial and early American periods have, so far, done a poor job of discerning the specific threads of Yuchi experience within the broader tapestry of Southeastern and Creek history. Even when the bias toward viewing Creek society as homogeneous is taken into account, the available historical works either fail to account for the social and cultural realities of Southeastern Indian life or distort social categories and cultural patterns described in twentieth-century ethnography when projecting them back into the eighteenth and nineteenth centuries. Anthropologically informed ethnohistories of the pre-removal Yuchi, as well as of the Southeastern situation more broadly, are a pressing need.[6]

Central to the analysis presented in the chapters to follow is the view that Yuchi ethnic identity has been sustained through social interaction with non-Yuchi peoples. Such a view, attuned to the larger social systems within which people reside, has for many decades been replacing the idealized, isolated community as the locus of anthropological description. The several-hundred-year period during which the Yuchi can be identified in the historical and archaeological record clearly illustrates the manner in which the persistence of Yuchi cultural patterns and social life is linked to interactions with neighboring peoples, as well as with representatives of large-scale, non-Native institutions.[7] The position of the Yuchi within the ethnohistorical record for eastern North America shows that their relatively recent relationship with the Creek Nation and with the U.S. political system in the nineteenth and twentieth centuries is remarkably consistent with Yuchi experiences extending over a longer duration (see Spicer 1992).

In eastern North America, the connection of identifiable peoples of the historic period with precontact societies known only through archaeology is difficult and uncertain. Particularly problematic is the equation of language groups (manifest in Native language names recorded in early documents) with cultures and localities that contact-period ethnohistory requires. With this reservation in mind, the earliest identifiable archaeological complex to be tentatively associated with the Yuchi is the late Mississippian Mouse Creek focus, located just west of the Blue Ridge Mountains in eastern Tennessee on the Hiawassee and Tennessee Rivers. From at least the early sixteenth century through the early eighteenth century, Yuchi people appear to have resided in this region and were settled in distinct communities close to the towns of Koasati-speaking peoples identified archaeologically as the Dallas focus. The identification, still open for question, of the Mouse Creek people as Yuchi and the Dallas people as Koasati speakers is based on the study of narratives left by sixteenth- and seventeenth-century European explorers, combined with linguistic and archaeological evidence. In this period, at the moment of contact, Cherokee settlements existed to the east of these Yuchi and Koasati communities, but the Yuchi and Koasati appear to have been in greater interaction with each other than either were with the Cherokee-speaking peoples (Bauxar 1957a, 1957b, 1995; Booker, Hudson, and Rankin 1992; Lewis and Kneberg 1949).

FIRST CONTACTS

Having situated at least some of the ancestors of present-day Yuchi people in eastern Tennessee during the period of European exploration, I want to pause briefly and precede the chronological account of Yuchi history with a reflection on Yuchi-European contact, inspired by my association with contemporary Yuchi people. It is a gross understatement to say that first contact between indigenous populations and European colonial powers had a tremendous impact on both types of community. The known history of the Yuchi is the history of this colonial encounter. The stories are multiple. There is the story, a favorite for anthropologists of the generation before my own, of drastic social change prompted by the European entrance into the Southeast. There is also the story, a genre more popular in our own time, and equally true, of Yuchi resistance and cultural persistence. There is also the less comfortable story of Yuchi participation in the colonizing process launched by the expanding European powers. Finally, in addition to the stories told by scholars, there are the stories that people, colonial and Yuchi, told and continue to tell themselves. Because so much of the cultural analysis presented in subsequent chapters hangs on the narratives, inherently historical, of contemporary Yuchi elders, it is worthwhile to pause at the beginning of Yuchi "history" and reflect on the collision of worlds that took place somewhere in the southern Appalachian mountains in the middle sixteenth century. The important questions, mostly deferred here, are the ones asked by Edward Schieffelin in his exploration of first contact in New Guinea. He opens his study pondering: "What is the nature of the experience of initial contact between peoples of utterly different worlds, and how do factors of social structure, cultural perception, and historical contingency affect it? How, in turn, does this experience affect the subsequent perceptions, relations, and actions of the people involved?" (Schieffelin et al. 1991:1). The experience of Yuchi-European contact is so distant in time that it remains speculative, but these speculations continue to shape "subsequent perceptions, relations, and actions."

The Spanish entered the Yuchi world in search of wealth, measured in precious metals. The first conquistador to hear of the Yuchi, then known to the Spanish as the Chisca, was Hernando de Soto, already wealthy from the conquest of Peru.[8] The Spanish never found the gold that they sought in the American Southeast, but on his expedition in 1539–40, de Soto got near enough to the Yuchi to hear about them and to learn of their trade in a metal, actually copper, which he mistakenly thought might be gold. Sending two of his men over the mountains to contact them, de Soto was frustrated when his men were unable to obtain conclusive information on Chisca gold (Hudson 1997:207). With these rumors, the Yuchi entered the European imagination as the mysterious possessors of inaccessible wealth.

This vision of the Yuchi continues into the present, where they fill a symbolically powerful role for some Euro-Americans interested in mystical fabrications of world prehistory. Now, according to Joseph Mahan and a group of fellow enthusiasts who have been inspired by the work of Berry Fell and other hyperdiffusionists, the Yuchi are the descendants of ancient Dravidian peoples of the Indus Valley and are the former inhabitants of Atlantis. They are believed to possess a secret wealth, not of gold, but of cultural knowledge explaining the mysteries of the ancient world (Mahan 1992:148–50). The creation of this new

European fantasy independent of the lived realities of Yuchi people, like the Spanish dream of Yuchi gold, has profound effects on contemporary Yuchi people, as Yuchi scholar Richard Grounds has begun to document (1996:66). The moral and scholarly problems created by this tradition of pseudoscholarship has begun to receive serious attention, mostly, however, with reference to claims of African influence in the pre-Columbian New World (de Montellano et al. 1997).[9]

Just as Europeans narrativized the Yuchi, Yuchi people constructed oral accounts of Europeans. Maxey Simms, a speaker of the Yuchi language who provided Yuchi texts to Günter Wagner for linguistic analysis in 1928–29, provided the following account of contact, presented here in Wagner's free English translation:

> A long time ago the red people may have lived somewhere under the rising sun. On this island there lived no pale faced White people, only red men were living there. Once the water rose, covered with much water foam; right there a person came out; that person was a White man; he came to the shore, it is told; every now and then the white man left and came back again. They asked for some land, only as much as one cow hide would cover, only this much they should give them, they said. They did not want to give it, and some said: "Let us kill them." Others, however said, "We will not kill them, as much land as one cow hide would not be much," they thought, and so they gave it to them. The White men threw a cow hide into the water, when it was wet they cut it in little pieces. And then they stretched it; when they measured the four corners they had taken very much land. When the Indians said they had not understood it was to be done that way, they answered that they had taken just as much land as one cow hide; very much land they had taken indeed. Further on more and more White people came across the water and they increased; when the Indians saw that they took their land away, they made war with each other. The White people drove them and their game backwards all the time. As time went on, there were many White people and they followed the red people. [quoted in Wagner 1931:157–59]

Mr. Jimmie Skeeter, the first Yuchi elder to struggle with teaching me about Yuchi culture, told a similar account to that provided to Wagner by Mr. Simms. In these stories, the trick played on Indian people by the whites comes to symbolize the entire history of Indian-European relations from the Yuchi perspective. This is an example of what Raymond Fogelson has called an "epitomizing event," an account of an event, real or imagined, that attempts "to encompass and make intelligible seemingly impersonal, inevitable, and insidious processes of change" (1984:261).[10]

While the written record indicates that de Soto himself failed to meet the Yuchi, Mr. Mose Cahwee, a learned Yuchi elder and an energetic proponent of Yuchi language and cultural preservation, epitomized the Yuchi encounter with de Soto differently. In a presentation on the history of the Yuchi stickball game to a children's Yuchi language class in the summer of 1995, he used the conquistador's travels to make a claim about the historical depth and cultural distinctness of his people's practices. To the students and their parents, he reported the following story.

TEXT 2

An account of Yuchi stickball games and the Yuchi encounter with the de Soto expedition. Delivered by Mose Cahwee to a gathering of the children's Yuchi language class in Sapulpa, Oklahoma, 7 September 1995.

Way back there in the <<cough>>
    in the
    in the [time]
    when the pilgrims
    came.

And when ah
    some of the settlers
    came.

And also
    like these
    famous explorers
    came.

They
    they had
    they witnessed
    this ballstick game.

And ah
    de Soto
    he was one of the great explorers.

And he came to the Yuchis
where they were at at one time.

And so the Yuchis
wanted to do
something
extra for him
while he was there.

So what they done
they got the ballsticks.

And that's what
that was one of the GAMES.

That was one of their SPORTS
that they had to use
during those days.

So <<cough>>
while de Soto was there
well
they played this game for him.

And ah so
when they got through playing
well some of the guys . . .

At the end of the game
some of the guys
had got cut on the head
arm
or hand.

They were bleeding.
And so
de Soto told 'em
said he'd seen
a lot of rough games.

Mr. Mose Cahwee (left) and Chief James Brown, Sr. (right) photographed during a Yuchi language class in Sapulpa, Oklahoma, 7 September 1995. The men hold pairs of "ballsticks" of the type used by the Yuchi and their neighbors in the two forms of "stickball" discussed in this study. It was on this evening that Mr. Cahwee recounted the story presented here in Text 2.

But he said
    this was one of the ROUGHEST games he ever witnessed
    he said.

So, but he . . .

So he had always remembered
    the Yuchis
    that they had this ballstick game.

And the Yuchis
    as far as he know
    that was the only
    TRIBE that ever had that
    ballstick game.

So

so what we're talking about now
it didn't happen yesterday.

This came from way back
back in the
maybe seventeen hundreds.

And this has been going on
a l l t h e w a y through.

Much of the recent work by ethnohistorians on the documents related to Spanish explorations of the Southeast has involved using archaeology and social theory to read between the lines of the documentary record, postulating reasonable guesses about the social and historical experiences of colonizers and Indians in the early historical period. As Mr. Cahwee's account reveals, anthropologists are not the only ones interested in such pursuits.

EARLY HISTORY

The European record shows the first extended encounter with the Yuchi (Chisca) to have been in 1567, when Sergeant Hernando Moyano de Morales, a junior officer serving under Juan Pardo, launched two attacks on Chisca towns on the west side of the Appalachians. These towns were in the same area where the de Soto expedition located the Chisca twenty-eight years earlier. Furthering the ambitions of the chief of the village where he was stationed, and apparently inspired by the de Soto reports of their gold, Moyano attacked and burned a Chisca town in the spring of 1567. He failed to find gold, but he did succeed in angering the Chisca, who in turn threatened to destroy him and his men in retaliation. Moyano preempted this attack and launched a second expedition against the Chisca, this time attacking and destroying a large, palisaded village (Hudson 1990). These Chisca encounters with Moyano foreshadow two hundred years during which the Yuchi would become a permanent thorn in the side of Spanish colonial policy, repaying the Spanish for their hostility with their own expeditions into Spanish Florida.

Knowledge of the Yuchi in the sixteenth century, limited and provisional though it is, points to eastern Tennessee as their common homeland at the time of European contact. Some Yuchi clearly remained there, west of the mountains, at least through the early eighteenth century, but other Yuchi groups began appearing throughout the Southeast during the seventeenth century. As they emerged sporadically in the historical record, groups of Yuchi seem to have formed, relocated, coalesced and divided quickly all the way up until the time they were pressured to remove to the West by the U.S. federal government. Throughout this period, those Yuchi groups formed temporary alliances with various other peoples, and they pursued their own strategies in dealing with colonial powers, sometimes in conflict with each other.

One group of Yuchi appeared in Spanish Florida near Pensacola in the early 1600s and continued to expand over the next hundred years. Here they began harassing the Spanish and their Indian allies, disrupting the mission system on which Spanish rule in Florida was based. They also appear to have been establishing trade relations with Gulf Coast groups and terrorizing pacified Indian communities. By 1677, these Yuchi were at war with the missionized Apalachee, from whom they captured slaves to trade with the English (Swanton 1922:299).

During this same period, other Yuchi groups were settled near the South Carolina frontier, where they were in conflict with various piedmont and coastal tribes. In the 1680s, Yuchi who were allied with the English were attacking the Spanish missions to the Gaule in coastal Georgia (Smith and Gottlob 1978:8; Swanton 1922). At the same time the Westo, whom Swanton believed to be another Yuchi-speaking group, were fighting with the English in the Carolinas.

Contemporaneously, Yuchi towns in what is today Tennessee, between the Chickasaw and Cherokee on the Tennessee River, as well as Yuchi parties roaming farther afield into the Midwest, came into increasing contact with the English and French west of the mountains. In 1674, agents for an English trader visited a Yuchi town in Tennessee and in 1700 a Yuchi party was encountered by a French Jesuit priest on the Mississippi below the Ohio River. Supporting the contention that the Yuchi have a long history of interaction with the Central Algonkian peoples, the priest, Father Gravier, was able to communicate with the leading Yuchi man in Illinois and Shawnee (Swanton 1922:297).

In the early eighteenth century the Yuchi in Tennessee appear to have come into increasing conflict with the English traders and their Cherokee allies. In 1714, at the instigation of an English trader, the Cherokee attacked and destroyed one Yuchi settlement in the Tennessee country. While this incident seems to have ended the autonomous Yuchi presence in Tennessee, there is some evidence that Yuchi people were incorporated at this point into the emerging Cherokee state, a pattern that would be repeated when Yuchi communities were encompassed in the ambiguous Creek polity (Mooney 1900:385–86; Swanton 1922:298).

After 1715 and the defeat of the Westo in the Westo War, the groups who had been opposed to the English in Carolina retreated west into Georgia and Alabama, becoming increasingly associated with various Muskogean towns. Almost simultaneously groups of Yuchi, together with bands of Shawnee, moved east, temporarily settling on the Savannah River above present-day Augusta, Georgia. More permanent than the joint Yuchi and Shawnee settlements were the Yuchi towns located on the river closer to the Atlantic coast. These settlements were closely associated with the Salzburger settlers in early colonial Georgia and also had close social relationships with the Muskogean town of Cussetah (von Reck 1990; Wallace 1996).

In this period, English and Spanish colonial policy was beginning to precipitate the social entity called "the Creek" out of the very fluid social world of autonomous ethnic towns existing in the lower Southeast. Muskogean-speaking towns, intermixed with Shawnee and Yuchi towns as well, began to consolidate after the Yamassee War of 1715 into a more tightly constricted geographical range in western Georgia, eastern Alabama, and northern Florida. To the north and east were the expanding American colonies, and in the Appalachians were the consolidating Cherokee, who sided with the English in the Yamassee uprising; to the west were the Choctaw and the French. The geographic constriction in Georgia and Alabama, the increasing debt and dependency generated by the escalating deerskin trade, the aftermath of the Yamassee War, and the need of the colonial powers to deal with a unified, multi-town government provided part of the basis for the increasing political centralization underlying the Creek confederation. Under these conditions, the only escape valve in the system was increasingly vacant Spanish Florida.

By the 1700s, slave raiding by the English and their Indian, especially Yuchi and Muskogean, allies had caused the near or total extermination of most Native North Florida peoples, thus effectively ending the mission system that the Spanish needed in order to defend northern Florida.[11] With the Yamassee War, the Spanish were prepared to reorganize their efforts, turning to the former allies and now enemies of the English. In the period 1715–18, seeking to fill the Florida population vacuum, the Spanish began courting their former tormentors, encouraging the Creeks to move into northern Florida and to take up trade with the colony. Groups of Yuchi and people from various Muskogean towns in Georgia and Alabama began entering Florida, seeking refuge after the Yamassee War and escaping an increasingly complicated and conflicted social world on the frontiers of the English colonies. As the nebulous Creek Confederacy emerged in Georgia and Alabama, these Florida colonies formed the foundation for its ethnic alter ego, the emergent Seminole tribe (Craig and Peebles 1974; Fairbanks 1978:165–66; Sattler 1996; Sturtevant 1988). In practice, all the towns in Florida, Georgia, and Alabama – Creek and Seminole – vacillated in their colonial allegiances, supporting or resisting the Spanish, French, and English (later Americans) differently at different times and places. Sometimes they were at dramatic variance with each other, a pattern that crystallized internal conflict within Creek society and solidified Seminole differentiation and ethnogenesis.[12]

In 1729 there was a clear indication of the Yuchi place in the evolving Creek sociopolitical system. In that year, some of the Yuchi from the Savannah formed a new town on the Chattahoochee River, in west Georgia. Swanton described the event as a complete westward relocation of the Yuchi in eastern Georgia. "After the establishment of a Yuchi settlement on the Chattahoochee by Chief Ellick of the Kasihta [Cussetah], in the year 1729 . . . they began to make their permanent residence more and more among the Creeks, using their old territories [in eastern Georgia] principally for hunting" (Swanton 1922:309). In contrast, Pamela Wallace (p.c. 1997) asserts that the founders of this town were only a portion of the Yuchi from the Savannah and that a considerable number remained nearer to the Georgia colony in alliance with General Ogelthorpe.

Although it was probably not the only major Yuchi settlement of its day, the new town did prefigure the future Yuchi-Creek relationship. Benjamin Hawkins, the American agent to the Southern Tribes from 1796 to 1816, provided the fullest account of this town and its founding. In describing the town, Hawkins noted: "In the year 1729, an old chief of Cussetuh [Cussetah], called by the white people Captain Ellick, married three Uchee [Yuchi] women, and brought them to Cussetuh, which was greatly disliked by his towns people; their opposition determined him to move from Cussetuh; he went down opposite where the town now is, and settled with his three brothers; two of whom had Uchee wives; he, after this collected all the Uchees, gave them the land where their town now is, and there they settled" (quoted in Swanton 1922:310). In singing the praise of the Yuchi town and its inhabitants, Hawkins also asserted: "They retain all of their original customs and laws and have adopted none of the Creeks" (quoted in Swanton 1922:310). He also described three subsidiary Yuchi villages in the region of the main town and noted that some Yuchi were settled with the Shawnee among the "Upper Creeks" in present-day Alabama.[13] He failed to identify those Yuchi that Wallace noted remained longer near the coast, but Swanton was of the opinion that Yuchi settlements during the late 1700s and early 1800s were distributed throughout the Creek country (1922:311).

Just days before I began writing the historical summary that is the foundation for this section, I visited with Newman Littlebear. With us was Simon Harry, the Chief of the Duck Creek Ceremonial Ground, Mr. Harry's wife Nancy, and Elenora Powell, daughter of James Brown, Sr., late Chief of the Polecat Ceremonial Ground. Mr. Littlebear and Chief Harry were discussing other communities that, in the past and present, had been allies to the Yuchi. After discussing their long relationship with the Shawnee, they began a discussion of the now inactive Big Cussetah Ceremonial Ground that they had both visited before World War II. They recalled that this ground had "taken the Yuchi in" and they were frequent visitors there. This prompted Mr. Littlebear to share an oral version of the Captain Ellick story recorded by Hawkins. He began by probing my memory of the work of my predecessors among the Yuchi, Wagner (1931) and Frank Speck (1909). As this story reveals, the direct connection of identity of the pre-removal Creek towns with the contemporary communities of the same name in Oklahoma is still very strong among Creek and Yuchi people, particularly ceremonial ground people who view the ceremonial grounds as the present-day manifestations of town organizations. The Cussetah Ceremonial Ground is presently inactive, but its identity is shared by several churches – Little Cussetta Baptist Church, Big Cussetah Methodist Church, and Little Cussetah Methodist Church.

TEXT 3

A story relating to Cussetah involvement with the Yuchi. Delivered by Newman Littlebear during conversation at his home in Kellyville, Oklahoma, 16 January 1997.

Did a –
    in Speck's writings
    in Speck's writings
    did he mention anything about Big Cussetah?
    or was it Wagner?

One of them mentions it
    but it was Cussetah.

It didn't say Big Cussetah or Little Cussetah
    it just said Cussetah
    I think.

And it told of an incident in there where a
    where
I guess I think they was talking about a ceremonial ground chief
    that married into the Yuchi
    married a Yuchi woman.

You remember that?

And then he had a brother
    this chief had a brother
    married a Yuchi woman.

And over that, over that situation
    them
    them ah Muskogee people
    or Creek round-about
    they kind of
    they didn't like it.

They didn't like what these
    Cussetah men did.
    'cause they took them Yuchi women.

And they had a falling out over that.

And they kinda
    I guess
    kind of disowned them
    you might say
    this Cussetah bunch.

So I guess that
    since we're Yuchi
    that kind begins tying in.

Like Mr. Cahwee's de Soto tale, this story illustrates the process by which Yuchi elders are capable of transforming their own study of ethnographic sources to create ongoing, publicly circulating oral discourse that serves social purposes in Yuchi community life. In this particular telling, Mr. Littlebear recasts the story to emphasize two points. First it supports the historical relationship of the Yuchi with Cussetah Town, which Chief Harry had, moments before, been providing. Second, it draws out the differences in worldview that separate Yuchi people from the Creek. A frequent motif in such stories is the flexibility and openness of Yuchi people to outsiders, in contrast with the more insular Creek towns. When he told the story, I could not recall where it originated, although I did not remember it appearing in Speck's or Wagner's works. All of us who were present when he told it placed the story in Oklahoma after the removal era, and it was only on reviewing Swanton's (1922) historical summary that I recognized it as Hawkins's tale and was able to reconstruct another piece of the text's natural history.

The life cycle of this story – from oral history recorded by Hawkins, to Swanton's ethnohistory, to contemporary Yuchi oral discourse – is indicative of the flow of cultural materials and concepts across the anthropological-Native American frontier. A concern underlying much of my interpretation of Yuchi cultural practices is understanding the degree to which Native communities and American anthropologists have collaborated in creating both the discipline and the ways in which "culture" is interpreted in American Indian communities.[14]

The situation of the Yuchi in the context of their Creek neighbors was also of interest to naturalist William Bartram, who visited the same Yuchi town on the Chattahoochee in 1775, forty-six years after its founding and twenty-two years before Hawkins. Citing the existence of the Creek Confederacy, Bartram noted the anomalous position of the Yuchi within it: "They are in confederacy with the Creeks, but do not mix with them; and on account of their numbers and strength, are of importance enough to excite and draw upon the jealousy of the whole Muscogulge confederacy, and are usually at variance, yet wise enough to unite against a common enemy, to support the interest and glory of the general Creek confederacy" (1955:313). Contemporary Yuchi people encountering Bartram's description find it resonant with their own understanding of their present predicament vis-à-vis the Creek government, yet now that they lack "a common enemy," they struggle with finding ways of withdrawing their "support." The push for separate federal recognition of the Yuchi is rooted in longstanding patterns of mutual othering by Creek and Yuchi people.

Beginning after the American Revolution and accelerating after the turn of the nineteenth century, the peoples who shared the Creek social universe were confronted by the same pressures faced by other Native communities in the East. Until this time, the survival of Woodland societies had hinged on trade and diplomatic relations with the three colonial powers as well as on the ability of Native leaders to play the interests of one European nation against the others. For a time, a common ground existed in which Europeans and Indians on the American frontier each had needs that could be met by the other. A common colonial culture briefly existed in which Native societies retained some room for movement by potentially, or actually, shifting their alliances and trade relationships. On a large scale, these shifts took place in alliances with the European powers, but on a local level, Native communities could shift allegiances between particular traders and could relocate themselves on the frontier to avoid enemies and rivals as well as to create new ties with Native and European communities. The creation of intertribal communities, and the adoption of new identities exemplified by the formation of the multiethnic Creek Nation, exemplifies a process that took place throughout eastern North America. With American independence, the kind of active equilibrium that had been established briefly on the frontier disappeared. The fur trade became secondary to American expansion and Native leaders were no longer able to trade Indian alliance in colonial conflicts for breathing room west of the American colonies.[15]

Internal and external processes of social change shaped a common Creek political culture emergent in the eighteenth century, but political consensus was never achieved. Creek society instead divided along lines that are still recognizable in Oklahoma today. The division was both geographic and ideological. In the river valleys of Georgia, closer to the American settlements, were the "Lower Creek" towns, including the Yuchi town on the Chattahoochee River and its satellite villages. To the northwest, in the valleys of central Alabama, were the "Upper Creek" towns. While the Upper Creek region possessed a larger population, the Lower Creek towns acquired centralized power through their closer dealings with the American and European powers. As American settlers flooded into Creek country and conflict with the new nation emerged, the Lower Creek leaders became the voice of accommodation and assimilation, while Upper Creek communities became centers of resistance and closer adherence to customary values and practices. As is the case today, the Yuchi were the notable exception to the general rules explaining the social division of Creek society.

Yuchi people were settled mostly in the Lower Creek region, but they also lived in the Upper Creek town of Sauwanogee, which was primarily a Shawnee town established near the other Upper Creek towns on the Tallapoosa River. After 1800 many Upper Creek towns began resisting the efforts of the Americans and their Lower Creek allies. That resistance intensified when Tecumseh, the Shawnee nativist, and his allies went among the Creek towns preaching a pan-Indian revolt against the Americans. Creek society divided over those teachings and the similar efforts of local, mostly Upper Creek, prophets (Dowd 1992). The Lower Creek communities, who were already more predisposed to the Americans, were also positioned to face the full onslaught of American retaliation. They rejected the revolutionary urgings, while the Upper Creeks generally accepted the prophets' teachings. Perhaps because they were so closely allied with the Shawnee, among whom they had so often resided, the Yuchi established a long-standing tradition of running counter to trends among their Lower Creek neighbors. Several hundred Yuchi from the Chattahoochee settlements relocated to the Upper Creek country and sided with the prophets in the conflict that followed, the Red Stick Revolt of 1813–14 (Martin 1991:137–38).

The Yuchi pattern of expressing greater cultural affinity with the Upper

Creek towns while existing in greater geographical proximity to the Lower Creek towns is another historical pattern preserved in the present. After removal to Oklahoma, the upper/lower division was replicated, with towns establishing themselves closer to their former neighbors, although the north-south pattern was reversed. The Lower Creek towns were established in the richer land of the Arkansas River valley in the northeast part of the nation, while the Upper Creek towns were relocated in the poorer southern and western regions, on the Deep Fork and Canadian rivers. Since at least the early 1970s, all of the active ceremonial grounds among the Creek have been those associated with Upper Creek towns. By that time, all of the Creek towns in the northern part of the nation had abandoned their ceremonial grounds, often replacing them with church congregations. The only exceptions were and are the three Yuchi towns that have, in contrast to their Lower Creek neighbors, retained their ceremonial grounds to the present (see Robbins 1976:5). The bonds of interaction between the present-day Yuchi ceremonial grounds and the Upper Creek ceremonialists will be discussed in chapter 6.

Just as Creek society was divided, then as now, by social and cultural differences, so was the Yuchi community divided within the Creek Confederacy. Some Yuchi people, feeling strongly about the cause of resistance, sided with the Upper Creek prophets. Others were loyal to the Lower Creek strategy of accommodation. A historical expression of this division is the case of Timothy Barnard and his family. A Scottish trader among the Lower Creek towns, Barnard was married to a Yuchi woman and served as Benjamin Hawkins's assistant. A slave holder, Barnard maintained a plantation on the Flint River east of the Yuchi town on the Chattahoochee. During this period of turmoil, Barnard attempted to raise his sons in two worlds. He was more concerned about mitigating the influence of his unscrupulous white colleagues than shielding his sons from Yuchi culture, yet their access to Yuchi values was undoubtably filtered through their father's experience and world view (Henri 1986:123). His most notable son, Timpoochee Barnard, became the Yuchi example of a well known political type within Creek society – the métis, middleman politician. When General Andrew Jackson's Tennessee militiamen rampaged through the Upper Creek country in 1814, putting down the Red Stick revolt, Timpoochee Barnard, commissioned as a major, led a company of Yuchi soldiers. When Jackson concluded one of a series of treaties (this one formally ending the Red Stick revolt; however, like those that preceded and followed it, in reality ceding Creek and Yuchi land), Timpoochee Barnard was among the signatories, signing as "Captain of the Uchees" (Thomas 1907).

Again, pre-removal history reveals patterns continued in more recent Yuchi social life. Throughout the late nineteenth and early twentieth century, there have been men, such as Timpoochee Barnard, who, living in two worlds, claimed, and in part were granted, the right to represent themselves to outsiders as Yuchi chiefs. Such men have been a focus of Wallace's work on twentieth-century Yuchi political history (1995, 1998, forthcoming). In light of the interests that I am pursuing here, I note only that these "chiefs" are quite different from the community leaders introduced in the next chapter. The métis chiefs and their authority were always in question internally. Their ability to make claims was just as much an artifact of the desire by outsiders for the Yuchi to have a single leader with whom to deal as it was a legitimate political reality acknowledged by Yuchi people. As Wallace has argued, the legitimacy that these men did have within the Yuchi community depended on the material aid that they could provide to Yuchi people. In this manner, they and their Creek counterparts perpetuated the system established by their white ancestors, the town traders who had married into Indian society.[16]

Defeated in the Red Stick revolt, the greatly reduced and impoverished Upper Creek population, including those Yuchi residing in Alabama, were faced with shrunken landholdings and diminished prospects. Some went into Florida to become Seminole, expanding that population and increasing its anti-American and anti-Lower Creek sentiments. Some remained in the constricted Creek territory, attempting reconciliation with their Lower Creek rivals, including the Yuchi who had remained on the Chattahoochee.

In the two decades that followed the revolt, pressure from Southern politicians and their constituents to open the remaining Indian lands intensified tremendously. Having failed in military resistance, Creek society reunified around diplomatic opposition to further American expansion. A stronger National Council emerged and passed laws preventing new sales of Creek land. This strategy did provide some time during which Creek society could regroup, but while political consolidation furnished the foundation for post-removal government, the pressure for complete removal of the Creek peoples from their lands became unstoppable during the 1820s and 1830s as Andrew Jackson rose from war hero to president (A. Wallace 1993).

Benjamin Hawkins possessed a detailed knowledge of Southern Indian affairs, and his long tenure as American agent during the years preceding the Creek revolt resulted in a documentary record that allows glimpses into Yuchi society. After Hawkins's death in 1816, no American official had the interest or time to understand Creek society in depth. For this reason, in the two decades preceding the removal in 1836, the Yuchi slip from view, and except for the notation of two Yuchi towns in the census of 1832 their history is not known separately from that of the Creek Nation as a whole. The American policies that led to the removal of the Southeastern tribes west of the Mississippi have been examined by a number of authors (Green 1982; A. Wallace 1993). Since little can, at present, be added to the Yuchi part of this story, it is perhaps better to jump ahead to the new circumstances that Yuchi people faced in Indian Territory. While little historical information is yet available on the Yuchi during removal, it is perhaps enough to note that memory of the hardships accompanying the Trail of Tears, handed down in vague but emotional grandmothers' tales, is just as resonant and powerful for Yuchi people as it is for members of the other Southeastern tribes.

The quintessential moment in the two-hundred-year history of American fraud and abuse in its dealings with the Creek peoples, removal took place in 1836–37. Thousands of Creeks, doubtlessly including a proportional number of Yuchi, perished in the process. Established in the West, the survivors began the task of rebuilding new lives in unfamiliar country. The locations of various tribes established in eastern Indian Territory after the removal period are presented in map 1. The tribal boundaries shown in this map are for the period preceding statehood. At the time of Creek and Yuchi removal, many groups had not yet been relocated to Indian Territory and the lands occupied by those who were there were larger.

CREEK NATION, INDIAN TERRITORY

Between 1836, the year of removal, and 1907, when its sovereignty was negated and its lands allotted, the Creek Nation in Indian Territory established a national government along patterns that had emerged in the East before removal.[17] In the West, the individual town communities that had been the foundation for Creek and Yuchi tribal life were reconstituted, many also reestablishing themselves as ceremonial organizations. Retaining their social and political functions, the towns became more diffuse as residential units. As today, a person identifying with a particular town did not necessarily reside within a narrow geographic precinct. Households were distributed across the landscape, often leaving the town's ceremonial square (or in some later cases, its church building) as the physical expression of its powerful corporate identity.[18]

After removal, the American Civil War provided the next major context in which the Upper Creek-Lower Creek, conservative-assimilationist division within the nation would manifest itself. The métis Lower Creek leadership, who were slave holders and individualist, plantation-style farmers, sided with the South. The Upper Creek people attempted to remain neutral, but as a practical matter, ended up siding with the North. Civilian refugees who relocated, both to Union Kansas and to the Confederate Choctaw Nation and Texas, re-

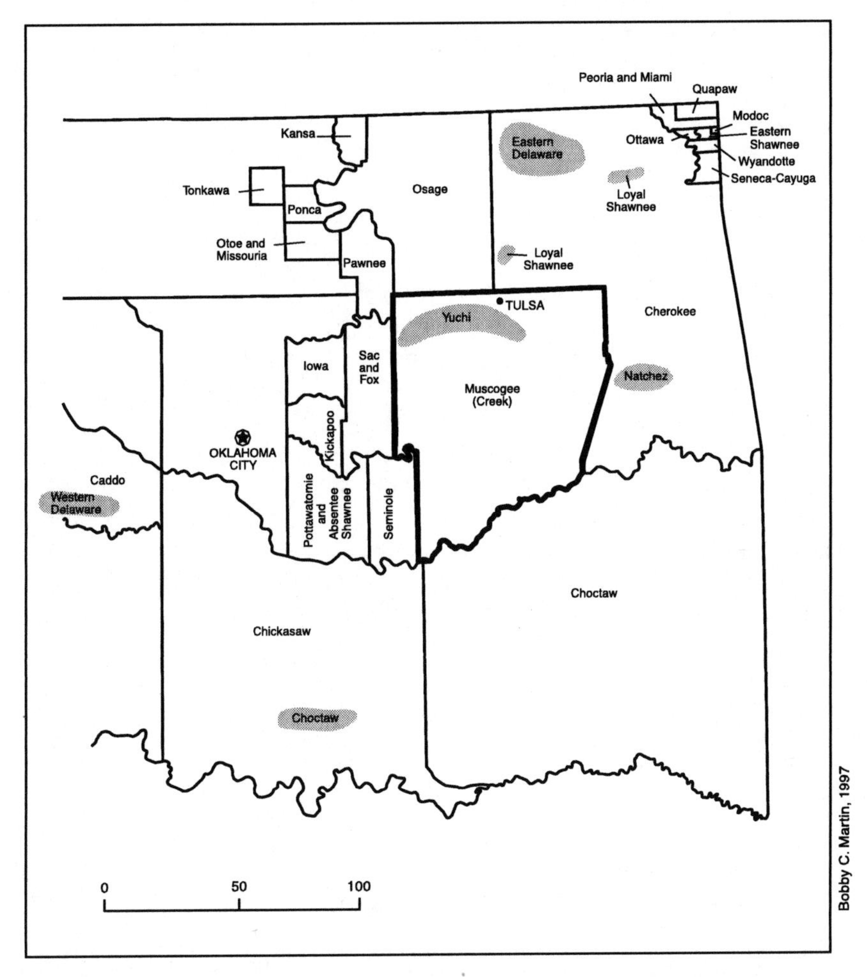

Map 1. Tribal groups in eastern Oklahoma after removal. Groups enclaved within federally recognized tribes are shown in shaded regions approximating their current locations. Recognized tribes are shown within their pre-allotment political boundaries. Tribal towns and other local divisions are not shown.

turned after the war to a decimated, burned-out nation reminiscent of the Upper Creek country after 1814.[19]

The Upper Creek leaders expected their loyalty to be rewarded in the postwar period, but the U.S. federal government, during the reconstruction of the nation after the war, empowered the pro-assimilationist Southerners instead. The Unites States used the Creek treaties with the Confederacy as pretense to invalidate prior U.S. treaties, opening the door for renegotiations detrimental

Table 1. Creek Nation Citizens, 1891

Yuchi Town population	580
Population of the 44 Indian towns (including Yuchi Town)	9059
Population of the 3 Black towns	4203
Total citizens	13,842
Average population of the Indian towns	206
Average population of the Black towns	1401
Yuchi population as a percentage of Indian population	6.4%
Yuchi population as a percentage of the total population	4.2%

Source: Debo 1941:333

to Creek interests. These new treaties resulted in the sale of the western half of the Creek lands to the United States, as well as the granting of Creek citizenship to the freed slaves within the nation. The culturally conservative Upper Creeks were punished for the decisions of the Lower Creek leadership, while again being shut out of decision making. In addition, the loss of land hurt the Upper Creeks more severely, as they used the western lands more extensively for subsistence and commercial hunting.

The Creek Nation in the West possessed a stronger national government than that it had had in the East, and it was further consolidated in the period after the Civil War. The system established in 1867, during efforts to reunify the nation, was patterned on the U.S. federal system. The national government included an overall chief and second chief, a judiciary, and two legislative houses to which the towns sent representatives.

In the period from removal to allotment, few historical documents present information specific to the Yuchi, although most observers continued to recognize their cultural and especially linguistic distinctiveness. Despite their size, their geographic spread across an extensive area, and their status as a culturally distinct people, the Yuchi were treated as a single town in the Creek national system. This meant that "Yuchi Town" was second only to the major Creek town of Tuckabatchee (numbering 785 in 1891) in population size, but the Yuchi, as a enclaved minority, were never in a position to mobilize politically within the Creek political structure.

Table 1 presents Yuchi and Creek population information collected in 1891. Comparison of the population of Yuchi Town with the average town population shows the Yuchi community to be the numerical equivalent of three average towns. This fact accords well with their known history in three major settlements, and contemporary population size and distribution.

To a greater degree than residents of the Creek towns, the Yuchi appear to have kept to themselves during this period. Noting the enclaved minority groups residing within the Creek Nation (Natchez, Hitchiti, Yuchi, Alabama, and Koasati), Ethan Allen Hitchcock observed in 1842: "The Uchees are more numerous, maybe 800, and preserve their distinctive character more than any other band or tribe. Not many of them speak Creek and they intermarry but rarely with the Creeks" (1930:121). Lacking control over the political questions faced by the Creek Nation, Yuchi people alternatively withdrew to their own communities or involved themselves in Creek affairs as individuals. With respect to the major political issues, they appear to have divided internally in ways familiar to their earlier history and characteristic of the divisions in the Creek Nation as a whole. Timpoochee Barnard's grandson, Timothy Barnett, provides another case for examining the position of the Yuchi in Creek national divisions. During the war, he sided with the South, serving as a colonel over the Creek troops, but after the war he switched allegiances and supported the cause of the conservative, Northern faction (Grayson 1988:134–35).

Located in the far northwest portion of the Creek Nation, the Yuchi were remote from the bulk of the Creek population and were more open to relationships with their Indian neighbors to the west. Writing just after allotment, Frank Speck noted, "They seldom mix socially with the Creeks, presumably because of their former enmity. A strong feeling of friendship is, however, manifested toward the Shawnee." He also reports: "With their neighbors on the west, the Sauk and Fox, the Yuchi have developed, since the removal, considerable intimacy. Their contact can be traced in trade, in attendance upon each other's ceremonies, and especially in the Plains practice of 'sweating' horses" (1909:11).[20] In a study of the Yuchi population as reported in the Creek census of 1898, Wallace found that a sizable proportion of the Yuchi population at this time had been enumerated, and appear to have been residing beyond the borders of the Creek Nation, near Stroud, on the Sauk and Fox reservation (P. Wallace 1993). She also found that present-day residence patterns in the modern settlements described in the next section generally mirror pre-allotment residence areas.

During this period the towns remained the central social unit for most Creek and Yuchi people, but throughout Indian Territory local leaders faced considerable forces creating a disorganized, and at times dangerous, social landscape. Missionaries, with the support of the Federal government and Creek métis politicians, yet opposed by many conservative leaders, began extensive work in the Creek Nation after the Civil War, opening boarding schools that took children away from their family and town communities. After emancipation, African Americans from bordering states flooded into Indian Territory reporting to be relatives of the Creek Freedmen and establishing themselves as citizens of the nation. An in-migration of white grafters, speculators, con-men, and outlaws proved destructive. After the Civil War, the transgressions of such people precipitated a crisis of sovereignty and social control in the Creek Nation, just as it had in the 1820s and 1830s. The building of railroads and an increasing number of cattle drives moving through the nation added to the social stress.

By the turn of the twentieth century, the pressures that the Creek Nation had faced in Georgia and Alabama had fully caught up with them in the West. Pressure for land and the removal of Native American communities from the national political agenda led the United States to abolish the national governments of the five large southeastern tribes and to allot tribal lands to individual citizens, freeing up land for white homesteading and paving the way for Oklahoma statehood. Creek politicians attempted legal resistance to allotment, and some conservative Creek and Yuchi people attempted armed opposition, but the dissolution of the Creek Nation as a sovereign state took place technically in 1898 with the passing of the Curtis Act. Enrollment and allotment was essentially complete by the time the state of Oklahoma entered the Union in 1907, effectively ending sovereign Creek government from the perspective of the United States, until 1971.

OKLAHOMA

Yuchi and Creek history in the twentieth century is less remote to the Yuchi today and more closely bound to historical events and patterns shared by other American Indian communities and American society generally. Wallace's (1998) dissertation, drawing on archival sources and contemporary oral history, presents a full account of twentieth-century Yuchi social history. As background to the ethnographic chapters to follow, a few features of twentieth-century Yuchi and Creek history need to be discussed here.

While statehood temporarily terminated the Creek Nation, most Creek and Yuchi people continued to maintain their own local communities without the interference or even the understanding of the federal government (see Opler 1952, 1972). For contemporary Creek and Yuchi people, local community life and social interaction with other Creek and Yuchi communities provide the salient historical backdrop for their lives. In contrast, knowledge of the old Creek national government is second-hand and the current modern national government is a recent phenomenon whose emergence and evolution are recognized as new and secondary to more permanent ties of family, community, ceremonial ground and/or church. For elders, the bureaucratic role that is today increasingly played by the Creek Nation was filled, during most of their lifetimes, by the Bureau of Indian Affairs, with which they interacted directly.

For the Yuchi community, World War II brought a watershed social transformation. Not only did a large number of Yuchi men serve overseas, but the war also marked the end of the period during which Yuchi families were focused economically on agricultural activities. Until this time, those families who retained their allotments or other landholdings were almost universally small-scale farmers, producing both modest cash crops and their own subsistence needs. In addition, most Yuchi people, those with or without land, worked as day laborers on the larger farms held by whites and sometimes by Indian owner-operators.

During the war Tulsa boomed with military manufacturing, and Yuchi men and women were drawn from their nearby settlements into industrial wage labor. After the war those young adults (today's elders) who had gone to war and to work in town remained in the wage economy. Those who tried to return to farming, after becoming fully engaged in the capitalist economy, discovered that small-scale techniques were no longer viable on land that had become only marginally productive.

That transformation is one of the most striking features of Yuchi oral historiography. When talking with elders in their rural homes today, they vividly describe the active agricultural life of their youth while they are now surrounded by abandoned fields in which virtually no productive agricultural activity is taking place, except for occasional small-scale cattle ranching. Although the shift in the 1940s from agriculture to urban work marked a dramatic economic change, the Yuchi community was spared the disruptive social effects that accompanied that shift in other Native communities. Because the Yuchi settlements were close to, but distinct from, urban Tulsa, many Yuchi people were able to obtain reasonably good jobs without relocating to distant urban centers or abandoning their landholdings. This enabled them to retain their own community activities, patterns of interaction, and cultural identity, although participation in the wage economy, as well as the boarding school experience, furthered the language shift from Yuchi to English and prompted other adjustments in social life.[21]

The New Deal in the 1930s began a reversal of federal Indian policy toward recognition of the value and legitimacy of tribal self-government. In incremental fashion, political progress came during the middle of the century. The Oklahoma Indian Welfare Act in 1936, and the work of the Indian Claims Commission beginning in 1946, preceded the return of popularly elected Creek national government in 1971. The reconstituted tribal government has increasingly played a valuable role in promoting the interests of Creek citizens (including most, but not all, Yuchi people), but the present form of government fails to recognize the ongoing significance of the town communities and the ethnic and cultural heterogeneity that they represent.

Under the constitution of 1867 the Yuchi were recognized as a single town within the tribal council, but the present constitution provides for representatives elected on the basis of eight geographic districts. This means that neither the Yuchi nor any of the Creek town communities that retain their corporate identity have any direct representation in the national government. Many Yuchi, as well as most of the culturally conservative Creek people, reject the abandonment of the town-based form of national government. The sovereignty and enduring significance of the towns, as symbolized most visibly by the ceremonial grounds, is a major theme of the public oratory examined among the Creek by Amelia Bell (1984) and among the Yuchi in chapter 4. In its reconstituted form, the new Creek Nation has perpetuated many of the social divisions characteristic of earlier periods. These divisions are most clearly expressed in the domination of the nation by métis politicians who are particularly alienated from the cultural values of the ceremonial ground communities among whom I have worked and whose beliefs are reflected in the chapters that follow.

YUCHI COMMUNITIES TODAY

Like conservative Creeks, Yuchi ceremonial ground participants identify closely with their local "town" communities, while recognizing a shared tribal identity as Yuchis. As among the Creeks, *tribal town* has a special meaning for the Yuchi. Not a geographic entity per se, a tribal town is a social entity whose identity is manifest in a ceremonial ground or church. Even without any institutional expression, Creeks and Yuchis may continue to identify with the name of their town and recognize their affinity to fellow townspeople (Opler 1972). Towns in this sense do have geographic locales, but people identify with their tribal towns wherever they go, and residence near the district associated with the town's institutions is not necessary to maintain ties of affinity with the town community (A. Walker 1981).

Another aspect of Creek belief related to towns that is shared by the Yuchi is the notion of *mother ground* (or *mother town*)(see Swanton 1912:594). For ceremonial ground people, the focal symbol of a tribal town is the sacred fire that each maintains at its ceremonial site. This fire is rekindled anew each year as part of the ground's Green Corn Ceremonies, and the sacred fires in Oklahoma today are believed to have been carried west during the removal from the Southeast. As before removal, some towns today trace their ancestry back to divisions of towns existing at earlier periods in tribal history. The common fire or town shared by a group of derivative (daughter) towns is called their *mother fire* or *mother ground*. Unlike Creek tribal towns, modern Yuchi towns in Oklahoma do not carry over names and identities from towns that existed in the Southeast. Nevertheless, the Yuchi do have a mother town. The Polecat Ceremonial Ground is considered by Yuchi people to be their mother town, and the other two Yuchi ceremonial grounds are believed to be derivative from the Polecat fire. All Yuchi people are encouraged to participate in the activities of the mother town, and it, more than any other institution, symbolizes Yuchi identity.

Overlaying the old tribal town system of the Creek Nation is a modern innovation instituted by the Creek national government. Recognizing the lack of local organization formalized in the modern Creek governmental system, Creek political leaders replaced the town system with a system of *chartered communities.* Chartered communities exist in association with most municipalities in the Creek Nation area. As formally recognized voluntary community organizations, they receive some financial and organizational support from the Creek Nation. Most possess community-center buildings, and they provide Creek citizens (including some Yuchis) living in particular locales with a local organizational framework for secular social activities and for locally organized community development projects. Services provided by chartered communities include meals for the elderly, access to federal food programs, social activities, and in some communities, limited employment associated with community businesses such as bingo halls and tobacco shops. The chartered community system was created, in part, to replace town loyalties, but for conservative people, it simply created another level of national governance without diminishing affiliation with the tribal town ideal. When the chartered community system was introduced in the 1970s, Yuchi people established their own separate community organizations, but these were systematically dismantled by the Creek national government and replaced with geographically specific chartered communities not tied to town or tribal identities.

The three modern Yuchi settlement areas described below fit into this broader social framework. My interpretation reflects the views of ceremonial ground leaders. Other Yuchi people may view this social system very differently. Some do not identify their churches with the tribal town system. Some are loyal to their chartered communities without participating in other social institutions. Not all Yuchi people are even aware of the existence of named Yuchi settlements and instead see themselves simply as residents of municipalities such as Kellyville or Sapulpa.

SETTLEMENT AREAS AND INSTITUTIONS

Since removal, the Yuchi have resided in a series of settlements located along a fifty-mile arc in the northwest corner of the Creek Nation territory. This settlement area is indicated in map 2 and discussed in turn below. Everywhere that Yuchi people reside, both in rural areas and in small municipalities, they live interspersed among Euro-Americans, African Americans, and Native people of Creek and other tribal ancestry. All of those groups have a considerable history of co-residence with their Yuchi neighbors. However, in recent years the rural areas where Yuchi people reside have undergone shifts in residence pattern. Rural, multiethnic agricultural communities have been transformed by the decline of farming activities. Historically rural non-Native families have been leaving these areas at the same time that new home construction has transformed them into rural suburbs on the fringe of Tulsa. This transformation is particularly noticeable to Yuchi elders who note that they no longer know their neighbors and express regret about the passing of a shared, inter-ethnic rural culture.

DUCK CREEK

In the eastern portion of their territory, Yuchi homesteads are located near Snake Creek, Duck Creek, and Euchee Creek in the Arkansas River Valley, near the municipalities of Bixby and Mounds. This settlement was known in the past as Snake Creek and has been known in more recent times as Duck Creek. Its identity as a tribal town and a formal community is expressed most visibly in the Duck Creek Ceremonial Ground and in the Duck Creek Indian Community, a local chartered community organized within the government of the Creek Nation. The Duck Creek Ceremonial Ground is one of three active Yuchi grounds. Almost all members of the ground and most members of the community organization identify themselves as Yuchi.

Also located in this community is the Snake Creek Baptist Church, a mostly Creek congregation that has had some Yuchi involvement in the past. An Evangelical church organized and run by Yuchi people opened recently on the allotment of a Duck Creek family, but most of its membership is composed of Yuchi people from the Polecat area, further west. The members and leaders of the ceremonial ground play a leading role in the community organization. Those Duck Creek residents active in Christian churches attend either the predominantly Yuchi Pickett Chapel United Methodist Church in the Polecat settlement area or non-Native congregations. The strength of the ceremonial ground community and the settlement's rural character provide Duck Creek with a clear community identity that expresses the tribal town ideal that the Yuchi share with the Creek.

While the Duck Creek community is, in certain respects, the Yuchi settlement that is the most internally cohesive and the one that most closely approximates the tribal town ideal, the community is also the least able to directly participate in the national government of the Creek Nation. The community

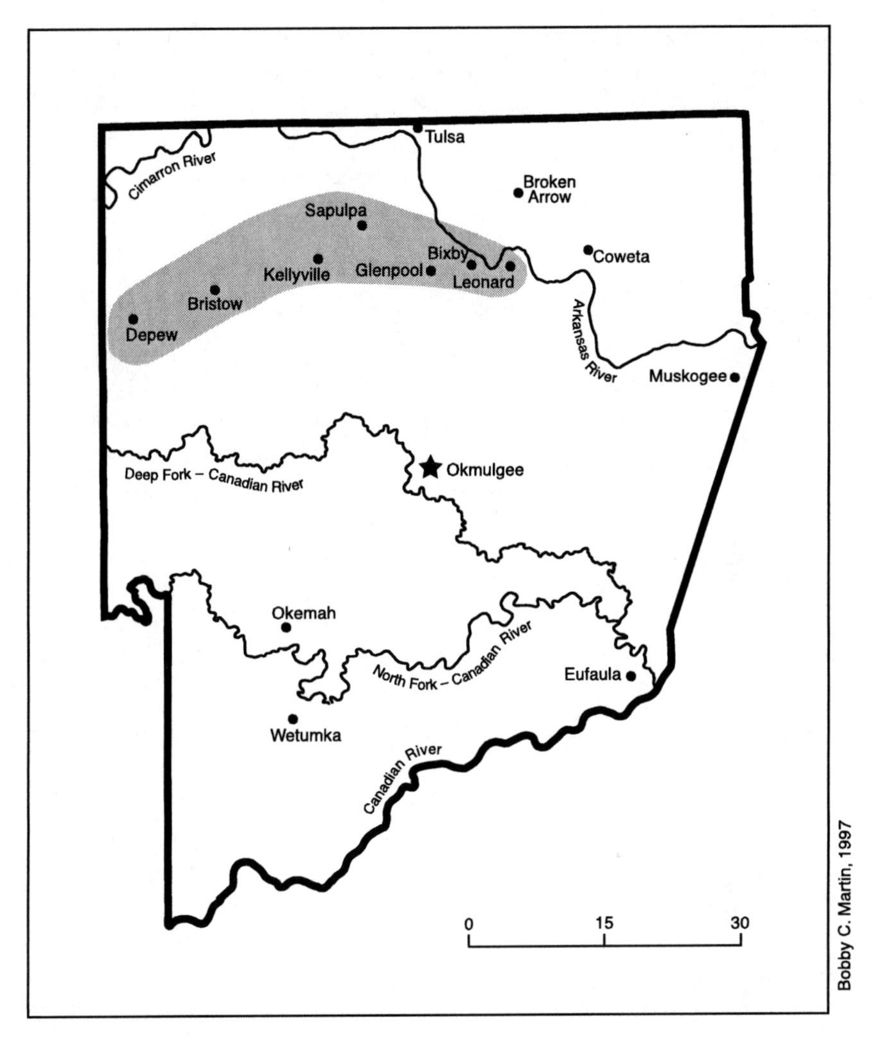

Map 2. The Yuchi settlement area within the Creek Nation

straddles the border separating Creek and Okmulgee counties, placing it in two electoral districts for representation on the Creek National Council. Unlike Sapulpa, which is the scene of much political activity during tribal elections, Tulsa's large and powerful Indian community politically dwarfs the Duck Creek area. Similarly, the Creek national capitol is located in Okmulgee, making it the political center of Okmulgee county. Although the marginality of Duck Creek provides the clearest picture of Yuchi alienation from Creek national politics, Yuchi people in all communities express frustration at their lack of voice in the national government. Yuchi dissatisfaction with their place within the Creek national government has many layers. In part it relates both to their unique status as a cultural enclave and to values shared by many Yuchi with culturally conservative Creek people, particularly ceremonial ground participants, who feel that the national government fails to respect their cultural practices and recognize their place in Creek society.

POLECAT

Northwest of Duck Creek, near Polecat Creek and the municipalities of Sapulpa and Kellyville, is Polecat, the largest of the Yuchi settlements. Although its identity as a Yuchi tribal town is symbolized by the large Polecat Ceremonial Ground, considered to be the mother ground for all Yuchi people, the community is geographically large and organizationally heterogeneous. Sapulpa, the settlement's municipal center, is a small city and a county seat, with a population of approximately 18,000. Until the school was closed in the 1950s, Sapulpa was the site of the Euchee Mission Boarding School, a prominent landmark in Yuchi historical consciousness.

In contrast to the situation at Duck Creek, the Yuchi political identity manifest in the ceremonial ground and its chief does not translate directly to the local community organizations in the Polecat area. Sapulpa and Kellyville both have separate chartered Indian communities within the Creek Nation, and their membership, leadership, and activities, while sometimes overlapping, do not match those of the ceremonial ground acting as a Yuchi tribal town. Additionally, the rural area south of Sapulpa, known as Pickett Prairie, has something of a distinct identity in Yuchi social thinking. Named after a prominent Yuchi family, it is the home of Pickett Chapel United Methodist Church. This church is the largest Yuchi congregation and the one with the strongest identity as a distinctly Yuchi institution. In addition to Pickett Chapel, Yuchi people have been involved in a variety of Creek congregations in the area, particularly Little Cussetta, a Baptist church, and the now disbanded Rock Creek church, an independent Methodist congregation.

Sapulpa serves a large population of both Creek and Yuchi people and is the site of a Creek Nation sponsored preschool program, a heavily utilized Indian clinic, and many homes built by the Creek Nation's housing program. Because of its own industrial base, anchored by two glass manufacturing plants, and its proximity to Tulsa, Sapulpa has attracted both Yuchi and Creek residents throughout the twentieth century.

Like other American towns of its size and circumstance, Sapulpa has witnessed an economic shift away from a self-sufficient service economy to a relationship of dependence on a nearby metropolitan area. Yuchi elders from Duck

Creek observe the transformation of a rural community, while Polecat elders narrate Sapulpa's civic decline. The Sapulpa of their young adulthood – straddling the famous U.S. Route 66 and a busy passenger rail line – was a town with a lively downtown life, featuring streetcars, movie theaters, and concerts on the courtyard steps. Sapulpa today is an exit off of Interstate 44 served by a complement of American chain institutions – Wal-Mart, McDonald's, and Motel 6. While its citizens are now well connected to Tulsa, the city's role as the seat of government for Creek Country, a county separate from Tulsa County, has enabled it to preserve some of its socio-economic autonomy.

SAND CREEK AND BIG POND

Duck Creek and Polecat are discontinuous settlements, but Yuchi homesteads and allotments stretch in a continuous band going west from Sapulpa and Kellyville on old Route 66. Fourteen miles southwest of Kellyville is the municipality of Bristow (population 4,062), the economic center of gravity for the Yuchi people of the Sand Creek community. The Yuchi political identity of this community is invested in its ceremonial ground located ten miles south of Bristow. Bristow itself is the home of the Bristow Indian Community, another chartered community composed of both Yuchi and Creek members. The second historic Yuchi church, Mutteloke United Methodist Church, is located in Bristow. While founded by Yuchi members of Pickett Chapel as a church to serve the Yuchi people of the Sand Creek settlement, the church is less steadfast in asserting its Yuchi identity and is today composed of people of Creek and other tribal backgrounds as well. Mutteloke, at present, shares a pastor with the Choska United Methodist Church, a Creek congregation located just south of Bristow.

Like the Mutteloke church, the Sand Creek Ceremonial Ground historically has had a small group of participants. Like the Church as well, the ground, as a Yuchi institution, has customarily exhibited the greatest mixing of Yuchi and Creek people and of Yuchi and Creek cultural practices. When Speck conducted fieldwork among the Yuchis of Sand Creek (1904–5), he observed that the nearby Creek town of Taskigi had abandoned its own ceremonial ground and Taskigi people were participating in the Yuchi ceremonials at Sand Creek. This pattern at Sand Creek has continued in the present and will be examined in fuller detail in the chapters that follow.

The Sand Creek settlement is considered to stretch from the area north of Bristow south to the area near Gypsy and Iron Post, two hamlets near the present site of the ceremonial ground. To the west, between Sand Creek and the Creek Nation's border with the old Sauk and Fox reservation, is the Yuchi area known as Big Pond. Unlike the other three settlements, Big Pond no longer has its own ceremonial ground. For all but the most historically aware Yuchi elders,

Big Pond has lost its distinct identity as a Yuchi community. The town of Depew is the closest municipality to the region considered to be the Big Pond area. In the early years of the twentieth century, Big Pond residents abandoned their ceremonial ground and consolidated their activities with the Sand Creek town. Big Pond is the name of a large and prominent Yuchi family whose allotments are scattered throughout the Sand Creek-Big Pond region. It is likely that the Big Pond community was always a satellite of the larger Sand Creek community, just as Yuchi towns before removal possessed satellite villages that sometimes built their own square grounds for the purpose of holding smaller local dances and ceremonies.

PAN-YUCHI ORGANIZATIONS

Cutting across the local Yuchi communities are other institutions and social networks that are tribal in scope. Members of the Native American Church among the Yuchi may affiliate with the Yuchi Chapter of the Native American Church of Oklahoma. In common with most Oklahoma communities, Yuchi peyotists practice the Little Moon form of the peyote ritual (Stewart 1987). Historically, Yuchi peyotists have had close relationships with the Shawnee and Sauk and Fox, but participants among the Yuchi, like those in most tribes, seek to host intertribal activities, valuing their relationships with friends from far-flung tribal communities (Jackson 1995). Yuchi involvement with the Native American Church has waned in recent years, perhaps due to increased activity in other sectors of the Yuchi cultural life, but also potentially mirroring national trends. Activity today in the church is strongest among Polecat community members.

While efforts to form a comprehensive tribal organization have arisen at various points in the past, the 1980s saw several significant undertakings that continue to shape the Yuchi community as a whole (for earlier efforts, see Wallace [1998]). First on the scene was the Yuchi Tribal Organization (YTO), established in 1989. It remained active until about 1993, although some of the group's members continued to work together less formally. The YTO was founded for the purpose of organizing the Yuchi community as a whole, and the group's primary focus was the pursuit of federal recognition for the Yuchi tribe, separate from the Muskogee (Creek) Nation. The organization had some initial success, receiving a grant from the U.S. Department of Health and Human Services for community organization and research in support of the recognition petition. However, the group's activity was hindered and the group faltered over divisions arising from the petition. In 1991 the petition was submitted to the Bureau of Indian Affairs (BIA) over the objections of some Yuchi community leaders.

After being evaluated as deficient by lawyers from the Native American Rights Fund, the petition was submitted without substantive revision and was subsequently rejected by the BIA (Bureau of Indian Affairs 1999).

In 1992, in response to increased awareness of Yuchi cultural preservation needs, but cautious in its attempts to avoid the divisions engendered by the YTO, Euchees United Cultural, Historical, and Educational Efforts (E.U.C.H.E.E.) was founded. This group has undertaken a range of successful projects. Most visible are its efforts sponsoring language classes and camps for children and families. It has also organized a photographic archive, produced annual photographic calendars since 1992, and published a tribal history in 1997 (E.U.C.H.E.E. 1997). It has also collaborated on a museum exhibition related to Yuchi culture and history and sponsored a series of annual tribal festivals together with the Euchee (Yuchi) Tribe of Indians. E.U.C.H.E.E. has been successful in obtaining grant funding for its efforts and is currently developing several new projects, including language activities on CD-ROM.

Working in close cooperation with E.U.C.H.E.E., and founded at about the same time, is a second organization attempting to unite the full Yuchi tribal community. Community activists concerned with addressing the original purposes of the YTO began the Euchee (Yuchi) Tribe of Indians. Uneasy about the lack of representativeness of the YTO, the Euchee (Yuchi) Tribe of Indians has sought to establish and maintain its legitimacy in the community as a whole by relying on the involvement of the chiefs and officers of each of the three Yuchi ceremonial grounds. These men serve on the organization's board of directors and act as representatives for the three major Yuchi communities. Although the Euchee (Yuchi) Tribe of Indians is not universally accepted, the view that the three Yuchi chiefs are the legitimate moral and political leaders in the communities has enabled the organization to achieve considerable success. This view combines the tribal town ideal, in which a ceremonial ground is taken as the manifestation of a legitimate Indian town, and the belief that the Yuchi constitute a unified people. Because it is based on the legitimacy of the ceremonial grounds as political entities, the Euchee (Yuchi) Tribe of Indians has its greatest influence among stomp ground participants, although church members are also involved in its activities. In founding itself upon the ceremonial grounds as tribal towns, the Euchee Tribe is in many ways comparable to the Tribal Towns Organization, a body that links the Creek ceremonial grounds and presents itself as an organizational alternative to the modern Creek national government.

The Euchee (Yuchi) Tribe of Indians avoided direct involvement in the recognition effort during the period in which the YTO petition was under review, but it has been particularly interested in facilitating research that will support future recognition efforts. The organization has formally collaborated with various researchers on projects to document Yuchi culture, genealogy, history, and language. My own invitation to work in the Yuchi community studying oral history and contemporary cultural life derived from these efforts.

The sketch of Yuchi history and culture that I have provided in this chapter is not an adequate substitute for a general ethnography of contemporary Yuchi life or a history of Yuchi society through time. My goal here has been to provide some cultural, historical, and social context for the understanding of contemporary Yuchi ritual. Chapter 3 provides more specific social and cultural contexts for interpreting Yuchi ceremonial ground life. If this chapter has accurately described any Yuchi reality, my hope is that it has explained some of the social forms and historical patterns characteristic of a people who, while not recognized as such, have been and continue to be a distinct people with a unique history and distinct society. In the chapters that follow, I hope to outline some of the cultural values that make life in this distinct society meaningful.

3 Ceremonial Life
General Frameworks

"Observe and realize the power of the Creator."

Having sketched the historical and cultural situation of the Yuchi community as a whole, I focus in this chapter more specifically on the social life and cultural values of the three contemporary Yuchi ceremonial grounds. Conceptually, all Yuchi people belong to a ceremonial ground and are encouraged to participate in its activities; however, only a subset of Yuchi people are actually involved in the ritual life discussed in the remaining chapters. In outlining some of the general features of Yuchi ceremonialism, this chapter provides background for the specific consideration of the ritual events described in the chapters that follow.

THE BIG HOUSES

The three Yuchi ceremonial grounds – Duck Creek, Sand Creek, and Polecat – have already been enumerated and located within the three major settlement areas. In Oklahoma English, these grounds and those among the Creek, Seminole, Cherokee, Shawnee, and other groups are often called "stomp grounds," a name that refers to stomp dancing, the prominent dance and music genre performed at them. In elevated speech, such as the oratory discussed in the next chapter, the Yuchi refer to their ceremonial grounds as "big houses." This translation of Yuchi *ju'a* may refer to the pre-removal practice of building communal town houses, but it is used today as a metaphor evoking the values of community and harmony expected of ceremonial ground participants. Encompassed by a common big house, Yuchi people are expected to interact with one another, with the Creator, and with their ancestors with the respect and decorum appropriate to a family.[1]

Since the turn of the century, the ceremonial ground in the Duck Creek community has been located at four different sites, and was inactive for about seven years during the 1930s and early 1940s. It was established at its current site in 1941 with John Brown, Sr., serving as chief. Subsequent chiefs were Bobby Gibson (1976–84) and Felix Brown, Sr. (1984–96). The current chief is Simon Harry (1996-present), who formerly served as second chief and is the nephew of Willie Fox, the ground's chief in the 1920s and 1930s. When reestablished in the 1940s, the ground's ritual program featured some Creek practices mixed into the general Yuchi ceremonial framework. During the 1980s and 1990s, specifically Yuchi dances and rituals, modeled on those performed at Polecat, were consciously reintroduced into the ground, in some cases replacing Creek forms. In 1996 this shift in the ground's program was virtually complete when the Duck Creek men, with the assistance of Polecat ground leaders, performed all but one of the Yuchi day-time dances found in the Green Corn Ceremony at the mother ground.

As will be discussed in chapter 6, Duck Creek is the most active Yuchi ground in its visiting of other ceremonial communities. Ardent dancers and socially cohesive, the Duck Creek ground sends out large delegations on every available weekend during the summer ritual season. The ground has ten active family camps, and most of this membership is active in community events throughout the year.

The Polecat stomp ground is the largest of the Yuchi grounds. With seventeen camps, it is one of the largest Woodland ceremonial grounds in Oklahoma. Considered the mother ground of the Yuchi people, it is thought to preserve the fullest and most authentic versions of the Yuchi calendrical rituals. While the ground was moved at least once during the twentieth century, it was never allowed to become inactive, although for a period in the 1960s, participation waned and the full ceremonial was not performed each year.

The earliest Polecat chief remembered by current participants is "Old Man" Watashe, who served at the ground's previous site in the 1930s. Several members of the Watashe family held the position of chief in the 1940s. Jackson Barnett served as chief during the 1950s and early 1960s. James Brown, Sr., whose wife was a member of the Polecat ground and whose father had been the chief at Sand Creek in the 1930s, took the Polecat chieftainship following Jackson Barnett, having previously served as the ground's second chief. In 1996 James Brown, Jr., became chief following the death of his father.

The Polecat ground has many members, but the bulk of the ground's yearly program is supported by a smaller core group of active participants. During the period of my involvement in its activities, only five or six of the Polecat camps were active year-round, with the remainder participating fully only during the Arbor Dance, Green Corn Ceremony, and Soup Dance. In contrast to Duck Creek, fewer Polecat members are active in visiting relationships with the other Oklahoma ceremonial grounds. When Polecat delegations participate in visiting, they tend to do so in coordination with Duck Creek.

The Sand Creek ground was founded at its current site during the 1960s by Madison Bucktrot's family, and the majority of its active members are linked to the Bucktrot family by kinship or marriage. Because the ground was inactive for much of the twentieth century (roughly 1938–61), many people who belong to the Sand Creek community (on the basis of genealogy) are now active in the Polecat ground. The Sand Creek membership has also, in the past, included members of the Big Pond community, who at the time of Frank Speck's fieldwork in 1904–5 were not performing their own Green Corn Ceremony (1909:78).

The Sand Creek ground was moved several times and was dormant for a period (or periods) in the 1910s and 1920s. During these early decades of the century, John Wolf and Clarence Brown served as chiefs. From around 1938 until the early 1960s, the ground was inactive. It was revived at this period by the family of Madison Bucktrot, who served as the ground's first new chief. He held this role until about 1972, when his son, Alvin Bucktrot, became chief. In 1974 his nephew, Wade Bucktrot, Jr., became chief, serving until 1996 when his brother Kelly Bucktrot assumed this role. Gary Bucktrot currently serves as Sand Creek chief. Although the figure has varied somewhat from year to year, the Sand Creek ground has had approximately seven active family camps over the last decade (1990–2000).

The present ceremonial program of the Sand Creek ground shows the greatest mixing of Creek and Yuchi patterns and, as discussed in chapter 6, that ground has the most extensive linkages with Creek ceremonialists. Unlike Duck Creek and Polecat, the Sand Creek ground does not, at present, perform Feather Dances or any other daytime "medicine dances" during its Green Corn Ceremony.

YUCHI POPULATION AND CEREMONIAL GROUND PARTICIPATION

Because Yuchi people are enrolled as members of the Creek Nation or another tribe, they have no formal means of determining just how many people self-identify with their community. Additionally, an undetermined proportion of the Yuchi people live outside the Yuchi region, dispersed across Oklahoma and the United States, increasing the difficulty of estimating their population. Recent work by the Euchee (Yuchi) Tribe of Indians directed toward collecting Yuchi genealogies may, in the near future, provide the information required to accurately assess the size and nature of the Yuchi population.

When discussing the nature of their community, the Yuchi people with whom I worked focus on the institutions and activities that provide the form and content for distinctly Yuchi society and culture. While descent from an ac-

Table 2. Estimated Yuchi Ceremonial Ground Participation, ca. 1995

GROUND	NUMBER OF CAMPS	ESTIMATED PARTICIPATION
Duck Creek	10	100
Polecat	17	170
Sand Creek	7	70
Total	34	340

Note: This estimate is calculated on the basis of extended family camps with an average of 10 affiliated members per camp.

knowledged Yuchi ancestor is all that is required for an individual to assert Yuchi identity, participation in community life is the most salient means by which Yuchi people go about actively being Yuchi.

Seeking to describe the stark difference between the number of people enrolled by the Cherokee Nation and the number of people living in socially and culturally distinct Cherokee communities, Albert Wahrhaftig (1968) adopted the term "tribal Cherokee" to characterize the latter. The label "tribal" is used similarly in the English of more conservative Indian people of eastern Oklahoma, usually in statements contrasting themselves and their communities with the more assimilated political leadership of their tribal governments. With the help of Cherokee speakers, Wahrhaftig identified seventy-four socioculturally Cherokee settlements in Oklahoma. As with the towns of the Yuchi and Creek, one or more ceremonial institutions provided the central focus for these communities. By determining the number of Cherokee community institutions, the estimated number of households belonging to each, and the average household size, Wahrhaftig was able to compile an overall estimate of the tribal Cherokee population. As the primary venues in which Yuchi cultural life unfolds, the ceremonial grounds and churches, taken together, similarly can be used to approximate the Yuchi "tribal" population count. Based on my experience participating in ceremonial ground activities, I am able to make a reasonable estimate of ceremonial ground membership and participation. These figures are given in table 2.

This overall estimate (340 ceremonial ground participants) measures participation based on regular attendance at the annual Green Corn Ceremonies. Participation in the full cycle of ritual events is less at all three grounds, although the amount of variance differs between grounds. Polecat has the largest participation at Green Corn, but suffers the most during other events. The difference between full participation and Green Corn participation at Duck Creek and Sand Creek is much less extreme.

According to 1997 figures compiled and published by the Oklahoma Indian

Methodist Conference, the total membership at Pickett Chapel was 187 with an average service attendance of 60 individuals. At Mutteloke Church, the membership for this year was 68, with an average attendance of 17 (Wilson 2000). Of this total (multi-tribal) membership of 255, it is reasonable, I think, to estimate the number of Yuchis not enumerated among the ceremonial ground members at around 150. This would suggest a total of about 500 "tribal" Yuchi. This figure accords well with the communities' own estimate of about 1500 as the total number of people able to claim Yuchi identity. Similar ratios of active tribal people to inactive (often out-of-state) tribal descendants are found among most of the smaller Oklahoma tribes, where those ratios are more easily demonstrated by comparisons of tribal rolls, voting patterns, and community activities.

CEREMONIAL GROUND ARCHITECTURE

The general architectural format for the Yuchi ceremonial grounds is similar to those of the Creek and Seminole, but several features are distinctively Yuchi and deserve special notice. While previous writers have focused attention just on the layout of the square at the center of each stomp ground, the construction and orientation of the entire site is culturally significant (see Howard and Lena 1984). The layout and use of different areas within the ground index Yuchi understandings of both social divisions and appropriate interaction patterns. Map 3, which describes the layout of the Duck Creek ceremonial ground, illustrates this discussion.

Each of the Yuchi grounds is located in a cleared grassy area, on land owned by an individual who provides it to the community for use as the ceremonial site. An outer boundary of forest or fenced fields separates the grounds from other parts of the landholding. The outer precincts of the ground itself comprise parking areas and family camps. The camps that surround the town square are the modern equivalent of the permanent households that once existed at the center of pre-removal Yuchi towns. Each camp is maintained by a different family that is active in the ceremonial ground, and each ceremonial participant affiliates with one of these camps through ties of kinship, marriage, or friendship. The camps provide the setting for domestic life during multi-day events such as the Green Corn Ceremony and they are the primary site for female activities on the ceremonial ground. As signs of family, motherhood, and domestic life, they are the architectural and behavioral counterpart to the central square where male-dominated ritual activities take place (Jackson 1998a).

Separating the camps from the square is a perimeter drive that provides access to all of the camps. Members park their cars on the outside of this drive in

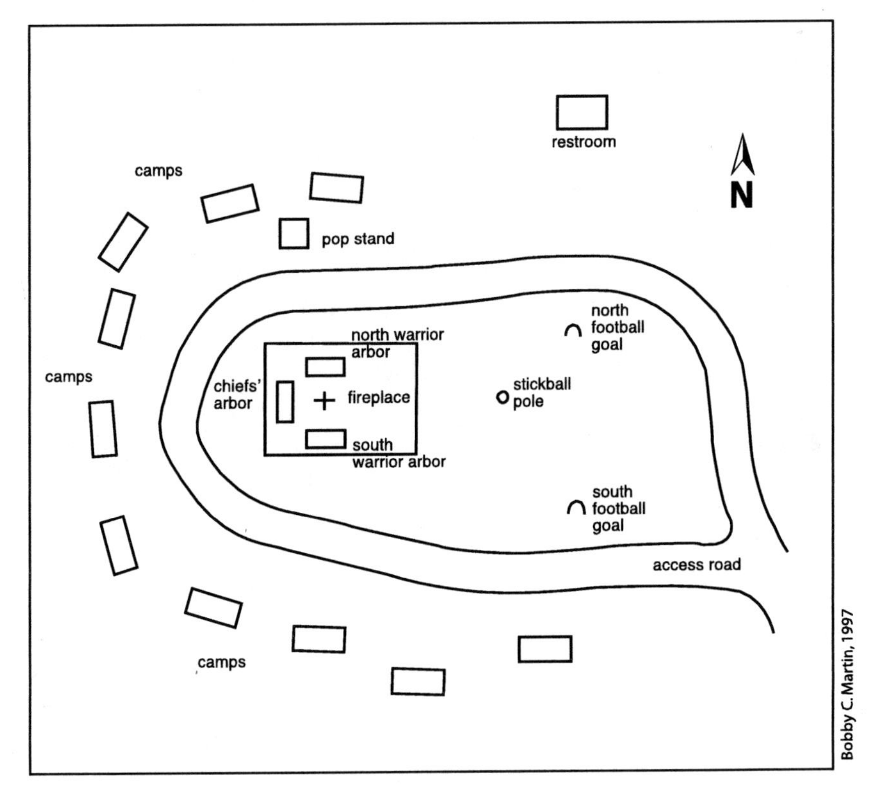

Map 3. Ground plan of the Duck Creek Ceremonial Ground

front of the family camps where they participate. Guests visiting the ground park on the inside of the drive, adjacent to the square. To the east of the square is the football field, oriented north-south. At Duck Creek, the pole used in the single-pole stickball game is located between the square and the football field, due east of the fireplace. At Sand Creek, this stickball pole is located north of the square. The Polecat ground does not have a ballpole at its current site.

At the center of the ground is the square. Like those of the Creek and Seminole, it is a plaza of cleared earth, ringed by a raised circular ridge created through the process of scraping the ground clean each year. The square, where dances and rituals take place, is the most sacred precinct of the ground, and the ring of earth serves to separate it from the remainder of the ground. The square's sacred character is most evident during the main day of the Green Corn Ceremony, when only men who are fasting and taking part in the rituals may cross the earth ring into the square.

At the center of the square is the fireplace. On the north, south, and west sides

A view of the Watashe family camp at the Polecat Ceremonial Ground during its Green Corn Ceremony, 12 July 1997. This picture illustrates typical family camp architecture.

stand open-sided brush arbors that house the patrilineal men's societies during formal events. The chief and his assistant(s) sit in the west arbor along with members of the chief society. The members of the warrior society are divided between the north and the south arbors. This organization of the arbors is fundamentally different from that found among the Creek, Seminole, and Cherokee. The ceremonial ground arbors of these groups are divided among matrilineal clans. In determining eligibility for specific ritual offices, these clans function in similar ways to the patrilineal societies of the Yuchi, but unlike the matrilineal clans of their neighbors, the Yuchi societies are not exogamous (Jackson 1996a).[2]

The manner in which members and visitors behave and interact within the space of the ceremonial grounds is highly structured, providing insight into Yuchi values and cultural suppositions. The descriptions presented in the chapters that follow can be foreshadowed here with a small example. When taking their seats beneath the brush arbors on the square, men are expected to sit down

The poleboys tend the new fire early in the morning of the Green Corn Ceremony. This image provides a view of the Duck Creek Ceremonial Ground looking north from the southwest. 29 June 1996.

from the front side of the bench and to not step over the bench from the back. For younger participants this expectation is just "one of the rules," but older men explain that during ceremonial ground events, the spirits of Yuchi ancestors return to the ground to participate with the living. To step over the bench is to risk rudely treading on such a spirit, while the proper technique provides the ancestor with an appropriate opportunity to move over and share the bench. In isolation such a rule may seem peculiar; however in subsequent chapters I seek to show that it is one expression of a fundamental concern in Yuchi ritual – respect for, and engagement with both Yuchi ancestors and the cultural patrimony that they bequeathed to the living.

RITUAL SOCIAL ORGANIZATION

Key building blocks of the ceremonial ground community are the extended family groups that establish and maintain camps at the ground. Unlike the informal campsites that spring up during powwows and other contemporary Native American gatherings, ceremonial ground camps are physically permanent and socially central to activity on the ground. At the center of a camp group is an older family member or couple, who are often the founders of the camp or who inherited it from still older camp members who have passed away or retired from ceremonial ground life.

Much of the activity that takes place within the camps is the responsibility of women. If the camp is owned and led by a couple, then the wife is typically the key organizer of its activities. A widow or single older woman may also lead a camp. If an older widower is at the center of the camp, then one of his daughters, granddaughters, or other female relatives will shoulder this responsibility. Around this central person or couple gather other family members and friends who are unattached to another camp at the ground. Typically, the leading woman will rely closely on a small, core group of other women (daughters, sisters, granddaughters, or friends) for shopping, gathering equipment, setting up, cooking, cleaning, and serving food. Other women attached to the camp will assist during events, contributing food and work, but their participation is less intense than that of the main helpers.

In the course of ceremonial ground events, the attention of the men is focused mostly on the dances and rituals that take place on the square, but each man belongs to his family's camp or to one where he is incorporated as a friend. While much of the domestic work of the camp is in the hands of women during events, men play a major role in preparing the camps for use during the week before the Green Corn Ceremony and the week before the Soup Dance, when the camps will be used. Repairing the camp buildings, moving in the equipment and supplies, mowing the grass around the camp, and obtaining and cutting firewood are the major male tasks.[3]

At the Green Corn Ceremony and the Soup Dance, the camps play a major role in negotiating relations with guests and visiting ceremonial ground groups. During these events, each camp takes on part of the responsibility for hosting and feeding visitors. In extending hospitality to visitors, the camps become the front line in negotiating inter-community relations, thereby establishing and sustaining bonds of reciprocity between ceremonial grounds. This topic will be explored in greater detail in chapter 6.

During stomp dances, the Arbor Dance, and football games, the ceremonial ground as a whole uses a single camp, often the chief's camp, for potluck covered-dish meals. Just as during the final two events, at these gatherings the welcoming and feeding of visitors is a priority. The women of the ground, led by the chief's wife and other camp matrons, will maintain this camp during the evening and throughout the night of a dance to feed dinner to visitors and to provide a coffee break to guests during the early hours of the morning.

Division into camp groups is one way in which the members of each ceremonial ground organize themselves for life at the grounds. In addition, Yuchi men are organized into a second grouping, a patrilineal dual division, the sides of which were called "societies" by Frank Speck and are called "arbors" by Yuchi people today. The Yuchi name refers to the role of this grouping in determining where men sit while participating in rituals on the square (Jackson 1996a:124–35; Speck 1909:74–78). Beyond determining seating under the arbors, arbor group membership determines eligibility for most ritual offices.

On the east side of the square is the chiefs' arbor. Men eligible to serve as chief or second chief are seated here. Within a ceremonial ground, men belonging to the chief society tend to trace their ancestry back to two or three prominent men, usually former chiefs of the ground.

The warrior society members sit under the other two arbors. This group shares membership in the warrior side of the dual division but is divided internally between the north and the south sides. In some respects, the north side is considered senior to the south side, but some central ritual offices, such as the official who ritually scratches the men and boys during the Green Corn Ceremony, are assigned to the south side. Men joining the ground community without society membership are often assigned by the chief to the south arbor.

Many of the offices filled during the Green Corn Ceremony fall to members of the warrior society, reflecting notions of reciprocity and the belief that the warriors have an obligation to assist the chief in making the ground a success. In undertaking this work, the men of each arbor retain a group identity that was probably stronger in the days when these divisions were the basic "structural pose" for Yuchi political life (Gearing 1962). Formally, the men of each warriors' arbor must consent to one of their members being put into service by the chief. If the chief chooses a man from the north warriors' arbor to serve as his speaker, he must ask the north arbor men, represented by their leading elder, before "borrowing" the man to act in this capacity. Thus borrowed, the speaker will sit with the chiefs while acting in this role. Similarly, the four "feathermen" who lead the daytime Feather Dances at Duck Creek and Polecat are selected from the two warriors' arbors. When they are ritually appointed on the Friday evening of Green Corn, their selection is publicly announced in Yuchi and their selection is ratified formally by the men of the ground.

OFFICERS AND OFFICIALS

The key official in Yuchi ceremonial ground life is the chief who leads each community. The chief is responsible for all activity on the ceremonial ground and for fostering the well-being of all community members. Formally, the chief is responsible only for the activities of the ceremonial ground; he is, however, ideally, and generally in practice as well, the moral leader for the local community. Because life away from the ceremonial grounds directly affects the social health and welfare of the community on the grounds, a chief is very concerned about the entire community, particularly active members of the ground. Although this concern for community well-being is typical of American religious congregations, it is enhanced by the tenets of Yuchi religious philosophy, in which the spiritual and physical health of ceremonial ground members is linked to the overall health of the community. To break a taboo or create social strife in this context is to endanger all ground members. This understanding creates incentive for a chief to both model and encourage appropriate behavior.

In contrast with current practice among Creek ceremonial grounds, where some chiefs serve set terms, Yuchi ceremonialists hold that a ground chief is expected to serve for life. In recent years, beliefs about chieftainship, especially the manner in which a new chief is selected, have been the subject of discussion within the community. Differing views have been expressed both in public discourse and in the political behavior that accompanied the recent selection of new chiefs at the Yuchi grounds. My account of political succession is based on the consensus view of the ritual leaders with whom I have worked. Typically, a change in leadership is an uncommon occurrence, and most participants have only been witness to a few such transitions in their lives. This fact, combined with the realization that the Yuchi grounds are small communities that privilege public consensus and are governed by face-to-face interaction, makes clear the sense in which political decision-making is flexible and pragmatic, as well as customary.

Deference to the views of elders, respect for understandings of tradition, the preservation of face, and the practical requirement that chiefs must have the necessary skills to lead communal ritual life all play a part in negotiating changes in leadership. The older norm, still privileged by most ceremonialists, is that the eldest son of the deceased chief becomes his father's successor. Alternatively, another son might be chosen if circumstance prevents the eldest son from serving. Lacking a son, another male relative of the chief would be sought. In the absence of a relative, an unrelated but experienced man from the chief society would be chosen.

In 1996, after the deaths of the chiefs of both the Duck Creek and Polecat grounds, discussion accompanied the appointment of new chiefs in each community. During these deliberations, both men and women stated their views publicly. After a period of open discussion held away from the Duck Creek ceremonial site, the male members of the ground, particularly members of the ground committee, consulted with the sons of the late chief in proposing a solution. Their decision was later ratified by all members in a formal meeting on the square ground. The eldest son of the recently deceased chief was appointed as second chief so that he might study under the tutelage of the former second chief, who was appointed chief. The new chief, while belonging to a different family than the late chief, was himself a descendant of the chief who had served before the ground became inactive in the 1930s.

In contrast, at Polecat, the son of the deceased chief did take his father's seat; however, his selection came after a meeting on the square in which other candidates were nominated and each member present at the meeting cast a vote. At both the Duck Creek and Polecat grounds, the new chiefs were ritually installed in a ceremony in which each member of the community in turn greeted the new leader, shook hands with him, and pledged support during his tenure.

Each new Yuchi chief selects a second chief to assist him and to serve in his place in his absence. At Polecat, the chief also selects third and fourth chiefs as assistants. While these chiefs are drawn from the chief society, the chief is also assisted by a standing committee of men, typically four in number, who are drawn from the warrior as well as the chief society. The committee advises the chief on matters such as the scheduling of events as well as on matters pertaining to ritual practice.[4]

The chief's speaker, whose work is discussed in detail in chapter 4, is an important officer who is drawn from any of the societies. His task is to speak publicly on behalf of the chief and the members of the ground. Characterizing the office at the turn of the century, Speck described the speaker as the master of ceremonies, and indicated that he was the highest official of the warrior society (1909:81). While not necessarily the case today, the two speakers with whom I worked – Newman Littlebear, the speaker at Polecat, and the late Jimmie Skeeter, speaker at Duck Creek – were both clearly the leading men of the warrior society within their grounds. As a matter of practice, the speaker normally serves as a member of the chief's committee, in addition to his other duties.

A host of offices are associated with particular phases of each of the Yuchi calendrical ceremonies, and eligibility for many of these jobs is determined by society membership. These ceremonial officials are introduced within the framework of the particular rituals described in the chapters that follow. In addition to the standing officers already enumerated, the chief may select members to assume responsibility for certain administrative duties on a regular basis. Today, each ground has a treasurer to oversee the finances of the ground, and unlike the jobs so far enumerated, this position may be filled by a man or a woman.

THE ANNUAL CEREMONIAL CYCLE

Ceremonial grounds are the site of a series of regular calendrical rituals. The Yuchi ceremonial grounds, in their role as town square, once served as the general meeting place for all community activities, but today they are, with few exceptions, used only for holding the prescribed calendrical ritual events. The

Table 3. The Yuchi Ceremonial Cycle

Event	Timing
a. Football Game	(late March)
b. Football Game	
c. Football Game	
d. Football Game/Stomp Dance	
e. Stomp Dance	
f. Stomp Dance	
g. Arbor Dance/Stomp Dance	(one week before the Green Corn Ceremony)
h. Green Corn Ceremony	(June-August)
i. Soup Dance	(late July-August)
j. Optional "Extra" Stomp Dance	(September)
k. Fall Dance	(at the change of seasons)

Note: The Fall Dance, which involved taking medicine, is obsolete but remembered by living consultants. The Soup Dance is held one week after the Green Corn Ceremony at the Polecat Ground and later in the summer at the other two Yuchi grounds.

Yuchi ritual season opens in the spring and continues into the early fall. Before removal, the Yuchi possessed round town houses (also called "hot houses") similar to those found among the Creek, but unlike some Creek communities that built them for a time in Indian Territory, the Yuchi appear to have abandoned them at removal (Swanton 1922:309, 1928d:177–81). Such town houses were once the site of winter ceremonial events, but today, both the Creek and Yuchi are ritually inactive during this season. Increasingly, Yuchi and Creek ceremonialists participate in indoor stomp dances of a secular character during this "off-season."

The Yuchi ceremonial cycle is outlined in table 3. Although this schedule, in outline, is shared by all three grounds, the timing of events and the form that each ritual takes vary. The variation in timing is indicated in appendix A, which presents specific dates for the events of 1996.

The Yuchi football game initiates the ritual season. The first game, held on a Sunday in early spring, is followed by three additional games spread over a period of six to eight weeks. Typically the football games are accompanied by a potluck meal and a meeting of the membership. The first ritual act of the ceremonial season, preceding the game, is washing with spicewood (spicebush, *Lindera benzoin*) medicine as a means of purification before entering the central areas of the square. As the start of the activity on the grounds, the Yuchi believe that the football game is a signal to the Creator that they intend to renew their ceremonials for another season. The form and significance of the game is explored in chapter 5.

The fourth football game is held on a Saturday rather than on a Sunday, and is followed in the evening by the first of four Saturday night stomp dances. These dances are the basic form of ritual performance in the contemporary ceremonialism of the Yuchi and their neighbors. Dances are preceded by a communal meal and, at Duck Creek and Sand Creek, by games of single-pole stickball played between the men and the women. The dance itself begins in the hours after sunset, usually between ten and eleven-thirty, and continues until sunrise on Sunday morning. Stomp dances are the primary event through which the Yuchi ceremonial grounds interact with each other and with the ground communities of other tribes. The stomp dance and its role in intercommunity relationships is more fully considered in chapter 6.

The fourth and final stomp dance in the series that comes before the Green Corn Ceremony is known as the Arbor Dance. The dance itself is preceded by daytime work to refurbish and purify the ground, especially the square and the arbors that border it. While the men are renewing the ceremonial ground in preparation for Green Corn, they fast. This fast is broken at the conclusion of their work with a feast prepared by the women of the community. On the evening after this work, a regular stomp dance is held. After the collective work of the Arbor Dance is completed, the families are permitted to renew and repair their own family camps in preparation for the Green Corn Ceremony. During the week before the ceremonial, families begin moving into their camps. Specific aspects of the Arbor Dance are discussed in chapter 7.

The high point of the Yuchi ceremonial calendar is the Green Corn Ceremony. Although this ritual event is found among many Woodland peoples, the Yuchi form differs in several significant ways from that of the Creek and other peoples. A complicated, multi-day ritual event, the Green Corn Ceremony serves a variety of practical and spiritual functions. It is, among other things, a harvest celebration, a new fire ritual, a world renewal ceremony, a means of ensuring community health, a purification ceremony, a homecoming reunion, a tribal festival, and a means of communicating Yuchi values. Among the rituals of Southeastern peoples, the Green Corn Ceremony has commanded the greatest amount of scholarly attention. The mythological foundation of the Yuchi Green Corn rituals is addressed in chapter 8.

The final regular calendrical ceremony taking place at the Yuchi grounds is the Soup Dance. While less elaborate than the Green Corn Ceremony, it is also a complicated multi-day ritual event. It reinforces some of the same themes expressed in the Green Corn, but the ceremony has ritual forms and cultural concerns of its own. In the Yuchi form practiced at Polecat and Duck Creek, the daytime ritual focuses on preparation, by the men, of a special corn soup on the sacred fire. This soup is featured in a large communal feast that the members share with the spirits of ancestors who return to join their living kin. A night of stomp dancing concludes the Soup Dance and the prescribed ritual season. The Yuchi Soup Dance is described and interpreted in chapter 9.

Although this basic outline of events is shared by the three Yuchi stomp grounds, each community schedules the events in differing ways. During the period of my work, the chiefs noted that they were more concerned than their predecessors in the past had been with coordinating the timing of their own events so as to not conflict with those of other Yuchi grounds. Easy transportation and communication through Pan-Yuchi community organizations have increased the ability of the chiefs to foster Yuchi identity through this reciprocity.

Duck Creek typically begins its ritual season with a football game in late March or early April. As a general rule, Duck Creek holds its Green Corn first, usually in June. Following the general Yuchi pattern, the ground holds its Arbor Dance on the weekend before the Green Corn Ceremony, but it refurbishes the ground before the main ritual on the Saturday (seven days before), rather than the Friday (eight days before), as at Polecat. The Soup Dance at Duck Creek is scheduled on a weekend later in the fall. A Fall Dance, during which members took a special medicine, is remembered to have once been held by the Duck Creek ground after the leaves fell.

Polecat has established the pattern of playing its first football game on Easter Sunday. The ground retains what is considered to be the older Yuchi pattern of holding the Soup Dance as the closing event of the Green Corn Ceremony. The Arbor Dance, Green Corn Ceremony, and Soup Dance at Polecat take place now on three consecutive weekends in July, and the members remain camped at the ground throughout this period. While these events remain consecutive at Polecat, they have been relocated to the weekends to accommodate the modern work week.

Whereas Duck Creek completes its dances early in the summer and activities at Polecat occupy much of the Yuchi community during July, Sand Creek spreads out its dances on open weekends throughout the summer and undertakes the Arbor Dance and the Green Corn Ceremony in August, after the Polecat ground has completed its events. As at Duck Creek, the Soup Dance at Sand Creek is held later in the season, but unlike current practice at Duck Creek and Polecat, the ritual does not involve preparation of a special soup, but is instead a second opportunity for purification through fasting and taking the same red root medicine featured in the Green Corn Ceremony.

The ritual calendar for 1996 is typical of the current Yuchi scheduling, except that during this year the Sand Creek ground skipped the two regular stomp dances that follow the first dance and precede the Arbor Dance. This modification of the schedule was the result of the death of a ground elder and a change in leadership within the ground.[5]

EXPRESSIVE FORMS IN YUCHI RITUAL

Yuchi ceremonial ground ritual encompasses a number of expressive genres. Like the ritual themes that I introduce in the next section, these forms are the material out of which Yuchi ceremonial events are constructed and made meaningful.

Food for the Yuchi is a primary expression of hospitality and celebration in community life, particularly at the ceremonial grounds. Eating accompanies virtually every Yuchi gathering and it is said to define the character of Yuchi events. At secular community gatherings and minor ceremonial ground events like stomp dances, the community will eat as a single group, usually buffet style, in potluck dinners. At major events like Green Corn and the Soup Dance, each family will prepare its own meals within its own camp. In every case, meals are focal events used to cement community and family solidarity. (For a discussion of secular Yuchi foodways, see Jackson 1998a.)

Clothing worn during ceremonial ground events ranges along a continuum from everyday street clothes, worn during informal periods and games, to ceremonial Indian clothes, worn during the major dance events of the Green Corn Ceremony. While distinct Indian dress is never a requirement for full participation in any ceremonial ground event, ground members enjoy dressing in Yuchi style. As in most clothing systems, individuals combine personal tastes with culturally patterned styles in creating their appearance. In general form, Yuchi ceremonial clothes are similar to those of their Creek and Seminole neighbors. Men's clothing combines commercially produced "cowboy" items – wide-brimmed hats, denim jeans, and western boots – with homemade Yuchi pieces such as cotton ribbon shirts, hunting coats, yarn belts, and feather hat ornaments. Women's clothing similarly combines commercial and Indian elements. Long, full skirts or dresses provide room for the wearing of leg rattles while dancing. Both the shirts, jackets, and vests worn by men and the skirts and blouses worn by women are distinguished by their full cut, the use of solid and print cottons, and ribbon trim. These features are holdovers from nineteenth-century-Woodland Indian clothing, which was itself influenced by early American "citizen's dress." Yuchi ceremonial ground dress is pictured in the accompanying photographs. (See also the description provided in Jackson [1998b.])

Meals are the focal point of activity in the family camps. In contrast, music and dance dominate communal interest on the square at the center of the cere-

Using a coconut hand rattle, Chief Simon Harry leads a performance of the Old Folks Dance during the Green Corn Ceremonial at the Duck Creek Ceremonial Ground, 27 June 1998. Ester Littlebear, who leads the Ribbon Dance at this ground, dances behind Chief Harry. Several styles of Yuchi dance clothes are illustrated. The empty seats behind the dancers are those of the women of the ground.

monial grounds. All Yuchi dances are line dances. The stomp dance, in which a single line of men and women spiral around the fire, is the basic dance form. Behind the leader, women and men position themselves in alternation. The leader and the men who follow him sing in a call-and-response (antiphonal) style. The men dance with a shuffle step and sing the responses, while the women provide accompaniment with rattles tied below their knees. For each step taken by the men, the women take a double step in order to produce the appropriate rhythm with their "shells" (rattles made from tortoise shells or evaporated milk cans). The daytime dances of the Green Corn Ceremony and the nighttime social dances performed at the Soup Dance elaborate on the stomp dance by varying music, choreography, and step.

The only accompaniment for regular stomp dance songs is the shell shaking of the women. The rattles that they wear are attached to a leather base, with laces used to tie them around the leg. During the nighttime social dances and the daytime Green Corn Dances, hand rattles made of coconut shells are used by male song leaders, as are water drums and, occasionally, dry hide hand drums.

Mrs. Mary Watashe, seated here with women of her family, leads the Ribbon Dance at the Polecat Ceremonial Ground. Mrs. Watashe is wearing the older style of Yuchi dress, a one-piece garment worn with a full apron. When photographed here, the women had just been escorted to the ground by the stickmen in preparation for the Ribbon Dance during the Green Corn Ceremonial, 12 July 1997. Seated, left to right, are Mary Watashe, Lou White, Pat Wildcat, and Valetta Anderson. Standing, left to right, are Katie Johnson and Leatrice Bearpaw.

RECURRING FEATURES OF RITUAL ACTION

In the specific rituals that comprise the calendrical ceremonies of the Yuchi, certain cultural themes and expressive forms occur repeatedly and can be introduced initially as keys to the cultural code underlying Yuchi ceremonialism. These themes relate to the general propositions and world view of Yuchi culture. Their configuration is distinctly Yuchi, but as specific patterns, many are shared by other Woodland peoples. These commonalities make Yuchi ritual intelligible to members of these other groups who participate in Yuchi ceremonies, while the distinct ways in which they are organized serve to define the distinctly Yuchi character of Yuchi events.[6]

The Creator, Witnesses, and Medicine

An ever-present observer of Yuchi life, the Creator pays particular attention to Yuchi communal ritual. Yuchis today hold a variety of views about the specific nature of the Creator. These range from fully normative Christian perspectives to understandings that seem to more closely approximate pre-Christian belief. For the practice of ceremonial ground ritual, these differences remain personal and familial matters. In public discourse, the Creator is understood and interpreted in general ways that allow room for variations in personal interpretation. Specifically Yuchi understandings of the Creator and of cosmology are most clearly articulated by the elders who, in overseeing the practice of Yuchi ritual life, have reflected most seriously on its symbols and concepts. Even among these leaders there is variation in thought, but little conflict arises from it.

The Creator is responsible for the specific existence of the Yuchi as a people. This creation is alluded to by the Yuchi ethnonym *Tsoyaha* 'Children of the Sun'. The sacred narrative that accounts for this event has been widely reported since 1893, when it was first published by Albert S. Gatschet (1893; see also Speck 1909; Tuggle 1973; and Wagner 1931). In 1996 Newman Littlebear recorded a new telling within the context of a discussion of the scheduling of the Yuchi Green Corn Ceremony. While summarizing quickly the events of creation, Mr. Littlebear provided an important explanation of the manner in which the Sun, the Sacred Fire, and human Spirit are viewed as manifestations of the Creator.

TEXT 4

Observations concerning the creation of the Yuchi. Delivered by Newman Littlebear during an interview at the Kellyville Indian Community Center, 15 January 1996.

. . .

We always have ours in July
 at Polecat.

It has always
 been that way.

It usually, you know . . .

I guess originally they used to have it at
 the full moon
 in July.

Whenever they would take their . . .
    or have their Green Corn Ceremonial.

And I guess you know
    we've
    we've
    we've talked about that
    and we've wondered,
    in our younger days,

    why?

But you know there is a story
    of that full Moon
    you know.

Its like some of the
    legends
    or tales
    about the early . . .
    you know,
    in the time of
    the beginning
    of the Yuchi people.

About their
    origin
    or whatever you might call it, you know.

It has to do with the full Moon
    and ah

    you know the Sun.

The Sun, that *Tsoyaha* business comes in there.

That name, *Tsoyaha* was the full
    full Yuchi.

And I think THEY always went by that
that sign
whenever that Green Corn Ceremonial came about.

And ah, it seems like in this . . .
in our generation now
it wasn't,
it REALLY hasn't been explained,
but to me,
I've heard it, you know, mentioned
or talked about
by one of my elders
but he didn't go into no fine, you know, detail explaining it.

But he said that was our Mother.

It was like

the Sun
causing that mother Moon to
to shed blood.

And
when the blood hit the, hit the earth
it became the
became the first Yuchi.

See that legend . . .

He didn't go into all this detail
but, you know, that was what he meant, you know,
that is where we come from.

And I just don't REALLY
know how all-of-this ties in
like, with the medicine – the redroot.

An ah,

But the whole ceremony,
I don't know if anyone can
you know, explain all of it.

But all of that ties in.

The medicine we have
and the
blood that we shed in our, in our sacrifice
and the fire.

And the sand.
As I understand it
it is the Sun rays of the sand
runs from the fire.[7]

And the fire
kind of like
represents
the Sun above.
And the Sun above
is light and like
that father
father
spirit
is light and
it is something, you know,
that the human,
human race can
observe
and realize
the power of the Creator.

And
through this way
and through the Sun
and through the Fire
and the Spirit,
which we are.

We are Spirit
and we get our,
like our,

inspiration
passed down through
through that situation.

Unlike the synthesized accounts that have been previously put on record, this version is more typical of the actual ways in which such sacred narratives are alluded to and evoked in contemporary discussions of Yuchi culture.[8]

In addition to the Fire and the Sun, a host of other spiritual entities are manifest and visible in Yuchi ritual life. The Yuchi refer to this class of spiritual expressions as "witnesses." The Yuchi view is close to that of the Shawnee described by Carl Voegelin. He describes witnesses as an "intermediary between Shawnee who are praying for assistance and the ultimate source of all assistance, the Creator. No Shawnee would care to give a categorically limited list of witnesses. Rather, the notion seems to be that if anything has been used as a witness, then it is a witness. But a feeling of relative importance prevails; tobacco is the leader of the witnesses; fire, water, and eagle are of first rate importance" (1936:7). The key witnesses for the Yuchi reappear throughout ritual activities, but appear most prominently in the Green Corn and funeral ceremonies.

Paint worn on the face is a prominent witness. Yuchi ceremonialists today assert that paint should only be worn in two contexts – on the ceremonial ground at the time of the Green Corn Ceremony and at death. In both cases, paint acts as a witness on behalf of the individual, vouchsafing to the Creator and to Yuchi ancestors that he or she is a Yuchi person, entitled in the first place to be acknowledged as one of the faithful, and in the second place to be admitted into the company of ancestors residing in the next world. Although Speck (1909) recorded a range of paint designs, they are today codified into two basic forms . For women, red circles are painted at each cheekbone. For men, horizontal bars of red are painted on each cheek. Some Yuchis feel that white paint may be used in laying a chief to rest. This view is in keeping with the strong symbolic association of chiefs with peaceful activities, identified in color symbolism with white.[9] The red circle or "women's design" proscribed by Yuchi ritual leaders is also used by the Seneca-Cayuga, Shawnee, and other Northeastern groups. Men's designs vary more among those groups, but the use of paint as a witness of Indian identity in the eyes of the Creator is held in common by at least the Yuchi, Delaware, and Shawnee (Howard 1970, 1981; Speck 1937:119). Red earth paint is the ideal medium for these uses, but modern commercial face paints are sometimes substituted.

Possessing a widespread significance in Native America, tobacco is an especially important witness for the Yuchi. Like paint, it appears prominently in both the Green Corn and funeral ceremonies. In the Green Corn ritual, tobacco is used to signal to the Creator that preparations for the ceremony have been made. It is also used ritually as a symbolic payment by the men to the singer who sings Ribbon Dance songs for the women during an important phase of the ceremony. It is used similarly in the funeral ceremony, in which the deceased on earth is given tobacco that is to be presented to the Yuchi ancestors at the completion of the journey to heaven. In this role it is a currency for spiritual transaction with the ancestors, a sign of Yuchi identity, and an indicator of the completion of appropriate ritual forms.

After tobacco and paint, a host of other elements with sacred connotations play less prominent roles as witnesses. Feathers, particularly of eagles, hawks, and cranes, are venerated and used throughout Yuchi ritual. One use of feathers provides a clear sense of what Indian people mean when referring to certain objects as witnesses. Many Yuchi people place specially prepared eagle feathers above the doorways of their homes. Such feathers can be read by an Indian doctor to discover the nature of any disturbances occurring within the home, such as a burglary. Feathers are used as literal witnesses in this way among the Creek and Cherokee, as well (Kilpatrick 1964:219).

In keeping with other North American Indian theologies, smoke, particularly tobacco smoke, is a witness in that it carries messages upward toward the Creator. Songs sung at the ceremonial ground function in the same way. Yuchi stomp dance songs, while composed mostly of vocables rather than words, are considered to be a form of prayer to the Creator.

Sacred things somewhat distinct from witnesses are the plants that function as medicines in Yuchi ritual. The two most important plants are red root (tall prairie willow, *Salix humilis*) and snake root (rattlesnake master, *Eryngium yuccifolium*). Both are made into teas that are consumed during the Green Corn Ceremony. A number of other plants also have ritual uses. Their efficacy in rituals of purification, as well as the value of the plants used in herbalism and doctoring, is attributable to the power and beneficence of the Creator. In English, Yuchi ritualists use the phrase "taking medicine" to refer both to the collective use of such plants in ceremonies (washing, drinking, or touching) and their use in more strictly medicinal contexts. Prescribed behaviors, such as fasting and prayer, accompany the collection and use of all medicine plants.

Directional Symbolism

Cardinal directions are significant in Yuchi ceremonies and cosmology, with east and west providing the main axis around which ritual unfolds. East serves as the primary direction. It has positive associations, most clearly expressed in the observation that the sun rises in the east. This linkage in turn connects the east with health, vitality, and the morning-time. Prayers are to be said, medicines are to be taken, and ritual songs are to be sung while facing east. This is the spatial logic underlying the positioning of the chiefs' arbor looking toward the east. Most ceremonial ground rituals orient the singers and dancers toward the east. Medicine plants, the poles carried by the poleboys, and the four logs used to build the new fire during the Green Corn Ceremony are cut facing east, and when trees are cut they are expected to fall to the east (see Hudson 1975:98).

The west is the symbolic opposite of the east. Yuchi funeral rituals are oriented toward the west and, while there is some conflicting evidence for the Yuchi and other Woodland groups, heaven, or the world of spirits, is typically located in the sky to the west. At the gravesite guns are fired westward, announcing to the ancestors the departure of the deceased. Overt associations with the west are omitted in ceremonial ground rituals, and no Yuchi ceremonial ground arbor faces the west.[10]

The east-west axis marks the path taken by the sun, and the directions together stand for the lifecourse of a Yuchi person. Older Yuchi sacred narratives stress the regularity of the sun's east-west path. In mythic time, the Yuchi had to defeat a strong sorcerer who temporarily caused havoc by making the sun alter its normal path. One version of this story, which continues to be told today, is found in the unpublished notes of Jeremiah Curtin, who visited the Yuchi in 1884:

TEXT 5

The Rescue of the Sun, an unpublished Yuchi story recorded by Jeremiah Curtin from an unknown consultant, circa 1884. Minor inconsistencies in punctuation and the spelling of Yuchi have been changed. Curtin used "Yutci" as his spelling of the tribal name in this manuscript.

After the Sun had agreed to give light to the world she used to rise in the East and go over the sky every day, but a great witch, a very long animal, came out of the ground and chased the Sun trying to catch and kill her. The Sun was terribly afraid of this animal.

When it followed her the Sun used to grow pale from fear and, weak in the knees, gave dim light and covered her face. One night the Sun called all the people together in council to decide how they could kill this animal. All came, among the number two Yuchis bringing a club and an ax. The Sun brought two bags of fog which were to be carried, she said, to where the animal jumped out of the ground, and opened there, the fog would come out of the bags and the animal would not be able to see her, then it might be killed.

When the Sun asked who would kill the animal no one came forward. The two Yuchi said nothing but took the club and ax and slipped out unobserved.

> After awhile they were missed. When the people saw that the club and ax were taken away they said, "These two men have gone to kill the animal, run after them with the two bags." They ran after the Yuchis and gave them the bags. The Sun was already up and running as fast as she could. The witch was hurrying close in her tracks. The Yuchis opened the two bags, the fog came out and hid the Sun. The Yuchis could not see the animal because of the fog, but they heard it strike its jaws together and tramp along with a terrible tread. When the animal came near, the man with the club was ahead and knocked it down, the other cut its head off with his ax. When the witch's head was cut off, the fog went away and the Sun shone out bright and happy. [Curtin 1884]

Whereas the east-west axis has cosmological associations, the north-south axis has social implications. The warrior society is divided between the north and the south arbors, with the north arbor often taking precedence. In the football game, the field is oriented north and south, with each gender guarding one end.

Pattern Numbers

As with most Native American communities, a familiar pattern number reoccurs at all levels of structure throughout Yuchi ritual acts. Among the Yuchi, as well as the Creek and most other Woodland peoples, this fundamental number is four. Songs and dances occur in sets of four. Four adolescent poleboys, four adult feathermen, and four designated whoopers serve during the Green Corn Ceremony, and preceding it are four football games and four stomp dances. During a stomp dance, the home members complete four rounds of stomp dancing before inviting visitors to join in the dance. Although such pattern numbers often go unnoticed in dominant cultures, the repeated appearance of the number four in the ritual life of the Yuchi and other contemporary Native North American peoples is consciously recognized and frequently commented upon (Dundes 1980; Farnell 1995).

Women and Men

The distinction between women and men is reproduced at various levels in every aspect of Yuchi ceremonialism. Historically, strict taboos governed the conduct of women (and male spouses and relatives) during menses, calling for their separation from men in both the ritual and domestic spheres. In present-day practice, the restrictions governing women have weakened, but they continue to be expected to withdraw from ritual participation during menses.

Beliefs about Yuchi cosmology are expressed in the prohibition of menstruating women from entering the central square of the ceremonial ground. This practice is associated both with beliefs about the power of the sacred Fire and of understandings of purity and sickness. Transgression of this rule endangers both the community, whose members are exposed to the danger of illness, and the woman, who risks being overcome by the power of the Fire. Dangers derived from the Fire's power extend to pregnant women and to children too young to walk on their own. Menstruating women, like unborn children and babies, are viewed as being in a weakened condition that makes them vulnerable to powerful forces. While the Fire is considered a positive, beneficial force and an expression of the Creator's power, it also has a consuming nature. In addition to consuming wood, the Sacred Fire is ritually fed sacred foods as part of the annual ritual cycle. It is its strength, combined with its capacity for "hunger," that most endangers people in a weakened condition.[11]

Just as women are separated from men in Yuchi cosmology, they are also separated in social practice. During ritual events, men and women have different roles. Yuchi women in everyday life have achieved considerable success, by mainstream American standards, in the world of employment in the cash economy, but they retain a powerful symbolic identity as cooks and mothers in the realm of Yuchi belief. Women are the leaders of domestic life and are directly responsible for the maintenance of children and the nurturing of family. As cooks and also formerly as gardeners, women are symbolically associated with corn, the staple food, and other produce. During many ritual events, women are involved in cooking and looking after children at the same time that men are undertaking dances and other ritual activities.

As Bell has noted among the Creek, the life-sustaining women's activities of cooking and child-care are balanced by the male activities of hunting, warfare, and woodcutting, all appropriate, socially sanctioned forms of killing (1990:336–37). Woodcutting provides fuel for fire. In the domestic domain, the cutting of wood sustains the work of women, and thus the family. In the communal domain, cutting wood sustains the sacred fire, and thus the well-being of the community. Cutting wood for the sacred fire is an important activity undertaken collectively by the men of the ground.

In the stomp dances that accompany Yuchi rituals, male and female worlds are communally juxtaposed. Men and women alternate in the dance line around the fire. Just as women support the men of their family in the domestic settings, they provide accompaniment to the singing of their husbands, brothers, and fathers in the dance line. Men and women are characterized by different abilities and roles, but the work of both is required to produce harmonious families and communities, carrying Yuchi society into the future.

Age and Hierarchy

As men and women are understood as different in Yuchi culture, older and younger adults are also conceptualized differentially. Age carries prestige both for men and for women. One example of rank ordering by age is manifest, among the women, in the Ribbon Dance performed during the Green Corn Ceremony. In this dance, the only Yuchi dance that the women dance alone, very careful attention is paid to the manner in which the women are positioned within the line. Each woman is stationed directly behind the same woman throughout her life. As a child, a girl dancing for the first time joins at the back of the line. Throughout her life, she moves forward through the line as she ages, and as those women in front of her pass on or retire from the dance. The leader of the dance is thus the oldest active woman of the ceremonial ground, holding this position for life. Responsibility and respect are similarly distributed among the men of the ceremonial grounds. The Yuchi exhibit great concern, respect, and deference for all older people, particularly the patriarchs and matriarchs of their own families and communities. As among other Woodland peoples, knowledge is seen as being accrued by individuals throughout a lifetime, making elders the appropriate leaders of communal ritual life.

Yuchi and Non-Yuchi

A final conceptual distinction, important in Yuchi ritual life, is the separation between Yuchi and non-Yuchi individuals and communities. Although they are divided into three separate ceremonial grounds and two recognized Yuchi Christian congregations, Yuchi people share a very strong common identity as Yuchi. While ceremonial ground communities found in the Creek towns make very clear distinctions between members and non-members, the Yuchi extend identification of members broadly among all the Yuchi people. As discussed in chapter 6, the first four dances of a stomp dance are said to be reserved for members of the home ground, after which all visiting groups are invited and encouraged to join in. Nonetheless, it is quite common for all Yuchi people present to join in the dance from the start, regardless of their ceremonial ground membership. In explanation, it is frequently said that all Yuchi belong at all of the ceremonial grounds. This is both a practical reality, in that the members of all three grounds are closely related to one another, and symbolically justified by the view that all three Yuchi grounds derive from the common fire at the mother ground, Polecat. The common identity of the Yuchi people is sharply contrasted with the ascribed Creek status that Yuchi people carry as citizens of the Creek Nation. The Yuchi have friendly relationships with the Creek people, but they constantly seek to reinforce their separate identity.

This common Yuchi identity is regularly emphasized in Yuchi public discourse, yet the Yuchi are surprisingly open to outsiders in comparison to other Native American communities. Whereas the ceremonial ground communities of many other groups in Oklahoma resist the participation of outsiders, particularly non-Natives, the members of the Yuchi grounds welcome visitors who demonstrate a sincere interest in Yuchi cultural life. Several non-Natives participate both in the cycle of Yuchi ceremonial ground rituals and in Native American Church services organized by Yuchi people. Yuchi elders take particular delight in stories that reveal how non-Yuchi people, particularly blacks and whites, mastered aspects of Yuchi culture, such as the language. Despite the fact that my singing of stomp dance songs is weak and my Yuchi fluency is meager, my Yuchi friends have been more enthusiastic about these attempts at Yuchi cultural literacy than concerned about my ethnographic diligence. As I suggest in several contexts throughout this study, Yuchi openness to outside influence is a part of the cultural dynamic that has enabled them to maintain their own distinct corporate identity.

RECIPROCITY

In the chapters that follow, I repeatedly emphasize the theme of reciprocity in Yuchi rituals. Reciprocity is a central concern in Yuchi ritual and it operates at a number of levels. In social life, reciprocity is evident at the individual level, as when ceremonial ground members support each other during stomp dance episodes, and at the collective level when stomp grounds reciprocally visit each other's ceremonies. Men and women (in some contexts) and the men's societies (in others) each perform services for the other in ceremonial ground life. Reciprocity is also manifest spiritually, with mutual obligations obtaining between the present-day Yuchi and the Creator. Reciprocity underlies Yuchi concerns with cultural continuity through time. Following tradition is a constant, ongoing transaction between the living and the ancestral Yuchi people.

The specific forms that ritual reciprocity and other important themes take in Yuchi ritual is the subject of the event-based chapters comprising most of this study. Before undertaking these descriptions, I present in chapter 4 a final preliminary account examining general features of Yuchi ceremonial ground life and belief. Ritual oratory, the subject of chapter 4, is a major resource for tying together the meanings and actions of Yuchi ritual. Public speeches made during ceremonial ground events have provided me with significant insights into the nature of Yuchi ritual. Those speeches will provide an important window on the individual events of the Yuchi ceremonial cycle.

4 "On behalf of our chief here . . ."

Speaking in the Big House

At the ceremonial grounds, oratorical practices long associated with Yuchi ritual life persist, but speakers now utilize a new language to pursue the purposes that their speeches have always served. My goal in this chapter is to introduce present-day Yuchi oratory and to examine some of the cultural functions and poetic devices associated with it as a genre. Several texts representing the norms of ceremonial ground oratory and its leading practitioner are presented and examined. Additional texts are considered in subsequent chapters. These performances are drawn from a larger corpus of speeches recorded between 1995 and 2000. Consideration of Yuchi oratory substantially expands the ethnographic record on formal speaking in Woodland communities, and it provides a rich window through which contemporary Yuchi ceremonialism and Yuchi ideas about culture, tradition, and identity can be viewed.

ORATORY AND CEREMONIAL GROUND RITUAL

In oratory, the Yuchi ceremonial grounds are called *big houses*. They are the site of formal speeches that are incorporated into all Yuchi calendrical rituals, as well as into other formal contexts in which members gather at the ceremonial ground; for example, in business meetings held on the town square. While a speaker may be called upon at any time to present a speech on behalf of the chief, the situation in which oratory occurs most regularly is during stomp dances, and within these events they most often occur in the morning at the conclusion of the night's dancing. The first oratory text considered here is an example of such a closing speech.

Throughout a stomp dance event, the chief and his assistant are seated under the west arbor, together with members of the chief society. If the speaker, by birth, belongs under one of the warriors' arbors, he must be borrowed from the warriors by the chief. Such a speaker sits under the west arbor while fulfilling his official duties. Before making any formal speeches, the speaker consults privately with the chief, with whom he sits under the west arbor. When delivering an oration, the speaker stands directly in front of the west arbor and addresses the assembled members and visitors. The speaker faces east, where the fire and most of his audience are located. This orientation is in accord with other ritual events, including speaking events, where ritual behaviors such as praying, singing medicine songs, collecting medicine plants, and drinking medicinal teas are conducted while facing east.

THE LANGUAGES OF ORATORY

During recent times, public speaking within Yuchi ceremonial ground events has drawn on three distinct and unrelated languages: Yuchi, Creek, and English. Multilingualism was common among Yuchi speakers before the widespread replacement of the language by English. Into the early twentieth century, fluency in Creek was common for Yuchi speakers, and additional knowledge of Shawnee or Sauk or both was not unusual. Since the tip toward English among the Yuchi (approximately 1935–45), the full repertoire of ceremonial ground languages has only rarely been the possession of any single speaker or audience member.[1]

Before 1994, Yuchi was the primary language used by orators in formal speaking. With the deaths of the last two orators fluent in Yuchi, English became the dominant language for ceremonial ground speeches. It is important to note that it was the loss of speakers, not the loss of fluent Yuchi audiences, that ended the practice of Yuchi language oratory. Yuchi was the privileged code for oratory even when no fluent listeners were present to interpret such speech events. In the recent past, English was used by speakers as an adjunct to Yuchi for the purpose of providing shortened summaries of Yuchi language speeches and for brief announcements, such as describing the rules to be followed by event participants, particularly monolingual members and guests.

Creek continues to be used as a third language in Yuchi ceremonial ground oratory events today. Some Yuchi grounds have Creek-speaking members, usually in-married Creek men, and all Yuchi ground leaders count Creek speakers among their close friends. A Yuchi chief can call upon the services of a man with the ability to speak Creek to address visiting delegations from Creek ceremonial grounds. The content of such a message would normally include words of welcome on behalf of the chief and ground, as well as explanations of ritual procedure. The example most widely cited by Yuchi ceremonial participants is an invitation, given in Creek, for visitors to join in after the evening's fourth round of dancing, the first four rounds being reserved for the home ground's members and other Yuchi people. A Creek speaker may also be called upon by

Newman Littlebear delivers a speech prior to the Saturday evening dances during the Green Corn Ceremonies at the Polecat Ceremonial Ground. Visitors from the White Oak (Shawnee) Ceremonial Ground are seated in the background, on the south side of the square. 10 July 1999.

the Yuchi chief to make an announcement on behalf of a visiting Creek chief, who, for example, wishes to take advantage of a Yuchi gathering with a large number of Creek visitors present to announce an upcoming dance or event at his ground. With the decrease in Creek language fluency and the concurrent rise (now universal) of English competence (among Creek, Yuchi, and other tribal visitors), these uses of Creek oratory within Yuchi contexts have diminished; however they will continue as long as the various Yuchi grounds retain Creek speakers among their memberships and as long as visiting Creek delegations continue to include Creek-speaking orators.

AUTHORSHIP AND AUDIENCES

A ceremonial ground chief chooses the man who will speak on his behalf. Usually, this is a person formally designated as his "speaker." This man is chosen to serve on the basis of his recognized speaking ability, his command of ritual knowledge, his skills in expounding upon the themes selected by the chief, his esteem within the community, and his ability to cooperate with and assist the chief. In speaking on behalf of the chief, the speaker is, by extension, representing the sentiments of all of the ground's members.[2] In ideal terms the Yuchi speaker speaks the words of his chief. But in practice, the speaker creates a complicated oral performance that combines the voice of the chief with his own as well as those of the Yuchi ancestors.

Just as the authoring of Yuchi oratory is more complicated than it appears initially, so are the types and roles of addressees. One audience for Yuchi ceremonial ground oratory consists of delegations of visitors from the other ceremonial grounds that participate with the Yuchi grounds in a common system of ritual and social interaction. By hosting visiting groups, a home ground strengthens its numbers for completing the hard work of continuing the stomp dance until morning. Visiting groups provide additional male dance leaders, as well as female shell shakers. The participation of visitors not only provides relief for the home members through the long night of dancing, but also improves the social qualities of the dance. Fellowship with visiting friends, and the ability for the host to select from a larger pool of gifted and spirited song leaders, increases the overall enthusiasm and enjoyment experienced by all participants. When visitors are present at a Yuchi event during the performance of a speaker's oratory, he will seek to cement positive relations between the visitors and the host ground by addressing their participation in the event and extending a message of appreciation on behalf of the home community. Patterns of stomp dance visitation are discussed in greater detail in chapter 6.

The most important audience for Yuchi oratory is the membership of the home ceremonial ground. While visitors may depart from the dance event early, the "home folks" are expected to remain until the dance concludes with the closing oratory. In the analysis below, I examine the social organization of stomp dance events implied in the oratory texts. The resulting model indicates the diversity of individuals and groups encompassed by the home ground membership. In the next section, I seek to explore the functions played by oratory for this diverse audience.

THE FUNCTIONS OF ORATORY PERFORMANCES

Oratory serves a variety of functions within Yuchi ceremonial ground society.[3] First, however, because most of the ceremonial ground speeches that I have recorded were delivered by Newman Littlebear, I preface his texts with a brief overview of his background as an orator. I then present an example of his speechmaking and begin consideration of some of the functions served by oratory in Yuchi ritual life.

Newman Littlebear, Yuchi Orator

During most of the time that I have known his people, Newman Littlebear has served as the main Yuchi speaker, not only for the Polecat ground where he has held this office for over a decade, but for the Duck Creek and Sand Creek grounds as a guest orator. Both of those communities lost their own elderly speakers during the 1990s. Mr. Littlebear regularly attends the activities of all three Yuchi ceremonial grounds and plays a major role in all of them. In addition to serving as speaker and advisor, he is one of the two principal singers at all of the Yuchi grounds. His career as a speaker began at the Polecat ground when he was asked to step in for that ground's ailing speaker. He eventually took on this role permanently.

Mr. Littlebear's mother was a Yuchi who spoke Yuchi and English. His Shawnee father was bilingual in Shawnee and English. Mr. Littlebear, now in his seventies, belongs to the first cohort of Yuchi to be raised as speakers of English only. In assuming the role of ceremonial ground speaker, he is the first monolingual English speaker to do so. Through exposure to and instruction from his uncle, the late Jimmie Skeeter, former speaker for the Duck Creek ground, and other Yuchi and Creek speakers, Mr. Littlebear has absorbed many of the stylistic conventions and thematic concerns of Creek and Yuchi language oratory. This lifelong experience was enhanced by a brief period of active involvement in the Pickett Chapel United Methodist Church. While a member there, Mr. Littlebear received formal training as a lay preacher. His experience as a preacher gives his oratories a sermon-like quality to the ears of some of his listeners. Those diverse life experiences are combined with a thorough knowledge of Yuchi customary practices and a widely recognized gift for speaking.

Mr. Littlebear's talent as an orator has enabled the Yuchi successfully to make the switch to English without diminishment of the power of ceremonial ground oratory as a cultural form. Among other Native communities in Oklahoma, this same transition has precipitated a crisis. In some cases, what were once marked styles of oratory in Native languages have dissolved into informal announcements and commentary in English, lacking the cultural force of the older genre. Other communities are having to go to increasingly complex lengths to hold to ritual ideologies that mandate the use of Native languages. For example, the Oklahoma Seneca-Cayuga now import Iroquoian speakers from Canada to speak during rituals where little or no local Cayuga-speaking audience exists (for background, see Jackson and Linn [2000]; Mithun [1989:244]).

Text and Context

The first text that I will analyze requires a comment on the context surrounding its performance. It calls on knowledge of subjects and circumstances, most notably the illness of the home chief and of the chief at the (North) Little Axe ground, which is not my focus here. This fact was salient in the context of the performance, but I am consciously avoiding this aspect of the talk in my interpretation here. This dimension of the speech does not seem to have changed the typical form or function of the text in the general areas that I am examining.

TEXT 6

An oratory concluding a stomp dance at the Polecat Ceremonial Ground. Delivered by Newman Littlebear, 25 May 1996 (Memorial Day Weekend).

(1) ((We're)) quitting a little bit early
    [with] holiday business and ah
    a lot a –
    lot of things going on
    maybe you've got some plans.

(2) Maybe you want to rest up.

(3) You might want to think about going to Duck Creek tonight.

(4) You might get an early
    start
    getting rested up.

(5) On behalf of ah
our chief here,
who carried things for us here
tonight
he say ah
((your)) women folks,
they did a good job for y'all,
dancing through the night.

(6) So.

[a brief passage occurring here is inaudible]

(7) I guess we can thank them for
what they did
and these young boys
on these sticks
doing everything here
'til morning.

(8) This young man it's the first time he ever
closed the door for us
but he done a good job.

(9) So.

(10) Us older ones, we're al – always willing to let them.

(11) If they are willing to try something
we like for them to try.

(12) That's how they learn.

(13) Anything in here,
they think they, you know
think they can
do it or do part of it
that's the way we like to see it
for 'em to take part.

(14) That way, why, they learn what –
what –
how to carry things;
to carry this
for a few more years longer,
prolong what we have.

(15) So, we're –
I say myself, I'm uh
I'm proud of these young ones.

(16) ((I know)) some of them, you are too.

(17) ((If)) you're a parent of some of these young boys
I know it makes you feel good to –
to see your
sons working in here and your
young daughters
busy in here shaking–
shaking the cans or shells,
helping out.

(18) So.

(19) I think everyone [has] given a good effort tonight
and [on] behalf of all of these men folks sittin' here
we thank everybody.

(20) And.

(21) I guess we'll meet here again
next Saturday
again.

(22) So.

(23) Try to carry it a little further.

(24) So in the meantime, maybe we can ah
think about
these people that come help us tonight.

(25) Like we said last year, you know ah
when Richard had
some of his people here from Little Axe
we said
down at Duck Creek and here
maybe we can all get together
and go assist them
somewhere this year
further down the line
and maybe again this year we might can do that
you know.

(26) They're a lot of help to us
and Duck Creek.

(27) So.

(28) If you have a chance to go
tonight
to assist
Duck Creek
we have that opportunity.

(29) So.

(30) I kind of urge you to go –
go and support them.

(31) Maybe several dances going on
tonight somewhere
and maybe Duck Creek bunch
need the help
be appreciated.

(32) They are just like we are,
you know.

(33) We got a lot of people
members here but uh
probably half of them not even here
you know.

(34) They're somewhere.

(35) I don't know, I can't say
if they
they're serving the Lord or not.

(36) Maybe some of them are, but there are some that's not.

(37) Some of 'em –

(38) Some of them wandering around.

(39) ALL –
all of our Indian people somewhere
young people
maybe all ages
wandering around in this world
when they've got a place to go.

(40) They got a home like this they can support
and be some –
some –
someway useful
in our traditional ways.

(41) Maybe you young boys hear my voice.

(42) Maybe you took a wrong step,
you might think about what
we talk about here sometimes.

(43) I'll try to encourage you.

(44) Be careful,
in this world.

(45) There is an old story that –
that says
the Almighty
prom – promi – – sed us

a prett – pretty long life
but you've got to be careful.

(46) But when you get to be
like my age
things become uncertain
for you
but you'll get some good years
like they have me
but I have reached my time
with what He said
after that, well
I might could have a few more good years
but He said that things become kind of uncertain
after a certain age.

(47) So you young people
make good use of your life while you are here.

(48) That's what He put you here for.

(49) The Creator didn't put you here just for nothing.

(50) He put us here to ah
take care of things
in this world
that He created.

(51) That He created this world
everything in it
was good
the way that He liked it.

(52) And He created humans
to take care of this –
take care of this
for Him.

(53) So.

(54) We might think of that.

(55) We see
that our Father's world has been [in]
turmoil.

(56) Sometimes we can't help it
but we don't have to be
helpless
to do things like that.

(57) He didn't create us
to be enemies.

(58) He created us
all equal
to be
friends.

(59) Good fellowship with one another.

(60) So that's what we like to say
when we come here.

(61) And we hope that you have
had a good fellowship.

(62) But they say
it's good fellowship
with
Grandpa. [referring to the fire]

(63) They say this is was our Grandpa.

(64) That's what some of the older ones called
this light:

Grandpa.
SPIRIT.

Light.

(65) For us,
our helper.

(66) Other things.

(67) Herbs
to help us
in this life
in our health.

(68) We have some of it here
that we use.

(69) Maybe we don't use it enough.

(70) And he said faith
in what we have here.

(71) We receive help
through faith.

(72) Through speaking
through talking
to the one above.

(73) They say
like this smoke
we talk
SING
this smoke go up
out of sight
deliver our words
our songs
our happiness
our prayers
our WHOOPS
OUR HOLLERS
WHATEVER WE DO
if we're in faith here
our Creator hears us.

(74) If we tell him we need help
we need something

tell him our needs
here
He'll help us.

(75) Maybe we think
we tell him
in faith
believe it
he'll help you.

(76) That's what I used to hear them say.

(77) So many of us need
help.

(78) Maybe you come
go around this circle.

(79) Maybe you have a good thought
for someone
or yourself
or your children.

(80) Maybe in your mind
in your heart
you walk around here and think about it.

(81) Maybe you'll get help.

(82) I'll pass that on to you.

(83) Maybe we think we're –
it's just dance.

(84) Have a good time.

(85) But faith comes in too.

(86) Some time we have difficulties

in this big house
amongst family members in –

(87) It happens.

(88) Maybe we don't realize.

(89) Maybe we think we're not
family.

(90) But if this be a big house,
all members here
visitors
welcome.

(91) I pass that on to you this morning.

(92) And just like us
our chief
our main chief
in the hospital
trying to recover
we think good things for him.

(93) Like Little Axe
we hear that their –
their chief,
like ours
has been stricken.

(94) Maybe we think good things for him.

(95) So, we know that, you know
that he comes sometimes
and be with us.

(96) But through this way,
what we did last night, we sing
maybe we think –
think about Richard
and Jim.

(97) Maybe that way they'll receive
a blessing
from what little effort we give.

(98) A l o t of things happen
around these – these fires.

(99) Sometime our people get careless.

(100) They got real careless one time
our Yuchi people.

(101) This almost went away.

(102) We almost lost it.

(103) They say if you don't take care of it, you know,
it could be that way.

(104) They let it go
al-most-went-a-way.

(105) But
they got together
to talk about it.

(106) Said they wanted to bring it back like it use – used to be.

(107) So they did.

(108) They worked at it.

(109) Took a lot of years.

(110) Finally it come back.

(111) Growed up again.

(112) And we have what we
have in our ceremonies
in our Green Corn Ceremony
built back.

(113) So you young generation can see
what we had.

(114) Perhaps if that had went
you never would've been witness to
what we still have
this day
if them elders hadn't got together
MADE SOME RULES that help out in here.

(115) And the light begin to grow light–
brighter for us.

(116) I tell you that little story this morning.

(117) Tell you a true story.

(118) You can see
what we have.

(119) We can see
some of our people
careless.

(120) Our young men are are careless.

(121) Some of their forefathers used to be here.

(122) A lot of the young men
ignoring what we have here.

(123) Ignoring the Creator's work.

(124) So, I say that much to you.

(125) Thank you all.

[men respond:] *Hõ*

Constituting Community and Cementing Social Relations

Drawing on fieldwork among Creek ceremonial ground people, Amelia Bell has offered the only detailed treatment of ritual oratory among a Southeastern people.[4] Her analysis (Bell 1983, 1984, 1985a, 1985b) focuses on a close reading of a single text, supplemented with observation of other speeches and with contextual exegesis by Creek-speaking consultants. The Creek speech examined by Bell is a closing oratory parallel with the Yuchi texts presented here and elsewhere in this study. In her analysis, the primary role of closing oratory (that is, the speech given at the conclusion of a stomp dance event) is to represent the outcome of the successful ritual event. In Bell's account, the purpose of Creek stomp dance ceremonies is to create health and peace by joining distinct categories and groups into a harmonious relationship. On a social plane, this means the establishment and perpetuation of friendly relations between the host community and allied towns present as visitors. The Creek orator recounts the course of the event itself, and if the dance was judged by the hosts to have been successful, he ratifies this success and makes clear to the guests (ideally from whose number he is drawn to speak on behalf of the host chief) the newly (re)-established friendly relationship between host and guest.[5]

In Yuchi oratory, the ratification of positive, reciprocal relations between the host ground and its guests is an important social function, but one less dominant than Bell's account suggests for the Creek.[6] The first text manifests this concern with intercommunity relations through reference (lines 24–32) to the participation of both the Shawnee ground of Little Axe and the Yuchi ground of Duck Creek.[7]

In the Creek context, the establishment of friendship between ceremonial grounds takes place within the context of many active Creek grounds. Each has a group of allies established within this larger set, which includes the Yuchi (Haas 1940; Spoehr 1941). The perspective of a Yuchi ground looking out upon this larger social world is somewhat different. There are only three Yuchi grounds and their membership is heavily intertwined, with close family linkages drawing individuals into participation, at various levels, in all three. The three Yuchi grounds – Polecat, Duck Creek, and Sand Creek – taken together are seen as constituting the whole of the Yuchi tribe. In Bell's account of Creek belief, Creek grounds are seen as potential enemies, a situation that must be overcome through stomp dance rituals and ratified in a closing oratory. In the Yuchi case, each Yuchi ground is a natural ally to the others. Within stomp dance events, the stance of a Yuchi ground toward its guests is one of appreciation and hospitality. When the men of the host ground gather to begin the dance, the speaker will often remind the men, on behalf of the chief, of their obligation to extend hospitality toward their guests. The men are expected to be attentive to the needs of visitors and the women of the host town work to prepare dinner for guests arriving early, as well as food for a coffee break for visitors during the middle of the night. Reciprocity among the Yuchi ceremonial grounds is the expected product of their common identity as Yuchi.[8] The ceremonial ground communities (Creek, Seminole, Cherokee, Shawnee, and others) that join with the Yuchi in their stomp dance events are welcomed as friends and appreciated for the help that they offer. Their presence enlarges the circle of fellowship and helps "carry the load" of the night's ritual work.

Although still expressed in Yuchi oratory, the negotiation of intercommunity relations is less significant today than it was in the remembered past. Today many visiting groups will not remain at a dance until its conclusion at sunrise. By leaving early, they are not present in the audience when closing speeches are given. Despite this fact, in his speeches Mr. Littlebear tends to address the participation of visitors. In doing so, he reaffirms norms of reciprocity and hospitality for the benefit of the ground members. Guests from other Yuchi grounds, because of their close connections to the host members, are in contrast more likely to remain in attendance until dawn. The cementing of relations among the three Yuchi grounds through oratory contributes to the formation of an overarching Yuchi identity.

"I'll try to encourage you"

A dominant goal of Yuchi oratory today is to provide encouragement to younger members of the Yuchi community. These words of encouragement seek both to build community and to outline a standard of personal moral conduct (cf. McDowell 1990). This is perhaps the purpose most commonly emphasized in Mr. Littlebear's oratory. This orientation appears throughout the text in a number of ways. In their first appearance, these words of encouragement emerge from the "thank you" normally expressed to the members by the chief. Here (5–7) the acting chief has singled out the women for appreciation. Next, Mr. Littlebear thanks the young men (mostly teenagers) of the ground, who in recent years have increasingly assumed a major part of the communities' ritual responsibilities. He singles out the young men who served as stickmen (7). At Yuchi grounds, the stickmen are responsible for the selection of new dance leaders throughout the night. Prior to each episode, they publicly signal each performer with memorized phrases announced in the Yuchi language. Serving in this capacity, they carry staffs that signal their position, hence their English title. Polecat is unusual in that the bulk of its active male members are younger men. For this reason, young men have taken on roles of ritual leadership.

Mr. Littlebear also singles out for recognition a young man who, on this morning, led the Closing-the-Door Dance for the first time (8). This dance is the last dance of the event and it serves to "close" the metaphorical door of the big house until it is "opened" once again with the Starting Dance performed at the next stomp dance event. Acknowledgment of young men for their assumption of responsibilities that typically would be held by older men leads Mr. Littlebear to a general discussion of how ceremonial ground practices can be carried on "a few more years" (9–19). In public discourse, Yuchi ritual customs are always framed as fragile, and their persistence is viewed as requiring effort on the part of all participants. Mr. Littlebear's words of encouragement seek to mobilize participants in this ongoing work of cultural preservation.

After cementing relations between the host and its Shawnee (Little Axe) and Yuchi (Duck Creek) guests, Mr. Littlebear returns to his goal of encouragement, but follows a new approach. Beginning with line 33 and continuing throughout the remainder of the speech, he weaves together a number of related themes. Initially he reflects on the wastefulness of Indian people who are living self-destructive lives, when they could commit themselves to service to the Creator and preservation of "traditional ways." In this and other speeches, Mr. Littlebear uses homelessness as a metaphor for troubles that befall some Indian people, particularly those of drug and alcohol abuse. Drawing on the metaphor of the ceremonial ground as a big house, he is able to equate participation in the ritual community with the experience of a fulfilling home (40) and family (86–90) life. To Mr. Littlebear, what is most wasteful about "wandering around" is that all Indian people, or at least all Yuchi and Creek people, have "a place to go" (39) and the definition of family includes both members and visitors (90). Introducing this theme in lines 34–36, Mr. Littlebear alludes, with approval, to Yuchi people active in Christian churches ("Maybe some of them are [serving the Lord]"). In other speeches, he has addressed this issue directly, indicating the acceptance by ceremonial ground participants of the church as another valid mode of worship and fellowship.

Oral History

Embedded within the extended treatment of moral engagement with tradition and community, Mr. Littlebear utilizes a specific historical example to bolster his argument. Such oral histories are often included within his narratives and serve both to enhance the point being made and to transmit the information itself. Much less frequently, myths associated with ceremonial ground belief are used in oratory in the same way. In this instance the historical narrative (99–117) concerns the history of the Polecat ground during the middle decades of the twentieth century, a period experienced by the ground's elders but not by the majority of members. Mr. Littlebear tells of how the Yuchi at Polecat "got careless" and how the fire "almost went away." He does not say it directly, but he is alluding to the drinking and reckless behavior that was allowed to become a problem at the ground. The ground developed a reputation among its neighbors as a place where one could go to dance and drink alcohol. For serious ceremonial ground people, drinking in the precincts of a ground is unacceptable, as it endangers the physical and spiritual health of the community and of all visitor participants as well. The reputation that Polecat had developed caused the devoted ritualists of other tribes, as well as many Yuchi people, to stay away from the ground. With the committed supporters of the ceremonial staying away, the ritual was almost lost until a group of men, determined to revitalize the ground, enacted strict new rules about alcohol consumption. As Mr. Littlebear indicates in his speech, the rebuilding of the ground "took a lot of years." To recover from its low ebb required decades of dedicated work, and visitors and members returned only slowly. To Yuchi people, the importance of this recovery is all the more salient because the Green Corn Ceremonies at Polecat are more elaborate and more distinctly Yuchi than at the other two Yuchi grounds. This explains the emphasis placed on the ability of the younger people today to see and experience the Green Corn rituals. Recounting this episode provides a historical frame for stressing the necessity of moral behavior for the good of the community in the present.[9]

In embedding stories within oratories, Mr. Littlebear frequently uses a number of framing devices. Most often the story (he uses the word "story" both for historical and sacred narratives) is closed with a variation of the lines appearing in 116–17: "I tell you that little story this morning. Tell you a true story." After such a closing, he will frequently attach a coda to the story that connects the account to the present. For instance, after concluding an account of the mythical origin of corn, he will return to quotidian time and relate observations on the continued importance of corn in everyday life. This rhetorical device connects the everyday experience of the audience with a significant past (cf. Darnell's [1989:335] discussion of this pattern in Cree narrative). Myths and historical stories, and the rituals that they describe, are mutually reinforcing. Because the Creator revealed corn to Indian people, the world can have an expanding wealth of valuable foods. This technique is exemplified in a small way in lines 116–18. Because the elders established new rules, the Yuchi ceremonies are still observable today. Narratives related to Yuchi ritual are discussed further in chapter 8.

Thanksgiving and Beseeching

The best-documented oratory practice among a Native Woodland community is that associated with the Iroquois longhouses of New York and Canada. Speeches designed to give thanks to the Creator for the various products of the natural world are a major focus of longhouse oratory (Chafe 1993; Foster 1974, 1989). The Yuchi share with the Iroquois the broad outlines of a common Woodland ceremonial pattern, one that is manifest in similar dance styles, musical forms, and calendrical observances. In is not surprising, in this context, that the Yuchi ceremonies reflect the same concern with expressing thanks to the Creator for his gifts of cultural practices bestowed in mythic time and natural products that reappear annually. Whereas emphasis in Iroquois ritual is placed on thanksgiving in the form of relatively fixed spoken texts, Yuchi ceremonialism places emphasis on the performance of dances and ritual acts as a direct signal to the Creator of the appreciation that Yuchi people have for his work. In a particularly poetic and beautiful speech performed at the Duck Creek ground, Mr. Littlebear explored those themes. The following excerpt comes from a longer discussion of the Ribbon Dance, which is performed by the women at each Yuchi ground during the course of the annual Green Corn Ceremony. The women wear long, multicolored ribbons in their hair, and the many bright colors motivate the way in which the dance is usually interpreted.

TEXT 7

Excerpt from a oratory interpreting the Yuchi Ribbon Dance. Delivered by Newman Littlebear at the Duck Creek Ceremonial Ground, 25 June 1994.

(1) It's about life.

(2) It's about creation.

(3) It's about
the different colors
in this universe.

(4) The sky above.

(5) The sun.

(6) The moon.

(7) The rain.

(8) The vegetation.

(9) All of creation.

(10) Perhaps that
head you see out there. [referring to the cow skull atop the ballpole]

The women of the Duck Creek community perform the Ribbon Dance during their Green Corn Ceremonial, 20 June 1997.

(11) Different colors.

(12) And our fire.

(13) And even our –
our colors
the colors of people
in the world
in this creation.

(14) And the colors that come from the Mother Earth.

(15) All the vegetation.
from different times of the year.

(16) You see many colors.

(17) And also
it –
it has been said

this is the way
our mothers
our daughters
and grandchildren
this is their way
the ladies' way
of honoring
us menfolks.

(18) It's sacred.

(19) This is their way
that our people had
to honor us menfolks
to perform for us.

(20) To show
the Almighty
that we are proud
of what –
of His creation.

(21) Like giving a thanks
for all of us.

This speech, while an expression of thanksgiving in what might be considered a meta-ritual sense, is really an exegesis on the subject of thanksgiving. Ritual speech directed at giving thanks can occur in Yuchi oratory, but it does not appear often and not in ways that approach the formalized nature of Iroquois speaking events. The following short excerpt from a discussion of the weather provides an example.

TEXT 8

Excerpt from a closing speech. Delivered by Newman Littlebear during the course of a stomp dance at the Polecat Ceremonial Ground, 1 June 1996.

Seem like
the Lord have ah
blessed us with real good
day and night.

Day started out yesterday morning it –
    we might thought it looked doubtful
    that we could be able to
    dance tonight
    but as it turned out
    why it turned out real good for us.

The ground was in good shape.

Didn't get dusty
    and it wasn't muddy.

So ah.

We can thank the good Lord for that
    blessing us like that.

As was the case with thanksgiving, comparison with Iroquois oratory helps explicate the beseeching function in Yuchi ritual. As Michael Foster (1989) has documented, Longhouse thanksgiving speeches are closely related to another major genre, one that is devoted to "begging" the Creator to provide the same products that are appreciated in the thanksgiving speeches. The two genres express the reciprocal relationship existing between the Creator and his people. People ask. The Creator provides. The people express thanks in order to maintain the relationship.

As with thanksgiving, beseeching in Yuchi ceremonialism is more closely bound to ritual action than to ritual speech events. Insight into the Yuchi view is provided by the first text (73–75), where Mr. Littlebear explains the means by which Yuchi people communicate their needs. Singing, dancing, playing ritual games, undertaking ceremonial observances, keeping positive thoughts, and achieving harmonious social relations – these are the ways in which people seek well-being from the Creator. In the spoken realm, beseeching the Creator is the province of prayer. While prayer occurs at ceremonial ground events, it is a distinct genre from oratory, although orators may be called on to pray publicly, as before communal feasts. Considered an important activity, prayer is ubiquitous in Yuchi social occasions and is practiced equally well by men and women (Jackson 2002).

Ritual Exegesis

In characterizing the role of ritual among the Shokleng, Greg Urban (1996) observed that ritual, as a tangible experience shared throughout this Native South

American community as a whole, was not the subject of circulating, referential discourse. Public discourse was reserved for subjects beyond common experience . In this case at least, rituals were embodied in experience, not in discourse. Characterizing their ceremonial tradition in the past, Yuchi elders describe it in similar terms. This change is explicitly addressed in the following lines from a speech about the Yuchi calendar ceremony that is presented fully in chapter 7.

> A lot of things we don't understand.
>
> A lot of things we –
> we take for granted,
> we don't explain.
>
> Some of us been here many years.
>
> Maybe they never HAD said.
>
> Maybe we just see, try to observe.
>
> But this morning the chief has ah
> said ah
> he wants you
> to see this,
> what we do at this time.

Here, Mr. Littlebear notes that in the past, specific rituals were not always explained, but now the chief wishes them to be explicitly explicated and demonstrated. Looking at a large corpus of oratory texts, a major theme emergent in recent English language oratory is the explanation of ceremonial practices. This cultural function is related to the conscious realization, by Yuchi elders, that changing social situations have hindered the ability of younger Yuchi ceremonialists to participate in rituals in ways similar to the manner in which they were experienced by older people, as well as by Yuchi ancestors.

The late Jimmie Skeeter, the last Yuchi-speaking orator at the Duck Creek Ceremonial Ground, is reported to have remarked: "I was a poleboy all my life." Poleboys are young men selected to serve as assistants during the Green Corn and other ground rituals. They are young, unmarried men, and their position is the entry-level ritual office. Their task is the difficult physical work associated with ceremonial ground rituals. In working as a poleboy, young men gain firsthand experiential knowledge of the details of ritual practice. In joking that he was a poleboy all his life, Mr. Skeeter refers to having learned what he knew of Yuchi ritual through a life of continuous, active participation as a vigorous helper. Only in his later years, after gaining a great deal of experience, was he called upon to serve as a key leader.

The inability of most younger Yuchi to participate at this level, due to the constraints of work and the distractions of modern American life, has caused Yuchi leaders to transform their understanding of appropriate methods of cultural transmission. Language classes, culture camps, the tape recording of ritual songs and video recording of ritual events, and the facilitation of ethnographic research all derive from a very real concern that much that is valued in Yuchi culture is being lost in the course of social change. The emergence of new forms of collective action aimed at cultural preservation was addressed in an oratory by Mr. Littlebear at the Duck Creek Ceremonial Ground in 1996.

TEXT 9

An excerpt from a speech given by Newman Littlebear before the Ribbon Dance at the Duck Creek Ceremonial Ground's Green Corn Ceremony, 28 June 1996.

How much longer can it last?

How much longer can all of our ceremonials
continue on?

I say to the young generation
its in your hands.

How well you respond
to what we still have,
that is the answer.

How well you learn,
pay attention.

Because some
of us people
had a little interest when we were young
we are still able to continue on
to this modern day.

There are many things in this life
in this modern time that can distract you

gets our attention
and causes us
to forget about our ways
our ways of life
that have been going on so long.

But nowadays we talk about it
we gather up
have meetings
and discuss
what we still have
and try
to find ways
that we can continue on.

The educational function of ceremonial ground oratory likewise emerges from this concern with the preservation of cultural knowledge and the creation of social commitment for its perpetuation. In the first text, this theme plays a major role.

Concluding his treatment of Shokleng ritual, Urban (1996:213–14) observes that shared rituals become a subject of referential discourse only when they are disrupted by conflict; however, it is this conflict that gives them their interest and makes them a subject worthy of public discussion. Thus, paradoxically, cultural disruption facilitates cultural continuity by making ritual the subject of public discourse. When ritual is represented in discourse as a source of conflict, interest in ritual itself increases. By making ritual more interesting, ritual's representation in discourse as conflicted serves the latent function of drawing people into participation and, in doing so, facilitating cultural continuity. Similarly, in the Yuchi case, public concerns over the loss of distinctively Yuchi cultural practices draws people into more intense participation in ongoing communal life. Once involved, participants are exposed to emerging forms of cultural activity designed to promote cultural continuity. Thus, concerns over culture change produce changed institutions, but these institutions are rooted in a concern with preserving cultural continuity. This reality of continuity through change underscores both the now-patent view that culture is never static and the emerging view that tradition is best viewed as an actively negotiated orientation toward the past, created by social actors in the present (Bauman 1992; DeMallie 1988; Glassie 1995; Jackson and Linn 2000).

POETICS

Having looked at some of the functions served by oratory in ceremonial ground life, the remaining sections of this chapter look more closely at the poetic and rhetorical forms used in oratory to make it an effective and artful means of achieving these ends. All of the issues raised in these remaining sections have been subjects of much recent work in the study of language in social context, and I have drawn heavily on this growing body of work in developing an understanding of Yuchi ritual discourse.

Keying Performance

Oratory performances are typically keyed or framed by a variety of mechanisms.[10] Even before his speech begins, a chief and speaker can call attention to the imminent performance about to unfold. In the space of the ceremonial square, a chief initiates an oratory by calling the speaker to sit at his side. Once seated together, the chief privately explains the themes that he wishes to have addressed in the speech. Especially at the end of stomp dance events, participants expect a closing oratory and these preparations signal the performance soon to unfold. When the conversation between chief and speaker concludes, participants notice this and conclude their own conversations. The performance itself begins when the speaker stands in front of the chiefs' arbor and begins to speak. The speaker begins by assigning responsibility for his words first to the chief. In the first text, this invocation is preceded by an explanation as to why the event is ending early, and hence why a closing oratory is being delivered at an unanticipated moment. Mr. Littlebear then speaks on behalf of the assistant chief, here filling in for the chief.

> (5)On behalf of our chief here, who carried things for us here tonight, he say, your women folks, they did a good job for y'all dancing through the night.

A more typical beginning appears in a text that is presented in full in chapter 7, the first lines of which are:

> The chief has asked me to say a little bit concerning
> this dance.

These formulaic openings are complemented by similar closings, such as those ending the first text.

> (124) So, I say that much to you.
> (125) Thank you all.

Oratories and other public pronouncements on the square ground are concluded when the male members seated on the square ratify the speech. Speaking in unison, they answer "hõ," meaning both "yes" and "agreed." This ratification by the male members closes the performative frame of the speech. Normal conversation, joking, or other quotidian talk follows closing speeches.

Opening formulae are typical of speeches by Yuchi orators and serve to make clear the fundamental relationship between the speaker's words and the chief's communicative goals. This coupling of chief and speaker begins a process of collectivizing the speaker's words that expands in various ways throughout the speech. As oratories unfold, many other voices are added to those of the chief and speaker.[11]

Once begun, a speaker will employ a number of poetic and rhetorical devices in his speech that both further key the performance and shape it as communication. One trope similar to the opening formula is a phrase widely used in Mr. Littlebear's speeches that typically acts as a marker between thematic sections:

(91) I pass that on to you this morning.
(116) I tell you that little story this morning.

These phrases, or variations on them, appear in all of the oratories that I have transcribed.

Parallelism

While the intense parallelism found in the ritual speech of other societies is not apparent in Yuchi oratory, Mr. Littlebear creates semantically parallel constructions that are highly poetic and form the aesthetic highpoint of his speeches. In the texts presented in this chapter, the best example of such a construction appears in text 7, where the symbolism of the Ribbon Dance is discussed (1–16).[12] Such constructions, in less elaborated form, appear throughout his speeches. A smaller example is in the discussion of the sacred fire in text 6 (62–65), where he provides the ancestral understanding of its nature and meaning.

Another variety of parallelism appears in the structure of the larger discourse. As with the Creek oratory described by Bell (1984, 1985a), Mr. Littlebear's speeches often unfold along the pattern of the ritual events he describes. In Bell's account, Creek "oration is structured as an index of its position in previous ritual action" (1985a:323). Mr. Littlebear's performances may, likewise, take the form of a retrospective summary of the preceding ritual event, but they also may use the order of future rituals as an organizing pattern. This method of organization is used extensively in a text presented in chapter 7. In this speech, presented at the close of an Arbor Dance event, Mr. Littlebear anticipates the unfolding of the entire upcoming Green Corn Ceremony. The content of these rituals is the subject of the talk, but their temporal organization also provides the form for its organization. In describing the Green Corn Ceremony, he begins with a semantically parallel set of descriptions, briefly worded and spoken in short, rhythmic bursts. These lines summarize all of the activity undertaken by the men during the daytime on Saturday of Green Corn. In the second half of this account, he uses more descriptive language to explain those parts of the ceremony in which the community as a whole, along with its visitors, will join together. The speech indexes the forthcoming event, and the parts of the event provide a structure for the speech, each part constructed verbally in a structurally parallel fashion.

Pronouns and Social Organization

In a critical rethinking of anthropological approaches to the social organization of small-scale societies, Urban has advocated looking at the way in which a community organizes and presents itself through publicly accessible talk (1996:65). Through his own ethnographic case, Urban provides an example of how anthropologists might discover such local understandings of social organization. His approach was to track the use of pronouns in publicly told mythic narratives. This technique revealed the lack of a clear group boundary, despite a long series of attempts by outsiders to discover a self-designation for the Native South American population with whom Urban worked. Instead of a group boundary, Urban discovered a culturally salient division separating the living and the dead, manifest in uses of the first person plural pronoun. The ethnic constitution of these groups was left unspecified. Urban argued that avoiding the demarcation of clear ethnic boundaries in discourse served to forestall the emergence of factionalism in a community governed by consensus politics.

In line with Urban's example, Mr. Littlebear's oratory texts can be examined for the image that they present of the social organization governing Yuchi Stomp Dance events and Yuchi society more generally. A quick glance at Mr. Littlebear's texts reveals them to be pronoun rich, implicating a complicated variety of individuals and groups. Locating these pronouns and situating them in their context of use reveals many salient social domains. The social units and actors addressed in the first text, augmented with additional groups addressed in the full text presented in the Arbor Dance speech appearing in chapter 7, are identified in table 4. While the account of Yuchi ceremonial social organization generated by Mr. Littlebear's speeches corresponds in general terms with my earlier structural sketch (Jackson 1996a), this brief account is richer because it illustrates the manner in which these structures are produced and reproduced in ceremonial ground ritual performances. It is in the combination of talk and ritual action that these social divisions are put to use and replicated in time. His account also reveals aspects of a conceptual social organization that is only manifest in discourse and in spiritual relations, notably with the Creator and with Yuchi ancestors. In addition, his account makes salient certain social categories that are not observable in the ritual context, but which are nonetheless significant to the Yuchi community (Yuchi people in church, those "wandering around," young men in danger of getting into trouble). The list of actors and entities presented in the table could be diagrammed as a series of overlapping sets, but the result would as likely distort as clarify the entities involved. What is made clear by the inventory is that each Yuchi ritual participant and each ceremonial community is embedded in a rich array of other actors and groups. From the individual actor, the social universe extends outward in social space to fellow ritualists (both Yuchi and non-Yuchi), to those who share Yuchi identity, and ultimately to all of humanity. Spiritually, this universe extends to venerated ancestors and ultimately to the Creator. Differences in group affiliation, gender, age, and world view all partition the Yuchi social universe.

Voices of Tradition

Recent work in linguistic anthropology has examined the ways in which speakers mobilize cultural and linguistic resources to achieve a variety of goals in social interaction. In particular, this body of work has refined our understanding of the creative ways in which individuals establish responsibility (Hill and Irvine 1993), regulate understandings of context (Duranti and Goodwin 1992), and manipulate generic conventions (Briggs and Bauman 1992). Central to many of these studies is examination of the ways in which speakers draw on social and cultural contexts, particularly preceding speech events, in the creation of new utterances. Valuable here is the notion of dialogue, not necessarily used in the everyday sense of conversation, but referring to how speakers incorporate the distinct perspectives and words of other social actors into their own speech. The use of quoted or reported speech is the classic example of the dialogical incorporation of other peoples' words into new utterances.[13] As the pronoun inventory reveals, many social actors and groups are implicated in Mr. Littlebear's speeches. In line with recent work on such reflexive language, I wish to consider briefly some of the voices represented in Mr. Littlebear's texts.

Uncovering the voices in the speeches relates to the issue of authorship already introduced. Most formally, Mr. Littlebear and other Yuchi orators speak on behalf of the chief of the host community. The process of delivering an oratory begins when the chief makes a request of the speaker to speak and explains what he wishes to have said. The role of the chief as an author is always evoked in these speeches, usually in a framing device such as those appearing in the line

Table 4. Social Groups and Actors Addressed in Ceremonial Ground Oratory
Drawn from text 6 with supplementary material from text 14 (presented in chapter 7).

FROM TEXT 6:

1. All event participants.
   (2) Maybe *you* want to rest up.
2. Visiting ceremonial grounds taken as a whole.
   (24) *these* people that come help us tonight.
3. The Little Axe (Shawnee) ceremonial ground.
   (26) *They're* a lot of help to us.
4. The Duck Creek (Yuchi) ceremonial ground.
   (30) go and support *them.*
5. The "home folks" from the Polecat (Yuchi) ceremonial ground.
   (32) They are just like *we* are.
6. Female members of the home ground (Polecat).
   (7) I guess we can thank *them* for
7. Male members of the home ground (Polecat).
   (5) they did a good job for *y'all,*
8. Young men belonging to the Polecat ground who are assuming responsibility for the ground's ritual.
   (10) us older ones, we're always willing to let *them.*
9. Yuchi people who belong at the Polecat ground but who do not participate in its activities.
   (33) probably half of *them* not here
10. Non-participant Yuchi who are serving the Lord (in a Christian church).
    (36) Maybe some of *them* are, but there are some that's not.
11. Non-participant Yuchi who are "wandering around."
    (38) some of *them* wandering around
12. Young boys present at the event but in danger of getting into trouble.
    (42) Maybe *you* took a wrong step,
13. Newman Littlebear as speaker.
    (43) *I'll* try to encourage you.
14. The Assistant Chief, acting on behalf of the Chief.
    (5) *he* say
15. The Creator.
    (48) That's what *He* put you here for.
16. All human beings.
    (58) He created *us*
17. Active believers in the stomp dance way.
    (60) So that's what *we* like to say
18. Ancestors (wise).
    (63) *They* say this is our grandpa.
19. Ancestors (unwise).
    (100) *They* got real careless one time.
20. You (individual event participant).
    (78) Maybe *you* come
21. The absent Little Axe (Shawnee) chief.
    (95) that *he* comes sometimes

22. The two ill chiefs.
    (97) Maybe that way *they'll* receive
23. Younger generation of Yuchi people.
    (113) So *you* young generation can see.
24. Older generation of Yuchi people plus ancestors.
    (113) what *we* had.

FROM TEXT 14:
25. Members of the chief society from the home (Polecat) ground.
    (27) *They* are the ones that are supposed to tie these knots.
26. Members of the warrior society assigned to the north arbor.
    (29) perhaps we can borrow off of *this*
27. Members of the warrior society assigned to the south arbor.
    (30) Or even maybe *this* side
28. The Yuchi people as a whole.
    (19) *They* did this.
29. The Sand Creek (Yuchi) ceremonial ground.
    (65) And *they* need help tonight too.

---

grouping numbered (5). The voice of the chief appears most obviously in these utterances or in the much rarer instances of direct quoted speech. More globally, as the formal sponsor of the speech and the ritual event it frames, the chief is the author of the entire oratory performance. Chiefs are typically quiet, reserved individuals, whereas speakers by their very nature are good talkers. The two individuals are combined in Yuchi and Creek ritual ideology, where the speaker is sometimes referred to as the chief's or the ground's "tongue." The ground as a whole is represented by the chief, and the speaker is a component or extension of the chief whom he serves. While similar chief-speaker arrangements are found in a variety of societies, the Yuchi chiefs do not rely on speakers as means of avoiding blame or saving face. I know of no instances in which a Yuchi chief publicly or privately contradicted his spokesman (cf. Duranti 1992:157). This may relate to the fact that stomp dance oratories are essentially confined to ritual matters. Topically, they rarely move beyond general cultural propositions accepted by most Yuchi elders.

The chief and his speaker formally combine their voices in speeches, but other voices intrude as well. Discussing oratory cross-culturally, Alessandro Duranti observes: "The most well-known and respected orators tend to be those individuals who establish relationship with their audiences by addressing current concerns while at the same time displaying an impressive knowledge of the tradition" (1992:156). For a Yuchi speaker, this "impressive knowledge of the tradition" is expressed through reference to past practices and beliefs, manifest in what "they," the ancestors, did and said. By locating present-day ritual in the historical stream of Yuchi cultural life, the speaker establishes the traditionality of his interpretation. A dense example of this process can be observed in a passage from the discussion of the Yuchi bark calendar presented fully in chapter 7:

> As we [elders] understand it, they [ancestors] said that this was their calendar when it comes to this ceremony which is coming ahead of us [all present members].

This passage draws on the voice of the ancestors in indirect, reported speech to provide warrant for present-day practices. The connection from the past to the present is provided by "we," here referring to the elders (Mr. Littlebear included) who have experienced this continuity throughout their lives. The social value of this continuity is created when the audience of young participants is included in the unfolding of Yuchi life. Many recent observations in discourse-centered ethnography are manifest here. Locating present-day interpretations of culture in the words and actions of respected ancestors has been identified as a key rhetorical technique for establishing and distributing responsibility and authority in oral discourse (Chafe 1993; DuBois 1986; Jackson 1997). In other words, Mr. Littlebear is not making up these practices and interpretations; he is relaying permanent and shared understandings. Such reliance on ancestral wisdom increases the believability and significance of his account. In speaking for the chief and by extension the entire ground, the authority of his account is further enhanced.

The linking of narratives in the present to speech and action in the past is an expression of what Richard Bauman, Dell Hymes, and others have called traditionalization. From this perspective, tradition is "a symbolic construction by which people in the present establish connections with a meaningful past and endow particular cultural forms with value and authority" (Bauman 1992:128; see Hymes [1975] and DeMallie [1988] for Native North American examples). From the point of view of Yuchi ritualists, few elders active in the ceremonial grounds remain. Most participants are young, and thus have not experienced direct contact with decades of ritual life. Thus, for elders wishing to foster continuity with the past and for young people trying to establish a connection with this tradition, such traditionalizing narratives play a key role in the maintenance both of cultural forms and of Yuchi identity.

In addition to enhancing the authority and historicity of ceremonial ground speeches, the combination of reported voices (speaker, chief, ancestors, elders, and Creator) serves to enhance the community-building function of such speeches. All of those voices posit a harmonious ideal community, manifest in an extended family housed in the sacred "big house." Despite temporary failures (almost letting one of the grounds dissolve), the Yuchi people in the past approximated this ideal. Their success is tangible in the persistence of past cultural practices, and the collective sense of community that they espoused is achievable in the present. The speaker's role in this work of tradition is central. "The performer is positioned at a complex nexus of responsibility. Taking command in the events out of which the future will rise, performers must, at once, keep faith with the past, with their deceased teachers, and with the present, the mumbling members of the audience who seek engagement now and might act later on what they learn" (Glassie 1995:402).

Describing the Green Corn Ceremonies at the Sand Creek Ceremonial Ground in 1905, Frank Speck provided an account of the closing speech given by Chief James Brown at the conclusion of the half-night dance held the day before the Green Corn rituals proper:

> At about midnight when things had quieted down a little, the town chief rose from his seat near the center of the west lodge, and silence was rendered him as he began a speech lasting about fifteen minutes. In this he referred to their ancestors who handed the ceremonies down to them; to the deities who taught them; to the obligations of the present generation to maintain them. He complimented the dancers, referred to the rites of the next day and called for the assent and cooperation of his town. The men shouted 'hó hó!' the sign of approbation. The town chief concluded with an appeal for good behavior and reverence during the celebration, exhorting them when the event was over to go to their homes in peace and to avoid getting into trouble or disputes with anyone. Then all dispersed for the purpose of sleep or carousing. [1909:119–20]

It is unusual and interesting, but not surprising, that the chief whom Speck came to know spoke for himself on this occasion. In 1993 I met his namesake and grandson, James D. Brown, Sr. When I met him he had served as chief of the Polecat ground for over three decades. When his old home community of Sand Creek reestablished its ceremonial, Chief Brown began participating there as well. Like Mr. Littlebear and the other present-day ceremonial leaders, Chief Brown believed that Yuchi people should support all of the grounds as much as they could. As the leading elder and the last speaker of Yuchi involved in the Sand Creek ground, he was asked by the young Sand Creek chief to serve as his speaker. Hence the oldest Yuchi chief and the leader of the largest Yuchi ground became the speaker for the youngest chief and the smallest ground. During my earliest visits to the Yuchi, I had the privilege of listening to Chief Brown speak at the Sand Creek ground. Like Speck before me, I had to glean the content of the speeches second-hand, in summary. My work was then too preliminary to involve serious work on the language in ritual context. While I wish that Speck and I had been in a position to obtain Yuchi language texts of the speeches that we heard, Speck's brief account paints a clear picture of the function that Yuchi oratory served then and now. The continuity between 1905 and 1995, when the Jim Brown whom I knew gave the last ceremonial ground speech in Yuchi, is striking. Yuchi ceremonialists feel an understandable sense of loss at the passing of the Yuchi-speaking orators, but they are encouraged that Mr. Littlebear, as well as younger men, are continuing to find ways to share the same messages in a new language. These speakers still refer to the ancestors who handed down the ceremonies to them. They still thank the Creator who provided them. They still exhort the present generation to maintain them. They still compliment the dancers for their good efforts. They still refer to the rites. They still secure the cooperation of the town. They still appeal for good behavior, reverence and harmonious social relations. And the men still shout "hõ hõ."

5

"It's a time that we let the spirits get gradually built up."

Indian Football

Signaling the Creator

Standing among his people on a spring afternoon, each of the three Yuchi chiefs opens the new ritual season for his ceremonial ground with the skyward toss of a handmade ball of denim, canvas, or leather. The game that ensues is a humorous rough-and-tumble contest between the men and women of the community. Watching the game from the sidelines are elders who remember games of their youth, and watching from above is Gohætone 'the Creator' (lit., 'master of breath'), who instructed the Yuchi in their ritual practices. Yuchi elders assert that Gohætone enjoys the game and is pleased to see them renew their ceremonies after another winter.

I witnessed the Yuchi football game for the first time in the spring of 1995. The members and guests of the Duck Creek Ceremonial Ground were gathered on a Sunday afternoon. Cars were parked along the perimeter of the ceremonial ground site, near the camp arbors that house the families of the community during extended ceremonies. Everyone waited in their cars or under the protection of one of the camps, as Sunday had brought rain in an alternating cycle of heavy downpours and light showers. At the west end of the ground the chief and his helpers, during a period of lighter rain, could be seen coming to a decision about the game. I had just returned to the Yuchi country to make arrangements for extended study with the elders who had introduced me to their community two summers earlier. As I moved from car to camp to car, visiting acquaintances, we heard a shouted call from the leaders to assemble on the ball field. The game would go on, rain or shine. With enthusiasm the young people gathered, while the older people were more circumspect about getting out into the cool rain. Felix Brown, Sr., at that time the ground's chief, walked slowly from the chiefs' arbor at the west end of the town square to the east, arriving with the football amid a cluster of eager young players.

In, under, and around the south goal a human wall of young women jammed themselves into position, preparing a firm defense against the sometimes-rough offense of the younger men. At the north end, one or two of the middle-aged men prepared to start, hanging back at the goal and hoping to avoid injury or exhaustion by leaving the rough play to the ground's younger men. As I watched, Chief Brown stood in the center of the field holding a stick for marking the score in one hand and the ball in the other. With a toss straight up, the game, and the ceremonial ground's ritual season, was begun. At the exact moment that the ball went skyward, the sun appeared and the rain ended.

In contemporary eastern Oklahoma, tribal rituals organized at community ceremonial grounds are the essential events through which specific tribal identities are given cultural substance – layering form and meaning on top of the brute genealogical facts of descent and tribal enrollment. In this chapter I examine the ceremonial game known in Eastern Oklahoma as "Indian football." This is a significant, yet poorly documented, cultural performance within the ceremonial cycle of the three modern Yuchi communities. It is also a game, played with various ritual motivations across the Native American societies of the Eastern Woodlands. Similarities and differences between the Yuchi game and versions found among those Woodland peoples not only reveal historical patterns of relationship and cultural variation, but exemplify the interesting balance between tribalism and intertribalism that still characterizes the social life of modern Oklahoma Indian communities.

PROCEDURE

For the Yuchi, spring football games begin the ritual season that climaxes with the midsummer Green Corn Ceremony. The chief of each community, in consultation with his assistants and advisors, formally selects the date for the first game, usually played in late March or early April. At the Polecat Ceremonial Ground, Easter Sunday customarily marks the first game. Regarding scheduling, Newman Littlebear remarked:

> Everybody knows that Polecat usually starts on Easter and it's kind of an automatically set date. Our people are aware of that, so the chief makes it official, then we have our first one. At our first ballgame, maybe we'll have a little council and talk about the next one and maybe other things for the coming year, such as encouraging the people to take part. It's a time that we let the spirits get gradually built up, as we move along. And we set a time for our next ballgame and then just kind of go from ballgame to ballgame. [15 January 1996]

Unlike the stomp dances that follow in the Yuchi ritual calendar, the football games are primarily community-internal events. To be measured as a success, the stomp dances require the participation of visiting groups from other ceremonial grounds, but the ballgames attract only members of the home community. Further explaining the scheduling of the games, Mr. Littlebear commented:

> Even if we have a game at the same time as one of the other Yuchi grounds, like Duck Creek or Sand Creek, we usually go right ahead, because it [football] doesn't involve dancing. We can kind of handle the ballgames alone, but our dances, we try to schedule them alternate with the other grounds, so that we may be able to accommodate one another by attending those. We try to play every week to allow for weather conditions. If we get rained out, we usually plan for the following Sunday. We usually play on Sunday, except the fourth one gets played on Saturday because that's the night we'll dance our first dance. [15 January 1996]

Because it is followed by a dance, the three Yuchi grounds typically coordinate the scheduling of the fourth (last) ballgame, and visitors from these other communities are more likely to attend.

The Yuchi football game is typically played to eight points – thought of in terms of a pair of fours, the Yuchi ritual pattern number.[1] The chief serves as referee and scorekeeper, marking points with a cane staff in the dirt.[2] These marks are made perpendicular to a scoring line. The men's score is marked on one side of the line and the women's score on the other. After a team reaches four points, points five through eight are marked by the erasure of the four marks made for points one through four, with eight points being counted as "four up, four down." As at the beginning of the game, each point is followed by a toss-up of the ball by the chief.[3]

The rules of play are simple. No set number of players is needed. If the women are grossly outnumbered, the men will loan them several boys.[4] There are no field boundaries either, although play is usually contained within the open rectangle bounded by the goals on the north and south sides and the ceremonial square on the west.[5] Passing the ball through the opposite team's goal scores a point. The goal is made of two green branches that are set into the ground, bent to form an arc, and tied securely. The resulting goals are about five feet high and six feet across. Women may carry the ball, throw it in the air, or pass it along the ground by rolling or kicking. However, as in the Yuchi single-pole stickball game, the men are handicapped with stricter rules. They may not run with the ball and must pass it along the ground by kicking or rolling it. Thus a man can touch the ball to intercept a pass or to wrestle it away from an opponent, but then the ball must be placed on the ground to be rolled or kicked.

While sometimes rough, games are played in a spirit of good humor and elders are quick to chastise teenagers who get too serious or physical.

Before entering the inner area of the square ground and playing ball for the first time each year, participants must wash, while facing east, with spicewood medicine (*Lindera benzoin* and water) prepared by the chief.[6] This washing is perhaps the most basic Yuchi ritual act. All participants in ceremonial ground activities, even the youngest children, are expected to wash when visiting the grounds for the first time each year. Newman Littlebear and Duck Creek Chief Simon Harry discussed the centrality of washing, noting:

> (Simon) You clean up before you get in the ground. That's . . . that's the way my old people told me. They said: "Don't go in there without cleaning up."
> (Newman) That's one of the first things they . . . they taught, even the young. "Always wash. Wash up before you enter that square." [4 February 1997]

Washing removes any harmful spiritual forces accumulated during the winter, which is spent away from the beneficial effects of ceremonial ground practices, and it ensures that the ground will be maintained in a pure state. This washing is also done after a Yuchi individual or funeral party returns from a gravesite, in order to counter any ill effects brought on by such a visit. The spicewood medicine is also drunk as a general tonic that promotes good health. If spicewood is unavailable, plain water may be substituted, as water itself is considered by the Yuchi to be a blessed medicine.

At some grounds, the football game is followed by a potluck supper with dishes provided by the members. Recognized as a recent innovation, these meals provide more opportunity for community members to fellowship with one another. With many younger people no longer residing within the rural districts associated with the three Yuchi settlements, such ceremonial ground activities have assumed an even greater role in fostering community identity.

SIGNALING THE CREATOR

Like other valued cultural performances among Woodland peoples, the Yuchi football game resists association with a single meaning or purpose.[7] When speaking of the game, Yuchi elders today note first that the game is a "signal to the Creator." In throwing up the football, the ceremonial ground chief asserts, on behalf of the community, the group's intention to undertake again the full cycle of Yuchi ceremonies. Relevant here are sacred mythic narratives that assert that the Creator looks each year to see that the Yuchi are performing the ceremonies provided to them; if they are not, it is believed that peacefulness will

Assistant Chief Felix Brown, Jr. (the man center left facing away from the camera), acting as referee, has just tossed up the ball following a score by one of the teams in a football game at the Duck Creek Ceremonial Ground, 25 April 1998. Photograph by Cecil Harry.

Elenora Powell (seated) and Viola Thomas (standing) watch the game downfield while resting from their work guarding the women's goal at the north end of the football field at the Polecat Ceremonial Ground, 2 April 1999.

end and world-changing catastrophes will ensue. In his dissertation research among the Yuchi, Frank Speck recorded several narratives that included this motif. In sacred narrative, the Yuchi were created through the agency of the Sun, which, especially today, is considered the most tangible symbol of the Creator.[8] Early in mythic time, the Sun created the Yuchi and provided them with their most central ritual practices – the consumption of red root (*Salix humilis*) and snakeroot (*Eryngium yuccifolium*) tea and the scratching rite, both of which remain the core events in the annual Green Corn Ceremony. The Sun explained to the ancestral Yuchi that the peacefulness of the world depended on the maintenance of these ceremonies. In one version that Speck translated:

> No trouble comes to the people when they have taken the medicines. When the Sun comes up he looks down to see if they are doing the ceremonies. If he comes up high here [above the ceremonial ground] and sees no Indians performing the ceremonies on the earth at high noon, he would stop. He would cry. It would be the end of peacefulness. The Sun would cover his face with his hands and go down again in the east. Then it would become dark and the end. It has been declared so. This is what we heard in the past. [1909:107]

Such explanations continue to inform Yuchi ritual practice today. During Green Corn, both medicine taking and scratching rituals are coordinated with the Sun reaching the apex of its climb across the sky. In contrast to the ritual medicines of the Creek, whose efficacy derives from the efforts of a medicine man using spoken formulas transferred into liquid medicine through a bubbling tube, Yuchi medicines are made powerful through the agency of the Sun. Rather than by medicine men, Yuchi ritual medicines are prepared by the young men who serve as poleboys during each year's Green Corn Ceremony (Jackson 2000a). The medicine plants are steeped in water while they absorb the heat and power of the Sun. They are taken at midday, when this power is strongest.

In signaling the Creator, the football game is another expression of a general tendency in Yuchi ritual to view ceremonies and their component acts as communications and transactions between the Yuchi people and heavenly beings. Foremost among these entities is the Creator, who originally provided the form and content of Yuchi culture; however, the departed ancestors who transmitted it down to the present are important as well. All tribal ceremonies, both life-cycle and corporate, explicitly address this theme, which is most obvious in the Yuchi Soup Dance, examined in chapter 9. Proper continuation of customary practices is the obligation of the living, and the Creator responds with continued health and well being for the faithful. The enjoyment of the game is one of the currencies, together with tobacco, food, paint, song, dance, ritual speech, sacrifice, and ritual gesture, that the Yuchi community put into circulation in their moral economy through ritual. The Yuchi view in these matters is in accord with belief about ritual reciprocity in the Woodlands generally, as in the beseeching and thanksgiving of Iroquois oratory and the exchange of symbolic goods (such as food and white beads) in Delaware rituals (Foster 1989; Roark 1978).[9]

GENDER AND RENEWAL

Commenting on the single-pole stickball game that the Yuchi share with the Creek, Seminole, Cherokee, and Chickasaw, Raymond Fogelson (1962, 1998) has repeatedly drawn attention to the game's importance for understanding the gender and role dynamics of Southeastern societies. Fogelson's insights into that game extend to Yuchi football, as well. It, like the single-pole game and unlike the Southeastern matchball game, "has a more religious, peaceful cast, symbolizing opposition between the sexes and a reaffirmation of traditional sex roles" (1962:247).[10] Yuchi elders report that this gender symbolism once extended to special feasts held in association with the games, in which the losing team provided gender-appropriate foods to the winner. Chief Simon Harry recalled that if the women lost the game, they had to cook corn soup, while if the men lost, they had to conduct a squirrel hunt, offering the quarry to the women.

The association of men with game hunting and women with horticulture, particularly with corn, is widely observed in the Woodlands and is reflected in the gender divisions of the game and in feast behavior. Gendered food exchange linked to the football game is reported among other Eastern societies. In a pattern similar to that recalled by Yuchi consultants, the North Carolina Cherokee teams bet on the outcome of the game. "If the men were beaten, they had to hunt and prepare a deer for a feast. If the women were beaten, they had to prepare bread for a feast" (Gilbert 1943:269–70; see also Speck and Broom 1983:82–83). While the losers among the Cherokee hosted the feast a week later, among the Chickasaw both the men and the women were responsible for providing such foods for a meal held soon after the game (Swanton 1928c:244). In the Shawnee football game, the losers provide firewood, and the same complementary and gendered food distributions reappear elsewhere within the ceremonial events that encompass the game (Howard 1981). For the Yuchi community as a whole, the ballgame indexes relations with the Creator. Within the social sphere internal to the community, it celebrates an understanding of gender that sees men and women as distinct and different types of cultural beings, both of which are required in order to maintain and renew Yuchi society (cf. Bell 1990; Caffrey 2000; Fogelson 1990; Miller 1980, 1997).

From such surface manifestations of gender relations, it is not hard to see deeper significances underneath. Among the Shawnee and Delaware, the football game is explicitly performed in the spring in order to bring the rains and to stimulate the fertility of crops. It also celebrates the end of winter and the return of life to the natural world. In the first published account of the Yuchi game, a lively telling of his adventures attending a game at the Polecat ground in 1884, Jeremiah Curtin (1948) identifies the game as a "planting festival." If today Yuchi elders do not consciously refer to it in such terms, it is perhaps that the notion is too obvious to require explicit comment. The conceptual shift from a planting festival to a more diffuse recognition of springtime renewal makes sense, as well, in light of current economic life, in which most Yuchis are no longer directly involved in agriculture.

At the time of the first game of the year, the ceremonial ground is brown and encircled with bare trees. With each game that follows, the land becomes greener and, when the final game is played, the ground stands once again at the center of lush growth. Regarding the symbolism of natural rebirth associated with Yuchi football, Mr. Littlebear commented:

> You might say that, in that time of the year, the things of nature are beginning to become new. And the Indians, the Yuchi and I guess maybe other tribes, observe that. There is the grass, it's just young and beginning to become mature, as time goes by. The trees are beginning to bud out and stuff like that. We're kind of things of nature also. We kind of take it like that. Well, that new year is really already started when that happens, the new season. [15 January 1996]

With these games, the community reassembles after what, for elders especially, had been a period of increased social isolation. The beauty, power, and joy of the change of seasons are continually in both the minds and the conversations of all community members. Renewed social intercourse and a renewed world go hand in hand.[11]

HISTORICAL RESONANCE IN CULTURAL PERFORMANCE

Like other genres of ritual performance, Indian football evokes a variety of intertwined associations, some widely shared and others regularly contested. Beyond the ideas about gender that the game reflects, it also, for the Yuchi, expresses local understandings of male leadership. When I began work with the Yuchi, my formal task was to elicit an oral history of the three ceremonial grounds as part of a effort to gather documentation in support of a petition requesting separate tribal acknowledgment from the Bureau of Indian Affairs. In my first interview ever as a fieldworker, I was fortunate to record an extended monologue by Mr. Jimmie Skeeter, then speaker for the Duck Creek ground. He recounted the entire history of his community from before allotment through 1993. Central to his narrative was a football game that reestablished the community's ceremonial ground after several years of inactivity.

During the 1930s, the Duck Creek Ceremonial Ground shut down after one of its members was involved in a killing. Before and during World War II, travel to the ceremonial ground in the Polecat settlement, over twenty miles to the west, was difficult for the Duck Creek residents. By the early 1940s, the young men who had participated in the old ground had matured enough to take an interest in its reestablishment. In this context, the old chief, Willie Fox, began enlisting the support of the young men and the approval of the remaining elders to reactivate the community's ceremonial activities. News and enthusiasm spread during the summer and fall of 1941, but the old chief took ill and died during the following winter.

At about this time, John Brown, a Yuchi from the western Sand Creek settlement, moved to an allotment in the Duck Creek area and began to take an interest in local affairs. Having been a member of the Sand Creek ground, he inquired about the possibility of reviving the Duck Creek ground. At this point, the men were still interested, but were assessing their situation after the loss of the old chief. During this period, John Brown began talking about reviving the ground, particularly when the men of the community gathered to cut wood or hold archery shoots.

On a spring day in 1942, John Brown hosted an archery tournament at his home after which the men were to discuss the next steps to be taken with respect to the ground. Mr. Skeeter finished his story this way:

TEXT 10

Excerpt from an oral history of the Duck Creek Ceremonial Ground provided by Mr. Jimmie Skeeter in Tulsa, Oklahoma, 16 June 1993.

I guess he had already planned what he was going to do, but he didn't tell any of the rest of us about it. So he wrote a letter; I think they lived over there southwest of Bristow, which is quite a ways and transportation wasn't very good. They had a little old Model T Ford, I think, and they came down. I seen that car there, a strange car to me, you know. I walked up there and I didn't say nothing. I kind of figured something was going to take place, but we went on ahead with that archery shoot. When we got through, we were supposed to hold a meeting. And John said:

"Say, these folks come from over yonder."

He says:

"They come a long ways 'cause they heard we was going to play football, and they all came down to help us play ball."

Well, that was good but I said:

"We ain't organized that yet."

I said:

"We got to organize that."

And I said:

"We got to find a place, and we got to select a chief, who's going to run it."

He said:

"Well, I hate to disappoint them people, they drove that far."

He said:

"We're going to go ahead and play ball."

I said:

"Well, that's up to you."

So he was already ready. He done made that ball, he'd already cut them poles for the goals and he had them stashed out there, you know. So, after the archery shoot, well, he put those poles up and said:

"We're going to play ball."

Maybe he told the bunch we were going to play ball. He got ready you know, they were all gathered up, and he throw that ball up. After he threw that ball up, that old man [Luke Fox] walked up there, that was-supposed to be the second chief, he would have been, you know. Well, he kind of grinned and walked up. He said:

"Man, you already got started."

"Yeah,"

I said.

"He got in a hurry. He wants to go on. What do you think about it?"

I told him.

"Well, I guess they'll go on, this is his place, this is what he wanted."

He said.

But, he said:

"He's got to go ahead now, he's done thrown the ball up. He can't back down now."

Knowing nothing of the Yuchi football game at the time that I heard it, Mr. Skeeter's story of how the ground was reestablished and how its chief was selected went over my head. Oral history is spoken history, generated by individuals with particular discursive styles, interests, and life experiences. Understanding it requires knowledge of how historical narrative reflects local culture and is shaped by the distinctive social dynamics of a community (see Fogelson 1989; Glassie 1982, 1994; Sahlins 1995). Whether or not John Brown fully recognized the significance of his tossing up the ball that spring afternoon remains a matter of interpretation and debate in Yuchi historical thought, but in spiritual and political terms, the result was clear. Like Jimmie Skeeter, the ground's current chief, Simon Harry, recalls the moment as an important transaction. He reports that his grandfather, Luke Fox, reminded them that day that John Brown was going to be chief because "he has done signaled to the Creator" by throwing the ball into the air. For over thirty years John Brown served as the ground's respected chief, a job that for the Yuchi is lifelong. In throwing up the ball that afternoon, he instituted a contract with the Creator and stated publicly his intention to serve his people. When the ceremonial ground faced difficult times, his people held him to this understanding and insisted that he could not step down as chief. The Duck Creek ground flourishes today on the site of that first ballgame and the contract between its chief, the Creator and the community is renewed each spring when the ball is again tossed skyward.

AREAL COMPARISON AND REGIONAL IDENTITIES

Woodland ceremonial events such as the Yuchi football games held each spring are meaningful from a number of points of view. For Yuchi people they represent complex social, spiritual, historical, and personal interactions. This local and personal point of view can be complemented and enriched through a wider comparative perspective. Although such a view may appear to be a hallmark of scholarly attention, it also represents an interest widely held among American Indian peoples generally and in Woodland communities in particular. The Yuchi ceremonial leaders who have taught me about the richness of their own world are curious ethnographers when it comes to the beliefs and practices of their Native friends and neighbors. They understand Yuchi culture not only in its own terms but also vis-à-vis contrasts and similarities found across a wider American Indian social universe.

Although the football game has not attracted the same measure of ethnographic attention commanded by the "little brothers of war" – stickball in the Southeast and its northern sibling, lacrosse, a surprising amount of comparative material can be gleaned from the accumulated work of twentieth-century ethnographers (Vennum 1994).[12] With the goal of situating the Yuchi game within this context, shedding light on its cultural history in Eastern North America, and suggesting the ways in which the game fits within a larger, vital world of inter-community social engagement and interaction, I draw out of this ethnographic record some comparative notes. My goal is to understand the Yuchi football game in a wider regional frame but my hope, as well, is to illustrate the ways in which the classic techniques of the historic-geographic method and controlled comparison can continue to complement ethnographic studies concerned with modes of expressive performance. Theoretically, a comparative examination of "Indian football" contributes to a reassessment of models of regional social organization and social change, particularly the widely used, but poorly understood, concept of "pan-Indianism." After assembling and reviewing the available published and unpublished sources relating football in the Eastern Woodlands, I will return to such theoretical considerations.

Longhouse Iroquois

Among the Longhouse Iroquois of New York and Canada, the game of football must have seemed minor to previous observers, as it gets only passing mention in descriptions of the Midwinter Ceremony at Sour Springs Cayuga Longhouse and elsewhere at Six Nations in Ontario and at Coldsprings Seneca Longhouse in New York (Fenton 1936; Shimony 1994; Speck 1995). While similar in form, the significance of the Iroquois game seems to be an inversion of the game among the Yuchi and their present-day neighbors. According to Speck's description of Cayuga football (like the tug-of-war game) it "functions as a rite when called for by a patient as an adjunct to herbal medicine or suggested as an auxiliary to treatment prescribed by a medicine-man" (1995:125). Describing the four games used as curing rites at Six Nations longhouses (the bowl game, lacrosse, football, and tug-of-war), Annemarie Shimony characterized the function of the football game as structurally similar to the lacrosse game:

> ... with the patient throwing out the ball to begin the game and also keeping the rag ball as a charm. The game may be played either by young men against old or by opposing moieties. Again, the outcome is immaterial to the curing, the most important act being the initial throw by the patient. Cookies and false face mush also accompany this game. [1994:279]

The game at Six Nations is played in winter, as opposed to in spring and summer among the Yuchi and their neighbors in Oklahoma. As in much Iroquois ritual, the focus is on healing, and the game is played between the ritually significant categories of men, although William Fenton indicates that at Coldsprings the game is played by women against women (1936:17).[13]

In understanding the divergence of the Iroquois game from the versions found elsewhere in the East, it is tempting to see the Iroquois form as a relatively recent transformation of what is likely the older, more widely distributed pattern. As the ritualized male and female game possesses a sexual overtone, it may have been modified, as were certain Iroquois social dances that were condemned as promiscuous in their older forms by the Seneca prophet Handsome Lake (Speck 1995:152). Fenton documented a parallel transformation in the Iroquois Eagle Dance which, in Handsome Lake's time, lost its warfare connotations and took on a curing function (1953:32–33).

As is the case with other aspects of their culture, the football game of the Oklahoma Seneca-Cayuga, who are separated by half a continent from the majority of the other Iroquois peoples in the Northeast, appears to be a mixing of Iroquois forms with patterns adopted from their neighbors in northeast Oklahoma. The only published description of the game is James Howard's account of the Seneca-Cayuga Green Corn Ceremonies held in August 1959. The game that he witnessed was played on the third day of the event, at the end of the Green Corn rituals proper, prior to the Sun Dance, which took place on the following day: "The crowd, however, did not disperse, for many events were to follow. That afternoon there was an Indian football game, boys against girls, sponsored by a crippled woman who sought to gain relief from her pain by attracting the Creator's attention in this manner" (1961:25).[14]

With so many of their congeners in northeast Oklahoma present at their celebrations, it is not surprising that the procedure of the Seneca-Cayuga game mirrored Shawnee, Delaware and Quapaw practice. Howard's account of the woman seeking relief for her ailments matches accounts of a longhouse practice in the north. The Seneca-Cayuga case is intermediate between Northern Iroquois and Oklahoma belief and practice. Howard reports that the woman's cure was obtained by "attracting the attention of the Creator" (1961:126), as opposed to coaxing "the withdrawal of some unfriendly spirits who are standing in the way of the successful action of the medicine administered" (Speck 1995:126) by a medicine man. As among most groups, information on the Seneca-Cayuga ballgame is minimal, and further ethnography would prove particularly interesting.[15]

Cherokee

Reports of the Cherokee game suggest Iroquois affinity through the linking of the game with the tug-of-war rite, but as in most things, the hints of a shared Iroquoian heritage are submerged beneath more prominent areal patterns (Fenton 1978). Both a tug-of-war contest between men and women and the football game were played by the North Carolina Cherokee in the morning following an all-night dance. Speck noted, "Quitting the dwelling [the house in which the dances took place], the celebrants assemble in the yard for a last social festivity. At this time one of the games or contests is held between the men and the women to decide who shall, within the week, give a feast to the community. Since the Big Cove people used to dance on Saturday nights, the feast was usually appointed for the following Friday night" (Speck and Broom 1983:82). The Yuchi game is occasionally played in the morning following a stomp dance, in this same manner. The single pole stickball game, similarly, is often held in the morning at Creek ceremonial grounds under the same conditions. While the tug-of-war and football games are linked components of Cherokee dance events, as among the Cayuga, the published sources make no mention of a healing motivation in the Cherokee contests.

According to Speck, each team is captained by a member of the opposite gender, whereas William Gilbert reports single-sex male teams, with the women usually "given one strong man on their side for additional assistance" (Gilbert 1943:269; Speck and Broom 1983:82). As in the other Woodland communities where it was played, the Cherokee football game was an intra-community game, unlike men's lacrosse or stickball, which often pitted rival communities against each other (Fogelson 1962, 1971). Gilbert reports that the challengers began the game by kicking the baseball-size ball, with twelve points constituting a game. Speck stated that one point completed the game, but Gilbert's data on team size (ten to fifteen per side) and points scored match unpublished notes collected by Frans Olbrechts and appear to be more reliable. Olbrechts's (1927) notes indicate that neither side was permitted to use hands, a contrast with the rules of the Yuchi, Chickasaw, and others among whom only the men are so handicapped.

Speck reports that the game was obsolete at the turn of the century. More recent field work, however, suggests that it continued longer, indicating that Speck's consultants in the Big Cove community had abandoned it earlier, and knew less about it, than people in other North Carolina communities. On the basis of the memories of living Cherokee elders from the Snowbird community in North Carolina and several towns in Oklahoma, the game was included in a revival of the Cherokee Green Corn Ceremony in North Carolina in 1989 (Fogelson 1998; Thomas 1990). An Oklahoma Cherokee friend from the Stoke Smith Ceremonial Ground has confirmed Robert Thomas's report that the game is remembered in Oklahoma as well as in North Carolina.

While available accounts are limited and descriptive, the Cherokee game emphasizes the same concern with gender role divisions and community celebration found to be associated with the game among the Yuchi, Shawnee, Delaware, and other Woodland peoples.

Delaware and Shawnee

Comparatively, the Yuchi game is closest in form and significance to the game among the Shawnee and Delaware communities in Oklahoma.[16] With them, the Yuchi version shares the status of the opening event in the ceremonial season that is initiated in the spring (Howard 1980:156, 1981; Speck 1937). As among the Yuchi, the game is closely watched by the Creator. Concerning the Shawnee Creator, Carl Voegelin noted: "She always looks through her sky-window while a game is in progress. She smiles with approval when in the speech preceding each game it is said that ball games are played because they were ordained by her rules" (1936:15). As a cultural performance, the game among the Yuchi, Shawnee, and Delaware expresses similar understandings of appropriate gender roles, of rebirth in the natural world, and of the thanks due the Creator.

The most detailed information on the Shawnee game is that compiled by James Howard. Based on work with Loyal Shawnee ceremonial leader Ranny Carpenter, he noted:

> The game is a sacred exercise. It is thought to be pleasing to Our Grandmother and also to the Thunderbirds and is therefore conducive to bringing rain and promoting the fertility of the crops. Because the first game takes place prior to the spring Bread Dance, around the first of May, and the last one during the latter part of June, the Season lasts about a month and a half or two months at the most. Other tribes that have acquired the game from the Shawnees, such as the Delawares, Oklahoma Seneca-Cayugas and Quapaws may play on into the autumn, but the Shawnees would not think of doing so lest they bring storms and bad weather. [1981:263]

While Howard's information on the significance of the game is certainly well attested, his historical reconstruction is less solid. The presence of the game among the Cayuga and other Iroquois people in the north calls into question his assertion of Shawnee diffusion to the Oklahoma Seneca-Cayuga. On the basis of early ethnohistorical references, Jim Rementer has argued that the game has a long history among the Delaware and was probably not, as Howard and Speck suggested, a recent borrowing from the Shawnee (Rementer 1993; Speck 1937:73). No information is presently available to me on the origins or form of the game among the Quapaw.

Howard's descriptions of actual games played at the modern Shawnee ceremonial grounds in Oklahoma are the most detailed available accounts of the game among any group. The actual play of the Shawnee game is very close to the Yuchi form. The main points of difference can be quickly summarized: an elder, man or woman, acts as referee, in contrast to the Yuchi chief. A separate scorekeeper distinct from the referee keeps score with a set of sixteen sharpened wood pegs (eight for each side), placed in the ground. The Shawnee and Delaware goals are large vertical poles in contrast to the arc goals used by the Yuchi. Among the Absentee Shawnee, kinship rules regarding which relatives of the opposite gender one can touch or interact with are reported to be enforced during the game, strengthening the kinship system and making the game more complicated and humorous.

Most distinct is the practice, associated with the Shawnee and Delaware game, of collecting individual bets. Those wagers work as follows: "The bets consist of comparable items wagered on either of these two sides by individuals. Each person's bet of say, a scarf, is knotted to a comparable bet from the opposite side, and paired bets are then tied to a long string. When all bets have been gathered the string of bets is suspended between two poles" (Howard 1981:264). After the game, individuals from the winning team reclaim their own items as well as the matching wagers. Such betting also accompanies the Delaware game. Goods that have accrued significance as old-time valuables, such as scarfs, cloth, and ribbons, appear to be the typical wager.

The basic form of the Delaware game is identical to the Shawnee contest, but additional information on its significance is available in the accounts of Speck and Rementer, both of whom present direct information from Delaware collaborators. Speck describes the game's significance.

> The ceremony, being a glorification over the return of spring, has certain formal requirements to be fulfilled, not only by the chief, but by the people at large. It is believed that if the rules governing the festival are not obeyed, floods, tornadoes, and storms will result, causing the destruction of grain and fruit crops. On the other hand, the proper conduct of the football game during the season of performance will strengthen the growth of crops. There is also a symbolical feature to the festival in the desire to indulge in a show of pure enjoyment of the people for the blessings of good weather and the returning warmth of the sun.[17] [1937:74]

Perhaps more valuable than Speck's discussion is the ballgame prayer provided by his consultant, C. J. Webber, a Delaware chief who supervised the game ritual. A prayer such as the following preceded the start of play. It is presented here in Speck's free translation:

> My kindred, I am thankful now as we are thinking upon the blessings received when our Father, the Great Spirit, remembers us. And we can see how up until now we have lived along so that we can all together observe the coming of springtime. Wherefore we rejoice when we see how everything is coming forth, and how our grandfather's trees are sending out their buds. And now everywhere throughout the land appears in beauty all the green growth and likewise our grains, while also the fruits that we gather show forth the beginnings of growth. And we also feel it as he is coming to send forth heat, that one our elder brother the sun. He has sympathy for us. And then, besides, those grandfathers of ours the Thunders as they give us an abundance of water. Everything is the doing of our Father the Creator. And it is even said that all the Spirit forces (manitu) pray, because sometimes we hear them, our grandfathers the trees, as they earnestly commune in prayer when the wind passes by through them. It is enough to set anyone thinking and should be a cause for happiness when

> he beholds the marvelous works of our Father, and how well they work for our benefit all the year through. And that now, my kindred, is the formula of prayer for this kind of traditional rite here. [quoted in Speck 1937:77–78]

Mr. Webber's prayer reinforces eloquently the thanksgiving aspect of the football ritual. As noted previously, in ritual events throughout the Woodlands, thanksgiving for gifts received and supplication for needs to be fulfilled are often closely linked within the same ceremonial events.

Creek and Other Muskogean Peoples

Customarily, anthropologists have sought Yuchi cultural affinities among the Creek with whom they have been politically linked since the late eighteenth century. Having established the ties between the Yuchi game and that of their long-time allies, the Shawnee, the game among the Creek and the other Muskogean peoples remains to be explicated.

In his study of Creek social organization, John Swanton makes passing mention of the football game: "In later times the Creek men and women also played against each other in a kind of game of football. Two goals were made, each of two sticks inclining to a point at a height of about four feet. The game was to drive the ball through these goals. It was thrown up in the middle and the men were allowed only to kick it while the women might use their hands also" (1928d:468). In recent years, Pam Innes has collected new information on the game among the Creek and Seminole. Her Creek consultants indicated that they remember playing pickup games of football "just for fun" between ritual episodes at the ceremonial ground events (p.c. 1996). The Oklahoma Seminole consultants with whom she has worked recall secular games of Indian football as family or neighborhood events at individual homesteads. While neither she nor I have been in attendance at either ground, our consultants among the Creek and Yuchi report that the game is still played by members of the Hillabi and Alabama ceremonial grounds. Asked why they do not play football at their own ceremonial grounds, Innes's consultants indicated that they now are aware of the game's importance to the Yuchi and feel that it would be inappropriate to perform a Yuchi ceremony as a game just for amusement. The religious or secular nature of the game in the Creek communities where it is still played has not been documented.

In a manuscript report based on fieldwork with the Koasati (Coushatta) in Louisiana, Lyda Taylor noted that football was played in that community. Like the Alabama residing in Texas, this community represents the people of towns that separated themselves from the main body of the Creek Nation before removal from the Southeast to Indian Territory. Taylor does not indicate the presence of gender-divided teams or ritual associations, but does indicate that the ball was kicked through goals like those used elsewhere (n.d.:37–38).

Swanton's brief mention of the Chickasaw game, like his description of the Creek game, is devoid of overt ritual association.[18] It would appear that the football game among the Creek and other Muskogean peoples lacks the rich associations of the game among the Yuchi and other more northerly groups. Not mentioned in early historical accounts, the game is perhaps a recent borrowing among the Creek, Oklahoma Seminole, and Chickasaw, although its presence among the Koasati in Louisiana suggests that such a borrowing would have taken place before removal to Indian Territory.

Other Woodland Groups

Various Native and anthropological sources note the presence of the football game among the Quapaw. This is not surprising in light of their intimate relations with the Seneca-Cayuga, Shawnee, and Delaware in northeastern Oklahoma. Beyond its presence though, the form and history of the Quapaw game are unknown to me. The only available report is in Sue Roark-Calnek's summary: "Quapaws play football 'for fun' at secular stomps [stomp dances] and war dances, but traditionally also at funerals and commemorative feasts, where it is said to please the deceased and console the bereaved" (1977:754–755). It is today played at their annual powwow (Gloria Young, p.c. 1997), but I have been unable to attend this event and witness the game.

In an earlier version of this chapter, published as an essay, I reported that no sources reported the game for the Kickapoo, despite their close association with the Shawnee (particularly the Absentee Shawnee and Oklahoma Kickapoo). Beth Dillingham's ethnography of the Oklahoma Kickapoo mentions a ballfield maintained by the tribe, but does not provide any information on the form that their ball game takes (1963:64–65). I also cited Felipe and Dolores Latorre's (1976) study of the Mexican Kickapoo, which provides information on a ball game that they describe as a transformation of Northeast-style lacrosse in which the racquets have been abandoned, except for a pair carried as tokens by the team captains. Like other Northeastern lacrosse games, it is played between men of opposed moieties. In the summer of 2001, I learned from Absentee Shawnee friends that the male-female football game *is* played among their allies the Oklahoma Kickapoo in a style similar to the Shawnee (contra Jackson 2000b:54–55). Despite other similarities in the ceremonialism of the Sauk, Kickapoo, and Shawnee, no sources available to me report the game among the Sauk.

Caddo acquaintances have also, since the publication of the football essay, reported that the game was once played among Caddo ceremonialists. Caddo play is described as similar to that of the Absentee Shawnee. As I came to know both communities better during 2000–2001, I learned that many social ties and cultural practices have linked the Caddo and Absentee Shawnee communities since their settlement in Oklahoma Territory. Additional fieldwork among the Caddo promises to reveal the shape and texture of this relationship through time.

Ann McMullen (p.c. 1996) reports that a game like football is played among the Mashpee at community celebrations. In their game, personal effort on the part of the players bestows the individual with health and well-being. Other Native peoples in contemporary New England are also reported to play similar ball games during powwows and community celebrations (Joan Thomas, p.c. 2000).

While my comparative effort has been a controlled one of the type advocated by his colleague Fred Eggan (1975:196–97), Fogelson (1998) has advanced a more wide-ranging thesis about the game's deep history and significance. He suggests that the Woodland game is related to ritual shinny games found in the Pueblos, and that it shares with those a common underlying concern with the fertility of crops and the division of society by age, gender, and moiety (cf. Ortiz 1989:66).

"EASTERN WAY" IN OKLAHOMA

Although it seems a small thing when viewed next to the overwhelming changes experienced by American Indian people in Eastern North America over the past 500 years, the football game represents an important thread in a larger tapestry of cultural continuity and persistence. For the development of a more refined theoretical perspective on the Eastern Woodlands and American Indian social interactions through history, the game also provides important lessons. It was in 1955 that both W. W. Newcomb (1955) and James Howard (1955) independently published accounts of the so-called Pan-Indian culture of Oklahoma. In Howard's treatment, distinct tribal cultures gave way to generalized Indian ones under the effects of acculturation. Pan-Indianism, as a theory, was especially attentive to what it perceived as the dissolution of American Indian cultural boundaries after World War II. Drawing on his own observations and on the work of Newcomb and Karl Schmitt, Howard framed Pan-Indianism as "one of the final stages of progressive acculturation, just prior to complete assimilation." He explained it "as a final attempt to preserve aboriginal culture patterns through intertribal unity" (1955:220).

In defiance of theories of Pan-Indianism, many Woodland peoples of Oklahoma have not permitted "their unique tribal characteristics" to be "withered away" (Hagan 1961:150). What has happened on the ground, particularly in the area of the ritual life of Oklahoma peoples during the twentieth century, has been much more interesting, for folklore and anthropology scholarship as well as for Native peoples, than the rise of the powwow and the bingo hall as universal institutions in Indian country. In eastern Oklahoma, where large numbers of Native people of differing tribal backgrounds reside, tribalism and intertribalism exist in a state of dynamic equilibrium. Among Woodland peoples in Oklahoma, ceremonialism has persisted in local communities as much *because of* inter-community contacts as *in spite of* them. Unlike the isolated enclaves of Native peoples located throughout the East, the different tribal and town communities in Oklahoma have been able to provide one another with the personnel and practical support needed to preserve the expressive forms that serve to define tribal identity.

As a ritual practice in eastern Oklahoma today, the football game varies between tribal and ceremonial communities in a contrastive fashion. Features such as field orientation, ball shape, goal shape, scoring method, and number of scores constituting a win vary according to local norms. As with other aspects of Oklahoma Woodland ceremonialism, the practices of local groups are distinct enough to provide a sense of tribal and often community (town/ceremonial ground) identity, while sharing enough features in common to foster a larger pan-Woodland ritual community based on intertribal involvement in what have remained identifiably tribal ceremonials. Intertribal and intercommunity marriage and participation provide local communities with needed personnel who share a common world view and ritual sense. Those outsiders conform to the broad outline of local practice, while undoubtedly shifting it occasionally in perceptible and imperceptible ways.

On the basis of my preliminary survey, it appears that the football game is, or at least was, played by most of the groups who participate in the broader system of Woodland ceremonialism most closely identified today with the stomp dance. This shared Oklahoma Woodland ceremonialism – what Roark-Calnek (1977), following Delaware practice, called "Eastern Way," – extends from the Quapaw and Seneca-Cayuga in the far northeast of the state southwest through the Yuchi country as far as the Caddo and Western Delaware country in central Oklahoma. Describing the dynamic of intertribal participation within tribally specific ceremonies, Roark-Calnek writes: "Indian football is played throughout northeastern Oklahoma by the Delaware and the tribes to their east, and by the Absentee Shawnee. It pits men against women with scoring rules that give women an advantage. While the game has everywhere the same rules and the same overtones of sexual joking, its rationale and appropriate occasions differ from tribe to tribe. Because these tribes are now so inter-married and participate together in the same overlapping regional circuits, the same players may move from ground to ground, observing the rationales and restrictions imposed by each tribe" (1977:754). It is within this interactional framework that the contemporary Yuchi game should be viewed. Although the basic form is widely distributed and many of the people who join in the Yuchi games could also claim identities as Creek, Shawnee, or white, the game at a Yuchi ceremonial ground remains a distinctly Yuchi event, governed by Yuchi norms and informed by Yuchi values.

The classic formulation of Pan-Indianism does not account well for the American Indian social networks existing in Woodland Oklahoma today or in the East during colonial times. As a theory especially interested in forms of cultural performance such as dance and ritual, Pan-Indianism assumes that individuals or groups engaged in social gatherings across tribal or national boundaries will increasingly lose their cultural distinctiveness. Such a view is based on an overly strong assumption of primordial boundedness, but it also ignores the capacity of communities to consciously maintain distinctive local practices in interactionally complex settings. Such cultural continuity is possible in Woodland Oklahoma because the locus of social action is the community, not the individual. Among Woodland people, communities and their traditions are conceived of in very superorganic ways. For instance, both formal oratory and condolence ceremonies, as public articulations of traditional culture and society, focus on symbols of the collectivity and its continuity with the past – chiefs, ancestors, and fireplaces. Little emphasis is placed on individuals or sociocultural innovation (Jackson and Linn 2000).

Returning to an external view of the Yuchi game's cultural history, the comparative picture shows the Yuchi as mediating cultural contacts between Northeastern and Southeastern groups. The Yuchi are the only modern ceremonialists practicing both football and the single-pole stickball game in their ritualized forms. While the single-pole game points to an affinity with their Creek neighbors, the form and significance of the football game connects the Yuchi strongly to their longtime allies, the Shawnee. Scholars have long seen Yuchi culture as a permutation of Creek patterns. Consideration of the football game, along with other patterns of social organization, social interaction, bilingualism, and ritual practice, point to ties with Central Algonkian groups that Yuchi people have always recognized, but which are only recently being noticed by students of Woodland culture history (see Callender 1994).

The Yuchi, as well as the Delaware and Shawnee, assert that the Creator appreciates observing the pleasure that the game brings to the people. While Simon Harry, Newman Littlebear, and other Yuchi elders have enjoyed exploring the ritual significance of the football game with me, they also recognize that the game's primary attraction, particularly for the young, is fun. Pitting women against men is a perfect recipe for Yuchi humor. This aspect is readily apparent when watching any game, and particularly humorous moments crystallize into stories that continue to circulate in families and communities. In a discussion of the game with her father, Newman Littlebear, and me, Linda Harjo recalled an old strategy that the women adopted. This prompted Mr. Littlebear to recall an anecdote about the game that, in his telling, left us breathless with laughter.

TEXT 11

Funny stories about Yuchi football. From a discussion between Newman Littlebear, Linda Harjo, and Jason Jackson, Kellyville, Oklahoma, 15 January 1996.

(Linda) They used to say too, some of them older women too, a long time ago the old women would play and stick that ball down in their blouses.

<<laughter>>

(Newman) Yeah. There was a story that said that . . . Well. I knew this lady. I don't know if you remember, but it would have been Martha . . . her grandmother or great-grandmother, I guess. Her great-grandmother I believe.

Anyhow, they said she . . . They used to wear them long skirts too, you know. Among those old ladies a long time ago, it was common.

They played ball and they say she, ah. She was playing and she was a tough old lady. But she stuck that ball way up between her legs like that. And all them mens, they didn't want to get . . . try to get that ball.

<<laughter>>

And her husband was down at the camp.

<<laughter>>

So they had to call him. They called him from camp out there to come and come out there and tackle his wife and get that ball.

<<laughter>>

There was a l l kind of comical things like that, you know.

> They . . . Oh, they would tell about it. Later years that . . . that story lived on. It still lives 'til today and oh, that happened over fifty years ago. It was before my time playing ball.
>
> <<laughter>>

This quotidian side of the game is the bedrock commonality that all the differing tribal forms share. That an always spirited, often humorous, and sometimes flirtatious game could simultaneously be a sacred act with a diverse range of symbolic associations is a telling feature of ritual life among all Woodland peoples. The Native ceremonies throughout the eastern United States that have been carried into the modern world are uniformly sincere, often exhausting, typically intellectually complex; but always rewarding to those who continue to invest in them. Playing ball attracts the beneficial attention of the Creator, of ancestors, and of friends and neighbors. It communicates appreciation for life's blessings and leads to a life in which such blessings continue to manifest themselves. For these reasons I am grateful to Yuchi friends who have pulled me out of the audience and onto the field of play in games that have left me winded and sore, but happy and thankful.

6 Stomp Dance
Reciprocity and Social Interaction

"They're a lot of help to us."

Between the months of April and October, each weekend poses a pair of linked questions for members of the ceremonial grounds of eastern Oklahoma: "Who's dancing?" and "Where are we going?" These questions acknowledge the fact that ceremonial grounds are both distinct communities of social actors and particular nodes in a larger social system. When stomp dance participants meet – in a shopping mall or supermarket, at a community center or health clinic, at a graduation ceremony or bingo game – the first question is usually easily answered. From weekend to weekend, word gets around quickly and active participants in the world of stomp dance cultivate detailed understandings of the workings of the larger social system. Answering the second question is, ideally and usually in practice, a corporate task invested in each ground's chief. The ways in which each modern stomp ground responds relate to longstanding patterns governing the social organization of inter-community relations among the Native peoples of the Eastern Woodlands. Examination of the system today provides a window on the ways in which the Yuchi stomp grounds sustain tribal identity and insight into the manner in which Woodland communities balance cultural commonalities and differences in social interaction.

In this chapter I describe Yuchi stomp dance events, placing special emphasis on social interaction and the negotiation of reciprocal relationships. The stomp dance is the central expression of contemporary Woodland ceremonial life in Oklahoma today, and its modern form has been described in varying degrees of detail by a number of authors, notably Amelia Bell (1984) for the Creek, Sue Roark-Calnek (1977) for the Delaware, and James H. Howard (1981; Howard and Lena 1984) for the Shawnee and Seminole. In describing the Yuchi form of the dance, I want to sketch some uniquely Yuchi features and provide enough context to understand patterns of inter-community interaction.[1]

VISITING

Previous students of stomp ground ceremonialism have marveled at the persistence of those practices into the contemporary era. From the perspective of his work with a Seminole ritual leader, Howard attributed "the surprising amount of traditional culture still remaining among today's Oklahoma Seminoles" to "the remarkable resiliency of Seminole culture" (Howard and Lena 1984:249). Less circular is the explanation provided by Lester Robbins (1976) on the basis of ethnographic fieldwork with the Creek ceremonial ground of Greenleaf during 1973–75. He argued, in line with Edward Spicer's (1971) work on persistent cultural systems, that the tenacity of Creek ceremonial ground ritual and belief was founded on the continuing significance of the town organizations, on the cultural value placed on ritual for maintaining collective health, and on oppositional tendencies within Creek society in which ceremonial activities express resistance to both the dominant society and assimilationist Creek politicians. While Robbins's explanations remain relevant, they do not address the social means that make this cultural persistence possible.

In considering the stomp dance as a focal event in Indian ritual life in eastern Oklahoma, I want to explore the ways in which the persistence of Yuchi ritual life, and Oklahoma Woodland tribal ceremonialism more generally, is facilitated in large measure through ongoing networks of intermarriage and reciprocal visitation sustained between communities. As Roark-Calnek (1977) has demonstrated in her work with the Delaware, it is these patterns that have provided the critical mass of participation that has sustained the Woodland ecumenicalism expressed best by the stomp dance. In addition, I suggest that tribally specific ritual forms, such as the Green Corn Ceremonies, are also sustained by the existence of this larger social sphere. Not only are intertribal stomp dances a central component of tribal ritual events, but all the ceremonial grounds (towns) rely on the experience brought by personnel whose community affiliations shift through time, especially through intermarriage.[2]

When discussing the social significance of visitation to their ceremonial grounds, Yuchi ritual leaders speak of the help visitors provide in "carrying the load." Stomp dances are the core events in the ritual calendars of the Oklahoma ceremonial grounds, and visitors play an important role in assisting local communities in the work that these dances represent. Stomp dances begin in the late evening and are expected to continue until sunrise. While a single community is usually capable of carrying off such a dance unassisted, a dance without visitors is a greater challenge for its members. Passing the night in dance and fellowship is enjoyable in the company of visitors but a dance becomes hard work when a ground is on its own. Alone, the male members of the ground must lead multiple dance episodes, while the women who shake shells must dance every round with little opportunity to rest and socialize.

Although additional participants, in the form of song leaders, shell shakers, and dancers, are the most obvious contribution that visiting groups make to a stomp dance, they provide other benefits, as well. Stomp dance visiting is the means by which news circulates, particularly news relating to developments in tribal politics. At dances, young people have an opportunity to court and socialize with other adolescents who share similar backgrounds. Most significantly, informal talk, as well as formal discourse, reinforces shared presuppositions and ideological tenets of culturally conservative Woodland Indian life.

During the period of my fieldwork I identified over twenty ceremonial ground communities that were active and acknowledged participants in the network described here. Previous researchers have compiled various other lists of active grounds. Those lists vary through time, both because grounds move in and out of active status, and because, from the point of view of any one community or cluster of allied communities, the boundaries of the system become fuzzy at the edges of the network. This is a problem recognized generally in mapping social networks, both for participants and researchers (Knoke and Kuklinski 1982:23). For Woodland ceremonialists, the problem is less acute because the practice of a clearly identifiable cultural form – the stomp dance – is the distinguishing feature marking inclusion in the network. Nonetheless, different participants and participating groups will have different maps of the stomp dance universe. A Yuchi teenager just being introduced to the stomp dance will have a limited knowledge of the system, while a well-traveled Seminole elder not only may know about the other grounds in Oklahoma, but may have experienced the cognate Seminole ceremonialism in Florida, as well. Similarly, the Oklahoma Seneca-Cayuga are in regular contact with their fellow Iroquois ritualists in Ontario and New York, as are some Oklahoma Cherokee who have established contacts with their tribespeople in North Carolina (Fogelson 1998). Even within the practical constraints of Oklahoma, no community can effectively participate in the full system. Most Yuchi, for example, have minimal knowledge of, and no experience visiting, some of the groups existing at the distant margins of the network, for instance the Caddo in the west near Binger and the Quapaw in the far northeast. As a result of the size and scope of the whole system, each community interacts with a smaller subset of other groups. Following the work of Roark-Calnek (1977:472), I refer here to these interactional subsets as *performance circuits.* For the purposes of this chapter, the eastern Oklahoma ceremonial ground communities active during 1995–1997 are shown in relative geographic position in map 4.

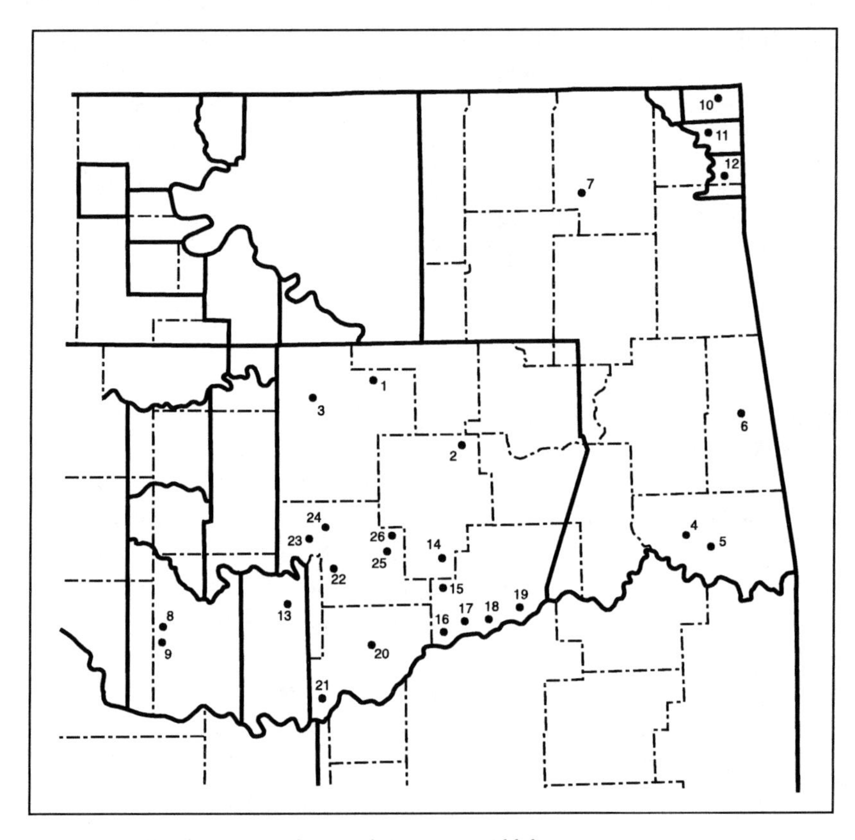

Map 4. Woodland ceremonial grounds in eastern Oklahoma, ca. 1996

KEY

NUMBER	GROUND NAME (COMMON ALTERNATIVES)	TRIBAL AFFILIATION
1.	Polecat (Kellyville)	Yuchi
2.	Duck Creek	Yuchi
3.	Sand Creek (Iron Post)	Yuchi
4.	Redbird	Cherokee
5.	Stoke Smith	Cherokee
6.	Flint Rock	Cherokee
7.	White Oak	Loyal Shawnee
8.	Little Axe (New Ground)	Absentee Shawnee
9.	Little Axe (Old Ground)	Absentee Shawnee
10.	Quapaw	Quapaw
11.	Ottawa	Ottawa
12.	Cowskin (Turkey Ford, Seneca)	Seneca-Cayuga
13.	Gar Creek	Seminole
14.	Arbeka	Creek

15.	Hickory Ground	Creek
16.	Muddy Waters (Weogufkee)	Creek
17.	Peach Ground (Pvkan' Tvlvhasse)	Creek
18.	Hillabee	Creek
19.	Tallahassee	Creek
20.	Alabama	Creek and Alabama
21.	New Tulsa (Tulsa Little River)	Creek and Seminole
22.	Greenleaf	Creek
23.	Fish Pond	Seminole and Creek
24.	Okfuskee	Creek
25.	Nuyaka	Creek
26.	Tallahassee Wvkokaye	Creek

Note: Caddo and Chickasaw ceremonial sites, located beyond the range of this map, are not shown. The author only began becoming acquainted with these communities after the conclusion of the fieldwork reported in this study. Additional Cherokee ceremonial ground communities are known to the author to have formed or (re-formed) during or since the period under discussion. The Eastern Delaware also established a new "dance ground" after the period examined in this study. The Miami, Peoria, and other groups in northeastern Oklahoma hold non-ceremonial stomp dances during powwows and other tribal events. The Tallahassee Wvkokaye ground (26) was formed by individuals previously associated with the Tallahassee ground (19). This founding took place during my initial period of study (1995–97). The Tallahassee ground (19) should not be confused with a currently inactive Seminole ground of the same name. As noted elsewhere in this work, a third ceremonial ground was also established among the Absentee Shawnee after the period of my initial research.

INTERMARRIAGE AND TOWN ORGANIZATION

In the week following their Green Corn Ceremony in 1997, the members of Polecat ground and the Euchee (Yuchi) Tribe of Indians sponsored a series of evening discussion groups at the ground. Held while the Polecat members were camped prior to their Soup Dance, these meetings provided an opportunity for all Yuchi people to gather and discuss tribal history and culture. During this meeting, Newman Littlebear discussed the nature of Yuchi identity within the context of intermarriage with other tribes:

> It is kind of difficult nowadays because so many of our members are married intertribe or even [belong to different] tribal towns and it is hard for them to just concentrate on just, on one. So some of them have to concentrate on both, if they are married in another tribal town, it kind of goes that way, both ways. We have some in that situation. They can't always be here or at Duck Creek. Different grounds are in that situation. [16 July 1997]

Intermarriage is one factor shaping patterns of interground visiting. Historically, marriages among the Yuchi and their neighbors tended toward matrilocal postmarital residence, in which a man joined in the communal life of his wife's town. While not prescribed, marrying outside the town was a practical byproduct of clan exogamy coupled with relatively small town size. The specific nature of Yuchi clans is unclear, but the pattern of matrilocal residence provided the central dynamic of Southeastern social organization (Fogelson 1990; Gearing 1962:21; Jackson 1996a; Swanton 1928a). Although the Yuchi exhibit some variance from the Southeastern areal pattern, the implications of matrilocality are present in historical Yuchi society, from the control by women of horticulture and other domestic domains to the elaborate systems of meaning embedded in sacred narrative and ritual symbolism. As Bell (1990) illustrated for the Creek, both the practice of matrilocal residence and the elaborate ideologies of gender that it indexes remain, to varying degrees, a key aspect of contemporary culture and society among Creek people. The patterns that she identifies for the Creek are less obviously manifest in Yuchi social practice, but the fundamental values that she identifies, particularly relating to gender role divisions, are equally significant for them and other Woodland peoples today.

In terms of actual social practice, membership and participation choices are more flexible today, particularly as place of residence is often determined by both access to employment and the availability of land and housing. The latter has been significantly shaped, in turn, by the allotment of tribal land at the turn of the twentieth century and by contemporary tribal housing programs. The replacement of ceremonial grounds by churches as the focal institutions in many local communities has also modified the form and function of the Woodland Indian towns. For example, a Yuchi woman raised in a church who marries a man from another community who is active in a ceremonial ground may choose to become active in her husband's ceremonial ground, bring her husband into her church, or attempt to negotiate participation in both religious settings. Despite the increased variability brought about by such twentieth-century transformations, the older pattern of matrilocality still governs many contemporary relationships, and continues to be recognized as a desirable form among Yuchi and Creek ceremonialists. Its continued relevance plays a role in determining patterns of visiting between ceremonial grounds (Bell 1984; Haas 1940; Opler 1972). In terms of the questions that I am addressing here, an important additional outcome of contemporary matrilocal ground affiliation is that at least a portion of the male members of each ceremonial ground will be drawn from a variety of other natal ceremonial communities. These men foster inter-town alliances and their presence as leaders in the affinal ground permits the circulation of ritual beliefs and practices and other forms of specialized cultural knowledge.

The current situation of the Sand Creek Ceremonial Ground illustrates the articulation of individual and group decision-making and demonstrates the effects of intermarriage. The ground maintains patterns of interaction more distinct from the other two Yuchi grounds, and this is best explained on the basis of patterns of intermarriage. The ground's closest non-Yuchi ally during the 1990s was the Fish Pond (Creek) Ceremonial Ground. A leading member of this ground was married to a Yuchi woman from Sand Creek. This man was widely regarded as a knowledgeable medicine man and he played a leading role in both his natal and affinal grounds. His role as a mediator between the two encouraged reciprocal participation in activities. This secondarily brought each of the two communities into sustained contact with the allies of the other. In this way, at the level of personal and corporate interaction, the relationship between the Sand Creek and Fish Pond grounds was the key point at which the Fish Pond ground connected to the other Yuchi grounds. Likewise, when considering where to go visiting among the Creek grounds, the predispositions of their Fish Pond allies played a guiding role for Sand Creek. Similar marriage relationships currently link Duck Creek with the Creek grounds of Arbika, Tallahassee Wvkokaye, and Muddy Water, among others.

Such links between communities change through time. When it reestablished its ceremonial activity around 1940, the first Creek ground to begin regular patterns of visiting with Duck Creek was the now inactive ground of Eufala. In recounting the history of this period, Duck Creek elders point to several interrelated factors. First, the wife of the new Duck Creek Chief John Brown was a member of Eufala town. In the period immediately preceding the reestablishment of the ceremonial ground, the men of the Duck Creek community were participating extensively with men from Eufala in weekly archery tournaments. This interaction, together with intermarriage with Creek men from other towns, is a source for the ground's former Creek character. Duck Creek's entry into the Creek system was through Eufala, but today it has shifted its ritual forms back toward Yuchi practice, while establishing new relationships with its Creek neighbors.

Intermarriage provides one link connecting the Yuchi grounds to the ceremonial grounds of neighboring tribes, but ground intermarriage also serves to bind the Yuchi community itself together as a tribal whole. Until recently, outmarriage to non-Yuchi spouses was less common than were marriages between Yuchi individuals. In most such tribal marriages, the spouses were affiliated with different natal ceremonial grounds (Pamela Wallace, p.c. 1997). This fact continues to shape Yuchi understandings of tribal and ground or town membership, and it governs the patterns of interaction that obtain among the three Yuchi ceremonial grounds.

The nature and strength of the bond among Yuchi grounds is illustrated both in interaction data collected during the summer of 1996 and in the life histories of many Yuchi individuals. The experience of the late James Brown, Sr., chief of the Polecat ground during my first several years of involvement with the Yuchi community, is a widely acknowledged case in point. Chief Brown was born and raised in the Sand Creek settlement near Bristow. His father, Clarence Brown, was a leader in that community's ground. As a young man, Chief Brown met his wife while attending stomp dances at his home ground and at the Polecat ground, where her parents were members. After marriage, the couple first settled on his family's land in Sand Creek, but they later moved to Sapulpa, where he took a job and they raised their family. Throughout this time, they were particularly active in the Polecat Ground, Chief Brown's wife's home community. At various times during this period, the Sand Creek Ceremonial Ground was inactive and its members shifted their participation to Polecat as well. At the age of fifty-six, Chief Brown was asked to take the position of chief at Polecat, and he continued in this position for twenty-four years until his death in 1996. When the Bucktrot family, former participants at the Sand Creek Ceremonial Ground and relatives of Chief Brown, reactivated the Sand Creek ground, Chief Brown and his family became active supporters of this ground as well. In his later years, Chief Brown became the most senior Yuchi man involved at Sand Creek and its last male Yuchi speaker. In this role, Chief Brown served as an important advisor to the ground's young chief. The Sand Creek chief also called on Chief Brown to serve as his orator. In doing so, Chief Brown used the Yuchi language for the last time in public ritual oratory. It was also during the last five years of his life that Chief Brown, recognizing the vitality of the Duck Creek Ceremonial Ground and wishing to safeguard an important part of the Yuchi cultural patrimony, undertook the task of instructing the members of that ground in the performance of the many distinctive Yuchi dances that take place during the Green Corn Ceremony as performed at the Polecat ground. His role as chief of the mother ground was decisive in his active commitment to all three grounds, and perhaps more than anyone else he symbolized a common Yuchi identity, but it was his kinship ties to all three Yuchi communities that provided the foundation for his involvement in all three grounds. The linkages that governed that interaction are typical of most Yuchi people who are older than middle age.

FORMAL ASSISTANCE AND RECIPROCAL SUPPORT

Chief Brown's role in the Polecat ground illustrates the continuing pull of marriage patterns, while his serving in the role of speaker at Sand Creek illustrates another social force that binds grounds together as allies. When he took on the role of speaker at Sand Creek, Chief Brown's family built a camp there, signaling to the community that they were taking on the responsibilities of full members in the ground. When members of one ground take on formal responsibilities at another, they bind themselves and their supporters more tightly in the web of reciprocal support.

During its Green Corn in 1994, the Duck Creek Ceremonial Ground performed, with the help of Chief Brown and Newman Littlebear, the Yuchi Buffalo Dance for the first time since the ground was reestablished. The use of this Yuchi dance at Duck Creek was the first step in the recent effort to introduce, or reintroduce, Yuchi dances and practices to the ground, while displacing cognate Creek forms previously followed there. By agreement, the Creek version of the dance had been led previously, for a four-year term, by Tony Hill, the chief of the Greenleaf Ceremonial Ground. Within the larger ceremonial ground community, such borrowings of personnel are not uncommon. While recovering from the death of a chief or other key leader, a ground may borrow an individual with the requisite skills from one of its allies. An individual may serve in this way with the approval of his fellow townspeople, and such a relationship usually strengthens the visiting relationship between towns.[3] During the period in which Chief Hill led the Buffalo Dance at Duck Creek, Greenleaf was among the most regular of the ground's visitors. The two grounds have continued as allies, but the bond between them has weakened without the increased reciprocity engendered by the Buffalo Dance arrangement.

DILEMMAS OF VISITING

Consideration of visiting behavior exposes a series of tensions within the system. Because the size and characteristics of ground memberships differ, some groups need more help than others and are thus more dependent on visits from their neighbors. In order to obtain this help, they must be more active in providing help to their supporters. In contrast, the ceremonial grounds with the largest memberships are less dependent on outsiders and can afford to be more insular.

The case of the Cherokee ground of Stoke Smith during the 1990s provides an example. During the middle and late twentieth century, this ground consolidated the activities of various subsidiary, and now inactive, Cherokee grounds with its own. The result of this process, which is as yet undocumented, is that the ground is presently the largest single ceremonial community in eastern Oklahoma. With its large size, the ground has developed an orientation and a reputation, as well as an interactional pattern, at variance with those of other communities in the area. During the lifetime of its oldest members, the Stoke Smith ground has increased the intensity of its own communal activity. At present, the ground holds gatherings on every weekend of the year. For its leaders, this heavy schedule is a way of ensuring that the ground is the central institution in the lives of its members. Participants, especially children and teenagers, have the maximum opportunity to join in communal life and acquire traditional Cherokee values, while hopefully avoiding the social ills that endanger young adults in the secular world. Because of its size, the ground does not need the support of other communities to successfully hold these events. At present, loyal Stoke Smith members are limited in the amount of visiting that they can undertake without neglecting their responsibility to support the activity of their own ground. The Stoke Smith ground is therefore no longer governed by the norms of reciprocity that sustain much of the stomp dance social universe. Discussing the ground in the 1990s, Yuchi and Creek people expressed disappointment that their Cherokee friends were unable to reciprocate the support provided in past visits. Lack of visiting on their part has not completely stopped intertribal visiting at Stoke Smith ground. The novelty of going further afield and participating in a wider range of venues remains a potential enticement to occasional visitors. Some intermarriage between Cherokees and other ceremonial ground peoples motivates visitation, as well. Nonetheless, the result of these patterns is that at present, the bimonthly dances held at Stoke Smith ground are largely members-only affairs (Roark-Calnek 1977:211). An exception is made twice a year, however, when Stoke Smith holds its two major dances – the council meeting dance on Labor Day weekend and the celebration of the birthday of Redbird Smith, leader of the Cherokee ceremonial revival (Thomas 1961). Some communities from beyond the Cherokee country continue to attend those dances, no longer drawn by reciprocal obligation, but attracted instead by the sheer size and novelty of the events.

The effect of the inward-looking orientation of the Stoke Smith ground illustrates some of the tensions at work in the visiting system. In seeking to meet the needs of its members, Stoke Smith ground has closed itself off from its neighbors. The case of Stoke Smith is extreme, but all of the ceremonial grounds are situated somewhere on this same internal-external continuum. The Polecat Yuchi ground and the Creek ground of Alabama are also both large grounds that tend toward an inward focus. As the performance circuit data summarized in the next section illustrate, Polecat has weaker ties to non-Yuchi grounds than do Duck Creek and Sand Creek. Similarly, the leaders of Alabama ground hold it apart from its peers by discouraging Alabama members from participating in secular, indoor dances during the winter.[4]

From the perspective of Yuchi elders, visiting is a positive aspect of stomp ground ceremonialism but one that is ideally an extension of participation in one's own ground. Elders express frustration with younger people who are more interested in visiting than in supporting their own ground's activities. Despite preaching against such behavior, in reality, most Yuchi stomp dance participants do dedicate themselves first to their own communities, despite the work and commitment that this entails. Furthermore, in maintaining their own communities and reaching outward toward others, they contribute to the maintenance of the larger ritual system of which they are a part.

ALLIANCE AND FRIENDSHIP

Based on important work with Creek people from various towns in 1938–39, Mary Haas described the manner in which the Creek towns historically divided into two rival "semidivisions," classified as peace (white) towns and war (red) towns. The distinction between the two has been noted in the historical and ethnographic record for several hundred years. Haas's discovery was that a town's membership was fluid rather than fixed and that the men's stickball game was the chief mechanism by which allies and enemies interacted. On the basis of informant testimony, she reconstructed a pattern that seemed to have only recently disappeared (circa 1920) in which towns changed sides after losing four consecutive matchball games to a rival. In this system, after four losses, the losing town switched sides, becoming a "friend" to the winner (Haas 1940; Spoehr 1941).

During the period of Haas's work on Creek social organization, Alexander Spoehr pursued field studies on Southeastern kinship systems. From his Creek consultants Spoehr obtained corroborating information on the place of the ballgame in structuring inter-town friend and enemy relationships. Connecting Haas's work to the problem of Yuchi involvement with these patterns is a bit of information preserved in Spoehr's fieldnotes, but not presented in the (1941) note that he published in supporting Haas's interpretation. Dan Cook, a Creek man of Laplako town and Spoehr's primary consultant on the ball game, reported: "In old times Alabama could play any town in match games, but Tuckahbahchee beat them four times and Alabama went on the Red side. The same was formerly true of Yuchi, but Kasihta [Cussetah] beat them and Yuchi went on the White side" (Spoehr 1938).[5] This comment concurs with modern Yuchi testimony, in which the Yuchi, like the Alabama, are described as existing outside the structures of Creek society until recent times, when they were brought in more fully through alliance with the Cussetah. This recalls the Cussetah narratives discussed in chapter 2. It also illustrates the way in which the Yuchi are viewed as a single town unit from the point of view of the Creek social system.

The Yuchi abandoned the matchball game during the early twentieth century, but Creek ritualists, during or just after the period of Haas's work, consciously transformed its social organization. Either in reaction to escalating violence and social pathology associated with the game or perceiving the incongruity of those features with twentieth-century life in Oklahoma, they ceased the practice of inter-town games, combining practical insight and Creek ritual symbolism to reconfigure the game, while retaining it as a significant cultural performance within ceremonial ground life. The new format that they established is the one presently in use at those Creek grounds that continue to play matchball. Rather than towns challenging their enemies to matchgames, a ceremonial ground may hold a matchgame following its Green Corn. The game is preceded by a stomp dance during which the preparatory ballgame rituals are conducted. As with regular stomp dances, visitors are encouraged to attend. The dance is concluded in the morning with additional ballgame rituals, and then the game itself takes place near the ceremonial ground. Rather than town playing town, all men present, hosts and guests, are encouraged to play. When a man plays matchball for the first time, he is assigned permanently to either the "west" or the "east" team and in subsequent games lines up with fellow team members from that side.

The unknown Creek leaders who instituted this transformation preserved the ballgame and its attendant ritual while enacting a dramatic transformation in its social organization. The east-west division is a different mode of dual organization, but one equally salient in terms of Creek symbolic categories. Just as red and white are the two key symbolic color opposites in Southeastern thought, east and west are the two cardinal directions emphasized in Creek and Southeastern cosmology. On a social plane, the ballgame was restructured to continue in a less antagonistic form. The older system, described by Haas, provided a mechanism for reconstruction after a protracted series of losses in what amounted to inter-town warfare. As "the little brother of war," the old game was predicated on animosity that could no longer be socially contained or publicly expressed in modern Oklahoma. Under the new system, brothers and fellow townsmen were now ritual rivals, decreasing the structural animosity of the game to a level akin with the joking relations manifest in the community-internal dual organizations found elsewhere in Native America. While the game remains a rough contest, with the change, it could be safely brought inside the bounds of the town as a ritual shared by the town and its allies, with the exclusion of its enemies.[6]

Haas described the ballgame as "one of the pivots upon which the relations between [Creek] towns of opposite semidivisions turned," but she also provided some additional insights into the nature of town alliances and present-day stomp dance visiting networks (1940:480). Today, as in the 1930s, geographically proximate towns may or may not be allies. On the testimony of John Hill of Hillabi, Haas noted:

> Hillabi [active], Ockchai [inactive] and Wiogufki [='Muddy Waters,' active] were friends and used to attend one another's ceremonies, but even though Pakantallahassee [also called "Peach Ground" in modern English, literally 'old peach tree town,' active] lived nearby, these three towns would not attend the latter's ceremonies, nor would Pakantallahassee attend theirs. The Creeks firmly believed that if any citizen of an opposite town attended their ceremonies, he would do something "to weaken the medi-

> cine." Since every town's very existence depended upon the strength of its medicine, anything which might in any way weaken it was strictly avoided. [Haas 1940:484]

The description provided by Mr. Hill is best interpreted with reference to map 4. No longer preserving its ceremonial ground, Ockchai town is located on the Canadian River east of Hillabi.

Modern Creek people do not discuss the red and white semidivisions explicitly, but they do, as Bell (1984) noted, place emphasis on the distinction between grounds that are "friends" and those that are not. With the transformation of the ballgame within the Creek sphere, the primary mechanism through which these relations are negotiated is visitation at stomp dances. Just as Peach Ground and Hillabi were neighbors but not allies in the 1930s, grounds today very distant from one another may be strong friends, while those close at hand may not support one another. An example foreshadowing the interaction data to be considered in the next section is the case of the Shawnee ground of Little Axe (North). This ground, located over 120 miles to the southwest of the Yuchi country, has a longstanding relationship of mutual support with the three Yuchi grounds. The members of all four grounds will literally pass by closer dance events to attend those of its partners. While stomp dances remain the venue in which friendships are ratified, there is no longer an institutional setting in which rival towns confront one another openly.[7]

YUCHI PERFORMANCE CIRCUITS

Before looking at the ways in which visitations are negotiated and alliances solidified within the interactional context of a stomp dance, the performance circuits in which the Yuchi grounds interact must be delineated. Although individual participants may visit dances freely, the phenomenon that I am describing here involves collective social action in which a group from one ceremonial ground visits another as a delegation, usually in the company of its own chief. In the course of my participation in Yuchi ceremonial ground life, I have noted the patterns of interaction that the Yuchi grounds, particularly Duck Creek and Polecat, have entered into. Yuchi visiting that took place during the summer of 1996 is characteristic of subsequent years, and forms the basis for my description here.

During 1996, the Duck Creek Ceremonial Ground continued its regular pattern of active visiting. Its own dances were also well attended by visitors. Through visits to other grounds and the attendance of visitors at their dances, Duck Creek connected with seventeen other communities during 1996. This count excludes connections through co-attendance at a third party's dance. Fourteen ceremonial grounds were represented by delegations at Duck Creek events during 1996. Duck Creek reciprocated eight of those visits during that summer and visited several more of those grounds during the following year. For example, the Seminole ground of Gar Creek, with whom the Yuchi have cordial relations, visited Duck Creek during 1996. Because of scheduling conflicts between the Yuchi grounds and Gar Creek, Duck Creek was unable to attend one of their dances in 1996, but throughout the winter the Duck Creek leaders anticipated visiting Gar Creek and did so during their Green Corn Ceremony in 1997.

In 1996, Duck Creek's strongest tie was with the Polecat ceremonial ground. Duck Creek members attended all of Polecat's dances except for the first dance of the year, which conflicted with their own second stomp dance. This pattern has been constant throughout the 1990s. Duck Creek also visited Sand Creek and Tallahassee Wvkokaye (Creek) grounds more than once. Based on activity in 1996 and 1997, other members of the Duck Creek performance circuit include: Little Axe (North) (Absentee Shawnee), Tallahassee (Creek), Gar Creek (Seminole), Greenleaf (Creek), Hickory Ground (Creek), Muddy Water (*Weogufki*) (Creek), Nuyaka (Creek), and Okfuskee (Creek).

In three cases, Duck Creek visited grounds who did not visit them. In each instance, a separate rationale for visiting can be identified. Duck Creek attended Arbika's (Creek) Green Corn in 1996. Although Arbika did not send a delegation to Duck Creek, several Duck Creek members have ties by marriage to Arbika members. This pull is complemented by the magnitude of the Arbika dance, which attracts a great many participants and visitors. Similarly, Duck Creek attended the Labor Day council meeting dance at the Stoke Smith ground. This is the largest Cherokee dance of the year, drawing many hundreds of participants. Duck Creek often attends this dance and their willingness to visit there has been strengthened recently by the participation, at Duck Creek, of an active Stoke Smith ground member, connected to the Yuchi by marriage.

The final visit that Duck Creek made during 1996 was on October 19, to a stomp dance sponsored by the Ottawa tribe near Miami. This dance took place outside of the regular Yuchi performance circuit and provided the novelty of visiting new people in a new setting. This dance was held outside, beneath a tin-roofed dance "shed" of the type shared with other northeastern Oklahoma tribes, but it was run in the style associated with secular, indoor dances in the Yuchi-Creek area. The dance was managed by a master of ceremonies utilizing a public address system and, unlike Creek and Yuchi dances, ended not long after midnight, rather than continuing until daylight. For the Yuchi, the indoor dance season began two weeks later with a dance sponsored by the Kellyville Indian Community. Illustrating how visiting patterns can carry over into the winter dance season, several participants in the Ottawa dance reciprocated and attended this indoor Yuchi dance.

Attending the Ottawa dance were Shawnee, Delaware, Seneca-Cayuga,

Miami, Peoria, Cherokee (Redbird and Flint Rock grounds), and Ottawa people. Those participating groups comprise the performance circuit centered to the northeast of the Yuchi (see Hamill 2000; Roark-Calnek 1977). Stomp dancing in this area is more secular and more heavily intertribal – typical features of cultural performances among the small Woodland tribes of far northeast Oklahoma. Indicative of the patterns of linkage in the Woodland ceremonial community, the Ottawa dance was scheduled on the same weekend as the Fall Bread Dances at the two Absentee Shawnee ceremonial grounds in central Oklahoma.[8] Those events drew several Loyal Shawnee families, who otherwise would have attended the dance of their Ottawa neighbors, away from their home community to those of their kinsmen several hundred miles to the southwest. Performance circuits are shaped in part by geography, but geography can be overridden by cultural or historical affinity, patterns of intermarriage, personal ties between leaders, and other factors.

The Polecat ground's performance circuit is almost identical to that of Duck Creek. When Polecat members go visiting, most do so together with Duck Creek. When the grounds visit together, they sit as a single unit and are treated as such by their hosts. A few families from Polecat have personal ties that facilitate visiting in a different circuit than the main body of Polecat members, but they do so as individuals. Ties established by these Polecat members through joint attendance at Native American Church meetings with participants from the Flint Rock (Cherokee) and Redbird (Cherokee) grounds explain some of this variation.

In contrast to Duck Creek and Polecat, with whom I have often visited other grounds, I am acquainted with Sand Creek visiting only through co-attendance with them at various dances and through participation in the events that they host. This means that my knowledge of their attendance patterns is more limited. In addition to Duck Creek and Polecat, Sand Creek's performance circuit includes Fish Pond (Creek), Greenleaf (Creek), Alabama (Alabama-Creek), Gar Creek (Seminole), and Nuyaka (Creek). Many of those grounds are located, along with Sand Creek, on the western edge of the Creek Nation area. During 1996 and 1997, the Sand Creek ground underwent changes in leadership and participation that disrupted its established patterns. During 1997, the Sand Creek members were active visitors, attending many dances throughout the Creek and Yuchi area. Such visiting helps a ground reestablish itself after a period of transition.

THE INTERACTION ORDER

Sociologist Erving Goffman has contributed a great variety of useful tools and concepts to the study of social interaction. In considering the interactional social organization of Yuchi stomp dance events, I want to begin by characterizing those events as what Goffman terms *social occasions*. The particular meaning that he ascribes to this concept is "a wider social affair, undertaking, or event, bounded in regard to place and time and typically facilitated by fixed equipment; a social occasion provides the structuring social context in which many situations and their gatherings are likely to form, dissolve, and re-form, while a pattern of conduct tends to be recognized as the appropriate and (often) official or intended one – a 'standing behavior pattern,' to use Barker's term" (Goffman 1963:18). Social occasions are intermittent, focused gatherings in which individuals conduct themselves under the guidance of shared norms and with expectations that persist across particular events. In this section, I describe what goes on when the members and guests of a Yuchi ceremonial ground gather and take responsibility for interacting with one another meaningfully over the course of an evening that is both a serious ritual act and an enjoyable social occasion. Each Yuchi ceremonial ground has its own variations on the common ritual pattern that all three share. In outlining the order of activity at a Yuchi stomp dance, I am presenting the procedure of the Duck Creek ground, unless otherwise noted. In most respects, the same procedure is followed at Polecat and Sand Creek as well.

Seating and Space

As evening approaches, the focus on the ground shifts from predominantly community-internal activities such as ballgames, meals, and visiting to the dance itself, with attention redirected outward by the arrival of visitors. As guests begin arriving at the ground, they park their cars in a patterned way along the perimeter of the square. Over the years, visiting delegations establish regular areas adjacent to the square, where they park and sit. How a visiting group positions itself will vary depending on how many members of the group are present and how many other groups are sharing the sidelines with them. Regardless, they will try to set up as close to their regular spot as possible. If many different groups are present and the ground is crowded, a delegation may set up its chairs several rows deep, while at a sparsely attended event, they will spread out along the edge of the square. As new arrivals appear, they park and set up their chairs with their fellow townspeople. All visitors station themselves just beyond the ring of earth that separates the square from the public areas beyond.

When I first became aware of the patterned ways in which visiting groups set up upon arriving at the dance, I was struck by the effortlessness of the process. The host ground does not need to provide direction to the visitors. The spatial organization of the event spontaneously unfolds on the basis of shared understandings of how the precincts of a ceremonial ground are symbolically interpreted and used.[9] The patterned way in which visiting delegations station themselves around the square may seem mundane; however, the regularity of the seating pattern is a crucial aspect of the interactional social organization governing the event. On a cultural level, the seating of guests just outside the perimeter of the square signifies the separation of the visitors from the hosts, who control the power of the square ground, the medicine, and the fire, as well as direct the unfolding ritual action. On a general social level, the seating of participants as delegations reiterates the ongoing significance of the town (ground) as a collective body, which is expected to act as a unit. Beyond these general presuppositions, the patterning of visitors assists the hosts in governing the stomp dance as an interactional event. It allows them to know which groups are in attendance, to monitor those groups, and to organize the action of the event in a dark setting lit only by a single fire burning at the center of the square.

In the early evening, visitors arrive slowly. If members of a delegation have close ties of friendship or relationship with members of the host ground, they will seek out their contacts upon arrival. If the visitors are less well connected to the host, they will remain seated in their position adjacent to the square, near their cars. During this period, the chief and other men of the host community will circulate among the visitors in an effort to welcome them—telling stories, catching up on news, and discussing tribal affairs.

After the potluck feast given earlier, the leading women of the ground will keep coffee warm at one of the campsites and make food available for visitors interested in a late supper. As the host men move among the visitors, they will direct their guests to the care of the women located in the camps.[10]

Informal fellowship in this vein continues for several hours after sunset, as visitors and those members who left the ground after the afternoon activities, or who are arriving for the first time, assemble. During this time, the women of the ground socialize with one another in the camps and at the perimeter of the ground, while the men begin to assemble under the arbors on the square. By about ten-thirty, the chief takes his place under the west arbor and begins making preparations for the dance, particularly assigning responsibilities to various assistants.

Getting Things Going

The chief formally initiates the dance by calling on an assistant to make the first of four "calls" that announce that preparations to dance are underway. Before beginning the dance, four such calls are made in the Yuchi language. Participants keep track of how many calls have been made in order to time their preparations so as to be ready and assembled at the square when the dance begins. Ideally, the calls are made by the ground's speaker. If this person is unavailable, another person makes them. Until recently, Yuchi-fluent speakers served in this capacity, but with the loss of fluent orators, the "caller" is now a language-learner who has memorized a series of fixed texts.

In the early stages of preparation, most of the those seated on the square are either members of the chief's committee or are other leading men of the community. They tend to sit as a single group, talking quietly under the chiefs' arbor, regardless of which arbor group (society) they formally belong to. When told to make a call, the appointed man rises from his seat near the chief and stands facing east in front of the west arbor. Here he makes his call in a loud voice.

TEXT 12

An example of the announcements used by a speaker or caller to summon the members to the square ground in preparation for a stomp dance. Presented by Chief James Brown, Sr. during a study session in Tulsa, Oklahoma, 19 January 1994. The recording session was arranged to teach the process of giving these calls to a group of younger Yuchi men. The text given here is based on interlinear translations prepared by Mary Linn, from a videotape of the proceedings. Chief Brown provided the English glosses. Clarifications by Linn and myself are given in brackets. The literal translation utilizes standard conventions for identifying grammatical markings on words. These are explained with regard to Yuchi texts in an extended analysis of this genre (Jackson and Linn 2000).

[nɑnde gowɑ̨ha 'ɑiyɔ̨́]
nɑ̨de *gowɑ̨-ha* *'ayǫ*
and member-PL 2PL.ACT
'All you members,'

[kɛde yu'æle 'ɑgonʌ̨́↘]
kede *yu-'æ-le* *'a-go-nǫ*
now.INCHO house-big-DIR LOC-come-IMP
'you all come back into the Big House!'

[nɑnde k'ɑk'oni keči]
nɑ̨de *k'ak'ǫne* *ke-či*
and work there.is-CL(SIT)
'There's work to be done here.'

[kɛle hɔ̨ɬɑ yu'æle 'ɑgonʌ̨́↘]
kele hǫ-ɬa *yu-'æ-le* *'a-go-nǫ*
there 3PL(Y).ACT-go house-big-DIR LOC-come-IMP
'Hurry up there and come into the Big House!'

[nɑnde	p’ɑ̨ɬ’ęnʌ̨	go’wedeni	hʌ̨dzowɑ̨]
nąde	*p’aɬ’ę-hęnǫ*	*go’wedene*	*hǫ-dzo-wą*
and	chief-CL(YM)	word	3SG(YM).ACT/DAT-1SG.PAT-give

‘The chief has given me these words’

[’ɑndɑsɑlɑ	’ɑdi	čudɑgowɑ̨́↘]
’ądze-sala	*’ą-di*	*čudą-gǫ-wą*
2PL.PAT-all	2PL-EMPH	listen-must-EXHORT

‘for all of you, listen!’[11]

As he concludes, the men seated under the arbor respond in unison, “hõ,” “agreed,” ratifying his call. Three more calls of this type will be made before the dancing begins. The time between calls varies between grounds and events, but typically the dancing is begun between eleven o’clock and midnight.

When the fourth call is made, the members of the home community all assemble at the square, the men seated under their appropriate society arbors and the women seated in chairs adjacent to the square, usually at the northwest and southwest corners – between and behind the three arbors. Ideally, a crowd of visitors has assembled in groups around the square on all sides, facing inward. Although individual visitors may arrive throughout the night, by this time all of the principal participants will have assembled. During the first stage, the visitors to a Yuchi dance are onlookers, as the members have certain responsibilities to fulfill before the visitors join in the dancing.

After the fourth call, the chief prompts the speaker to gather the local men together in front of the chiefs’ arbor. With the men huddled together, the speaker delivers a speech that only they can hear, analogous to pre-game pep talks delivered by coaches of sporting teams. He directs them to be attentive to the needs of the visitors and exhorts them to participate enthusiastically, to give a good effort and to carry themselves appropriately. The message of this talk may be illustrated with reference to a customary tale or practice, or the speaker may address a particular issue relevant to the circumstance. Like the public oratories that the speaker delivers at other times during the dance, his speech to the men is delivered in the name of the chief, whose views it represents.[12]

When the speech has ended, the men reply “hõ.” Then, much like a sports team breaking up from a pep talk in huddle, they separate with whoops and shouts. These Yuchi cheers are the same characteristic whoops and turkey gobbles that have long been described for Southeastern groups.

With continued whooping, the men move from the area in front of the west arbor to the east edge of the square.[13] Here they form a line facing east. More senior or experienced men take places toward the front, while young men stand

A pair of Yuchi women's leg rattles made from condensed milk cans, commercial leather, and hardware by Clifford Littlebear, 1997. Such rattles are tied around the lower legs atop a pad made from a towel or a piece of foam. In this pair, each rattle measures 10″ × 9 ½″ × 6 ½″ Courtesy of the Gilcrease Museum, Tulsa, Oklahoma. Cat. No. 84.2884 a-b. Photograph by Shane Culpepper.

toward the back, with young boys at the rear. The chief, or his designee, positions himself at the front of the line in order to lead the Yuchi Starting Song that begins the dance. The leader uses a single coconut-shell hand rattle while leading this song.

As the men progress through the series of song episodes that form the whole piece, the women of the ground take a position to the north of the men. Here they line up facing the men in rough order of seniority and experience, although the lineup is not fixed as it is in the Ribbon Dance performed during the Green Corn. All are dressed for the dance, wearing a full skirt or dress and a pair of turtle or can rattles on their calves.

The Yuchi Starting Dance is composed of several strophic songs linked together. The leader sings the initial verse of each song, and the other men join in as this verse is repeated and elaborated upon. The leader and other dancers are in a stationary, double-file line while these initial songs are sung, but after a number of songs (the number used varies between leaders), the song changes and becomes antiphonal and the line becomes a single file. Joining hands behind the leader (left hand back, right hand forward), the men begin dancing forward. The leader moves the line forward into a counter-clockwise spiral. As the men turn into the spiral, the women join the line on the north side, interspersing themselves between the men. After all of the women dancers have joined the line, there are usually several extra men and boys at the end of the line. They join hands, completing the formation of the dance line.

Several songs are sung in the spiral formation and then the leader reverses his progress and unwinds the line clockwise. Reaching the outside of the group, he moves the line toward the fire with all of the dancers still holding hands. Reaching the fire, he dances the line around it from the east and north. Once the dancers are in position, spiraling around the fire, the leader stops singing and places the coconut rattle that he has been holding in his right hand on the ground at the east side of the fire. He then leads the first of the four introductory stomp dances.[14]

The men and women of the home ground are seated after the Starting Song and the stomp dance episode that concludes it. Three more stomp dances are reserved for the home members. The "stickmen," whose responsibilities are described in the next section, announce that another man has been chosen to lead the dance. The members of the home ground dance these episodes in quick succession, allowing just enough time between dances for the members to be seated briefly and the new leader to be announced. These stomp dance episodes have the same basic song and dance form as the dance that concluded the starting song and those to be performed throughout the night.

After the fourth round, the chief will often prompt the speaker to give a brief oratory in which visitors are welcomed and invited to join in the dancing. After this, the stickmen, who control the progress of the dance, will select dance leaders from among the visitors, and the visitors then enter the square for the first time.

Stickmen

When hosting a stomp dance, the chief selects a group of experienced male members to serve as stickmen. These men act in a number of capacities, all of their responsibilities revolving around regulating the progress of the dance event. Stickmen are appointed in an ad hoc manner by the chief on the occasion of each dance, but in making his selections he will tend to choose from a pool of men who have proven their ability to fill the role. The title *stickman* derives from the staff or "stick" (usually a cane pole about four feet in length) that each carries while acting in this capacity. The ground chief possesses a set of sticks as part of his ritual equipment, and he presents one stick to each man when assigning him to the task. Today, fulfilling this role at night, the lead stickman will also carry a bright flashlight.

Typically, two or four stickmen will serve during a night of dancing. At most grounds they work in pairs, one pair serving during the first half of the dance, the second covering the second. Normally, one stickman in each pair will be more experienced and will take the lead. A chief will pair a younger or less experienced man with a more experienced partner in order to provide training to the novice. Sometimes a single man will serve alone, but working in pairs is more common, especially during well-attended dances. Doing the job alone is more difficult as there is often more than one task to be handled at a given time. For the men serving, working in pairs is also more enjoyable.

The main task of the stickman is to select and announce new dance leaders between episodes. The job requires detailed knowledge of the many ceremonial grounds that participate in reciprocal visitations. Acquaintance with the officers and prominent dance leaders from those communities is essential. The best stickmen use their knowledge to work the crowd effectively in a number of ways.

In creating a lively dance, the stickmen seek to select an interesting mix of dance leaders. As the dance progresses, they will note which visitors and members are present and, while circulating around the edge of the square ground, engage the visiting delegations in talk and jovial banter. As they move around the square, they select dance leaders from each of the visiting groups, occasionally mixing in men from the home community. In doing this their strategy will vary depending on the number of visitors present. If there are many guests, they will postpone selecting home members in order to give visitors ample opportunity to lead dances. If fewer visitors are present, they will more freely call on home ground members, providing opportunities for visitors to rest between leaders and intermixing young and novice men with more talented singers.

Each leader is selected one or two rounds ahead of time to allow him the opportunity to muster the assistance of his townspeople. When one dance leader concludes his set of songs, the dancers who have followed him break up the dance formation and return to their seats. As they do, various men will utter drawn-out words of encouragement and approval – *sǣ::le* ('good' [Yuchi]), *mato:* ('thank you' [Creek]), *wato:* ('thank you' [Cherokee]) (see Roark-Calnek 1977:249).

When everyone is seated, the stickmen station themselves in front of the chiefs' arbor on the west end of the square. From there they walk, one behind the other, in a counter-clockwise circle around the inside of the square. In front of each of the three arbors, the leading stickman announces, in Yuchi, the selection of the next dance leader. The Yuchi phrases used for this purpose vary and most are memorized as fixed units, as most stickman are neither fluent speakers nor active language learners. As they pass each arbor, the men seated there respond to the announcement in the same way that all public pronouncements on the square are affirmed, with a loudly spoken "hõ." After passing each of the three arbors (south, north, west), the stickmen return to their original station just to the south of the chiefs' arbor. From there they repeat the announcement a fourth time, this time directing their words beyond the arbors to the assembled guests. All of the men under the arbors respond "hõ." After making this announcement, the lead stickman will turn on his flashlight and aim it at the next dance leader, signaling to him that it his turn.

Leading

Having been called to dance, the leader rises from his seat, readies himself, and begins to file into the square. As he stands, the men and women of his town arrange themselves behind him; the line enters the square and moves toward the fire. The group lines up according to a variety of loosely followed strategies. After the leader, the second-most important person in line is the woman following him, his shell shaker. In rough order of precedence, this woman is the man's wife, partner, daughter, or female relative. In the absence of a qualified person in one of these roles, another woman, one recognized as a good shell shaker and on friendly terms with the leader, will fill this role – sometimes at his request, sometimes volunteering spontaneously. After this first couple, other men and women line up in alternation. Close to the front will be the leader's closest relatives, the chief and officers of the ground, and other good singers. Toward the rear of the line, less experienced singers and shell shakers will follow. There does not need to be an even number of men and women, as other participants will join the line, filling in holes in the leader's group before joining the end of the line.

As this group arrives at the fire, the leader begins his dance by walking counter-clockwise around it. The typical leader will walk around the fire several times, as dancers line up behind him and his supporters. When he is ready to begin, he initiates the dance with a series of call-and-response vocables. Among the Yuchi and their neighbors, this beginning phase is more standardized than the songs that follow. For descriptions of stomp dance music, see Heth (1975) and Schupman (1984).

During the middle of these introductory phrases, the leader will progress from a walk to the stomping step that is characteristic of the dance. The woman shaking shells behind him will follow, beginning the double step that is used by the women to accompany the singing of the men. One at a time, in order, the men and women behind the leader fall into cadence. Meanwhile, the leader continues his introductory song while the dancers join his dance rhythm and the men reply to his singing.

Once all of the dancers have joined in and he has concluded the introductory song, the leader then moves into a series of interchangeable stomp dance songs. Many of these songs are sung by many leaders, but each singer orders them into his own pattern and sings them in his own style. Most leaders pause briefly between songs, indicating to the other dancers that they are about to stop by rais-

A typical stomp dance episode is difficult to photograph because it is performed at night in the dark. The exception to this pattern is found in the ceremonials of the Sand Creek and Duck Creek communities. The stomp dance is performed in daylight during the late afternoon dances of the Green Corn Ceremony in these communities. This image, illustrating the general organization of a stomp dance, shows one of four rounds of the dance following the performance of the Old Folks Dance and Buffalo Dance episodes in the Duck Creek Green Corn Ceremonial, 21 June 1997. Children are seen toward the back of the spiraled dance line. The male "leader," who is singing at the front of the line, is obscured in this photograph. Photograph by Amy Jackson.

ing their left arm, bent at a right angle, upward. A variation on this pausing signal is to touch one's hat brim with the fingers of the left hand. Signaling in this way causes the women to jump in place for a moment and then pause as the next song episode is begun. With the next song, the men reply to the new calls from the leader and the line begins moving again. While waiting to begin stepping again, dancers will walk forward quietly until the person in front of them once again begins stepping in time. Most leaders pause in this way between song episodes, but some change songs without breaking stride. In those cases, the line continues to move seamlessly and the songs change without break.

When a leader is dancing, the stickmen alternate between searching for new leaders and regulating the activities of the dancers. If the dance is crowded, especially in the early stages when many young people are present and participating, the stickmen must pay close attention to the dancers and activity at the fireplace. At a large dance, when a good singer is leading, many dancers will join the file behind him. Many others, who wish to hear the singing and watch the dancers, will stand around the outside of the spiraling rings of dancers. This crowd of onlookers is drawn inward by the fire and the singing, while the ring of dancers continues to expand as participants hop into line, either joining the end of the line, or cutting in before friends. Under these conditions, the stickmen will work the crowd to ensure that the dancers have space to comfortably dance. Carrying their sticks, the stickmen will dance in a circle around the ring of dancers, forcing onlookers to step backward and make room for the dancers.

Monitoring the dance in this way, the stickmen are also on hand to regulate other aspects of the dancing. Sometimes a dance leader will form the innermost ring of the dance line too far from the fire. When this happens, the dancers will follow his lead and space the rings too far apart, reducing the overall space available. While correct management of the dancers is one of the skills possessed by a good leader, talented stickmen can control the dancers almost imperceptibly. In this instance, the stickmen can station themselves between the rows of dancers, coaxing or corralling them toward the fire. In a similar way, the stickmen keep an eye on the activities of the small children who dance at the end of the line, making sure that they are safe and not disruptive.

The dance unfolds in a cycle of stomp dance episodes, alternating song leaders from various visiting groups and the host community. This rhythm is punctuated by particularly gifted leaders who attract the attention and participation of all present. Men who sing older songs, songs associated with distant tribes, or who sing "blues songs" – a melodic variation on normal stomp dance vocal technique – are all particularly appreciated by participants. The basic spiral dance formation of the stomp dance is also varied by some leaders who conclude a regular "lead" by having the dancers join hands, then unwinding the spiral at the fire and leading the line away to the edge of the square, where a new spiral is formed. When a leader begins such a dance, sometimes referred to as a "Snake Dance" because of the serpentine movement of the dancers, the stickmen clear onlookers away to make a place for the leader to conclude his dance. A stickman will mark the spot by holding a flashlight high in the air and shining its beam on the ground at the appointed place. As the leader winds the spiral tight, the dancers are quickly pulled around the outer circumference. This is a particular delight to the kids hanging on at the end of the line, as they run, skip, and get pulled quickly around the circle. The stickmen take particular care to watch that the kids are not injured in this stomp dance variation of the child's game "crack the whip."

Between dances, visiting chiefs sometimes will ask the host chief to announce their own upcoming events. For this purpose, the host chief will call on his speaker, or may ask a speaker of Muskogee to make the announcement in the language of his Creek guests. The chief may also ask his speaker to deliver longer speeches addressing particular topics, although such long talks are typically reserved for the conclusion of the dance.

At Yuchi grounds, visitors are invited to have a coffee break sometime after about 1:00 A.M. The stickmen organize this effort at the square, while the leading women of the host ground oversee activity in one of the camps. In order to keep the dance moving during this break, the stickmen select visiting groups one at a time to take breaks in shifts. The stickmen will invite a visiting chief and his members to take a break and will direct them to the camp where the women have prepared food and drinks. As one group finishes up, the stickmen will direct another group to the camp. Typical coffee-break fare includes cake, danish, doughnuts, frybread, *sofkee* (corn soup or drink), coffee, iced tea, and soda, as well as leftover foods from the evening meal served earlier.

Early Morning

Older people hold that visiting delegations should remain at a dance until its conclusion at sunrise, but many visitors slip away during the early morning hours, changing the tone of the dance.[15] By this time, most children have fallen asleep and the crowds of onlookers have dwindled, leaving the active singers and dancers alone at the square. Many visiting leaders have taken their turn leading, so more men from the host ground are selected to sing. As participants grow weary, men make jokes, and the comment "it's almost daylight," spoken prematurely in jest, never fails to produce laughter. Good stickmen will have held some lively leaders back in order to keep spirits up as the group becomes drowsy.

As sunrise approaches, the chief prepares to conclude the dance. He confers with his speaker, instructing him in preparation for the closing speech. He also selects a man from his ground to lead the Yuchi Closing Dance that metaphorically "closes the door" to the big house, ending the dancing until the door is opened at the next dance with the Starting Song. Before calling him out into the square, the stickman places the coconut shell rattle on the ground just east of the fire. The Closing the Door Dance reverses the order of the opening dance. It begins with the leader leading a regular stomp dance episode, following which he picks up the coconut rattle. Joining hands with the line of dancers, the leader leads the dancers away from the fire to each of the four corners of the square (northeast, northwest, southwest, and southeast). Throughout this dance he sings a single, repeating antiphonal song. Arriving in each corner, he winds the dancers into a spiral, at which point all sing a brief passage in unison. The leader then unwinds the line, resuming the same call-and-response song. He leads the dancers to the next corner, where this process is repeated.

The dance ends in the southeast corner of the ground, near where the dance event began. After concluding the Closing Dance, the dancers return to their seats. Sometimes the closing speech precedes this last dance; at other times it follows it. Examples of closing speeches were presented in chapter 3 and additional oratory excerpts appear in later chapters.

After a stomp dance concludes, the ground members visit with any remaining guests, thanking them for their participation. The chief may call a business meeting or request that members clean up the ground before departing. After the Green Corn Ceremony or Soup Dance, many members will remain on the ground and prepare breakfast in their camps before packing up and departing for home.

STOMP DANCES AS INTERACTION RITUALS

As a central *social occasion* in the community life of the Yuchi and their Native neighbors in Oklahoma, the stomp dance is a complex ritual, both in the classic religious sense of the word and in the social interactional sense associated with Goffman's notion of interaction rituals, that is, complex engagements among people guided by shared moral norms. In keeping with Goffman's analysis, stomp dances have participants "defined as responsible for getting the affair under way, guiding the main activity, terminating the event, and sustaining order" (1963:18). Among the Yuchi, these tasks are invested in the host ground and its chief. Achievement of these ends not only produces a successful dance, but testifies to the strong spiritual and social health of the host community. A dance that is interpreted as a success supports ongoing relationships, and fosters new ones, among individuals and groups who are identified as friends, allies, and supporters.

Shared norms ensure that stomp dance events unfold predictably, even though participants differ in various ways. In addition to distinctions between host and visitor, participants vary in tribal background, age, experience, language facility, ability, and interest. Differing tribal backgrounds and ceremonial ground memberships produce different interpretations and understandings of ritual procedure and meaning. A Creek chief visiting a Yuchi dance will normally accept and support a local rule, such as not to carry an infant in the dance line, even if his own ground views this matter differently. This general acceptance of cultural variation within the common framework shared across the stomp dance universe is typical. In cases where differences in ritual interpretations are considered more serious, groups will not visit one another, although they may, in part, overlap in the same performance circuit by mutually supporting other grounds.

Age and engagement are two primary differences affecting how individuals participate and interpret stomp dance events. These variables shape not only the strength of participation and the roles that individuals fill, but also the seriousness with which participation is interpreted. In part, variations in engagement reflect the constant cycle of cultural replication. Both full participation and active involvement through time exposes an individual to more detailed cultural information, including ritual and ethical exegesis, a variety of cultural forms, and incorporation into leadership roles. Casual participants believe that there is less to the stomp dance as a cultural performance than do full participants, and they are less likely to be concerned with, or knowledgeable about, the rules and beliefs that inform the organization of the dance. Such individuals pose the greatest concern to ground chiefs and other leaders because they risk endangering both themselves and the progress of the dance event with inappropriate behavior. The degree to which a stomp dance is a highly ritualized event governed by strongly shared moral norms is most apparent when those norms are violated. An individual behaving oddly within the event is a cause of great unease, prompting the concern and action of the host. In handling a drunk individual or a problem of a similar nature, the stickmen and other men of the host ground seek to remove the disruption as quietly as possible, both to save the face of the individual in question and to avoid further heightening the unease of their guests.

Such disruptions produce discomfort in participants not only because of the practical danger that they represent in a large social gathering held in considerable darkness, but because they undermine the positive emotional structure of the dance as well as endanger the spiritual health of participants by creating interpersonal tensions and threatening the ground's medicine. When a dance is successfully underway, the host creates and sustains good feelings among participants by organizing spirited dances, extending hospitality to its guests, and displaying confidence and solidarity. These expressions put guests at ease and engender positive feelings toward the host.

In this realm of social interaction within the stomp dance, individuals and groups negotiate and renegotiate their ties with one another. Although the characterization of such relationships as reciprocal exchanges that are at once "social and religious, magic and economic, utilitarian and sentimental, jural and moral" (Lévi-Strauss 1969:52) has become commonplace in anthropology, the interpretation fits with Yuchi understandings of the multiple meanings and levels of social action that unfold within their stomp dance events, (Lévi-Strauss 1987; Mauss 1990).

RECIPROCITY

Within the stomp dance, expressions of reciprocity operate at several levels at once. In an intimate way, each dance episode is a test of the social bonds that hold groups and individuals together. When a man is called out to lead a dance, he relies on his kinfolk and fellow ground members to support his effort. These are the men and women who know his songs best, who wish to see him succeed, and who wish to demonstrate a strong sense of community solidarity. Without the support of his peers, a leader is weakened and his performance is lessened.

When his townspeople enthusiastically file behind him, they indicate that he is a man of esteem, whether or not he is a particularly gifted singer. This indicates to other participants that the ground is a unified whole. In spiritual terms, this solidarity is evidence that the group's own medicine is strong and that they are thus a safe and worthy ally. At an individual level, to attract the support of one's own townspeople requires a man to have been a supporter of the other men of his community. This means having danced enthusiastically and having offered encouragement when others acted as leaders. In addition, a man must retain the respect of his peers by behaving in socially appropriate ways. In this way, each dance is a transaction in which those individuals who join behind a leader are registering their support for him and his community.

In contrast, an individual who has failed to support the other members of his ground will face the sanction of not having the enthusiastic support of his townspeople. This lack of solidarity likewise registers with the other participants who watch the action of the dance unfold. Such an instance is a sign of internal division within a ground. Division within a ground prompts other groups to temper or withhold their support out of concern, expressed socially as "avoiding another group's conflicts" and cosmologically as fear that the disrupted group's medicine is unhealthy and thus potentially dangerous. This withdrawal by a ground's allies is understandable in terms of the relationship between a ground's social solidarity and the health of its members and associates. The withdrawal of support makes the recovery of a weakened or lapsed ceremonial ground difficult, as it must struggle alone until members can prove to their potential allies that their medicine and their social relations have returned to a healthy state.

At a larger level, the attendance of a visiting group at a dance is a collective transaction. For most ceremonial grounds to build or sustain their reputations and the vitality of their activities, they must actively seek to support the dances of other groups. This support is reciprocated as hosts who have benefited from the participation of a regular guest in turn become visitors.

Documenting cultural performances among the Delaware, Roark-Calnek has suggested that the stomp dance has played "a considerable role in the construction of Indian Way," by which she refers to the overarching cultural system that the Delawares share with the Yuchi and with other Indian peoples of eastern Oklahoma. It is the primary institution that defines what she has called the "Woodland cultural sphere" (1977:265–66). In the twenty years separating our experiences in Oklahoma, her observation has remained true. For many Indian people in eastern Oklahoma, the stomp dance provides a point of balance at which specifically tribal and generically Indian identities meet.

On the tribal side, contrary to the expectations of both mid-century anthropology and some tribal elders, the specifically tribal ceremonialism characteristic of each Oklahoma stomp ground has not disappeared or become generically intertribal, as have the war dance performances of the Plains tribes. Actually, movements counter to the patterns of Pan-Indianism seem to be characteristic of ceremonialism in the region, at least during the 1980s and 1990s. The efforts made at Duck Creek to reintroduce the full Yuchi Green Corn Ceremony testify to this tribalism, as does the ongoing elaboration of Cherokee ritual away from common patterns shared with the Creek.

As the foundation for what Roark-Calnek calls "Eastern Way," I suggest that the stomp dance, by linking the ceremonial communities of eastern Oklahoma, has ensured the survival of specific local cultural practices. In isolation, no stomp ground community possesses enough personnel to sustain its activities for longer than a generation. Even the large and active Cherokee ground of Stoke Smith has built its current success by consolidating with smaller grounds. Through time, the stomp dance ensures the circulation of personnel among those communities, maintaining their vitality. Although Yuchi elders recognize a greater dependence on non-Yuchis to carry their ceremonials, as in the all-night stomp dances that must follow daytime rituals, this pattern is not new. The simultaneous existence of tribalism and Eastern Way is a recognizable feature of Woodland Indian life throughout history, from the activities of the Shawnee prophet in the early 1800s back to the so-called Southeastern Ceremonial Complex characteristic of pre-contact cultures known archaeologically. As Yuchi elders are quick to note, few Yuchi fullbloods exist today. Yet, for the perpetuation of local ceremonial practices, the existence of fullbloods is not a key criterion. As Newman Littlebear remarked at the Polecat meeting, "Even though there is not hardly no fullbloods, we consider ourselves Yuchi even if we're just a quarter or maybe an eighth, because we take part in some of these Yuchi grounds" (16 July 1997). While they are the products of collective social action replicating cultural patterns through time, ceremonial grounds themselves have identities that take on superorganic characteristics, persisting despite the flow of people through them. This idea is expressed in the way that ceremonial ground people talk about the agency of the fireplaces associated with their grounds, but it is also a social phenomenon rooted in shared cultural forms such as the stomp dance, combined with a respect on the part of Woodland ceremonialists for the perpetuation of the "locally distinct ground rules and thematic emphases" perpetuated in the ceremonialism of tribal or town communities (Roark-Calnek 1977:207).

7 Arbor Dance
Community and Renewal

"To renew all of this . . ."

Yuchi elders describe all of their ceremonials as a valued kind of work. The ceremony referred to as the Arbor Dance most closely actualizes this metaphor. In it, hoes, shovels, and chain saws are put to ritual use in renewing the ceremonial ground and by extension the community that calls it home. While preparing the stomp ground site for the Green Corn Ceremony, this collective work also binds together the men of the community, preparing them as a group to coordinate their efforts in the elaborate ceremony that follows one week later. In chapter 6, I viewed the stomp dance from the perspective of social interaction, emphasizing its place in inter-community relations. In this chapter I examine the Arbor Dance preparations from the perspective of ritual action, emphasizing their significance within the local social group and Yuchi cosmology.

ANTICIPATION

At the close of the season's third stomp dance, the Yuchi chiefs prepare their members to undertake the work of the Arbor Dance. Frequently, the chief will ask his speaker to publicly announce the upcoming event. As noted in chapter 4, this is a specific example of a more general tendency in oratory of reiterating the unfolding of the ritual cycle. To the corpus of examples of ceremonial ground oratory presented so far can be added a portion of a speech delivered at the close of the stomp dance proceeding the Arbor Dance at the Polecat ground in 1997. In it, Newman Littlebear speaks on behalf of the Polecat chief, articulating, among other things, what is expected to take place during this next event in the cycle. This discussion of the upcoming event is woven into the broader tapestry of concerns addressed in the text as a whole.

Immediately before this portion of the speech, Mr. Littlebear discussed the moral dimensions of ceremonial ground participation, drawing on the history of the Polecat ground to construct a comparison of the community's past successes and failures with those of the present, addressing in particular the failure of some ground members to participate fully in its activities. Then, as shown in text 13, he combines the announcement of the upcoming Arbor Dance and wood-cutting events with encouragement for the young men to both participate in this work and attempt to learn the ritual procedures that accompany these events. The wood-cutting session that he mentions is another feature of the ceremonial season prior to the Arbor Dance, held either early in the season, or as in this case, immediately before Arbor Dance. Because it preceded the Arbor Dance events of the Duck Creek ground and this ground's members were present, Mr. Littlebear's speech was relevant to both groups, a point that becomes clear at the conclusion, in which the upcoming Duck Creek events were also announced.

TEXT 13

An excerpt from a closing oratory. Delivered by Newman Littlebear at the conclusion of the third stomp dance of the season at the Polecat Ceremonial Ground, 1 June 1997.

Sometimes we say
    we don't know what to do next.

Like our next time we are going to meet here
    to renew this place
    to prepare it again.

In this new year
    we are going to renew this
    all of this.

So,
    that is ahead of us.

We say it is going to be July the
    fourth.

So all you
    menfolks

young boys
come
early that morning.

We are going to do this
make an effort again.

Bring your tools
whatever you need.

Womenfolk
perhaps
are going to bring something
and cook
when we get through here.

This is the way we've been carrying it.

And ((we))
encourage the young ones
when we come that morning
there are many things
you could observe
that we do in here.

Sometimes we talk about
what we're going to . . .
what's the next move is that we make.

Sometimes we are in that position.

So it is time
for the young generation to observe
while we still got some understanding
about the movement [ritual procedures]
all the way through.

I say that to you
        young generation.

((I)) pass it on to you young ones.

Some of our young ones
        picking it up already.

They know.

They try to learn
        but there's others
        need to know too.

So we find ourselves in that situation.

But we still have something good here.

We had a lot of help last night
        from Grandpa [the Fire]
        give us inspiration
        help us along.

That's the way we want to believe it.

That's the way we want to carry it
        carry it.

We know that there was a good joy here last night
        because of
        the good effort.

We hope that this
        this Grandpa
        messenger
        to the One above

knows
in our hearts
how we feel.

Have a good feeling.

That's the way
he want us to be.

Many of our people
a long time ago
they sang around here
they talk our language
they say something to Grandpa.

Maybe in the future ((and))
in our time now
[that] word
is still carrying on.

That's the way they believe.

So,
it is not all playthings here
some things are SERIOUS.

But it's a joy
when you serve the Master.

You are going to get a joy
when you do that.

There are some other kinds of joys out in this world.

You think you have a good time
but it ain't going to last always.

But the joy in here
is going to live on.

It's going to be with you.
It's going to help you.

so

I just
say that much to all of us this morning.

Like I said before
sometimes
we are running out of old people to talk to us
to encourage us.

In my young times there was older people
several of them.

Maybe you could ask them something
they could give you the answer.

Now
a lot of answers we can't . . .
we don't have.

Someday
somebody might say ((that)) to you
in years to come.

Some of these younger ones
if you continue on
it is the way it is going to be.

They are going to be working in here
carrying it on.

We don't know who it is going to be.

When I was a young man I never dreamed I was going to stand
before people
and try to encourage 'em.

But I find it like that
in my life now.

The ones sitting in these seats [the chief and his assistants]
they didn't know it either.

We thought we was always going to have some older people
where we could sit on the side and just
maybe help.

But you are going to find yourself a leader
that is the way it is
in this kind of a life.

Simon knows. [Simon Harry, Duck Creek chief, present in audience]

Committeemen knows.

They know that.

But it is good.

[We] Do the best we can.

So,
the chief say ((to)) the home bunch.
"Think about this wood."

Maybe
it would be easier for the poleboys
if we gather up
and cut wood
the last Saturday
in this month.

Maybe it would be
open.

And ah
in the meantime

if you got
if you got time
to go ahead
to bring some wood here
and accumulate it.

But at that time we need to come
on the last Saturday of this month and
be here
at nine o'clock
that morning.
so we can take care of this.

Get some good wood
to use for Grandpa.

We need to do that.

Pass it on.

There's some not here
that can help.

But we need to make a good effort.

It will make it easier on ourselves
when it comes time to camp in.

So.

Also I announce on behalf of Duck Creek
they're going to renew their ground
the fourteenth
two weeks.

So,
they face the same thing.

They need help too.

They need help
when they get ready to dance.

They're making an effort
to go
carry our ways.

Some of us go and assist them.

And so far it has been
good for 'em
but there still
[is] some more to go yet.

So, you all might want to think
think about that
and come join them.

I know they would be glad
if you do.

Fourteenth and twenty-first
Arbor Dance and Green Corn Dance
at Duck Creek.

So I guess that is all.

So
thank you all.

[men answer:]*Hõ.*

After such a speech, the chief may also call the members together at his arbor for a brief planning meeting. In such a meeting, the men will work out any specific details that remain to be addressed in order to facilitate the upcoming work.

FIXING ARBORS

The Yuchi Arbor Dance is an event with two distinct episodes. The first component is the work, undertaken by the men, of repairing and renewing the square ground. This phase is concluded with a community feast. The second part, held on the evening following this work, is the fourth and final stomp dance preceding the Green Corn Ceremony. This stomp dance unfolds in a manner similar to those described in the previous chapter.

Arbor Dance activities vary slightly among the three Yuchi ceremonial grounds, but they share a common ritual form and significance. Since this aspect of Yuchi ceremonialism has not been documented, is distinctively Yuchi, and is highly significant in the view of the Yuchi ritual leaders with whom I have worked, I preface my interpretations with an outline description of its procedures, based on the practices of the Duck Creek community.[1] The Duck Creek Arbor Dance of 1996 is taken as an example, and that event was typical of those that I have participated in since 1993. After describing the Duck Creek version, the features of the Arbor Dance unique to the Polecat community will be presented.

At Duck Creek, the men begin assembling at the ground before dawn on the appointed Saturday (22 June 1996), having begun fasting the night before, as in other ritual contexts. As men arrive, they begin work under the direction of the chief. Several tasks lie before them. The old willow coverings from the arbors must be removed. The arbor's forked posts, stringers, and benches must be checked, and any in poor condition will be replaced. The ground will be weeded with hoes, giving the plaza a neat appearance with squared corners. In this annual scraping, earth is moved out to the edge of the square, enlarging the boundary ring that encircles the square and separates its sacred space from the surrounding secular precincts. In this work, rocks will be removed and the surface of the square made smooth. During their work, the men will also clean and organize the woodpile, preparing it for use. Concurrent with this work, the practice at Duck Creek is to mow the grass in the common area demarcated by the perimeter driveway.

During these preparations at the ground, part of the work party will be away gathering the materials with which to rebuild the arbors. Because most of the large landholdings in the Yuchi area belong to non-Indians, in the days before Arbor Dance the chief will have made arrangements with local landowners to permit the men to gather willow boughs and post oak trees for the ground. Usually these landowners are from longtime farm or ranch families familiar with their Yuchi neighbors, but obtaining those materials is increasingly difficult as these holdings are being sold and developed by exurban homeowners who are unfamiliar both with the Yuchi and with the shared folkways that once governed these rural communities.

In addition to fasting, a number of constraints are placed on the men during their work. Outlining the procedures followed during Arbor Dance, Newman Littlebear recalled this point for Simon Harry and me.

Men of the Duck Creek Community toss green willow boughs onto the roof of the west arbor during the ground's Arbor Dance, 14 June 1997.

> (Newman) See on that Simon, I think that we might mention that during that time, the cleaning up, we got all the old leaves off and we're raking around, you know, sometimes if you don't think, you might not give it a thought, but they say you are not supposed to sit in those seats while that is going on. We got into that last year.
> (Jason) (laughing) He [Newman] and I got chewed out!
> (Newman) I knew that too, you know.
> (Simon) Slipped your mind, din'it. You forget sometimes and you just can't think of everything. [4 February 1997]

During arbor fixing at Polecat in 1996, Mr. Littlebear got winded and sat down for a moment. Having been working next to him, I followed his lead and sat as well. The humor of the anecdote derives from the fact that he is now the oldest and most experienced ritual leader at Polecat and we were chastised by a younger man with a reputation as a stickler for such detail. This prohibition is based on the observation that, until doctored, the new arbors are not yet purified and fit for use.

Sitting in the square is prohibited and there is a general feeling that the workers should try to keep working straight through until all of the work is done. Some slack is given to younger boys, but peer pressure and a desire to complete the work keeps the older boys and men working with only brief pauses. This ethic has direct social implications, minimizing discord among the adult men. It also indexes and promotes a spirit of community that is at the core of the event as a whole.

This ideal is also expressed in the prohibition against preparing individual family camps until the work of the Arbor Dance is completed.

> (Newman) I guess that . . . we never do stress it, I guess, but I think everybody kind of knows that, that ground comes first. That is the first thing you take care of, before you clean up your, your individual campsites. They said it was a no-no to clean up or touch your, touch your camp, as far as cleaning up. Renewing it. You don't do no work to renew your camps, you take care of that square first. [4 February 1997]

In this prohibition, the members are restrained from pursuing their own goals and desires, in favor of collective interests.

At the arbor fixing, as in other ground events, the medicine of spicewood (spicebush, *Lindera benzoin*) steeped in water is used to wash those participants visiting the ground for the first time during the season or those who have visited a funeral or gravesite since last coming to the ground. Men break occasionally during the work to drink a dipper of this medicine.

If they have not been slowed by bad weather, the men at Duck Creek begin completing their work between noon and 1:00 P.M. After the physical preparations are completed, a series of spiritual ones, aimed at purifying the square where the Green Corn Ceremony will take place, are undertaken.

PURIFYING THE GROUND

As the work of the men nears completion, the chief takes leave from the ground to obtain several armfuls of a flowering plant known locally as horsemint (wild bergamot, *Monarda fistulosa*). The blooming of horsemint is one of the factors shaping the timing of the Yuchi Green Corn Ceremonies, and typically the Arbor Dance at Duck Creek occurs just after its flowering. In 1995, the ground's arbor fixing was scheduled slightly earlier in June than is typical and the ground's leaders discovered that the horsemint was not as fully in bloom as is considered desirable. At Duck Creek, horsemint grows on the ground property, so collecting it is relatively easy. At other grounds, it must be obtained at a greater distance. Taking an assistant to carry the horsemint, the chief uproots the entire plant, selecting plants from several locations. In this work, he is care-

Chief Simon Harry, assisted by Cecil Harry doctor the north arbor at the Duck Creek Ceremonial Ground during its Arbor Dance, 14 June 1997.

ful not to take all of the plants in an area, so as to ensure their return in following years. Collecting these plants, Yuchi ritual theory holds that one must remove them while facing east, although inattention may cause an individual occasionally to forget this detail.

Returning to the ground with the horsemint, the chief and his helper enter the square from the northeast side, going first to the southeast corner of the north arbor. Taking a handful of the plants from his assistant, the chief begins doctoring the arbors by tapping and sweeping the flower blossoms over the bench, holding the clutch of four or five flowers close to the roots. Facing the front of the arbor (looking away from the ground), he sweeps, in alternation, the benches and the post oak fork supporting the arbor's roof. At each arbor he begins with the right front bench, followed by the right front post. This process continues with the chief alternating between the posts and bench sections. In order, he doctors the right front bench, right front post, middle bench area, middle post, left bench area, left front post, back right bench area, right back post, back middle bench, back middle post, back left bench, and back left post. After doctoring each pole he pauses and folds the bunch of flowers in half. The crosspole resting in the post's fork is lifted and the chief places the flower bunch beneath it, in the fork, with the blossoms facing in toward the square. In this way, each section of bench and adjacent fork is doctored with its own bunch of horsemint. The chief and his helper retrace their steps within the bench row of each arbor, leaving each arbor from the rear on the right side, before moving counterclockwise (north, west, and south) to the next arbor.

The members rest and wait outside the square during the time when the arbors are being doctored. After the chief and his assistant have completed their work they rejoin the other men and the chief instructs them to go into the woods to the west of the ground to cut brushes. Led by the chief in rough order of seniority, the men file into the woods, taking several axes with them. They return individually, each carrying a piece of post oak or other small tree with the leaves left on at the end. Younger boys carry branches, while adult men carry whole trees.

When all of the men have returned and assembled on the edge of the square, the chief leads them into the square, again single-file organized by seniority, with the youngest boys lined up at the rear. The chief enters and leads the line from the west, entering between the west and south arbors. Each man carries a brush over his shoulder. Arriving at the center, the chief leads the line around the fireplace counterclockwise, as in a stomp dance episode. When the chief arrives at the west side of the fire, he stops and turns, facing eastward. Once all of the men have joined the circle at the fire, he turns again and begins circling the fireplace counterclockwise. With his members following in line behind him, the chief circles the fireplace four times. As in a stomp dance line, the circle does not close, but the men and boys at the tail of the line walk to the outside of the front of the line. Completing the fourth circuit and arriving back at the west side of the fire, the chief faces inward (eastward) and places the leaf end of his brush on the ground. The other men and boys face inward and do likewise. As everyone faces inward, the line becomes a closed circle. At Duck Creek, the chief typically asks his speaker to speak to the men at this point. In 1996, Newman Littlebear was absent and the chief, Simon Harry, spoke briefly on his own behalf, thanking the men for their work and encouraging them to conserve their strength for the dance to take place that evening. At the conclusion of this talk, the chief directs the men to begin sweeping. From their position in the circle, each man backs up toward the edge of the square, sweeping the ground with the brush as he goes. After the men have reached the perimeter of the square, they come back inside and place the brush on top of one of the arbors.

Now that the square has been rebuilt and purified, the chief typically asks the men to sit in their arbors. With their work completed, the ban on sitting in the square is lifted. Having finished their preparations, they hold a brief business meeting. The meeting in 1996 was typical of the others that I have witnessed. The main item of discussion was making arrangements to obtain redroot (tall prairie willow, *Salix humilis*), one of the two principal medicines used during the Green Corn Ceremony. As this medicine is difficult to find and collect, and because, ideally, the roots used in this medicine are collected no more than a day or two before the ceremony takes place, the chief was concerned with assigning this responsibility to a capable work party.

Rather than conversing loudly back and forth across the square, the chief will call particular men over to the west arbor to discuss the business at hand with them. Those representatives of the north and south arbors will report whatever news emerges to their fellow arbor members. Once all decisions have been made, the chief will ask his speaker or another man acting as spokesman to close the meeting with announcements and dismissal. After being released from the square, the men join the women, who have been preparing the feast that breaks the fast that they have maintained throughout the work.

Both the feast and the work that precedes it provide an extended opportunity for the men to socialize with one another, as well as to make plans and arrangements for the Green Corn Ceremony. This social component of Arbor Dance preparations is important not only because the upcoming ceremonial requires a large amount of preparation, but because to be a success, it demands both coordinated effort and harmonious personal relations. Strife or tension among ground members is thought to weaken the ground's medicine, and personal problems will hinder the group's efforts to complete the many dances and ritual actions that make up the ceremony.

At the conclusion of the feast, the members typically retire from the square ground to rest and clean up before gathering in the evening before the stomp dance. When they come together again in the late afternoon they will have a second communal meal, welcome visitors to the dance, and resume the socializing begun earlier in the afternoon. At Duck Creek, the members will often play the single-pole stickball game before sundown, although the chief will encourage his members, who have already worked hard in the morning, to take it easy so that they will have an easier time making it through the all-night dance.

It is indicative of current Yuchi interest in cultural preservation and revitalization that, in 1996, the Duck Creek ground held an additional meeting after the conclusion of the feast, before members departed for the afternoon. In it, the members, both men and women – particularly the ceremonial ground's elders – were asked to make comments and observations about the history and practices of the ground. Modeled on the focus group discussions that the Yuchi have introduced to their community life in collaboration with the ethnographic research of outsiders, this meeting provided an opportunity for individuals to speak about their belief and commitment to the ground's activities and to share their own remembrances of its history and rituals. Such discussions are seen as creating new opportunities for younger Yuchi participants to ask questions and to be exposed to the stories and experiences of the community's elders. Like language classes and other emerging forms of cultural activity, such gatherings are seen as a way of mitigating some of the effects that changing lifestyles have had on the transmission of Yuchi culture. At their request, I video-recorded this meeting on behalf of the chief and community. The resulting recording is one of many such documents created and preserved by the tribe in its cultural preservation efforts.

WOMEN AND MEN

In the Arbor Dance, the general patterns of gender division characteristic of all Yuchi ceremonialism are manifest. Just as the men's work is community-centered, in that it is undertaken as an isolated social unit (rather than in cooperation with other grounds), so is the women's contribution to the event. Generally, the women of the ground awake before dawn with the men of their households, and while the men go to the ground and begin work, the women remain at home to prepare for the communal feast to be held after the men's work is complete. Those women whose health permits join the men in fasting during this period.

Beginning around 11:00 A.M., the women begin arriving at the ground. In either the chief's camp or another camp with convenient facilities, the women of the ground assemble and make preparations for the feast. The activity of the men working on the square and the women working in the camps mirrors and anticipates the division of effort to be replicated during the daytime of the Green Corn Ceremony.

Just as the work of the men helps bring them together as a group in anticipation of the Green Corn, so too does the collective work of the women in preparing the feast. At the same time, the men and women of each family are working in parallel, in their own domains. The men and women of a family have a strong bond to one another. In the families that I am closest to, the women feel strongly that their own fasting helps ease the burden of their male relatives. Were they to eat during the fasting of Arbor Dance and Green Corn, their male relatives would experience greater difficulty in their own fasts. From the Yuchi view, the men and the women both commit themselves to their customary responsibilities, both representing their families and serving their community.

The balance between male and female responsibility is often the subject of Yuchi ceremonial ground discourse, as are expressions of appreciation and pride in the accomplishments of both groups.

FEASTING

Almost all of the communal meals that Yuchi people share have an air of celebration, but those that conclude a fast at the ceremonial ground have special importance. The feast during Arbor Dance, like other potluck meals held in the Yuchi community, has an informal but regular order.

While elders remember a time when this was not done, a prayer of thanks to the Creator precedes most meals today. Typically such a prayer, in addition to expressing thanksgiving for the meal, includes a petition for the good health of the ground's members and leaders and expressions of gratitude for the many gifts provided by the Creator to the people, including the natural world, the Yuchi cultural patrimony, family, and community. Normally men selected on the spot by the chief deliver these prayers. At the Duck Creek ground in 1996, Simon Harry made a special point of asking a woman, one of his daughters, to say the blessing. He noted that in his memory this was the first time that a woman had said the blessing at the ground. A similar change took place at the Polecat ground soon after. In both communities, this innovation was well received, acknowledging the important contribution that women make to the spiritual life of the ground.

The same principles of ordering that obtain in other domains of Yuchi ritual life govern the pattern of eating. Women take responsibility for serving and setting up. The older men of the community and any visitors are served first, followed by younger men, women, and children. During such events, children play among themselves and are supervised primarily by women. Men and women usually eat and socialize in separate groups.

THE POLECAT ARBOR DANCE

Although the Arbor Dance of the Sand Creek ground is similar in outline to that of Duck Creek just described, the event at Polecat ground is differentiated and further elaborated, reflecting Polecat's status as the Yuchi mother ground, where the Yuchi rituals are considered to be most detailed and traditional. Yuchi elders recognize that the scheduling of the dances today represents a twentieth-century modification of an older pattern to accommodate the constraints of the modern workweek. While this change has taken place at Polecat, as well as at the other grounds, the Polecat schedule preserves the memory of the older pattern. Prior to the Second World War, when many Yuchi entered the wage economy for the first time, the Arbor Dance took place eight days before the Green Corn and the Soup Dance was held four days after the "medicine day" of the Green Corn. The total event comprised twelve days, thought of as two sets of four, followed by an additional four-day period. The whole process could begin on any day (rather than on a weekend), and the timing of the full moon, combined with the ripening of the corn and the blossoming of horse-mint, were the key determinants for the chief's decisions. After the war, the Polecat ground shifted the Soup Dance back three additional days, so that all of the events could take place on weekends. While the Soup Dance was rescheduled to fall on the weekend after Green Corn (itself permanently installed on a weekend), the Arbor Dance at Polecat has continued to be held eight days before the main day of Green Corn. This retention preserved the ritual to be described in the next section. At Duck Creek and Sand Creek, Arbor Dance is held seven days before the Green Corn Ceremony (both on Saturday), and the Soup Dance is postponed until later in the summer.

Because many Polecat members must work on the Friday of Arbor Dance, the pattern has developed of beginning this work just after midnight, in the early morning on Friday. Working in the dark of early morning with gas lanterns, the men assemble and follow a similar work plan to that described for Duck Creek. The overall common area at the Polecat ground is smaller than that at Duck Creek, but the area of the square is considerably larger. Thus, while there is little mowing to be done, there is much work with hoes removing grass and weeds from the square. Working in the dark, this hoe work is the focus of the earlier activities, while obtaining willow boughs and repairing the arbors is done closer to dawn, when more light is available. During the period of my participation at Polecat, the doctoring of the arbors was undertaken by one of the younger assistant chiefs, working under the supervision of the chief. In outline, the procedure followed is the same as that of Duck Creek.[2]

Rather than a midday meal, the work of the men at Polecat is concluded with a breakfast prepared by the leading women of the ground, who, like their counterparts at Duck Creek, arrive during the period when the work is winding down to a close. If enough members have participated and the weather has been favorable, the work at Polecat is concluded by about eight or nine in the morning, allowing those men who must do so to go to work.

THE POLECAT CALENDAR CEREMONY

As at the other grounds, Polecat members reassemble during the evening to hold the final stomp dance prior to the Green Corn. While the form of this dance follows the general Yuchi pattern, a final ritual, unique to the Polecat ground, takes place at its conclusion on Saturday morning. In 1995, imme-

Gladys McCall (right) and Josephine Madewell (left) prepare breakfast for the men soon to finish their work on the square ground during Arbor Dance at the Polecat Ceremonial Ground, 4 July 1997. Photograph by Sharon Skeeter.

diately before that proceeding, Newman Littlebear delivered a speech with the goal of explicating it. As in other oratories, the description of the particular ritual itself is augmented with an anticipation of the other events that will follow in the cycle.

TEXT 14

An oratory concluding the Arbor Dance at the Polecat Ceremonial Ground. Delivered by Newman Littlebear, Saturday, 30 June 1995.

(1) The Chief has ah
asked me ah
to say a little bit ah
concerning
this dance.

(2) We have ah
come here and prepared what we call

Arbor Dance,
to prepare our ground.

(3) And this morning
as
the Master
has let us see another –
another daylight,
we gather here
this morning
and I want to say just a little bit.

(4) A lot of things we don't understand.

(5) A lot of things we –
we take for granted,
we don't explain.

(6) Some of us been here many years.

(7) Maybe they never HAD said.

(8) Maybe we just see, try to observe.

(9) But this morning the Chief has ah
said ah
he wants you
to see this,
what we do at this time,
this bark and this stick.

(10) We always do this
at the Arbor –
Arbor Dance.

(11) When we finish up
we're going to do that this morning
after we dance the last round.

(12) I guess in the old, old time
we could say that when our –

our people –
when there was no calendars
to hang on the wall
to go by,
as we understand it,
they said that this –
this was their calendar
when it comes to this
ceremony
which is coming ahead of us.

(13) Like he said ah:
"They count eight days
when we finish up
counting today."

(14) EIGHT DAYS.

(15) The m a i n day.

(16) The main time of the year.

(17) For our people
came
gladly
from ALL communities
'round about.

(18) *YUJIHA* [the name Yuchi as rendered in Yuchi]
people.

(19) They did this.

(20) They looked forward to that day
when they could a l l come together and join.
and WE MIGHT SAY CELEBRATE
in a good way
the things that the Almighty had provided,
the blessings
He had bestowed upon 'em.

(21) And this morning we are going to do that.

(22) We're going to tie
to this –
this calendar, they called it.

(23) Put eight knots in it.

(24) And we'll go around the ground,
this square.

(25) Before that,
the CHIEF
he will call –

(26) As I understand it
the ones that ties these knots
are supposed to come from this
chiefs –
chiefs' arbor
chiefs' clan.

(27) They are the ones that are supposed to tie these knots.

(28) But in this day in time
sometimes, we don't –
we don't have enough
of those people.

(29) So,
perhaps we can borrow off of this
warrior side. [points to north arbor]

(30) Or even maybe this side [points to south arbor]

(31) To do what we are supposed to do.

(32) But we always do that.

(33) That's why he wanted me to explain it

a little bit
to you.

(34) So our young people
can continue on
to carry this out.

(35) Eight days.

(36) Maybe they called it a big –
big *busk*.[3]

(37) That main time we come and
be here that day.

(38) Dance that day.

(39) Take our herbs.

(40) Our medicine.

(41) Get scratched.

(42) Sacrifice.

(43) Then
when the men get through
the ladies' time.

(44) It's their Ribbon Dance.

(45) And after that
we all join
in this square
starting over here
for our Buffalo Dance.

(46) Then we have a break
for supper
a little while.

(47) Then we come back to the ground again

(48) Finish up that night again.

(49) So that is ahead of us.

(50) And all of this tells us
when that takes place.

(51) I suppose they
could have had other ways.

(52) Maybe they could ah
put a mark somewhere
each – each sunrise
and had other ways.

(53) But this is the way that they chose to do.

(54) So.

(55) Somebody has to
untie these knots
each day
so when that l a s t knot comes off
it will be that day.

(56) So.

(57) He want me to explain this to you a little bit.

(58) Maybe some of you already know
perhaps.

(59) But we now – we thank all of you.

(60) We thank you young folks
'round about.

(61) See a lot of the Duck Creek.

(62) Very helpful.

(63) We're thankful.

(64) And Sand Creek.

(65) Also they need help tonight too.

(66) They're going to have a dance.

(67) I don't know
some of us try to help them.

(68) There are just a few of 'em
*Yujiha*s over there.

(69) But they are still trying to carry on.

(70) So.

(71) Even our
leader here
that's where his ground is.

(72) His old folks.

(73) His father.

(74) So I tell you that much
[so] that we can continue to help one another.

(75) And we invite you back
next Saturday

if you wish to come
and be with us
and join with us
in what we have
ahead of us here.

(76) If you want to join us
men
ladies
if you want to come
we always try to welcome
somebody
if they want to participate with us.

(77) Because if
it is the Almighty's way
it's not just us
His ways are for everybody
the way we look at things.

(78) So.

(79) We say that much to you this morning.

(80) We thank you again for
all your good help
you visitors.

(81) You all come back again.

(82) So we'll do now what we got to do.

(83) Thank you.

[men respond:] *Hõ.*

This speech is the most direct example that I have recorded of ritual exegesis, highlighting this dimension of oratory described in chapter 4.

The chief prepares the bark calendar being discussed here during the evening of the Arbor Dance. It is made from a long elm branch, from which the bark is removed, in a single long lengthwise piece. This length of bark is tied again to one end of the stick from which it has been removed. The chief holds the other end of the stick in the air, suspending the bark strip like a flag. Holding the calendar in this way, men are then selected to individually tie a total of eight knots in it.

After this calendar described has been made, all of the male members form a line behind the chief. As in similar processions, the men line up in roughly hierarchical order based on age and society membership. Carrying the bark calendar for all present to see, the chief leads the men in a procession around the square, while announcing, in Yuchi, the upcoming Green Corn Ceremony. The men together answer "hõ," indicating their agreement with the chief's decision. Once the Green Corn is scheduled in this way, the ground community is committed to completing it, regardless of bad weather, deaths in the community, or other potential disruptions.

PURIFICATION, PLANTS, AND RITUAL REITERATION

The specific events that take place within the Arbor Dance preparations are unique, but the acts and symbols that combine to form its rituals of renewal reiterate those found in other Yuchi ceremonial episodes. Thus the Yuchi ritual cycle shares the quality of repetition common to ritual action generally. This feature was crucial to the symbolic approach to ritual studies developed by Victor Turner. His general observations orient my examination of the themes of Arbor Dance within the broader context of Yuchi ritual performances: "Some symbols recur throughout the different types of ritual forming that system, ritual roles are repeated, certain crucial values are expressed in different parts of the system by different symbols, and some of the ends or aims of different types of rituals are often the same or similar or overlap or are complementary" (1975:62). Turner's approach to symbolic acts and objects can be reconciled with a discourse-centered approach to ritual in the recognition that these expressions have a dual life, at once both part of the physical world of nature and ritual action, and also a part of the discourse that circulates in ceremonial ground life. It is through public exegesis and more focused discussion that interested individuals come to learn the meanings associated with physical symbols and ritual acts (Urban 1991:5–7).

Primarily viewed as a route to, and expression of, physical and spiritual purification, fasting among the Yuchi possesses a wider range of rich associations and is linked to other related practices and ideas about purity. While fasting, combined with emesis and medicine taking, is among the central acts of the Green Corn Ceremony itself, it occurs in related contexts where the well-being of the community and its members is at issue (see Hudson 1975).

At Duck Creek, in the early spring of 1996, the men undertook the task of replacing the ground's stickball pole. As in the Arbor Dance preparations, the men began early in the morning, not long after sunrise (associated with health and life), and fasted while they worked. Also as in the Arbor Dance, this project involved both working in the central, sacred area of the ground and acquiring materials from outside the ground for ritual use inside. By fasting during such activities the men ensure that they are spiritually clean, so as to both protect the square from contamination and ensure that the powerful spiritual forces that reside there will not overpower them.

Everything that relates to the square ground and its rituals is expected to be in a pure or purified state. This logic underlies both the preparations that take place in Arbor Dance rituals and many of the features found generally in Yuchi ritualism. The same dual logic that underlies fasting – keeping the ground in a pure state while safeguarding the individual from the power residing there, informs the taboo, discussed in chapter 3, that bars women experiencing their periods from entering the square during dances.

The impurity thought to adhere to such women has forced some modification in the Yuchi ritual program. One of the core aspects of the Green Corn Ceremony among the Yuchi and other Woodland peoples is its role as a new fire ritual. Among the first activities to take place on the main day of the Green Corn Ceremony is the clearing away of the old fireplace and the ritual building of a new fire. At Polecat ground today and customarily at the other grounds, this fire is made with flint and steel, rather than with matches.[4] Once established, this fire would be taken from the square to the camps at the ground's perimeter. This act replicated the pattern of bringing the new fire to the households in the compact, preremoval towns. Today, among most Yuchi families, this practice has been discontinued because it is not possible to monitor the condition of the many women who visit a family's camp during ground events.

Related to purification through fasting is washing. The first act of the ritual year for ceremonial ground participants is washing with spicewood medicine before coming in contact with the square. Arriving at the ground for the first time during the ritual year, members are careful to walk around the perimeter of the ground away from the square on their way to be washed. Washing removes the spiritual contamination that occurs during life away from the ground, and particularly during encounters with sickness and death.

During the Green Corn Ceremony itself, the four adolescent poleboys each carry a large pole cut from a tree, with the top leaves remaining. These poles are like the brushes used to sweep the square at Arbor Dance. One of the primary tasks assigned to the poleboys is to protect the square while the rituals are underway. Only those men taking medicine, and therefore fasting, are permitted within its bounds. With their brushes, the poleboys scare off any dogs that might enter and defile the square, either because they have eaten or because they possess some other harmful influence. Similarly, the poleboys warn women, children, and visitors away from the square.

In contrast to Creek and Seminole practice, these four poleboys, rather than a lone medicine man, are responsible for preparing the medicines used during the Green Corn. As young men without "experience with women" (to employ the Yuchi euphemism), they are considered to be in a purer state, suitable for the important task of preparing the snakeroot (rattlesnake master, *Eryngium yuccifolium*) and redroot medicines that will, in turn, further purify the other ritual participants. Themes of purification are at the core of all Yuchi ritual activities and warrant more comprehensive consideration.

In contrast to the various agents of impurity recognized in Yuchi ritual thought, plants have a strongly positive association. All of the major undomesticated medicine plants of the Yuchi (redroot, snakeroot, spicewood, horsemint, cedar (*Juniperus virginiana*), and *tsodasha* (*Gnaphalium obtusifolium*) have purification as their main function. Similarly, the arbors on the square, unlike their counterparts in the camps, are constructed completely out of unmodified plant materials – post oak and willow – without recourse to manufactured products, such as rope or nails.

In the fall of 1996, an interesting Yuchi community gathering was held. A delegation from the World Council of Churches was touring the United States visiting minority communities and trying to learn about the relationship between Christianity and local cultures. Invited to the meeting were the children's Yuchi language class and various elders recognized for their knowledge of Yuchi culture and history. The elders took this opportunity to address both audiences and explain some fundamentals of Yuchi belief and practice. In one of his observations to the group, Mose Cahwee recalled the story of how his grandparents took him into the country and instructed him in the fundamentals of Yuchi herbalism and medicine. The introduction and closing of his story reveal the beneficent role of plants in the understandings of Yuchi elders.

TEXT 15

Excerpt from a personal narrative about learning the significance of plants. Delivered by Mose Cahwee during a meeting of Yuchi people with representatives of the World Council of Churches at the Kellyville Indian Community Center, 21 October 1996.

And so, my grandma used to tell me, she said,

"One of these days, mornings, after breakfast, we're going to go out."

And grandpa, he told me, he said, after breakfast one morning, he said, after we got through eating, he said, we had a porch, he said,

"Come here."

He said,

"Open that door."

And he opened the door and he said:

"What do you see?"

I said,

"I see trees, grass, horses, cows, dogs."

He said,

"Is that all you see?"

I said,

"Yeah."

Ok now, I want to teach you, tell you something my parents taught me. And so what I learned from them, well I'm going to tell you, so you can pick it up.

Well, he said,

"When I look out that door and look out into the country, I see
a l l k i n d s o f t h i n g s out there
that the Yuchis live by.
Especially what the nature has provided for the Yuchis to live."

Ok, he said,

"There is medicines out there. There is a l l kinds of herbs. There is a l l kinds of fruits. And there is just everything out there that we can use when it is in season. We don't have to go out there with a chopping hoe and take care of it. Nature does all of that. So the nature provides all of these things for the Indians and the Yuchis, and so this is what they live by."

We went out and he said,

"I am going to take you."

He had a little hatchet and we went out.

After describing the plants that he and his grandfather collected and their use in Yuchi herbalism, Mr. Cahwee closed his account by reflecting on the spiritual aspects of Yuchi medicine. This discussion also reflects on the place of animals in Yuchi belief. The medicine-collecting trip that he describes here had only recently taken place and was an effort to instruct younger Yuchi people in a way similar to his own apprenticeship.

(TEXT 15, CONTINUED)

When you go out you got to be r e a l FAITHFUL. You can't have anything else on your mind when you go out to dig medicine, look for it. You always have to pray about it and on your way, some strange things will happen. And so, that morning that we went out into the country, we got together and we prayed and we started out, no more than the time we got started out a redbird came and joined us. And that redbird came and stayed with us a l l the way with us on that trip. And at the end, that bird would sit just a little ways from us. So, that's one of the things that the o l d timers, they are gone now, but what they taught me, I'm telling you. And these, what I have experienced, it is real, it's true.

For present-day ritual leaders all animals, but particularly birds, have a special interest in Yuchi spiritual affairs. Bird songs are sometimes interpreted as spoken Yuchi, and sightings of birds, particularly white cranes, near the ceremonial grounds are interpreted positively. These beliefs are most clearly articulated in the sacred narrative concerning the feather dance presented in chapter 8. Unlike some Southeastern tribes, present-day Yuchi ceremonialists do not possess a story accounting specifically for the bestowal of medicine plants or attributing an antagonism between animals and plants. Like the other core elements of Yuchi cultural patrimony, plant medicines are viewed as one of many gifts bestowed on them as a people by the Creator in mythic time (cf. Mooney 1900:250; Speck 1909:132; Swanton 1928b:636–38).

The general pattern of raking and sweeping the ground used as ritual space is reiterated in the other major Yuchi ritual series, the one accompanying funeral and burial. While no longer practiced, elders remember that elaborate cleaning and sweeping procedures were undertaken at the home of the deceased, where a funeral feast and all-night wake would take place. Not only was the home of the deceased completely emptied and cleaned (down to the detail of removing nails from inside walls), but the outside area adjacent to the house was scraped clean of weeds and swept in the same manner as the square during Arbor Dance.[5]

Within ceremonial ground ritual, such sweeping concludes the Lizard Dance that opens the Green Corn Ceremony at the Polecat ground. In this dance, the men reenact a series of sacred narratives that deal with the defeat by the Yuchi of a menacing monster lizard. After the lizard is driven from the square, a designated man restores it to a pure state by sweeping it again with the same type of brush used in the Arbor Dance preparations. While the square is cleaned in this way, the men who have enacted the role of the defeated lizard go to the woods to the east of the square and wash with water, purifying themselves after having been exposed to the monster lizard.

One of the most diffuse ritual motifs, reoccurring in Yuchi ritual of all kinds, is the regular appearance of the pattern number four. Viewed as a cycle, the Arbor Dance concludes the series of four stomp dances held before Green Corn. In the Arbor Dance, before sweeping, the chief leads the men around the fireplace four times. On the Friday of the Green Corn Ceremony in Polecat Town, the four poleboys are formally selected to serve during the Green Corn when the chief presents each with a stick made from *sagedi'tæ* 'bearpaw' (ironweed, *Vernonia fasciculata*) (Jackson 2000a). All of the daytime dances of the Green Corn Ceremony occur in repetitions and divisions of four. Constantly recognized and discussed by Yuchi ritualists, the regularity of the number four is primarily interpreted as an original feature of Yuchi ritual initiated by the Creator. When the pattern is reflected upon, it is done so in terms common to contemporary pan-tribal Native American symbolism, which links it to cultural patterns imposed on such natural phenomenon as the delineation of four cardinal directions and the four seasons.

Closer to the context of Yuchi ritualism, the number four is encoded in the four-sided shape of the square ground and its square-shaped arbor buildings. Many treatments of North American Indian theology have tended to emphasize the salience of the circle, but the ceremonies of the Yuchi and their neighbors show instead an emphasis on squares and corners. Most Yuchi dances are circular in choreography, but these circles are contained within squares. As noted in chapter 6, each Yuchi dance event is concluded with the Closing the Door Dance, a dance that has the same choreography as the Four Corners Dance. In both, the group of dancers visits each corner of the square repeating the same song and choreography. The pattern of dancing in the corners of a square-shaped area is replicated in the daytime Feather Dances of the Green Corn, which are also referred to as "Corner Dances."

The processionals led by the ground's elders, particularly the chief, reappear in various formal and informal contexts. This pattern is most often repeated during stomp dances. The chief of the home ground is normally the first man to lead a dance. When visiting another ground, the ground chiefs are the first men chosen by the host from each visiting delegation. In both of these contexts, the men of the ground file into line behind their chief, ordering themselves according to age, office, seniority, and kinship – categories that often overlap. This same principle is manifest in the daytime dances of the Green Corn Ceremony, all of which elaborate the basic line dance form of the stomp dance. These acts tangibly express the support of the members for their leader. Extending this principle, any man who leads a stomp dance is called a "leader." To do so is to walk into a public arena with the expectation that others will fall into line behind and follow. While the reciprocity governing the relationships among individual ground members is tested in this way during the stomp dance hundreds of times each summer, the more formalized processions make clear statements about the consent to lead accorded to chiefs and elders. The clearest example of this process in Yuchi ritual is found in the calendar ceremony held at the Polecat ground, in which the chief announces the date of the Green Corn Ceremony and the men who file behind him ratify his decision verbally.

Yuchi elders hold that the regularity of the counterclockwise movement around the fire found in their ritual acts, processionals, and dances is appropriate because by moving in this way, the human heart is closest to the fireplace, and thus in more direct communication with the Creator as mediated by the Fire (Grandfather) acting as a witness.

SOCIAL RENEWAL AND RECIPROCITY

As the formation of lines behind leaders reveals, community-centered ritual events, such as the Arbor Dance, Green Corn, and Soup Dance, are particularly important moments when ongoing social relations among both individuals and the ground's constituent groups are negotiated.

For ground participants, the three major ritual events are the primary opportunity during the year for entire extended family groups to gather together and act as units. In this context, fathers and uncles encourage the ritual participation of younger men, while mothers and aunts pass on their own experience and experiences of camp life to the young women of the family. As family reunions, these events, especially Green Corn, are the primary opportunities for young cousins, as well as occasionally for grown siblings, to interact with one another. Particularly for individuals living outside Oklahoma, Green Corn is a major opportunity to reunite with family.

While these events are opportunities to express the reciprocal obligations of family life, families are also engaged in relationships with other families, particularly during Green Corn and Soup Dance, when each family is camped independently and feeds visiting groups. Over the years, friendships emerge between particular families belonging to different grounds. These families become regular visitors to one another's camps. This pattern is manifest both in relationships between Yuchi families of different grounds and between Yuchi families and those of other tribes participating in the stomp dance.

These family-to-family relations are part of the foundation of ground-to-ground relationships. Reciprocal visiting and its expression in oratory are associated with all Yuchi dance gatherings, but the three major events, particularly Green Corn, are special opportunities for visiting. Visiting delegations are particularly interested in attending the Green Corn Ceremony of a host, not only because of the attendant camp life, but because the stomp dance and other activities held within it are especially elaborated and enthusiastically organized. The interaction data presented in chapter 6 indicated that the Green Corn Ceremonies in 1996 were more widely attended by non-Yuchi visitors than any of the other Yuchi dances.

Part of the attraction of the three major events is the larger number of people who attend. One source of increased attendance is less active family members who join their kinsmen for the major events, but who are not fully active in the ground. The larger number and size of visiting delegations is another aspect of this phenomenon. A third is the participation of certain whole families who only participate in the major events, sometimes only the Green Corn Ceremony. The reaction of Yuchi leaders to this phenomenon is understandably mixed. On the one hand, during the remainder of the ritual season they feel the absence of those members, both in the practical difficulty of carrying on the football games and dances with fewer people than ideally should be involved and in the recognition that these families are missing a large proportion of the positive social and spiritual benefits that accrue to participants. On the other hand, some participation is better than no participation, and there is the recognition that Green Corn does provide one strong opportunity for the Yuchi to gather yearly as a people. This sentiment is particularly strong in association with the Green Corn at Polecat, which is attended, at least in part, by most culturally affiliated Yuchi people. In light of these particular patterns, regular participation in the Green Corn Ceremony is the minimal test of ground membership.

As I have already indicated, strongly articulated norms emphasizing harmony are central to ceremonial ground belief. In their actions and words, ceremonial ground leaders work to avoid compromising the health of their members, the viability of Yuchi cultural performances, and the integrity of the ceremonial ground community in which they must be embedded. Public expressions of interpersonal conflict are almost non-existent and what conflict discourse does occur between members is confined to gossip, which the leaders of the ground also seek to keep in check by constantly articulating, particularly through oratory, the norms and need for a harmonious community. During the period in which I have attended Yuchi ceremonial ground events, I have been witness to only one public exchange of disagreement, and this was a relatively minor one. In a pattern shared by the Cherokee and other Woodland peoples, the Yuchi reaction to protracted interpersonal difficulties is withdrawal from mutual interaction rather than open conflict (Thomas 1962).

THE ARBOR DANCE IN COMPARATIVE PERSPECTIVE

The Yuchi Arbor Dance event is distinct from the rituals of the Creek and Seminole cycle. At most Oklahoma Creek and Seminole grounds, ritual practice includes renewal and purification activities similar to those of the Yuchi Arbor Dance, but these most often take place within the Green Corn Ceremony itself (Bell 1984; Howard and Lena 1984; Schupman 1984; Robbins 1976). At most Creek and Seminole grounds, the rehabilitation of squares takes place on the morning of the Green Corn rituals and, unlike with the Yuchi, Creek and Seminole grounds permit new family camps to be established prior to the first stomp dance of the spring. Like the Yuchi, the Seminole (and probably the Creek as well) doctor the arbors after rebuilding them, but, according to Howard's description, they utilize a different medicine plant (Mexican tea, *Chenopodium ambrosioides*) and slightly different ritual for this purpose (Howard and Lena 1984:125–26). The Yuchi prohibition against sitting on the square during the work is also differently observed in Seminole practice, in which, during the work, the chief and his assistant sit on the square making preparations for the Ribbon Dance, to be held at the conclusion of the repairs (Howard and Lena 1984:126).

The Yuchi Arbor Dance presents a contrast with the Creek and Seminole, but Howard's consultants among the Absentee Shawnee drew a direct connection between their own Arbor Dances, held just prior to the midsummer War Dance, and the Yuchi Arbor Dance, held prior to the Green Corn Ceremony (1981:280). In both events, a renewal of the ceremonial ground is concluded with a stomp dance in anticipation of the major ritual event to follow soon after. This common framework and its absence among many modern Creek and Seminole grounds adds an additional piece of evidence to the case for viewing the Yuchi as a people both distinct from their Creek neighbors and even more closely affiliated with the Shawnee than has previously been acknowledged.

8

"We didn't have songs at that time."

Green Corn Ceremony

Sacred Stories

Yuchi elders today use the English word *story* to describe a whole range of customary narratives, combining in this term those genres classified comparatively by folklorists as myths, legends, and folktales (cf. Valentine 1995:188). Viewed externally, the stories with which I deal in this chapter are all clear examples of myths. Because so much difference continues to exist between the everyday conception of a myth as a falsehood and its anthropological definition as a culturally prescribed, foundational truth, I have sometimes used the alternative label *sacred narrative* (Dundes 1984:1). For their tellers, the stories presented here have a clear relationship to ceremonial ground ritual. In this, they are canonical examples of myth, providing "the ideological context for a sacred form of behavior" and supporting ritual's capacity to "bring the creative events of the beginning of time to life, here and now in the present" (Honko 1984:51).

Once a primary focus of research, the study of myth and its relationship to ritual has suffered a measure of neglect as ethnographic and theoretical horizons shifted in late-twentieth-century anthropology. It is convenient to point to a rapidly changing world as the source of declining anthropological interest in myth, but it is probably more correct to associate that decline with a growing lack of interest in the social theories that came to dominate modern mythology – functionalism, structuralism, and Freudianism. Mitigating that decline, though, are several emerging insights that have reconnected the study of narrative, particularly in socially powerful forms such as myth, to a larger set of anthropological interests, especially in the nature of communication and its role in shaping the conduct of social life. This body of new work begins by considering actual tellings of myths, rather than the idealized paraphrasings that have served in much mythological study (Bauman 1986; Urban 1991).

In this chapter I draw on this recent work in exploring specific Yuchi sacred narratives as they relate to the rituals of the Green Corn Ceremony – the most elaborate and important Yuchi public gathering. In focusing on myth, I recognize that much of the Green Corn Ceremony's cultural meaning and social significance will go unconsidered. The richness of the event warrants both a general survey and specific treatments of features such as music and dance, social interaction, and ritual behavior. An outline of the Green Corn activities at the three contemporary Yuchi ceremonial grounds is given in appendix B. For general descriptions of the form of the Yuchi Green Corn Ceremony, see Speck's account of the ceremony at Sand Creek (1907a, 1909) and especially Ballard's (1978) focused account, which presents both a description of Green Corn at Polecat and a symbolic analysis of it. Witthoft (1949) remains the basic comparative account of Green Corn Ceremonialism in the Eastern Woodlands.

While contributing to the development of enactment-centered approaches to myth and ritual, I also seek to accomplish a more basic goal in this chapter. Review of anthropological work conducted among Woodland peoples in the second half of the twentieth century presents, I suggest, a false picture of "traditional" verbal art as moribund. The performances of sacred narrative transcribed here should make clear the fact that mythology remains a vital aspect of Yuchi ceremonialism, one that also spills over into other areas of community life.

CORN

Before myths became a source of insight into human psychology and sociology, the sacred narratives of Native American peoples were of interest to anthropologists for linguistic and historical reasons. A great many of the available sacred narratives from American Indian communities were recorded in the early twentieth century by anthropologists seeking to document Native languages while at the same time collecting texts that captured glimpses of culture as articulated by the members of a society themselves (Briggs and Bauman 1999; DeMallie 1999; Hill 1999). Secondarily, those collections of texts contributed to the study of American Indian culture history. Through comparison of similar stories found among neighboring peoples, patterns of interaction and relationship through time could be established. Closely similar myths, like other commonalities of language and culture, can be viewed as evidence supporting historical ties among groups. Alternatively, a sharp difference between the mythologies of neighboring peoples might suggest the maintenance of clear cultural boundaries, a very recent association, or both. These observations were grounded in the recognition that myths, like other human products, circulate among communities and thus possess their own histories of movement and change. In early American anthropology, this circulation was inferred from patterns of occurrence in space. In what has been viewed as the model of this type of study,

Franz Boas examined the mythology of the Tsimshian in comparison with other mythologies from northwestern North America. By comparing a large body of stories and motifs, he found evidence suggesting cultural ties between the Tsimshian on the coast and inland Plateau peoples. In contrast, comparison of Tsimshian mythology suggested less intense, or historically more recent, interaction with more southerly tribes on the Pacific coast (1916:872).

Today, diffusional studies, and the historical reconstructions that they generate, are of secondary interest to the study of cultural forms interwoven in the context of particular societies. Yet contextual study of a specific narrative within the life of a community can occasionally reveal how the processes underlying diffusion take place. The first Yuchi story that I wish to consider provides an example.

As its name indicates, the Green Corn Ceremony marks the ripening of the new corn crop. In the past, corn was the foundation of Yuchi diet and today, although few if any Yuchi grow their own corn, it remains symbolically powerful to Yuchi people and is the featured food in communal meals. As a first-fruits ritual, ceremonial ground participants are expected not to eat the new corn crop until they are purified by the fasting and medicine consumption undertaken during the ceremony. In the ritual of the Duck Creek community, corn itself serves as a collective medicine. As their last act of the daytime ceremonies, the men of this community roast four perfect ears of corn in the sacred fire and then touch these as a means of transferring the blessings of the fire and the new corn to themselves.

Like their ceremonies, songs, and dances, corn is, for the Yuchi, one of the blessings bestowed upon Indian people by the Creator. At the October 1995 community gathering with leaders from the World Council of Churches introduced in chapter 7, Newman Littlebear presented a narrative accounting for this gift of corn to Indian people. The story was embedded within an overview of ceremonial ground religious belief and practice. For the children who made up most of his audience, this was a first opportunity to hear a telling of such a sacred story.

TEXT 16

An account of the revelation of corn. Delivered by Newman Littlebear to a public gathering at the Kellyville Indian Community Center, 21 October 1995. The transcription is arranged in order to highlight the different voices and speech events occurring in the narrative. Left-aligned text presents Mr. Littlebear's own words. Middle-aligned text presents those of his father, while the text aligned furthest to the right selects out the corn spirit's own words articulated in mythic time. This formatting approach and its rationale are explained in detail in Dinwoodie (1999).

This was their life.
It was their life, and today it is
it is the life of many of us,
that is living today
although
you might say that it is gradually fading away
but (uh)
it involves (uh)
many good things
such as the fire
such as the fire and our vegetables
mainly the corn
that we was blessed by the Almighty with corn
And I'll tell you a story that I heard
Maybe some of you all . . .
My father told me this story about corn.
Said that:

> When we didn't have corn.
> and (uh)
> This fella, he heard a voice
> He was out in the wilderness
> He heard this voice
> of a tiny baby,
> whining, crying.
> like a newborn baby crying
> and (uh)
> he begin to listen and he heard this sound of a baby crying and
> he went
> he went to investigate
> but he didn't know where it was coming from
> but he went to the direction of the sound and (uh)
> As he got a little closer the sound got a little bit louder
> and he was getting close to the sound
> of this baby crying
> so
> as he did and investigated around
> he looked in some bushes
> and he saw that when he did, why
> he saw a little-bitty stalk of corn
> a little baby corn.

And that was where that voice was coming from.
And that was where that voice was coming from,
and that little . . . little stalk of corn spoke, spoke to him
and said to him.
and he asked for help
The little stalk of corn asked for help.
He gave him instructions what to do
Clean up and cultivate that . . .
cultivate that corn
And that little corn said:
"I'm here to help your people."
"I am going to help you all through your life."
"You must remember and never forget"
"I am going to help a l l o f y o u r people."
And so, that story was true.
We have many dishes today that comes from that corn.
That was the first story of
the corn that I ever heard.

Maybe you have never ever heard that, but my father told me that, and it was a story that I enjoyed
and I can see today that we celebrate that event
every year,
That was a blessing from the Master
Putting his voice into this . . .
And giving him instruction,

We may say that it is a fable, but we live it
we live it, and all of the things our people do, we observe
and remember what the Creator
has provided for us
in this life.

Like a significant number of the most culturally conservative Yuchi people, Newman Littlebear is also of Shawnee ancestry. His Shawnee father was involved in both Shawnee and Yuchi ceremonial ways, serving as a stickman and dance leader at the Polecat Ceremonial Ground and as a member of the Native American Church. Faced with an opportunity to discuss the importance of corn, Mr. Littlebear drew on his father's account of the origin of corn, strengthening his argument for the importance of corn in Yuchi life and belief, and more generally illustrating, for his guests, that the Yuchi are a spiritual people who recognize and appreciate the gifts provided to them in this life through the agency of the Creator.

Perhaps unexpectedly, the entire body of published and unpublished Yuchi myth texts collected by anthropologists does not contain a single example of a narrative accounting for the origin of corn. This is not to say that one never existed. All of the tribes that once were, or are presently, their neighbors have some such account, and it is logical that the Yuchi people in the past would have possessed some thoughts about the subject themselves. Yet, on 21 October 1995, as an elder and ritual leader, Mr. Littlebear took responsibility for interpreting Yuchi belief and performed a Yuchi sacred narrative into existence, filling an otherwise empty slot in the current Yuchi mythic repertoire. Although other ritual participants and leaders are aware of the story's Shawnee provenance, they accept it as representing ancestral "Indian" experience. I am unaware of any alternative stories, or criticisms of this one, circulating presently in the Yuchi community.

Such an innovation within tradition is possible for several reasons. For his audience, Mr. Littlebear is among the handful of elders who are almost universally respected for their knowledge of Yuchi culture and ritual practices. This respect provides him with the latitude needed to interpret Yuchi belief in accord with the general cultural framework transmitted from Yuchi ancestors into the present. The small number of Yuchi people in the audience who recognized the story's genealogy back to his father also recognized that, while a Shawnee, his father was a participant in Yuchi cultural life and had a valid understanding of Yuchi belief. Floating behind those observations is a recognized closeness of the Shawnee and Yuchi people to one another and their own sense of cultural commonality. Just as James Howard's Shawnee consultants drew on the example of the Yuchi Arbor Dance to provide an analogy to their own Arbor Dance, Yuchi people repeatedly comment on the similarity of Shawnee belief and practices to their own. In those comparisons, they often characterize the Absentee Shawnee community as a more conservative reflection of their own society. An example commonly articulated among the Yuchi today is the view that present-day Absentee Shawnee funeral practices mirror older Yuchi funeral rites that have been reduced since the deaths of the last Yuchi medicine men.

Although this public performance was the first time that I heard this story told, Mr. Littlebear recalled for me that he had narrated it one time previously, at a intertribal Peyote meeting. Interestingly, he recounted that several Shawnee elders were present for this telling and concurred that it is found among the (then) contemporary Shawnee. I was also present at a later telling of this myth during the Duck Creek Green Corn Ceremony in 1996. On this occasion, the story was used directly to elaborate upon the concern for corn expressed in the ritual.

Even more illustrative of the patterns of biography and cultural interaction that I am describing was a visit to the 1999 Spring Bread Dance at the Loyal Shawnee Ceremonial Ground near White Oak, Oklahoma. Mr. Littlebear and I were among the few visitors present at the conclusion of this dance. Before departing, Mr. Littlebear was inspired by the success of the event to deliver a formal ceremonial ground speech on his own behalf. His goal was to encourage the young members of this community in their efforts at carrying on their own ceremonial ways. In the course of this oratory, he again recounted the Shawnee story of the origin of corn. In discussing Mr. Littlebear's speech with these Shawnee ceremonialists, I learned that they had not heard it previously but that they especially appreciated learning it and its relationship to their own ceremonies.

The nature of much early anthropological fieldwork in Native American communities often precluded any opportunity to trace the *natural history* of stories, either as they evolved within a teller's repertoire or in their transmission within families, tribes, or intertribal communities. Diffusion was only observable through the comparison of stories, treated as impersonal objects, as they varied in historical time and social space. In a small way, Mr. Littlebear's account of the origin of corn, performed sequentially for elderly Absentee Shawnee peyotists, cosmopolitan Christian bureaucrats, Yuchi school children, Yuchi Green Corn participants, and young Loyal Shawnee ritualists, provides a glimpse into the processes that are at work in the life course of narratives that are closely associated with understandings of tradition (see Silverstein and Urban 1996).

'MAYBE YOU'VE HEARD DIFFERENT VERSIONS'

Sitting lifeless on the printed page, the myth texts that I read, or more often skimmed, in graduate school did not fully prepare me for the performance of sacred stories in the context of real human relationships. As a student, the myths that I first knew were either boxes of text presented without comment or objects of analysis embedded in webs of interpretation usually richer than the pared-down story abstracts on which they were based. These encounters with decontextualized or intellectualized myth meant that I was simultaneously over-prepared and unprepared to hear a sacred story actually transmitted from oral sources. When it happened early in my first visit to the Yuchi, I was so excited and overwhelmed that the moment has crystallized as the dominant memory of both my first efforts at fieldwork and of Jimmie Skeeter, the man who shared the story with me. The narrative that he told concerned the origins of the Yuchi Lizard Dance and his telling served as the basis for my first attempt at writing about Yuchi culture.

The story was prompted while Mr. Skeeter and I watched a videotape made of the previous year's Lizard Dance at the Polecat Ceremonial Ground. I listened excitedly as Mr. Skeeter relayed a story that accounted for both the dance and other features of Yuchi ceremonialism. On the basis of the notes that I made afterward, I compiled the following summary account, which served as the basis for my initial essay, later incorporated into an M.A. thesis in folklore (Jackson 1996b).[1]

> Back east, the people were living in a town. The town's medicine men chose three boys for training in medicine knowledge. One medicine man was selected to take them out a great distance away from the village to begin their training.
>
> The man and the boys began their trip. After a long day of traveling, the medicine man told the boys to stop, as they were going to make camp. While they waited at the campsite, the medicine man scouted in a circle surrounding the site. In surveying the area, he discovered a tree with a large hole in it. Returning to the campsite, he warned the boys to stay away from the tree with the hole. He sent two of the boys to go and chop wood for their camp. Discovering it for themselves, one of these boys attempted to chop down the tree with the hole. A large lizard emerged from the hole and grabbed the boy, dragging him into its nest to feed its young. The other boy returned quickly to the camp to explain what had happened. The old man declared that their party was now forced to abandon their expedition in order to stay and deal with this problem.
>
> The man and the two boys built a fire in the campsite. On one side of the campfire they built an earthen mound. The man prepared medicine and placed the medicine between the fire and the mound. He then told the two boys to sit with him, across the fire from the mound, and he warned them not to run in fear. After nightfall, the boys and the man heard the monster lizard approach. The monster drew near to the party and crawled over the hill, attracted to the medicine. After tasting the medicine, the lizard died.
>
> The party cut the head off of the monster and disposed of the body. They returned to the tree and killed the lizard's young. [The incident required that they return to the village, with the lizard's head.] When they rested on

the return trip, they placed the head on the top of various trees. In each instance, the tree on which the head was placed was destroyed. Finally, the party discovered that the cedar tree was unaffected by the power of the bloody head. With this discovery they returned to the village.

After telling his story, Mr. Skeeter went on to explain how it refers to various features of the Lizard Dance and other aspects of Yuchi ritual.

Held today on Friday evening at the start of the Polecat ground's Green Corn Ceremony, the Lizard Dance is the first dance to take place during the event. Danced by the men alone, it begins with two singers taking seats on the back bench of the chiefs' arbor. The dancers line up in the northwest corner of the square. Positioned in the southwest corner are four men carrying shotguns loaded with blanks. Over his shoulder, each dancer carries a green bough similar to those used to sweep the square during the Arbor Dance preparations. When the dance begins, the line of dancers enters the square and dances around the fire counter-clockwise, using a toe-heel step. As they dance, the dancers, in turn, repeat a somewhat guttural, somewhat musical call [we:e:e:ye:ye:ye:ye:]. Each call is answered by the dancers, [we::].[2]

After circling the fire several times, the riflemen enter the square and begin running at a jog around the circling dancers. As they encircle the dancers, they begin firing their guns skyward toward the east. After a time, the leader of the dancers breaks away from the circle and leads them out of the square, running to the southeast. When they arrive at the bottom of the hill on which the Polecat ground is located, each dancer washes in a tub of water placed there for this purpose. As the dancers depart, the gunmen face east and discharge any remaining rounds. After the dancers have exited the square, a designated man enters the square and sweeps its entire area in a manner similar to the sweeping at the arbor fixing.

Beyond explaining how cedar was revealed as a Yuchi medicine, Mr. Skeeter linked the lizard story to the Lizard Dance just described. In his explanation, the dancers collectively represent the lizard, with his long serpentine body and monstrous sounds. Each dancer carries a tree, symbolic of Yuchi medicine plants and the trees that appear in the story. The gunmen symbolize the power of the Yuchi doctor who was able to defeat the lizard, although the specific feature of using modern guns was never explained to him. Because the lizard's presence is contaminating, the men wash themselves and the square is swept at the conclusion of the dance.[3]

When I returned to Oklahoma in 1995 to continue research with Yuchi elders, I was particularly interested in exploring more fully the sacred narratives that were related directly to the Yuchi dances and ceremonies. In particular, if

The men and boys to perform the Evening Lizard Dance during the Polecat Ceremonial Ground Green Corn Ceremony kneel waiting to begin. They face the Chief's Arbor where the two singers will sit. They carry green "brushes" and wear white handkerchiefs "turban" style, 12 July 1996. Spectators can be seen beyond the south edge of the town square.

possible, I wanted to make recordings of such stories in order to learn not only about their content, but about their form and the norms governing their performance.

From Newman Littlebear, I first learned of several story motifs that were also linked to the Lizard Dance. I asked him if he was familiar with Jimmie Skeeter's account, hoping that I could record a version from him. Although they were relatives, Mr. Littlebear was unaware of the story that Mr. Skeeter shared with me. In this initial discussion, he related instead the following incidents.

TEXT 17

Observations on Yuchi Lizard Dance stories. Comments by Newman Littlebear during an interview in Kellyville, Oklahoma, 15 January 1996.

I've heard two stories
in my time.

They're not real long
stories.
But ah,
the first one I heard
I think it was from . . .
I heard him speak a little bit
up there in front of the chiefs' arbor
before, before the Lizard Dance was to take place
on the same evening.
And this was from Jackson Barnett
he was the chief, I guess, before Jim. [James Brown, Sr.]
And the way he ah
he stated . . .
And both stories could . . .
It has something in that dance that
you could kind of pinpoint a situation
such as that gun.
Now, if you think about it
we didn't have guns way back there.
What did they replace?
What did the guns take place of, if they did.
Well, it could have . . .
like he said,
our people started this dance.
Either after the Civil War or during the Civil War
when they was using guns, see.
And they made a dance out of
out of this situation
what they encountered
they was in the Civil War, some of our people.
And ah, it appears that all of our dances has
has something to do
origination with some encounter that our people was involved
within history.

And then this
the other story
goes further back than that.
And it also has something in the dance that resembles
what was in the story.

It says that
    back in the . . .
    maybe what modern books call it prehistoric
    times
    the time of the big giant lizards
    or dinosaurs.
They called them lizards
    our people didn't know the word for dinosaur
    but maybe them small lizards and stuff
    they had names
    for them.
But these were the giant lizards
    and they said that when they roamed the earth
    that the
    the timbers
    the trees
    they shook the earth.
They were so huge, that they shook the earth.
They cause the trees to shake.
    and this is why we use those brush.
The dancers use those brush.
They whoop and holler
    and that is what the brush remembers.
But then that gun comes in
    you know,
    see, it kind of throws you off
    from that story.
So but whenever
    whenever in
    in my time
    the things
    the movements that we do
    we do it by some action
    to send a signal
    to Above.
To like, you might say,
    alert them of what we are doing.
To me
    just from experiencing what I've experienced
    from one of the elders

about the gun,
that's not the only time that
in my life that I've seen our people use the gun
as a signal.

[JJ] Don't they do that at funerals?
[NL] Yeah.

The connection between the gunshots of the Lizard Dance and those fired at several points in old-time Yuchi funeral rituals led to a general discussion of funeral ritual, spiritualism, and the manner in which Yuchi rituals place emphasis on signaling both the Creator and the spirits of the Yuchi ancestors.

Later in 1996, Mr. Littlebear told me that another participant at the Polecat ground had told him an additional story related to the meaning of the Lizard Dance. Between then and 1997, he contemplated this story and added it to his repertoire. At the conclusion of the 1997 Green Corn Ceremony at Duck Creek, he included an invitation to the Duck Creek members to participate in the upcoming ritual at Polecat. Describing the events to take place, he explained that the Lizard Dance would be held on Friday evening. This discussion prompted a telling of the additional story, which he used to conclude the speech.

TEXT 18

Oratory excerpt dealing with the performance and significance of the Yuchi Lizard Dance. From a closing oratory delivered by Newman Littlebear at the conclusion of the 1997 Green Corn Ceremony at the Duck Creek Ceremonial Ground, 22 June 1997.

We have Ribbon Dance and Buffalo Dance on Saturday.
On Friday we have a Lizard Dance.
There's some old stories
about that Lizard Dance.
Maybe you
maybe you heard.
Maybe you heard different ways
about Lizard Dance.
It's for men,
a men's dance.
I heard a story one time about that.
They talk about,

        maybe dinosaurs or giant lizards
        roamed this earth.
They said it was like two of 'em.
One came out of the water
        and one on the land.
And they had a battle.
Them giant lizards,
        when they
        they scuffled
        they
        were battling
        the earth
        they shook the earth.
Them trees
        them treetops
        they shake.
It was like that, they said.
So,
        they made a dance.
They call it Lizard Dance.
The men folks
        the boys
        they go into the woods
        they cut
        a little brush
        resembling them trees
        when those animals were battling.
They said, when one of them . . .
        they battled
        the one on the land
        run one of them into the water.
One of them went back into the water.
And when they made a dance,
        when them animals was fighting
        [it was] like lightning and thunder.
Then when they made a dance
        they said
                "our medicine people
                they had gifts."

They said,
"they could make it lightning
and make it thunder
our people."
So that was the way
they said
it was.
In the modern times to resemble that lightning and thunder
we use them guns
in that dance
four of 'em.
They dance,
dance start here [at the northwest corner of the square]
go around the fire
and them shooters
with the guns
they come around
resembling what those old men did.
They use them guns to resemble the lightning and thunder.
And when they get through they run down to the
to the water.
They got water down there to where they a l l wash up.[4]
I tell you all that story.
Maybe some of you heard it.
Maybe some of you didn't.
Maybe you have heard different versions.
But that's what we're going to have on that Friday.
Maybe you want to take part.
Dance with us.
We'll allow you to dance.
If you want to take part with us.
We'd be glad to have you
in any of our dances.
If you believe you're one people
then come.
It's for our people.
Anyone that wants to come and join
with us.
That's the way it is for us.

So I tell you all that much.
Thank you.
[Men respond:] *Hõ.*

Like the other narratives examined here, this story is a variation on a widespread theme in Woodland mythology. It explores the eternal contest between the forces of goodness and order, most often personified by creatures of the air and land (eagles, the thunders, panthers) and agents of contamination and disorder, symbolized by monsters existing underground or underwater (snakes, serpents, the great horned snake, the *Uk'ten'* of Cherokee mythology). Although both contestants here are reptilian, the narrative shares with this larger corpus a general outline and a resolution in which the source of conflict is driven back underwater, restoring order, if only temporarily (Hudson 1978).

In explaining his version of the lizard story, Mr. Skeeter indicated that the gun firing element of the dance was something that he had puzzled over and never heard adequately interpreted. Mr. Littlebear's story provides additional exegesis on this point, as well as on the iconography of the green boughs carried by the dancers. The multiple meanings attributed by narrative to ritual elements, such as the guns (thunder, commemoration of Civil War experience, spiritual signal) or the boughs (acknowledgment of the gift of medicine, reenactment of the lizard battle), illustrates the richness of the semiotic relationship existing between myth and ritual.

The potential for multiple, even potentially conflicting interpretations of ritual in sacred narrative is inherent in a view of culture as a phenomenon distributed among a community of individuals characterized by varied backgrounds and experiences. One source of confusion in the study of myth and ritual derives from a hesitation to acknowledge this potential for diversity. Clark Wissler and D. C. Duvall were honest about this perplexity in their study of Blackfoot mythology: "A large number of [Blackfoot] myths function as ritualistic origins, the rituals themselves being in part dramatic interpretations of the narratives. Yet, while the rituals are fixed and rigidly adhered to, the myths show the same wide variations in details as those of other groups. This is contrary to expectation" (1908:12).

The meanings and understandings customarily viewed collectively as a group's culture are, in reality, distributed unevenly within a society. An appreciation of the distributed nature of cultural knowledge within communities had already emerged in mainstream cultural anthropology in the 1970s and 1980s (see Fowler 1987; Wallace 1970:110; Wolf 1994). In this context, the special contribution of scholars exploring the work of discourse in social life has been to investigate empirically the relative degree of variation in cultural sharing characteristic of particular societies (Urban 1991, 1996). Such an approach is founded on the premise that the locus of culture, as an abstract system of meanings guiding social action, is the individual and that culture is realized and transmitted through discourse and other concrete expressive forms. The variable distribution and circulation of discourse within a community creates situations, such as the Yuchi and Blackfoot cases, where a collective ritual is replicated through time in a relatively consistent form, while the narratives that explain it are localized in individuals and may vary one from another more freely.

Hearing Jimmie Skeeter's Lizard story was for me a powerful personal experience and the textual history of this story has continued to teach me about the dynamics of oral tradition in social life. More importantly, on a personal level, it initiated a lesson in the responsibilities that accompany exposure to, and participation in, such a tradition. In the January 1996 interview with Mr. Littlebear, I had sought to discover if he knew the same story that Mr. Skeeter had told me in 1993. After exploring the resonances of the stories that he knew, I asked whether there were similar stories related to other dances, but Mr. Littlebear returned to the Lizard Dance. Concurrent with this interview, I had been circulating copies of my M.A. thesis within the Yuchi community for comment. While I had not been self-conscious about writing the story down and including it there, Mr. Littlebear was justifiably curious to hear my version. The following exchange among him, his daughter Linda, and myself captures the audible part of the moment, although it misses the bashfulness showing on my face and Mr. Littlebear's eagerness to make the trade in stories more reciprocal.

TEXT 19

Interview excerpt dealing with Yuchi Lizard Dance stories. From a dialogue with Newman Littlebear during an interview in Kellyville, Oklahoma, 15 January 1996.

[JJ]
Maybe we got time for one more question?
The . . .
I asked you about the Lizard Dance
    and if there is a story about that.
Is there a story about the . . .
    any of the other dances?
[NL]
Well like that Lizard Dance now I was going to . . .
    Simon [Chief Simon Harry] mentioned something about

he heard about that Lizard Dance,
but that involved these lizards
and the medicine.
I was going to say, you might
have him touch on that.
Have you ever questioned . . . talked with him yet?
You might make a notation of
what he heard.
That it seemed like his grandpa told him, but
it involved something about this
the Yuchis and these giant lizards chasing
and they come up on maybe the redroot or something
or maybe the ceremonial site or something
and they stop.
The medicine
it was too powerful.
They had to stop.
Something along those lines.
Did he ever give you?

[JJ]
Jimmie Skeeter told me the story like that.
His story was . . .

[To Linda Harjo, Newman's daughter, who had read parts of my thesis.]

This is the one that was in there. [M.A. Thesis]
Did you read that yet?

[LH]
Uh-huh.

[JJ]
Jimmie Skeeter's story . . . and see I didn't have the tape player and that is why I was asking if you had heard the story that Jimmie Skeeter told because . . .
I don't like trying to just get it out of my head.

[NL]
It's all right . . .

[JJ]
Jimmie Skeeter said . . .
I feel funny telling . . .

Recognizing my predicament, Mr. Littlebear gestured that it would be all right if I turned off the recorder. Then, for the first time in my life I told a myth, not as an object for anthropological discussion but as a story, albeit one performed in a particularly odd and interesting framework. Discussing such hedged or negotiated performances, Richard Bauman (1993) suggests that performance involves the assumption of responsibility toward an audience. In Yuchi society such narratives as those considered here are held to be context-free enactments of Yuchi culture. Comparison of the range of collected stories, covering more than one hundred years of Yuchi narration, reveals that this ideal of replicating fixed cultural texts has been reasonably well achieved. In situations such as this where close attention is paid to replicating earlier performances of traditional stories, part of the responsibility that a performer has toward an audience centers on the expressive materials themselves. In some communities, attention to replication produces an active practice of meta-commentary on the authenticity of retellings. While some discussion of this type occurs among Yuchi elders, most current retellings are to audiences who lack a large body of previous experience in hearing sacred stories. If a person is active in current ceremonial ground life or in Yuchi cultural preservation efforts, sheer knowledge of a narrative places a responsibility on the individual to perform, or at least to report previous tellings of the story. In this instance, having been told a Lizard story placed me in such a position of responsibility. The Yuchi elders with whom I have worked have been quite open to my desire to learn about Yuchi culture. The more complicated and personal lesson that they have taught is that such learning requires reciprocity measured not only in diligent ethnographic work, but in participation in (and responsibility for) the same social and cultural system within which these materials are embedded.

My telling of Jimmie Skeeter's Lizard story is one moment when this reality was exposed for me. Having been led across this threshold, I should have expected further developments. At the Polecat Ceremonial Ground, the weekend of the Green Corn Ceremony is followed by a week during which the members of the ground remain camped there. During this week, which concludes with the ground's Soup Dance on the weekend after Green Corn, the members, particularly the younger people, have an opportunity to visit and socialize. This week features stomp dances lasting two or three hours each evening. Organized primarily by the teenage poleboys, these dances provide an opportunity for younger participants to practice singing, shaking shells, and dancing the special dances performed at the Soup Dance. During one such evening dance in 1996 I was invited to sit under the chiefs' arbor, where Newman Littlebear and some of the younger men were seated.

A young ground leader, then in college, mentioned having read some Yuchi stories drawn from an ethnographic collection, Albert Gatschet's (1893) tales, I think. This opened up a discussion of such myths as they relate to the Yuchi dances and rituals. The discussion landed on the Lizard Dance, and after telling some of the stories that he knew, Mr. Littlebear stated that "Jason's got a good story on that," setting me up this time to tell Mr. Skeeter's story in its natural context. Growing more accustomed to being placed in this position, I went ahead and did my best.

I end this review of the Lizard Dance stories and storytelling with Chief Simon Harry's version. As Newman Littlebear anticipated, it was the same version told to me by Jimmie Skeeter. These two men were neighbors and both served together as officers in the Duck Creek Ceremonial Ground, so it is not surprising that they shared the same story. It is likely that each heard the other telling it and that they had one or more sources in common.

TEXT 20

An account of the Yuchi encounter with the big lizard. Told by Chief Simon Harry during an interview in Hectorville, Oklahoma, 24 January 1996. Chief Harry's telling was acoustically more like everyday conversation than Mr. Littlebear's speeches, so I have presented it in prose format, highlighting reported speech through indentation.

Well they tell that story different. About that big lizard, you're talking about? Dinosaur?

Yeah. Well, I don't know. This doctor he had these warriors out with him. Young men, you know. They was out. I don't know what they were looking for, but anyway, they was out. They had dogs. And they found this place there, where they were going to camp.

I don't know what they were looking for, but that is the way I kind of how I hear it. But when they made that camp, this doctor he talked to these young fellas. He told them not to go out by theirself, you know. Wander off by theirself. Just stay around the camp here, around the fire. Well, that evening he went out and looked around. Looked a l l around.

He knowed there was something around, this doctor. He was a powerful doctor.

The men of the Duck Creek community perform the daytime version of the Lizard Dance during their Green Corn Ceremony, 21 June 1997.

He might be hunting medicine, I don't know what they was hunting. But anyway. He already had already done told them about not going out, you know, but these two boys, young boys, they went out.

And there was a big old hollow tree. I guess back in them days, there was b i g trees, you know, giant trees, I guess. There was bound to be things staying in those hollow tress, you know.

So they, these two young boys they went out. One of them was kind of hard headed. He wouldn't . . . , you know. You couldn't hardly tell him anything, you know. I guess, I guess that is why he got . . . that lizard got him, you know.

This, when they was out, well, this boy, he seen that big old tree over there. And he told the other boy:

> "Let's go over there and tap on that tree."
>
> "No."

This other one said:

> "No."

He said:

> "Well, I'll go over there and tap on it."

This boy, he stand back, you know, watch, you know.

He tapped on that tree. And when he tapped on that tree, well that thing came out of that big tree. Got him right quick and shoved him back into the tree. This boy, he run back and told what happened.

And this doctor told 'em:

> "I told you all not to wander off."

He said:

> "You all won't listen."
>
> "It done happened now."

He told them. He told them in their language, you know.

So, I guess this thing is going to come, you know. [unclear] 'cause it done caught that boy, you know. So that night, that big lizard, he come just so far, and then it would go back. The dogs, they were barking, you know. So the next night, well, that lizard would come a little closer. So, that old man, he was going to, you know, fix it. I think that fourth night, he fixed that redroot. Doctored that redroot. And when that thing come again, the fourth night, well, the closer it came, it got weaker. It come to that medicine, it smell that medicine, and that thing, he fell over. Keeled over.

They cut its head off. And they put it on a pole. They were going to take it back to the camp. So, when, everytime they laid that head on a tree, that tree, it would die. Different trees, you know, it'd die. So they came to a cedar tree. They laid that head in that cedar tree. That cedar tree didn't die. So they brought it to the camp.

Chief Simon Harry (right) and Newman Littlebear (left) begin singing a Feather Dance song at the front of the line of dancers during the Duck Creek Ceremonial Ground's Green Corn Ceremonial, 29 June 1996. The four feathermen carry their poles immediately behind the singers. Three of the four poleboys are visible to the left of the double file of dancers.

That's why they have that Lizard Dance. That represents that lizard they killed, way back there.

That's the story I heard. Maybe Jimmie told you a little different.

CRANE SONGS

As far back as memory reaches, the ritual program of the Polecat Ceremonial Ground has included the performance during the daytime of the Green Corn Ceremony of a series of dances known as a group as Feather Dances. In 1995, these dances were also reestablished in the Duck Creek ground's Green Corn program.[5] In all of these dances, four wands decorated with white crane feathers are carried by four dance leaders known as "feathermen." One sacred narrative that I recorded deals explicitly with the origin of the songs used in these dances.

In Creek ritual practice, the redroot and snakeroot medicines consumed during the Green Corn Ceremony are prepared by a medicine man who empowers them with songs blown into the medicine with a cane tube. While the Sand Creek ground today uses the services of a Creek doctor for this purpose, Duck Creek and Polecat communities make the medicine in a different, distinctly Yuchi manner. The medicine itself is prepared by the four teenage poleboys and is activated by a combination of two forces. In the place of the medicine man, the Sun, which looks down on the medicine and the ceremony, is the primary agent empowering the medicine.[6] Instead of the bubbled songs used by Creek medicine men, Yuchi practice relies on the songs of the Feather Dances to further empower the medicine. In the daytime dances, the men encircle the medicine, which is placed on the east side of the square. By putting forward strong efforts in their singing, dancing, and whooping, they strengthen its beneficial power.

The following narrative, which I have recorded in several public tellings, accounts for the origin of these Feather Dance songs.

TEXT 21

The story of how the Yuchis learned their Medicine Songs. Delivered by Newman Littlebear during an interview at the Kellyville Indian Community Center, 30 November 1995. As in text 16, the format used here seeks to represent the various speaking events represented in the narrative. Read progressively from the left, these are: the Speech Event (= Newman Littlebear's words), the Narrated Event (= Mr. Littlebear's account of Mr. Bummy James's description of the mythic events), and the Narrated Speech Event (= reports of conversations occurring in mythic time).

We received this story, I guess, (uh)
I am not definite about the time, but maybe
three years ago
and it (uh)
it happened right here in this building.

And (uh)
it came from (uh)
Bummy James, this information about the . . .

He asked us,
the question about the . . .
our ceremonial songs
in our day ceremonial dances
and we couldn't (uh)

we couldn't give him an answer to the question
but he (uh)
he informed us that what he was told
by his (uh)
elders or grandfather he called him.
Grandpa Willie Tiger.

And (uh)
I think most of us knew, knew the man he was talking about, because he
he was one of the singers, from time to time, up there at . . .
at Polecat.
But from his information,
he said, his information came from him
and (uh)
what he was told,
from someone beyond, beyond his time.

So (uh),
He said this was
about our songs that:
> "We didn't . . .
> We didn't have songs
> at that time, and well the Yuchi people was wanting
> wanting songs for their ceremonies."

And (uh),
He said:
> "at that . . . , in that . . . , in those times, our,
> our people was able to (uh)
> communicate with (uh)
> birds and (uh)
> animals."
>
> "And they went (uh)
> they went about,
> seeking the
> songs, that (uh)
> they could use in their ceremony."

"They had went to different (uh)
animals and had them to (uh)
sing in their ways;
and (uh)
the birds."

"And there was none that they (uh)
had that was pleasing to 'em."

"So they continued on,
and (uh),
and they came to the white crane."

"And they asked the crane to sing."

"And he agreed to."

"So he sung for the Yuchis and (uh)

And (uh)
They told the crane that (uh):

> "These are the songs that we want to use,
> we want to use in our
> our ceremonies."

"And the crane answered and (uh)
agreed
to let 'em use his songs."

And also the crane informed 'em that (uh):

> "If you use my songs,"

he said

> "I want you to also use my feathers."

[A younger Yuchi participant in the discussion breaks in to make an observation, unclear on my recording, to the effect that this is why the Yuchis use white crane feathers in the Feather Dance. Mr. Littlebear quickly continues:]

And also (uh)
Its been said that (uh)
the white
white feathers represent (uh)
peace
peace to people.

And (uh)
like (uh)
being dedicated and (uh)
pureness.

That's what they say the white feather represents.
And to this day that (uh),
we continue to use those songs. So,
according to that story, they don't belong to us
they belong to the
the crane,
We're just
on loan,
for those songs
and the feathers also.

So, but we still, we still continue on, to this day.
And that sounds like, you know, a good story.[7]

This account of the Feather Dance songs shares with the Corn story and a range of other Yuchi sacred narratives a common structure in which the Yuchi people of mythic times existed initially in a precultural state of need. In this condition, sacred objects (witnesses) are cumulatively presented to them for their benefit by some manifestation of the Creator, acting either directly or indirectly, through the agency of the objects themselves (feathers, songs, corn, fire, tobacco, redroot, snakeroot) (see Speck 1909:106–7, 146–47).[8]

Loosely applying the distinctions of agent- and patient-centricity developed in Greg Urban's studies of American Indian mythology, the Yuchi appear as patients in all of these narratives (Urban 1981). The prime actor throughout is either the Creator or other powerful entities who are derived from the Creator's actions and purposes. Each episode in this mythological corpus tells of a particular encounter in which the Yuchi were presented with another part of their cultural patrimony. As Newman Littlebear remarked in his Lizard Dance commentary, "It appears that all of our dances has something to do [with or an] origination with, some encounter that our people was involved with in history." Taken as a whole, the body of Yuchi myths fulfills the general function of explaining the current form and content of the Yuchi cultural patrimony, while suggesting a general proposition that the Yuchi are a unique people with a distinct configuration of sacred beliefs and practices. Theologically, these stories reinforce a sense of thankfulness that the Yuchi people owe the Creator for bestowing these gifts upon them as a people.

This reading of Yuchi myth may seem applicable to sacred narrative universally, but examination of other mythologies reveals vary different understandings of the ordering of the cultural world. The super-animacy attributed to the Yuchi Creator is in sharp contrast to the creative events of the Central Brazilian narratives described by Urban: "Shokleng mythology includes a lengthy origin account, wherein we hear how the tapir, jaguar and snake were created. What is of interest, however is that the creation in each case is effected not by a single super-animate actor, but always by a succession of actors" (1981:341). Also, in contrast to other North American mythologies, this group of Yuchi narratives does not explain the creation or bestowal of sacred power via accidental occurrences in the adventures of their ancestors or a culture hero. Thus, even the revelation of the cedar motif in the lizard story, which seems like an accidental discovery in Chief Harry's account, appears elsewhere as the direct outcome of the Creator's instructions, as in a variation of the tale collected by Albert Gatschet: "To insure success, the Unknown then made them tie it [the head] to a red cedar tree. There it remained, and its life became extinct. The blood of the head ran through the cedar. Henceforth the grain of the wood assumed a reddish color, and the cedar tree became a medicine tree" (1893:282).

Introducing his collection of stories, Gatschet made an extended remark that bears reconsideration. He presents two versions of the creation of dry land (the earth-diver) myth, in which the crawfish succeeds in retrieving earth from under the waters. Introducing these stories, he noted, "I have obtained one of these relations . . . from a pupil of the mission school at Wialaka, Creek nation, on the Arkansas river near the present settlements of the Yuchi. Here the Creator is introduced as agent, although he is scarcely in any way helpful in the creation of the land. The other land-creation story below differs in some particulars from the first one and omits the mention of a creator or great-spirit, whose existence is illogical in this connection" (Gatschet 1893:279). In light of subsequently collected narratives and my discussions with Yuchi elders, I suggest that Gatschet's criticisms are misplaced. This same pattern occurs in Newman Littlebear's corn story, where he opens the narrative stating that the Yuchi were "blessed by the Almighty with corn." The Yuchi had, and continue to have, a strong belief in an ultimate power at work in the universe. The power of the Creator is manifest in a variety of spiritual forms, including the sacred fire and the heavenly Sun, and it can also work indirectly through agents such as the crawfish or the crane. The earliest European visitors to Southeastern Native communities recognized this aspect of their cosmology and I see no reason to discredit it by suggesting, as Gatschet implies, that it is a modern corruption of an earlier belief.

STORIES AS NARRATIVES

Although a full consideration of the rhetorical strategies and poetic devices used by Yuchi story tellers is beyond the scope of this work, some brief comments can connect story telling with the practice of ritual oratory as described in chapter 4. As the Feather Dance story and the story of the two battling lizards reveal, when sacred narratives are embedded in ritual speeches, they take on the poetic and rhetorical features of oratory. Conversely, when stories are told publicly in non-ritual settings, speakers may borrow conventions associated with ritual oratory, especially when the stories relate to ceremonial ground belief. By making public story tellings oratory-like, tellers index the sense of seriousness with which the story itself should be interpreted. Both story-filled oratory and oratory-like story telling suggest the ways in which generic conventions are resources used by speakers in socially useful ways. In these cases, the two genres are mixed in order in increase their rhetorical effectiveness as explanations of Yuchi culture (Bakhtin 1984; Bauman 1992).

As in ritual oratory, narrators in public and semi-public story telling frequently utilize the impersonal pronoun *they* when telling stories. In doing so, story tellers are making reference to their own recent ancestors, from whom stories were learned, and the more ancient body of tribal ancestors stretching back in time to the events that the stories describe. As in oratory, this usage shifts responsibility away from the narrator and emphasizes that these stories are not recent or individual creations, but are instead timeless and collective (Jackson 1997).

In contrast with ceremonial ground oratory, stories utilize direct reported speech more frequently. In closing talks and other ceremonial ground speeches, orators typically represent the words of the chief in indirect speech. In sacred stories, key incidents are often highlighted by directly quoting verbal exchanges between the participants. In this way, the directions given to the ancient Yuchis by the baby corn plant and the crane are quoted for listeners in the present. This use of quoted speech brings these powers to life and focuses attention on the critical points within the narrative (Hill and Irvine 1993; Moore 1993). In both of these instances, and in other Yuchi narratives, the key moment is the act of giving, by which the Yuchi obtained their cultural patrimony in mythic time.

While quoted speech is used in reporting conversations in mythic speech events, it is also sometimes used in reporting earlier tellings of the mythic narrative. In the oratory dealing with the battle of the two lizards, Mr. Littlebear quotes the voices of the recent ancestors directly, recalling what they said about earlier generations of Yuchi people. "They said, 'They could make it lightning and make it thunder.'" Much like the events of mythological time, this usage focuses attention on powers that Yuchi people controlled in the past. They also distribute responsibility for the narratives beyond the speaker, connecting them to the authority of knowledgeable ancestors.

These rhetorical uses of pronouns and reported speech are enhanced by artful repetition, changes in tense, parallel constructions, interesting framing comments, and a range of other features worthy of further consideration. Rather than focus on these details here, I instead suggest that, like ritual oratory, the performance or reporting of Yuchi sacred narratives is an important means by which Yuchi cultural knowledge is replicated in time and made powerful through processes of traditionalization that connect stories told in the present to stories told in the past. These stories told in the past and retold in the present are about the ultimate beginnings of Yuchi culture, history, and identity, and such storytelling is an important social practice through which Yuchi life is imbued with meaning. Present reference to past tellings not only provides a kind of assurance of authenticity, but also imparts a sense of enduring continuity to Yuchi culture. Independent comparison of Yuchi sacred narratives collected through time suggests that this feeling of continuity is a warranted textual reality, as well as a product of the storyteller's art.[9]

COMPARATIVE ANALYSIS

As in previous chapters, comparison of Yuchi cultural materials with those of their present and historic neighbors provides insight into Yuchi cultural affinities and the nature of areal cultural patterns in eastern North America.

Some Creek and Seminole ceremonial grounds in Oklahoma retain their own Feather Dances, and these communities share with the Yuchi the belief that the Feather Dance songs were taught in ancient times by birds, most centrally the crane. Yet the music and choreography of their dances differs from those of the Yuchi, among whom the dances and the beliefs associated with them are more elaborate and extensive. The normative Creek-Seminole Green Corn incorporates four Feather Dance episodes, while the full modern Yuchi Green Corn contains nine Feather Dances, each with its own song and choreography.[10] Some of the Yuchi dances classed with and danced among the Feather Dances, such as the Bead Dance and the Jumping the Hill Dance, have additional ritual associations of their own.[11]

While the Yuchi Feather Dance and its associated narrative are more elaborate than the cognate forms found among the Creek, Mr. Littlebear's account of the origin of corn presents a marked contrast with the stories of other Southeastern peoples. Among both the Cherokee and the Muskogean tribes, a highly elaborated myth accounts for the origin of corn. Among these peoples, Corn Mother is the original provider of corn, generating it secretly from her own body, usually by scraping it off her legs. When her secret is discovered, the people are disgusted and reject or kill her. Before departing (or dying), Corn Mother explains how corn seed can be planted and cultivated, ensuring its future availability, but, for their ingratitude, the people must now work and worry over their corn crop.[12]

The Shawnee corn origin story told by Newman Littlebear not only fits into the overarching pattern of Yuchi mythology, but has identifiable parallels with stories among other Algonquian tribes. I do not have access to any other Shawnee versions, but a very similar Delaware narrative exists. I present it here, as abstracted by John Bierhorst:

> A youth refuses to hunt because the animals are his friends. Disgusted, his father, the chief, drives him from camp. Winter comes. The boy is about to starve. Then he sees a "large light." It is the "Great father Jesus," telling him to go to a certain stump (where he will find corn to eat?) but to leave seed for planting. Next year, after his corn has been harvested, he returns to camp and becomes a hero. From then on the people have corn – a hollowed-out stump is used as the mortar. [1995:63][13]

The Delaware are neighbors of the Yuchi to the north and they have long maintained close cultural ties to the Shawnee, with whom they share many customs.

The story that Jimmie Skeeter and Simon Harry told of the ancient monster lizard residing in a hollow tree appears elsewhere in the mythologies of various Southeastern tribes. Not surprisingly, the story is most elaborated among the Shawnee and Yuchi. Retaining a concern for medicine power, the Creek versions lack any explanatory function. In a Creek variant, one man has medicine power enabling him to race the lizard unharmed. A companion mistakenly believes himself capable of the same feat and is caught by the lizard (Swanton 1929:26). In a second variation, collected among the Creek and Hitchiti (Oklahoma Seminole), hunters discover the lizard and, unable to defeat it, are rescued by a powerful panther (tiger) (Swanton 1929:27, 96). Linking these Muskogean variants to the Shawnee-Yuchi narratives are two versions collected by John Swanton among the Alabama and Koasati in Texas. In these, hunters find the lizard and are unable to defeat it. At a later point, it is destroyed through the medicine power of the Shawnee (Swanton 1929:153, 196). As Swanton, among others, has suggested, these tales are connected to widespread beliefs about the heightened powers of Shawnee doctors and tribal medicine. "Shawnee doctors were in particular esteem among the Creeks, an esteem shared by all the other peoples in contact with them" (Swanton 1928b:627; see also Schutz 1975:169; Hudson 1978:63).

Jack and Anna Kilpatrick recorded a version from an Oklahoma Cherokee narrator that shared features with the Yuchi and Shawnee versions (1964:69–70). In it, the lizard is discovered and, following some losses, is defeated (by shooting into its mouth, rather than through medicine power). Inside the lizard's mouth are brown spots that are preserved and used as powerful medicines. This final motif links the story to tales from the Cherokee and Creek about the collection of scales from powerful monsters, most notably great monster snakes, to serve as powerful medicines.

The most comprehensive treatment of this story is in Noel Schutz's dissertation on Shawnee mythology (1975:157–61). He presents an unpublished version collected by C. F. Voegelin in 1933. It is a long narrative, combining elements found in many of the available Lizard texts. Since it demonstrates the closeness of Shawnee and Yuchi accounts, I summarize this telling here.

Men hunting discover a tree with what appears to be an animal den. The lizard chases and captures six of the seven men in the party, the seventh man remaining unnoticed in a tree near the monster's nest. When the seventh man runs away he encounters the powerful panther who fights the lizard, sacrificing himself and allowing the man to escape. When informed of these events by the escapee, the leaders of his people prepare to go and defeat the lizard. With them they take a medicine bundle and a young girl who is soon to begin to menstruate. On the expedition, the young girl has her period and cooks for herself. The leader obtains ashes from her cooking fire and places them in a rag bundle. The medicine men place these ashes in a mound before the lizard's tree and the men sit and wait to confront it. Singing medicine songs, they await the lizard, which eventually comes out and is overpowered. In order to determine if the lizard had medicine power, the medicine men wait to see if its tree will fall on noon of the following day. When it does, they discover the lizard's young inside the nest. They burn the tree and the lizard corpse. The burning takes four days and four nights, and afterward small pieces of the lizard remained alive. These are taken and used as medicines by the people, each of whom gains powers of his own choosing.

This Shawnee tale collected by Voegelin and reported by Schutz is a masterpiece, and it is regrettable that another version that Schutz indicates that he collected, comprising 136 manuscript pages with commentary, is unpublished. The use of menstrual blood and burning to dispose of the monster, along with the acquisition of medicine power, are motifs shared by both the Yuchi Lizard stories and the widely discussed Cherokee myths concerning the cannibal ogre Stoneclad (Mooney 1900:320; Fogelson 1980).[14]

In light of these comparisons, the stories of the monster lizard break into two groups. The Muskogean stories, while retaining a concern with power, do not relate directly to its provision in the form of collective ritual or the revelation of medicine plants or objects. In contrast, the available Cherokee, Yuchi, and Shawnee narratives share these dimensions and are generally more fully elaborated than the Muskogean stories.[15]

As a topic with a long history of study by scholars, the relationship between myth and ritual has been approached from a myriad of perspectives. In looking at the myths associated with the Yuchi Green Corn rituals, I find their association comparable to Ellen Basso's characterization of Kalapalo myth and ritual, which she describes as possessing thematic homologies. She goes on to note that, among the Kalapalo, "No ritual in its entirety as it might be observed today is ever described in myth, and certainly never in connection with an instrumental goal. The most obvious way, then, that Kalapalo myth and ritual are connected is that myth describes something which we can observe in the present as the most fundamental aspect of ritual performance" (1981:275). I suggest that the same can be said of the Yuchi stories that are used as explanations for ceremonial ground ritual. Many Yuchi dances and ritual episodes lack any explanatory narrative, but these cultural forms are just as significant as those for which there are mythic justifications.

Yuchi ritual leaders sometimes lament that the ability to explain fully the meaning of ceremonial ground rituals passed away with the deaths of earlier generations of ritual leaders. There is a sense in which this is no doubt true, but interpretation is an ongoing process and new insights about the meaning of ritual forms remain to be discovered through contemplation and discussion among current ritualists. This is a process that I have witnessed firsthand and it is a process that was just as likely characteristic of earlier periods in Yuchi ritual life. In thinking about sacred narrative, Franz Boas recognized that each generation in a society forms new readings of inherited cultural materials: "The forms in which the sacred teachings appear at the present time are therefore the cumulative effect of systematic elaboration by individuals, that has progressed through generations" (Boas 1915:340). Earlier investigators among the Yuchi documented many of the same stories that I have recorded, but in those times,

Mary Watashe leads the women of the Polecat Ceremonial Ground in the performance of the Ribbon Dance during their Green Corn Ceremony, 11 July 1998. While a central part of the Yuchi Green Corn Ceremony, no known sacred narrative accounts for the Ribbon Dance in the ways that the Feather and Lizard Dances are explained.

they seem not to have been so closely linked to ritual forms. The present generation of ritual leaders, passionately committed both to cultural preservation and to making ritual knowledge and activity accessible to the Yuchi people at large, have a particular interest in drawing the threads of Yuchi belief together into a coherent narrative that they can articulate to an increasingly interested and inquisitive community.

In looking at Yuchi sacred narrative, it is clear that these stories, even when the narratives of different speakers are similar, possess a range of varied associations and meanings. While the polysemous quality of Yuchi ritual narrative is probably characteristic of such interrelated systems in general, what I have found most rewarding about exploring these questions with Yuchi ritual leaders is their own deep interest in these matters. They possess a strong willingness to make new inquiries among themselves, to reflect upon and refine their own interpretations of myth and ritual, and to extrapolate deeper interpretations based on further consideration and new evidence. In this process they have recently begun to draw on available written accounts, supplementing the oral tellings available to them. During the history discussions held at the Polecat Ceremonial Ground in the summer of 1997, Newman Littlebear linked his knowledge of the published examples of the earth-diver stories that account for the creation of dry land to the Jumping the Hill Dance performed during the Green Corn Ceremony. Admitting that this was only his observation and not a traditional explanation, he went on to note the similarity in the conical shape of the dirt mound built on the square and the dirt mounds that crawfish build in nature. Such refinements and reflections on the meaning and significance of Yuchi ritual and beliefs are constantly emerging. Some are picked up by listeners and circulated as expressions of Yuchi culture, while others remain private or transient. For the Yuchi today, the ethnographic record, rather than codifying belief and stifling this process, provides another resource enabling contemporary ritualists to maintain a dialogue with the old people who served both as consultants to earlier researchers and as the previous generation of Yuchi community leaders.

9 Soup Dance

"Think about the old men that used to be in here."

Men, Women, and Ancestors

Like all Yuchi ceremonies, a variety of meanings and purposes are associated with the Green Corn Ceremony. In exploring some of those in previous chapters, I focused on what I consider to be a dominant concern – the responsibility that Yuchi people feel to perpetuate the beliefs and rituals bestowed by the Creator. In this chapter I examine a prominent theme in the ritual that follows the Green Corn: the Soup Dance. Whereas the Green Corn can be viewed as a moral transaction between the Creator and the Yuchi, the Soup Dance focuses special attention on the ongoing relationship between the present-day Yuchi and the ancestors who passed Yuchi culture and identity down to them.

Within anthropological thought, some of the general social dynamics underlying the rituals of the Yuchi Soup Dance have been well known for some time, at least since Marcel Mauss's (1990) landmark study of ritual exchange, *The Gift*. Despite recent shifts away from his general theoretical outlook, Claude Lévi-Strauss' elaborations upon Mauss's ideas about reciprocity remain useful and can be further extended to explore the meaning of exchange in Yuchi ritual from a semiotic perspective (Lévi-Strauss 1969:52–68, 1987). In the classic social theory of reciprocity developed by Mauss and Lévi-Strauss, the exchange of symbolically manifold goods and services is one of the communicative processes through which social orders are made real and perpetuated through time.

Building on Bronislaw Malinowski's study of the Melanesian "Kula ring" and Franz Boas's exploration of the Northwest Coast "potlatch," the greatest amount of anthropological attention in studies of ritualized exchange has focused on exchanges between individual and corporate social actors (Boas 1966; Malinowski 1961). Nonetheless, ample documentation exists attesting to the diverse ways in which the discharge of obligations of reciprocity may extend beyond a living, human community to encompass a range of other entities including gods, spirits, animals, and ancestors. In this chapter, I wish to describe the Yuchi Soup Dance ritual and some of the social significance that attaches to it. By directing ritual attention toward their ancestors in the Soup Dance and in other events, present-day ceremonial ground members also focus attention more generally on the persistence of Yuchi culture through time. In this aspect, the Soup Dance provides an opportunity for further consideration of how Yuchi people think about Yuchi culture generally.

RITUAL OUTLINE

The Green Corn is a busy ritual event with many parts. The full Yuchi Green Corn Ceremony practiced at Polecat, and more recently at Duck Creek, is exhausting in its fullness, as one ritual episode follows right upon another. The rituals of the Soup Dance are less complicated and demanding. As the major ceremony of the calendar, Green Corn is characterized by an excited mood, whereas the Soup Dance that follows is more slow and contemplative. Although the Green Corn Ceremony attracts marginal participants in ceremonial ground life, only active members of the ground attend the daytime activities at the Soup Dance.

The sketch of the Soup Dance in this chapter is based on the current practice of the Duck Creek and Polecat Ceremonial Grounds. The Sand Creek ground also holds one dance after its Green Corn, and while this event is called a Soup Dance, Sand Creek does not at present follow the soup making and feasting ritual described here. Instead, this last dance provides a second opportunity to fast and use the same redroot medicine taken during the Green Corn Ceremony. While this medicine taking mirrors Creek practice, certain Yuchi elements are retained in the Sand Creek ceremony. Among these are the use of poleboys and the prohibition against dancing nighttime social dances until after the Green Corn Ceremony. Unless otherwise noted, this chapter describes the soup making and feasting of the Soup Dance as performed at both the Duck Creek and Polecat grounds.

As during the Green Corn, families at Duck Creek and Sand Creek prepare for the Soup Dance by refurbishing their camps, moving their equipment back in and cleaning up the site during the week preceding the dance. At Polecat, the Soup Dance follows the Green Corn by one week and families will have remained camped at the ground during that time. In both formats, families often hold meals at the ground during the week before the Soup Dance. In 1997 the Polecat Soup Dance was held on 18–20 July, the Duck Creek Soup Dance on 22–24 August, and the Sand Creek Soup Dance on 20–21 September.

At all three Yuchi grounds, the events of the Soup Dance usually begin on a Friday evening with a half-night of stomp dances. Typically, the only visitors present for this first night of dancing are from the other two Yuchi grounds. Because the Green Corn has already taken place, the restriction on dancing the special nighttime social dances is lifted and one or more dances from this class (Garfish, Sheep, Turtle, Duck, Four-Corners, or Bean) may be danced. In contrast to the Green Corn Ceremony, the Soup Dance rituals held on Saturday are not extensive and strenuous. For this reason, the chief is less concerned about ending the dancing early and the dance may continue until members begin to tire in the early morning. In the absence of visitors, the Friday evening dance provides an opportunity for younger members to practice leading and shaking shells. At the Polecat ground, this dance is the final mid-week dance, culminating the series of dances organized by the poleboys and led by the ground's young people. Most members retire to their homes at the conclusion of the dance, but some may stay over at the ground, spending the evening in their family camps.

On Saturday morning, the chief and his assistants supervise the work of the poleboys, who prepare the corn soup that is the focus of the event. Not long after sunrise, they build up the fire at the center of the square and begin cooking a large iron kettle of corn soup. The soup combines a large quantity of cubed pork and kernel corn, either fresh, frozen, or dried. While the soup cooks directly on the fire, the poleboys tend to it under the supervision of the chief. It will cook for three or more hours and is stirred with a large, paddle-shaped wooden spoon.

As the soup cooks throughout the morning, members continue arriving at the ground. During this time, women prepare a variety of foods in their camps. Some of this food will be contributed to the collective feast, while the remainder will be served to family and visitors in each camp during the evening meal. As men arrive, they begin gathering under the arbors at the square.

Ideally, the Soup Dance feast is held near noon on Saturday, soon after the soup is finished cooking. Most often, the feast actually takes place around 2:00 P.M., when most of the membership has arrived at the ground. As before the Ribbon Dance, and at other times when the chief wishes to survey the progress and preparedness of the campers, before beginning the feast he designates two men as stickmen and instructs them to circle the ground and visit the camps. When called before the chief at the west arbor, they are given the cane sticks that indicate their position. Visiting each camp, they inquire with the cooks about their readiness for the feast. After the first round they report this information back to the chief, who estimates a starting time for the feast. On the following three rounds, the stickmen alert the campers of the time remaining before the feast. After each round, the stickmen return their staves to the chief. He calls on them again when he is ready to make another round to the camps.[1]

After the fourth round of camp visits has been made, the chief or his designee

The poleboys tend the special soup prepared on the square ground fire during the Polecat Ceremonial Ground's Soup Dance, 19 July 1997.

goes to the east side of the square to call in the food. During this phase of the ritual at Duck Creek in 1997, Jimmie Littlehead, a member of the chief's committee who sits under the north arbor, was given the job of calling in the feast. The procedure that he used is identical to that used at Polecat and at Duck Creek in previous years. Having been called to the chief's seat, he was given a hand drum, which he carried to the east side of the square. He began by beating a quick roll on the drum to attract attention. While still drumming, he made four loud whoops and then called out the Yuchi word *k'õdi*, "meat," four times. This was followed by five whoops (four were probably intended) and four calls of the word *k'athl'o*, "bread." After four more whoops, he stopped drumming and the men seated on the square answered "hõ" in unison. Having finished this summons, the caller returned the drum to the chiefs' arbor. Following such a summons, men who have not already done so retrieve plates, cups, and utensils from their camps, bringing these to their seats in the square.

The women bring bowls and plates of food from their camps to the earth berm at the edge of the square. Arriving at this boundary, men seated in the square meet them and receive the food that they have brought. These dishes of food are arranged buffet-style. At Polecat, a table covered with a tablecloth will have been borrowed from one of the camps and placed by the poleboys on the

Chief Simon Harry (standing) oversees preparations for the feast held on the town square during the Duck Creek Ceremonial Ground's Soup Dance, 23 August 1997. At Duck Creek, the foods that are contributed by the women of the camps are placed under the chief's arbor, as has been done here.

square just north of the chiefs' arbor. At Duck Creek, the food is placed on the ground between the front and back benches of the chiefs' arbor. If there is not enough room here, food will also be placed similarly under the north warriors' arbor. Ideally, each camp contributes four items (typically bread, meat, vegetable, and fruit) to the feast on the square, but the amounts and types vary in practice.

Having brought the food to the edge of the square, the women retire to their camps. When the men are settled in their seats, the chief typically calls on his speaker to deliver a short oration on the meaning and themes of the soup feast. As both an example of the genre and as exegesis on these points, I present Newman Littlebear's Soup Dance feast speech at the Duck Creek ground in 1997. It is comparable to the speeches that he gave at Duck Creek in 1996 and at Polecat in 1996 and 1997. As in other speech-making situations, this speech was delivered in front of the chiefs' arbor following a brief conference with Simon Harry, the ground's chief.

TEXT 22

A speech made before the Soup Dance feast at the Duck Creek Ceremonial Ground. Delivered by Newman Littlebear, 23 August 1997.

All right, well.
Let me have your attention.
The chief asked me to say something to you all, this . . .
    again.
I talked to you all last night, you know, about this.
What we're going to do today.
So
    it has come to this time and
    we're here again
    still trying to carry on.
And
    we call it Soup Dance, we said.
And
    the boys prepare
    food
    corn.
We might say it is a new year.
Then we always have a new crop
    new harvest.

So we use that new corn at this time too
also.
We use it maybe after we took medicine. [during the Green Corn
Ceremony]
And
again,
but this time we are going to share
feed the fire
what the boys cooked.
We always say we have to take care of this. [the fire]
Old ones called
called this
Grandpa.
It is just like a human.
We talk to it just like
a human.
When you <<make>>
songs and prayers
they go on from here
like through this way,
goes on to
above
to the Creator.
And he knows
what we're doing.
He understands it
because he
he provided this
this way to our
forefathers.
And too
we can think
ever since
like
some of us [were] young boys like y'all
Simon and me and maybe Virgil and somemore.
We was here
working like some of y'all
young boys.
And

many of our forefathers
used to make tracks here.
Visitors
friends
come and join here.
But they always . . .
they always believe
maybe we don't believe that way.
maybe we don't think
maybe we don't think too strong
maybe we are weak.
But that was the way they believed.
They say,
when you used to be here
when something is going on
they are going to
they're going to return.
Spirits are going to return
take part with us.
So
we can look
we can think
we can
sometimes talk about
some of those
elders that went on.
We still talk about them.
They used to be here.
Maybe sometimes something they said or
maybe in here or
maybe around-about in our lives
well, we remember.
But a l l of them
maybe they was close to us.
They might have been our
father
some of them was
brother
or sister

or mother
or grandma.
But this, they say,
is how we all join together
at a time like this
in fellowship with one another
in a good way.
So
I just pass that on to you.
So
and fellowship with this one. [the fire, representing the Creator]
They say, when we sit around here like this
this one
is glad.
Feels good.
Got feelings.
That's the way they talked.
And ah
they know everything.
They said conduct yourself
in a nice manner
always.
Perhaps, you know
sometimes we have a lot of fun in here
sometimes we talk
maybe
maybe tell a funny joke or something, you know
maybe about some of them that's gone on even.
That's how we fellowship.
That's the way they say.
And we take it in a good way.
So
I guess these boys now they are going to take care of that business.
They said, like
this one has got to have a drink
has got to have food
to be strong.
This is the way they say.
So

        we're still trying to do that
        we're still trying to carry on.
So
        you young ones
        you remember
        remember that
        you have to take care of this
        because it is the main one
        and the medicine
        all goes together.
But, it is for us to use.
And, our friends come and join with us
        relatives.
Sometimes we don't see relatives for
        maybe
        once a year
        maybe
        but they come here sometimes.
That is the way that it is.
But we can think about . . .
        I can think about them OLDMEN
        that used to be in here and work
        work around in here and be with us.
Perhaps we say spirit
        why, that is the way it is.
We don't see 'em
        but they say they are in here
        they be with us
        help us
        help us along.
When there is just a few of us
        we think about that
        and maybe brace up.
Maybe we are going to get tired sometime tonight.
But
        we won't, we look forward to tonight.
We said it's going to be good.
No matter,
        no matter what

it is still good
for us.

So

we're going to go ahead now with what them boys got to do.

So, I thank you all for your attention.

[Men answer:] *Hõ.*

In 1997, Simon Harry did not call a business meeting for the ground, but if he had, he would have asked for the time of this meeting to be announced.

At Duck Creek and Polecat grounds, Soup Dance is the time, as Mr. Littlebear noted in his speech, at which the sacred fire is "fed." This takes place after the men have assembled and any speeches have been delivered. From his seat under the west arbor, the chief directs two poleboys in this task. First a ladle of corn soup is taken from the pot resting in the northwest corner of the square. The poleboy moves to the fire, and standing on the west side facing east, pours the soup on the coals. After this action is completed, the men acknowledge it by responding "hõ" in unison. After the poleboy retires to the west, the second one carries a dipper full of medicine, usually spicewood medicine, to the west side of the fire and pours this on the coals. The assembled men also acknowledge this offering of a "drink" to the fire.

At Sand Creek, where the soup feast is not conducted, the fire is fed in a similar manner during the Green Corn Ceremony. As among the Oklahoma Creek and Seminole, the red root medicine and a beef tongue are used for this purpose. The same rationale is given in all three cases.

After the fire is fed, the men begin their meal, filling their plates from the buffet and returning to their seats. Before eating, the chief or another elderly man will typically remind the men to face forward in their seats while eating and visiting under the arbors. In this way they are physically in fellowship with the Creator's spirit, manifest in the fire, and with the ancestral spirits who are then present in the square.

During the meal, there is normal conversation among the men seated under each arbor. If a speech was not delivered before the meal, the speaker might be asked to speak as the men conclude it. While the men are still gathered on the square, but before they are dismissed, women will approach the square with empty bowls, which they provide to their kinsmen. The men fill those bowls with the corn and pork soup and return them to the women. This soup is carried back to each camp, where the women add it to the food prepared there. The women of each camp will also eat a brief mid-day meal that includes the soup. Meanwhile, they continue preparations for the evening meal.

As men finish their meal, they return to their campsites and, after depositing their utensils, many will return to the square to continue socializing. At Polecat the men are obligated to return with a piece of wood. This wood is placed on the woodpile to the south of the chiefs' arbor. After each man places his wood on the pile, those men remaining under the arbors or lingering in the vicinity of the square acknowledge this contribution by shouting "hõ" in the same manner that public proclamations and speeches are ratified.[2]

After all of the men have finished eating, the chief directs the poleboys to clean up the remains of the meal. Women are now permitted to enter the square and reclaim the empty bowls and dishes. The poleboys at Polecat remove the table and throughout the remainder of the afternoon, the poleboys at both grounds maintain the fire on the square.

During the recess between the feast on the square and the afternoon ground meeting, the members socialize informally. At Duck Creek and Polecat, several games of horseshoes are usually played, perhaps even in an organized tournament. At Duck Creek, stickball may also be played during the afternoon. In the past, elders remember informal games of Indian football being played as well.

An end-of-the-season business meeting is optional and is called at the discretion of the chief. If it is to be held, the members gather at the appointed time on the square. All of the men sit under or adjacent to the chiefs' arbor, regardless of arbor group membership. The chief and his assistants take their normal places on the front bench. The women sit in lawn chairs in the corners at the northwest and southwest. During this meeting, the chief, speaking for himself or through his speaker, summarizes his feelings about the outcome of the year's ceremonial activities and relays any decisions or instructions that he wishes be made known. If he has appointed new people to serve as assistants or as committeemen, he makes those changes known at this time. In all of the annual meetings that I have observed at Duck Creek and at Polecat, the chief has always made a point of praising and thanking the members for their efforts and contributions during the year.

All members, both men and women, then are given an opportunity to speak. Usually older individuals begin making statements, but all adults have the right to stand and speak. Problems or concerns are aired, and members who wish to testify to the successful outcome of the year's activities may do so as well. In addressing problems, everyone can take turns at speaking and the meeting can be as short or as long as necessary. Within the context of the square and in a ritual setting, disputes and concerns about problems are typically aired very cautiously and nonconfrontationally. In such instances, open discussion among

The members of the Polecat Ceremonial Ground assemble in and around the Chief's Arbor on the square for a community meeting during their Soup Dance, 20 July 1996.

the members moves the group toward consensus, with the chief intervening only to keep the discussion focused and on track. Ground meetings normally wind down rather than fill a set period of time, as everything that is going to be said, is said. At the conclusion of the ground meeting the chief or speaker will announce the time at which the evening dance is expected to begin.[3]

Following the meeting, the members break up and return to games and socializing. Around sundown, the patterns characteristic of a regular stomp dance begin to resume. Arriving guests from other communities are invited to join individual families for an evening meal in the camps. After dark, the chief begins preparations for the evening dance. In addition to the regular stomp dance episodes, a feature of the evening dance is special performances of the nighttime social dances. Although they may be practiced during the week at Polecat and on Friday evening at all of the grounds, those dances are fully performed on the Saturday evening dance during the Soup Dance when all of the adult membership of the ground is present.

RESPONSIBILITIES OF THE LIVING

The Soup Dance feast is not the only Yuchi ritual episode focusing on reunion with the ancestors. In the Bead Dance, the fourth of the Feather Dances danced

Signaling the spirits of the deceased that it is time to return to the square ground to participate with the living in the Green Corn Ceremony, the women of the Duck Creek community toss white beads on the heads of the men while they perform the Bead Dance, one of the Feather Dances. 21 June 1997.

during the daytime of the Green Corn Ceremony, the women approach the edge of the dance area east of the square. They position themselves in the corners of the area where the men dance a circular figure around the two singers. As the men dance, the women toss small white glass beads over and onto their heads. These beads are a signal to the ancestor spirits that they are invited into the square to participate with the living in the remainder of the ceremony.

In the course of community oral history discussions in the summer of 1997, several older Yuchi people recalled that beads were similarly thrown over the heads of the women while they danced the Ribbon Dance. Current ground leaders from Polecat and Duck Creek took this information and discussed their intention to reintroduce this practice during the 1998 ceremonies. In discussion, participants reasoned that the throwing of beads during the Ribbon Dance served as an invitation for the female ancestors to participate and worried that this omission had excluded them in recent years.

The throwing of beads as a signal to ancestors in the Bead and Ribbon Dances is related to a practice featured in the ceremony used to give a Yuchi name to a child. In this ritual, which is only rarely practiced today, a child is presented with a string of tiny white beads. When given a Yuchi name by an elder selected by the family, the string is tied around the child's wrist or neck and is worn until it breaks off. According to some informants, the string is dipped into water before being given to the child (Speck 1909:93–94).[4] With the exception of aspects related to the Shawnee clans or name groups, the Yuchi naming ceremony is identical to the ritual of their allies (C. Voegelin and E. Voegelin 1935). Although the use of beads in the naming ceremony was not explained to contemporary Yuchi elders, their use as ritual currency in ceremonies associated with ancestral spirits and themes of inter-generational continuity is widespread in the Eastern Woodlands, occurring in the rituals of the Tutelo (Speck 1942; Kurath 1981), Nanticoke (Speck 1937), Delaware (Miller 1997; Roark-Calnek 1977), Cayuga (Speck 1995), and other tribes.

Communication with, and the hosting of, ancestral spirits is also a primary feature of Yuchi funeral ritual. The firing of guns as a signal to ancestors before and during funeral ritual was mentioned incidentally in chapter 8. In addition, an obsolete practice that was once the focal event in old Yuchi funerals was a ghost feast in which the spirit of the deceased joined with returning ancestral spirits in a feast prepared by older women and accompanied by detailed rituals directed by a medicine man chosen to oversee all aspects of the funeral.[5] Older Yuchi people who participated in the old funeral feasts equate the two events as variations on a common theme. In both the funeral feast and the Soup Dance feast, the spirits of the Yuchi ancestors return to the world of the living. Here they consume the spirit essence of the food offered to them and celebrate with their living kinsmen who partake of the food's physical essence. The primary difference in the two ritual forms, something that Mr. Littlebear noted in an extended oratory on the evening previous to the speech presented above, is that young boys have always been welcome to participate in the Soup Dance feast, whereas children were always kept away from the funeral feast, and particularly kept from eating the food, because it was considered too spiritually powerful for them.

In some of its manifestations in Woodland ritual, the spiritual transaction in ghost feasts and related phenomena is conceived explicitly as a payment by the living to the dead, made in order to maintain harmonious relations with them and to avoid the sickness or disruption that lonely or hungry spirits might cause. While some Yuchi elders articulate these themes, particularly regarding the funeral feast, the Soup Dance feast today, as well as the bead-tossing invitations extended to the dead to participate in the Green Corn, are mostly interpreted more positively as proper behavior toward the "old people." When Yuchi people discuss Yuchi ancestors, they frequently do so in the context of explicitly discussing overt Yuchi culture, framed as tradition. Both in its poetic structure and overt content, the concern with ancestors and with cultural continuity through time is the dominant theme both of Mr. Littlebear's speech and of much formal and informal ceremonial ground discourse.

MEN AND WOMEN, AGAIN

In addition to the reciprocal relationship expressed in the rationale for the Soup Dance feast, another central social relationship is highlighted in its ritual form. As also evidenced in the obsolete practice of food wagering in the Yuchi football games, one central form of Yuchi ritual exchange rests "on the equations general among Woodlands people between men, hunting, and wild game, on the one hand, and between women, agriculture, and corn on the other" (Roark-Calnek 1977:173). In dramatic form, the Soup Dance feast highlights the basic complementary gender divisions that underlie the ceremonialism of the Yuchi and all of the horticultural peoples of the East. As in cognate performances among their present and former neighbors, the exchange of male and female foods is an important act within the Soup Dance Ceremony.

The ongoing gender beliefs expressed in the Soup Dance feast illustrate the capacity for cultural patterns to persist within changing social contexts. Yuchi women today obtain corn and corn meal at the supermarket, while men obtain pork or beef tongue at the butcher's shop.[6] Despite these changes, the overt patterns and covert dispositions related to gender, expressed in Yuchi belief and ritual, retain close continuity with the past. This phenomenon was well described by Clyde Kluckhohn: "The substantive aspects of a culture may alter in important features, but to the observer with experience of that culture even the new overt content somehow has a familiar tone. The same holds on a synchronic plane for different sectors of the same culture. One may be attending the Navajo chant 'Beauty Way' for the first time, but if one has had a fairly rich experience of other chants one feels quite at home" (1941:127). They are sometimes conscious and sometimes unconscious in nature, but the existence of such deep, general cultural premises about the world, like the appropriateness of Yuchi gender differences, have profound effects. Like the first-time visitor to the Beauty Way chant described by Kluckhohn, other Woodland ceremonialists can recognize shared concerns built into the pattern of Yuchi ritual. This factor supports the intertribal participation in tribal ceremonialism that I began describing in chapter 5. For Yuchi ritual leaders, the existence of general patterns and configurations underlying specific ritual forms allows them to adjust and maintain communal ritual life in ways attuned to the general ethos of Yuchi culture through time.

A brief example, relevant to the larger discussion, can be brought forward to illustrate this point. In 1997, the Polecat chief introduced an innovation in the ground's social organization. Responding to longstanding difficulties (found at all three grounds) in regulating the Ribbon Dance and other activities focused on women during the Green Corn, the chief appointed a new women's committee to provide communication among the ground's women and to provide information and suggestions to the chief and ground committee. The leading woman in the Ribbon Dance was appointed to chair this committee.

Although new to the Yuchi, similar women's committees are a longstanding feature of ritual congregations elsewhere in the Woodlands. The Yuchi innovation during the Soup Dance meeting at Polecat in 1997 suggests latent preexisting cultural dispositions. Other alternatives, such as appointing female representatives to the general committee, were not even discussed. The chief's solution was congruent with the existing framework, in which women undertake separate activities with distinct purposes in a fashion appropriate to women.

The problem prompting the creation of this committee – regulating the Ribbon Dance – is itself an outcome of the general orientation under discussion here. The stickmen and other men who assist in directing the Ribbon Dance during the Green Corn tend, not unexpectedly, to be hesitant to intervene or impose their will on a markedly female activity. Lacking a formalized means of organizing themselves, the women did not have a mechanism for sorting out conflicts, particularly disputes over precedence in the dance line. The Polecat Ribbon Dance is perhaps the largest such dance in Oklahoma (among the Creek, Yuchi, and Seminole) with over sixty dancers in 1996 and 1997. Because many women see each other only once a year during the Green Corn, disagreements, taking the form of differing interpretations of appropriate behavior, are understandable. Unlike the case of the men, who have many opportunities for the exchange of views on ritual matters, the women are isolated in their camps during much ceremonial ground activity. In contrast to the men, they lack an opportunity to collectively discuss women's aspects of ritual culture. Thus the women at present rely on family-based understandings of what is appropriate, distributing women's ritual knowledge much more unevenly than among their male counterparts.

The case of Polecat, which, as the mother ground, combines high Green Corn attendance with low general participation, has some unique features and the institution of a women's committee will probably not be replicated at the two smaller grounds. Nonetheless, the innovation fits well with the general ethos of Yuchi ritual culture. The new committee arrangement, emerging out of the town hall democracy of the Soup Dance business meeting, is a very Yuchi (and very Woodland) solution to the kinds of challenges that all communities, ritual or otherwise, face in maintaining harmonious social relations.

THE SOUP DANCE IN COMPARATIVE PERSPECTIVE

The specific configuration of ritual forms found in the Yuchi Soup Dance is unique, yet the event, as already suggested, shares patterns, episodes, and concerns with ceremonies among other Woodland Indian communities. Those rituals fall into two functional groupings: harvest ceremonies and memorials to returning ancestors. All share with Yuchi ritual the same capacity for manifesting multiple meanings and significances simultaneously. Consideration of the Soup Dance comparatively provides a richer context within which to understand both the themes that it shares with related ceremonials and those features that mark it as a distinctly Yuchi event.

In its concern for reuniting with tribal ancestors and satisfying their desire for fellowship with the living, the Yuchi Soup Dance is closely related to the Ghost Dance practiced by the Cayuga and other Longhouse Iroquois on the Six Nations Reserve in Canada (Speck 1995; Fenton and Kurath 1951). In this ceremonial, a feast is prepared by the women, but a special corn soup is cooked by a pair of male officials. As among the Yuchi, this is the only instance in which men prepare food for a ceremonial occasion. This feast is both presented to the spirits who return for the event and is eaten in a celebratory mood by the living congregants. Special dances are held and "it is believed that the dead are present in the Longhouse during the ceremony to receive the various forms of sacrifice and to participate in the song and dance" (Fenton and Kurath 1951:160). Unlike the Yuchi Soup Dance, the Iroquois ritual is organized by female officials. Despite this structural difference and a host of specific variations in dance and ritual performance separating the Iroquois and Yuchi rites, several overarching themes are clearly shared. In addition to a common focus on assembling with the ancestors, both reiterate the division of male and female roles. Also shared is a common mood, articulated for the Iroquois rite by William Fenton and Gertrude Kurath: "The Dead Feast is clearly more than a mourning ceremony. One might infer this from the lack of mournfulness: In fact, the dignified gaiety which pervades the gathering highlights the social nature of such communal rituals which also include the dead. . . . Thus the community unites in a pleasant evening of song, dance and feasting, including the living and visible and also the great invisible assembly of the nation since time immemorial" (1951:164). While the Iroquois ritual possesses unique dances and ritual actions (although these share with Yuchi forms a common Woodland style), Fenton and Kurath's observations characterize the Yuchi Soup Dance so well that the same motivations appear to underlie both events. Both ceremonies represent a manifestation of common themes found throughout Woodland Indian religious practice.

Not unexpectedly, a cognate ritual event is also found among the Shawnee.

Like the Yuchi Soup Dance, Shawnee Ghost Feasts are held during the weeks following the midsummer ceremonial (the Green Corn among the Loyal Shawnee, and the War Dance among the Absentee Shawnee). Shawnee feasts are a family event rather than a collective ritual, as is the case with the Soup Dance. The Shawnee form mirrors the ghost feast found during Yuchi funeral rites. A meal is prepared and then left alone for several hours or overnight to be consumed by the spirits of deceased family members who return to the world of the living for this occasion. After the family returns, the living then may consume the food on which the spirits have feasted (Howard 1981:286–87). According to James Howard, the Oklahoma Seneca-Cayuga, combining aspects of Yuchi and Shawnee practice, perform a similar family-based ghost feast in their family camps after their Green Corn Ceremony but before departing the ceremonial grounds (1961:27).

Although the cultural rationale of maintaining friendly contact with tribal ancestors demonstrates Yuchi affinities with Northeastern peoples, the specific form that the Soup Dance ritual takes echoes ceremonies of their Southeastern neighbors that are concerned with celebrating the end of the agricultural phase of the year, characterized as female and symbolized by corn, and the beginning of the hunting season, characterized as male and symbolized by wild game. Some modern Oklahoma Creek and Seminole grounds also have a ceremonial event known as the Soup Dance, or the Squirrel Soup Dance. Howard describes it as follows:

> The final event of the year is the Soup Dance. This is essentially just another all-night Stomp, but soup, cooked in a single large cauldron, is served to the dancers toward morning, together with loaves of Indian corn bread. The soup must be from wild game, such as squirrels, or in default of this, from "home raised" chickens (not supermarket poultry). The Creeks serve these foods right in the dance ground, but the Seminoles in one of the adjacent camps. In either case, preparation of the food is a ritual act, and two respected matrons are appointed for the task. Another distinctive feature of the Soup Dance is that it ends in the morning with a performance of the Morning or Drunken Dance, not otherwise performed. [Howard and Lena 1984:121–22]

As Howard suggests, correctly I believe, the modern Creek Seminole Soup Dance is derived from the older, obsolete Horned Owl Dance that was described in 1928 by John Swanton on the basis of informant testimony (1928b:525–27). What Howard failed to note is that this event has been preserved in a fuller form among the Florida Seminole and Miccosukee.[7] Available descriptions of this ceremony shed comparative light both on the corresponding Shawnee event (the Fall Bread Dance) and the Yuchi Soup Dance.

Swanton's description of the Creek Horned Owl Dance and Feast can be summarized as follows. Danced in September, it was administered by two men who carried long cane poles decorated with a wooden hoop, deer tails, "and sometimes a loaf of bread" (1928b:525). Like the male officials in the Iroquois Ghost Dance, those special stickmen visited each household, informing members of the upcoming dance. The use of special staffs as badges of office for ritual officers mirrors the case of Yuchi poleboys and the stickmen among the Creek, Yuchi, Shawnee, and Seminole. A special serpentine dance was associated with the event. At one point in the proceedings, the old man who served as singer took one of the hoop batons and placed the hoop over the heads of various women. While placing the hoop on their shoulders, the old man commanded each to "make bread." Another man counted off the women so selected "and when he made the last count all of the men said 'Oh' in a very high pitched tone" (1928b:526). This last feature mirrors the Yuchi practice of collectively ratifying formal selection of ritual officers by a chief or appointed leader.

After appointing these cooks, the dance broke up and the men departed on a hunt for venison and other game. Two weeks later they returned with roasted meat. On their return to the square, they announced their arrival with a gunshot and then prepared a special scaffold on which to place the meat. The women arrived with dishes of bread. The men and women formally exchanged their symbolic food contributions. For several nights the ritual exchange of gendered foods took place and the spiraling Horned Owl Dance was danced. Another account obtained by Swanton noted that this dance took place after summer, when the snakes returned to their holes. Parallels to the Yuchi Soup Dance practice can be found in most of these features and Swanton's description makes sense in light of fuller materials available on the Florida Seminole and Miccosukee Horned Owl or Hunting Dance. My description of the procedures draws first on the Seminole Hunting Dance participated in by Louis Capron in 1943.

In Florida the early fall timing of the dance matches Oklahoma practice. As in Oklahoma, several days of dancing are interrupted by a collective hunt by the men, during which the women cook corn foods. As in Oklahoma, two poles decorated with hoops and deer tails are focal symbols carried by the two heralds. Like the Yuchi poleboys serving during the Green Corn, the young men who carry these poles in the Florida Hunting Dance must carry them "when ever they were on official business" (Capron 1956:71). As Capron notes, "This was sometimes awkward, especially when they were carrying the food brought by the women onto the dance ground" (1956:71). The transfer of food from men to women at the edge of the dance ground also parallels the Yuchi Soup Dance technique. Capron was told that the hoops represented snakes and that the deer tail was used because deer are never bitten by snakes.

As among the Oklahoma Creek, the Florida ceremonialists build a platform for the products of their hunt. After returning from it, the men prepare the meat and then make arrangements for the feast. Among their activities is another Yuchi-Seminole parallel: "At 3:15 P.M. about 22 men and boys gathered at the dance ground and marched off in a single file. About 5 of the men had axes. In course of time they returned, still single file, each carrying a log or a large branch of wood. This seemed to be more ritualistic than otherwise, since there was already a big pile of wood, and they contented themselves with one trip, and no one came back heavily loaded. This procedure took about 20 minutes" (Capron 1956:74). The token contribution of each male participant of one piece of wood occurs not only in the Yuchi Soup Dance, but in the Friday afternoon feast held before the Green Corn at the Polecat ground. The single file march of men, in this case into the woods with axes to cut wood, is another familiar ritual image. This instance is most reminiscent of the cutting of leaf brooms during the Yuchi Arbor Dance clean-up.

Once ready, the men in the Seminole ritual assembled the meat near the benches on the edge of the dance ground (as in the Yuchi practice of setting the feast). The women brought the food from the camps to the perimeter of the dance area, where it was claimed by the two male officials.

Before eating the feast foods, the evening dance was begun. Four poles were erected at the corners of the dance area, around which the dancers were led in a spiral figure. Before setting up the poles, the two boys swept the square with leafy boughs. Capron was unable to remain at the dance and departed before the feast was eaten.

While Capron's (1956) "Notes" has the value of a first-hand observational account, William Sturtevant's interviews with Mikasuki-speaking Florida Seminoles produced more detailed information on the meaning of the dance. He indicates that the Hunting Dance is "a circumlocution to avoid offending snakes," and that the dance is also known as the Snake Dance, Horned Owl Dance, Twisting Dance, and Holding-Hands Dance.[8] In the dance itself "the dancers impersonate a snake, and the dance figure represents the snake's motion; it is also said that the dance represents the horned-owl, the 'friend' of the snake according to the myths" (1955:411). A feast takes place near midnight on each of the evening dances during the first four days. After the communal hunt of the fifth day, the activities observed by Capron take place and climax with the feast. In the first phase, a special soup is eaten. In the second phase, pairs of men and women exchange meat and corn bread loaves. In the third phase, the feast foods are eaten by the men seated in the arbor and the women seated separately, nearby.

Sturtevant learned that the staffs are made and exchanged by the two moieties, reflecting in ritual a second dual division in addition to the gender distinction. The hoops, according to his informants, represented the loaves of bread, while the tails represented the deer. The rationale given for the whole affair is that it placates the snakes. The dance pays the snakes for the game that Seminole hunters take and assuages their displeasure with the people, thus helping prevent both snakebite and sickness induced by snakes.

A different collection of data further expands the areal context for the Horned-Owl/Hunting/Soup Dance complex. Documenting Native ceremonial life in nineteenth- and early twentieth-century Louisiana and east Texas, Victoria Levine has drawn upon a range of unpublished documentary and oral historical sources. Among these are ethnographic field notes that Swanton made among the Koasati in 1910 near Kidder, Louisiana. For the multi-ethnic Indian community there, he reports that the Horned-Owl Dance

> lasted four nights and [participants] played ball all day. [Participants] did not sleep all this time. Men cooked the meat and the women bread during this dance. At supper time all sat down to eat cross-legged around the fire. Four men cooked and brought meat and put it in front of the women. Four women cooks brought bread and set it down in front of the men. After that the chief talked and then all sang, men and women. They sang the song of the Horned-Owl Dance. The Chief then talked again and told them, "Now get up." The women picked up the meat and the men the bread. They went to another place (the dance ground) and mixed the food all up and they ate. After that they danced all night. [quoted in Levine 1991:195]

Swanton's description, based on the testimony of Jackson Langley, both reveals the existence of the Horned-Owl Dance ceremony among the Koasati and their neighbors and captures the significant place of gender-marked food exchange within it.

In addition to drawing attention to an interesting and as yet little-noticed Southeastern ceremonial event, this extended description of the Creek and Seminole Horned Owl/Hunting Dance provides a noteworthy case illustrating the complexities of local variation in Woodland ritual life. The modern Yuchi Soup Dance shares its primary ritual rationale with cognate ceremonies found among the Iroquois and historically related Northeastern groups, but its form closely parallels a second set of rituals, having a different primary purpose, found among the Yuchi's Southeastern neighbors. I have, throughout this work, suggested that the Yuchi occupy a median, transitional position in the

Woodlands between Northeastern and Southeastern peoples. In this context, the case of the Soup Dance and its analogs is valuable in illustrating how complex local configurations of areal patterns result in cultural forms and performances that are simultaneously familiar and unique across community contexts. This sameness and differentness is the same balance that supports intertribal participation in social occasions like the stomp dance, while maintaining tribal boundaries in the preservation of locally specific ritual complexes.

In rounding out this sketch of parallel ceremonies, mention should be made of the Shawnee Bread Dance. Held both at the beginning (spring) and end (fall) of the ceremonial year at all contemporary Shawnee ceremonial grounds, it shares features of ritual form with the Yuchi, Creek, and Seminole Soup Dance and the older Creek-Seminole Horned Owl Dance. In it, a party of male hunters and a group of female cooks are selected to obtain and prepare the gendered foods of wild game and corn bread. Pointing to its connection to the Horned Owl (or Hunting, or Snake) Dance is the particular feature of appointing the officials by placing a hoop, decorated with seeds and animal fur, over the heads of the twelve men chosen to serve as hunters and the twelve women chosen to serve as cooks. Among the other features held in common between the events is the firing of guns as a signal by the returning hunters. The Shawnee Bread Dance is in turn closely related in form and purpose to the Iroquois Harvest Dance, to aspects of the Delaware Big House Ceremony, and to a phase of the Oklahoma Seneca-Cayuga Green Corn Ceremony in which foods are displayed in the center of the ceremonial ground before a feast.

NIGHTTIME SOCIAL DANCES

The daytime feast is the focal ritual event of the Soup Dance, but a second distinctive feature of considerable importance to the Yuchi is the performance of their repertory of special nighttime dances. Just as the Soup Dance feast has been examined in light of its expressions of concern with cultural continuity, the performance of these dances, whose primary function is social, can also be understood as a manifestation of Yuchi concern with the maintenance and preservation of their ceremonial patrimony.

The category of named social dances is shared by all of the Woodland tribes in Oklahoma and the eastern United States. In most cases, the music and choreography for these dances is shared, with local modifications, across the whole region. The Yuchi today perform five dances belonging to the social dance category. These are the Four Corners Dance, Sheep Dance (also called the Doubleheader Dance), Duck Dance, Garfish Dance, and Turtle Dance. The first four dances are known to be performed by other groups, but the Yuchi possess their

Table 5. Social Dance Performances during the Yuchi Soup Dances, 1997

Polecat	Duck Creek
Yuchi Old Folks Dance	Creek Guinea Dance
Yuchi Sheep Dance	Yuchi Four Corners Dance
Yuchi Turtle Dance	Seminole Bean Dance
Yuchi Duck Dance	Yuchi Turtle Dance
Yuchi Four Corners Dance	Shawnee Bear Dance

own song and choreographic variations for them. The Turtle Dance is the most complicated of the Yuchi social dances and is viewed as unique to the Yuchi.[9] In addition to these dances, those of other tribes, led by visitors, may also be danced during the nighttime dance at the Soup Dance. There is no mandated order of performance and some dances may be omitted during a given year. The social dances performed during the Yuchi Soup Dances during 1997 illustrate typical performance patterns (table 5). Tribal affiliations are those of the lead singer. Dances are listed in the order of performance during the night.[10]

In addition to dancing these at their own Soup Dances, Yuchi leaders are sometimes requested to lead social dances while visiting the grounds of other tribes, which they are willing to do after the Yuchi Green Corn Ceremonies have been held. During 1996, visiting Yuchi delegations led the Turtle Dance twice, with Newman Littlebear acting as lead singer on both occasions. The first occurrence was at the Little Axe (North) War Dance and the second was at the fall stomp dance sponsored by the Ottawa Tribe. This generalized practice of reciprocity is evident in the list of dances performed during the Duck Creek Soup Dance in 1997. Visitors from many different communities led those performances. In organizing a program and inserting social dances into the ongoing series of dances, the chief will consult with and guide the stickman, who makes the necessary arrangements.

As has already been mentioned, the Polecat ground's practice of camping in and dancing during the week between the Green Corn and the Soup Dance provides additional opportunities to practice and perform those dances at that ground. In addition, they are sometimes also included in the recently developed indoor dances that are held increasingly during the winter season when the ceremonial grounds are inactive.

The specific conditions under which social dances may be performed away from the ceremonial grounds have not been fully established. In 1993, the Duck Creek Ceremonial Ground was recruited to present a short stomp dance demonstration in June at the annual Creek Nation festival. Having agreed to lead this short, daytime dance, the leaders were later startled when the publicity provided by the festival organizers in the Creek Nation government stated that the Duck Creek members would perform the Turtle Dance and other social dances. Anxious not to seem ungrateful for the invitation, the Duck Creek leaders nonetheless refused to perform those dances, explaining that they were not to do so prior to their Green Corn Ceremony. In 1997, during planning for their own, first ever, Euchee Heritage Days festival, the Yuchi ceremonial ground leaders discussed the appropriateness of performing those dances. The event was scheduled for late November and the elders involved in festival planning thought that to do so would be acceptable, especially since it would provide exposure to those dances for a large number of Yuchi people in the context of a celebration of Yuchi traditional culture. This discussion raised questions about the specific nature of the rules governing the performance of those dances. An interview that I conducted in 1995 with James Brown, Sr., chief of the Polecat ground, became a component of this debate:

TEXT 23

Comments on Yuchi social dances made during an interview with Chief Jim Brown. Tulsa, Oklahoma, 18 November 1995.

We don't ever dance other dances until we go through with our medicine days.

[Jason] Can you dance them at a wintertime dance, inside, since that is after Green Corn?

Well, like that, I guess you could dance them, yeah. You could dance them if there was somebody to lead it. At the beginning of a New Year, we don't sing those songs. Before that, I guess you could go ahead and have it, different dances, like we dance on the inside, you know, or outside, if it is not too cold.

While providing approval for dancing the social dances after the end of the ceremonial ground season, the interview with the respected late chief left the meaning of "New Year" unclear. Some participants in this ongoing discussion perceived this to mean the calendar New Year, effectively banning the dances after midwinter. Others define "New Year" within the ritual cycle, pointing to the first football game as the beginning of a new ceremonial year. This situation is a prototype for the kinds of decisions that Yuchi ritual leaders must make in continually adapting an ancient culture to a modern time while keeping faith with the (always partial) instructions handed down from the past.

Sympathetic observers of Woodland music and dance have commented repeatedly about the decline in the practice of social dances in Oklahoma and elsewhere. On Creek dances, Claude Medford wrote, "The simpler stomp dances became more popular, and fewer and fewer of the shell shakers learned the complicated rhythms and dance movements necessary in the animal dances. Each Green Corn season sees more and more of these animal dances dropped from the Ceremonial, and many towns and stomp grounds have few or none of them as the songs have been forgotten" (1970). Writing about the same dances in the 1980s among the Seminole and Shawnee, James Howard echoed Medford's pessimism (1981:315; see also Howard and Lena 1984:180). Their negative assessment derives from the fact that, among each of the Oklahoma tribes, specific dances are known to have become obsolete during the twentieth century. From his work in 1904–5, Frank Speck identified the following Yuchi social dances: Big Turtle, Duck, Horse, Buzzard, Rabbit, Catfish, Leaf, Chicken, Owl, Drunken, and Shawnee (1909:124–30). Yuchi elders know the Drunk or Morning Dance, or at least some of its songs, today, but the dance was consciously discontinued as part of mid-century efforts to discourage drinking at the ceremonial grounds.[11] Of the other dances, the Horse Dance is remembered by most present-day elders and was last led by Clarence Brown, father of Chief James Brown, Sr. The other named social dances have not been performed at least since the 1940s, when current ceremonial ground leaders began active, adult involvement in the ceremonial grounds.

As Medford suggests, the loss of these dances derives from the failure of younger men to learn the necessary songs and movements. The loss of social dances is acknowledged by current Yuchi elders and motivates their own strong desires to see the remaining dances preserved. Chief Brown's public comments are typical of the period of my work: "I told those guys that we better sing some of those old songs, different songs, let this younger generation learn them or if we don't, we'll lose them, like the rest of them. We lost a lot of songs that we should have been singing" (18 November 1995). Less pessimistic than Howard and Medford in earlier decades, I feel that the loss of these dances has stopped among the Yuchi and in most other Oklahoma communities since at least the 1980s. Two forces are at work. First, cultural awareness and concern for preservation is perhaps stronger now than at any point in Oklahoma Indian history. This corollary to the anxiety of culture loss has been buttressed by widespread adoption of tape recorders within the context of active efforts to facilitate the transmission of songs, dances, and other expressions of Yuchi culture. During the period of my involvement with the Yuchi, formal public meetings with the purpose of teaching and recording songs, discussing ritual procedure, and passing on community history have progressed from novel to occasional to regular occurrences. Focus group discussions, language and culture camps, speaker-apprentice relationships, dance rehearsals, language revitalization projects, and tape-recorded interviews are all emblematic of Yuchi social life during the 1990s. Similar responses have taken place among the Eastern Delaware and other tribes in recent years (Lee 1995:72). Conscious efforts at pursuing ethno-education, instruction in traditional cultural forms through a cross between western and indigenous methods, was a defining characteristic of cultural work in Native America in the late twentieth century (cf. Jean Jackson 1995).

Among the Yuchi, Shawnee, and Creek today, it is not uncommon to see men in their early twenties, or even teenagers, leading social dances. Viewed from the perspective of the present, this is a new phenomenon. According to contemporary elders, it is a change from earlier practice in which young men, even though sometimes prepared to assume responsibility for some aspect of ritual performance, deferred to the leadership of elders until after the latters' deaths. This pattern was shared with the Longhouse Iroquois, where each generation has mistakenly appeared to be the last in which anyone is capable of reciting the ritual prayers and speeches. Michael Foster has written: "The notion of 'crisis' in the taking up of ritual roles tends to engender a pessimistic view. But despite the enormous loss to the Longhouse community in the death of many key ritualists in recent years, the remarkable process of succession – of young men stepping forward at the right moment – goes on. I have seen it happen at Six Nations over the last three years, even though most of the speakers who contributed to this study have died during the same period" (1974:252). Foster's experience among the Iroquois ritualists at Six Nations mirrors my own sense of the older Yuchi pattern.

Audio tape recorders have commonly been used at Yuchi stomp dances by Yuchi people since at least the 1970s, but it was not until the 1990s that recording became a formal tool used by ground leaders to teach ritual and social dance songs. While various efforts preceded it, a noteworthy development took place at the Duck Creek ground's third stomp dance in 1997. Before the dance began, while the men were gathered informally under the chiefs' arbor, Newman Littlebear and Simon Harry made a series of recordings in which they sang the songs for almost all of the Yuchi daytime ceremonial dances and nighttime social dances. Because I was present, I was recruited to make the recordings, but the project was facilitated by Newman Littlebear and his son Clifford. Afterward, I indexed the tapes and made extra copies for both grounds. Within a short time, several younger men, including all of the teenage poleboys from the Polecat ground, had mastered sizable portions of the song repertoire. For the first time in my experience, Yuchi elders, impressed with the quick mastery of the songs by various young men, began to speak more confidently about the future health of the social dances. This shift is a part of a larger context in which the public discourse of ceremonial ground leaders consistently dwells on themes of cultural continuity and preservation.

MORAL ECONOMICS

While acknowledging the limitations of extending market metaphors to all areas of social life (see Silverstein 1993 *contra* Bourdieu 1991), Sue Roark-Calnek's description of Delaware ritual as transactional exchange within an ongoing moral economy provides helpful comparative and theoretical material for further interpreting both the Soup Dance and Yuchi ritual generally. Among Delaware ritualists, she suggests that "In the absence of formal organization, Delaware religiosity achieved community from transactional interdependence. In private and public ritual conduct a kind of moral economy obtained in which certain sacred currencies were exchanged in return for services, blessings, and/or as a propitiary hedge against misfortune. The exchanges were public, and in their consummation a number of other transactional relationships, with less overt emphasis, were sometimes encoded" (Roark 1978:327). In the case of the Yuchi, who possess the kind of enduring formal ceremonial organizations that she sees the Delaware as lacking, the same conditions also hold (Jackson 1996a). The kinds of reciprocal ritual services commonly associated with dual organizations are found in Delaware and Yuchi ritual; indeed, in most Woodland religious practice. The same bonds of mutual moral obligation obtain between the genders, between the living and the dead, and between humans and the Creator. From the point of view of Yuchi culture, such bonds of obligation as felt by individuals and expressed communally in public ritual provide the motivation for Yuchi people to reassemble at their ceremonial grounds each year.

Roark-Calnek describes four material currencies used in Delaware ritual exchange – wampum (shell beads), deer hides (later cloth goods), tobacco, and food (Roark 1978:327). The place of white beads and food in Yuchi ritual have already been mentioned. One of many uses of tobacco in Yuchi ritual transaction is in a "payment" made to the singers by each male member of the ground during the Ribbon Dance, held during the Green Corn Ceremony. Completing the parallel, the Yuchi also customarily use cloth goods as a ritualized payment for the services of a medicine person, as once occurred in baby namings and funerals, as well as in treatments of illness. Roark-Calnek identifies five transactional uses of these materials within ritual contexts, and these too are directly comparable to Yuchi uses. The two forms of transaction on which she focuses most closely are also those of interest in further considering the Soup Dance:

> *Compensatory solicitation* initiated a transaction by offering the other party advance compensation for some specific good desired. It was most often made with food or tobacco.
>
> *Propitiatory solicitation* differs from the preceding in its intention as preventative therapeutics, the avoidance of negative outcome. It also made use of tobacco and especially food, and was perhaps emotively the most powerful of the uses of ritual currency. [Roark 1978:327–28]

She found these forms of transaction most fully expressed in the Delaware rituals that most closely mirror the Yuchi memorial feasts. These efforts at solicitation "made use of a complementary opposition of social parties, each of which had actual or potential transactional relationship with ancestral or supernatural patrons. The relationships required solicitation of the patrons by offering them food. In return for this each side received benefit (or escaped harm) from its patron. But each transaction required for consummation some activity of the opposite side" (Roark 1978:328). In Delaware funeral and memorial ritual, groups of kin and non-kin provided reciprocal services for each other. Each group provided food for their partners, which they ate on behalf of the giver's ancestors. Recalling the Yuchi funeral feast, and less explicitly, the Soup Dance feast, "failure to feed the ancestors incurred their wrath and made their descendants ill" (Roark 1978:329).

The class of exchanges that Roark discusses also provides a linkage between propitiation of ancestors and the exchange by men and women of gendered foods. Delaware ritual divisions and gender separation intersected, as the men of one group exchanged symbolic foods with the women of the other. Such a permutation is not present in contemporary Yuchi practice, as the Yuchi division of men into the chief and warrior societies does not extend to women, who are the undifferentiated counterparts of the men of the community viewed as a whole.[12] Roark explains this social division among the Delaware with reference to the existence of male and female spirit forces that are subservient to the Creator. For the Yuchi, in contrast, human ancestors are instead the focus of attention and the social organization of ancestral spirits is presumed to mirror that of the living.

A moral economy encoded in ritual, like a literal economy, requires the ongoing involvement of individuals who both feel a commitment to the larger social system and derive a personal sense of worth, value, or benefit from participation in it. Many religious communities rely, in varying degrees, on an element of coercion in sentiment or in action, but Yuchi ceremonial ground practice shows little of this, beyond the ever-present reference to custom as authority. Many Yuchi people choose not to participate in ceremonial ground ritual and do so without experiencing any serious social sanction. In contrast, active involvement in ceremonial ground life presents practical difficulties that participants actively decide to accept. They do so in part because collective ritual and discourse create for them a feeling of obligation toward their fellow community members, toward the Creator, toward an abstraction called Yuchi culture, and toward the Yuchi people who modeled this culture in the recent and the distant past.

CULTURE AS TRADITION

In considering the cultural themes associated with the Yuchi Soup Dance I have focused on what I feel to be its dominant concern – the acknowledgment of responsibility on the part of the living for maintaining a meaningful connection with the dead.[13] This attachment to the ancestors is expressed tangibly by putting on a feast, the most salient expression of hospitality in Yuchi culture. In the Soup Dance feast, the living and the departed commingle and together celebrate the ongoing practice of Yuchi religious life. In doing so, they draw attention not only to the specific transactional requirement placed on the living to provide the feast, but to the broader task of replicating Yuchi ritual culture and Yuchi values through time. By focusing on departed ancestors, the living draw attention to the past and to the temporality of Yuchi social life. While the Creator is credited with the creation of the Yuchi and their ceremonies, it is the ancestors of the contemporary Yuchi people who are responsible for bequeathing to them the practices that I have been describing throughout this work.

It is in this classic sense of "handed down through time" that Yuchi people understand the nature of their cultural tradition. Their use of tradition is of some interest to questions of identity and changing social phenomenon, such as the formal programs that the Yuchi are developing to facilitate cultural preservation. More interesting, in my view, than the ways in which *tradition* is a Yuchi category for and of culture, are the ways in which, through ritual and public discourse, Yuchi understandings of culture and history can be created and recreated in specific instances of social interaction. This is the *how* of tradition. It is tradition-making as a process, not in the ironic sense associated with the so-called *invention of tradition* characteristic of socially complex nation-states (Hobsbawm and Ranger 1983), but in a manner that is communicated within a small community governed by face-to-face interaction. The general nature of Yuchi ritual as tradition and traditionalization will be considered more generally in chapter 10.

The foregoing analysis of the Soup Dance has described the event as a singularity, while suggesting closely similar practices and beliefs among other Woodland communities. Widespread themes such as ritualized gender division, feasts of reunion with ancestors, and marking the transition into autumn from the agricultural summer, together with more basic and reoccurring ritual patterns, are uniquely configured in the Yuchi Soup Dance. I have called attention to those commonalities as a means of illustrating the ways in which the tribal rituals of the Yuchi and their neighbors are capable of fostering a larger system of ritual inter-participation across local communities. Drawing out those parallel practices also further situates the Yuchi within the general cultural history of Native peoples in the eastern United States. While these comparisons are of anthropological relevance and are also of considerable interest to Yuchi ritual leaders, who are themselves enthusiastic comparativists, the unique qualities of Yuchi ritual are what matter most to Yuchi people. Discussing mortuary ritual in Belau, both ethnographically and comparatively, Richard Parmentier has articulated a position that I share. "I think that each society needs to be studied in terms of specific patterns of intersection involving kinds of meaningful objects, social roles and groups brought into play during the ritual and modalities of transaction or exchange which couple these objects and social relations" (1994b:68). When Mr. Littlebear speaks of the ancestors who return to the ceremonial ground during the Soup Dance, he refers, from a Yuchi point of view, specifically to Yuchi ancestors. Those forefathers represent a line of continuity in personnel and practice stretching from our own mutual friends—from elders recently departed back in time to the original recipients of Yuchi cultural forms. In this aspect, traditional ritual serves as a defining feature of Yuchi identity. Yuchi people are conscious and proud of what is unique about their ritual practices and it is not difficult to see the broader implications of this awareness for a small community encompassed not only by a general North American social order but also by the large and sometimes indifferent Creek Nation.

10

"... and have an account of it."

Conclusion

In the first extended text presented in chapter 1, Mr. Littlebear said: "We are trying to keep history moving and have an account of it." I took this to mean that those Yuchi people whom I know are presently concerned about doing two things with their cultural inheritance. The first is to continue to live it to the best of their ability. This means participating in all those activities that are distinctly Yuchi, particularly those bestowed upon the Yuchi by the Creator in ancient times. The form and significance of these ritual practices has been my focus in this work. The second point that Mr. Littlebear was making regards an innovation in Yuchi life, albeit one aimed at furthering the first goal. To "have an account of it" means to do something new. Mr. Littlebear's speech on this occasion was not given at the behest of a ceremonial ground chief at the end of a stomp dance. It was delivered as his personal view of the Yuchi circumstance at the end of the twentieth century. The setting for his comments was a new kind of gathering – a public discussion in which Yuchi people were encouraged to contribute their own knowledge of Yuchi cultural life. The assembled group was both source and audience for this information. Present as well were tape recorders and video cameras in significant numbers.

Why such attention to formal documentation linked to cultural preservation and renewed engagement with community life? Mr. Littlebear went on to say: "There may be able to come a time when our ... the younger generation can refer back to something that is useful when it comes to this ... ceremony." Yuchi people of all ages today are acquainted with the work of earlier anthropologists who visited their community. Although they consume such sources with the critical eyes of people who know the meaning of being Yuchi from the inside, they appreciate ethnography as a valuable link to ancestors and knowledge no longer otherwise available to them. If ethnography has some use to Yuchi people (and my primary hope is that mine might have some) then their own self-documentation has even greater potential value. Yuchi people today are reflexive enough to know that if video recording could have been made of Yuchi storytelling, dancing, or conversation in 1896, then such a document would be priceless today. If this is so, then a visual record made of the teachings of contemporary elders in 1996 will have great potential interest to the Yuchi in 2096. What separates such records from my own anthropological ones is that they preserve not only the content of Yuchi knowledge and practices but also the modes of expression, the thematic concerns, and the local documentary approach that is emergent in the present generation of Yuchi community members.

Between 1989 and 1999, the Yuchi people assembled a comprehensive photographic archive, organized four "Euchee Heritage Days" festivals, published a tribal history and many photo-historical calendars, held language classes and summer camps beyond count, completed a major museum exhibition on Yuchi culture and history, and undertook a series of master-apprentice relationships (two for language, one for traditional plant medicine, and one for social dance songs). During this same period, the tribe completed several major grant projects for developing governance procedures, documenting and teaching the Yuchi language, undertaking cultural preservation activities, and studying health care decision-making. In addition to these projects, Yuchi people also undertook collaborations with at least six outside researchers in ethnomusicology, linguistics, and anthropology, as well as with a documentary film production company. All of this activity outside of the ceremonial ground context is in addition to developments within that domain, such as the reestablishment of Yuchi dances within the Green Corn Ceremonies of the Sand Creek and Duck Creek towns. The total picture that this frenetic activity reveals is of a dynamic community proud of its culture and eager to make that culture accessible and understandable to all Yuchi people who wish to embrace it now and in the future. I am pleased that Yuchi people see, in this process, a role for an outsider such as myself and for an undertaking such as anthropological study. Clearly, the period of cultural intensification and revitalization that I have just described is worthy of a comprehensive history in itself. My goal here is simply to suggest that such concerns are directly implicated in my own research and in the Yuchi ritual practices that I have explored in this work.

In concluding this study, I wish to provide both some further interpretive frameworks for placing my research in context and some disclaimers acknowledging its limitations.

COMPARATIVE CONTEXTS

In this study I have attempted to present Yuchi ritual and belief within the larger field of Woodland Indian culture and society. In situating Yuchi ritual practices within a comparative context, frequent mention was made of similar Shawnee ritual forms. Yuchi ritualists frequently make such comparisons themselves, and several centuries of close contact provide a reasonable basis for this pattern. In noting these parallels here, my goal is not to suggest that the Yuchi are somehow Shawnee. Shawnees and Yuchis recognize their separate histories, languages, and cultures, just as they note common viewpoints, values, and ritual practices. In fact, Shawnee ritualists feel close bonds to other communities, particularly other Algonquian-speaking tribes such as the Kickapoo, with whom the Yuchi have had little contact. The practical purpose, both in Yuchi discourse and in my own, for making such comparisons is to draw attention to the distinctiveness of Yuchi culture and society. Making clear to outsiders that they are not Creeks, and that Yuchi culture is different from Creek culture, has been a dominant concern of Yuchi people since at least the eighteenth century. My hope is that by outlining some of the cultural and social patterns characteristic of Yuchi ritual life and placing these patterns into a larger context, a more realistic understanding of the Yuchi as a people will emerge.

I have a second purpose in drawing out such comparisons, one related to a more recent anthropological concern with understanding the larger social systems within which local communities interact. Although Yuchi people are very concerned with describing what is unique about their community and asserting their identity as Yuchi, Yuchi social life is far from closed off from other peoples. There is no neighborhood in any Yuchi settlement where only Yuchis reside. In everyday life, Yuchi people are in constant contact with non-Indian Oklahomans, as well as members of many other tribes. While this larger social world has not been my subject here, the same diversity of interaction is characteristic of Yuchi ritual life. As I have sought to document, practice of Yuchi ceremonial ground ritual articulates Yuchi society with similar ritual communities among a large number of tribes. This creates a larger social universe of (partially) shared or overlapping meanings that facilitates intertribal gatherings in which tribal distinctiveness, a shared Woodland heritage, and generalized Indian concerns are all articulated and reproduced. In trying to understand this social world, made up of other "stomp dance people," I have tried to suggest the ways in which the maintenance of a strong local identity and locally distinctive ritual practices does not require that communities cut themselves off from their neighbors. In eastern Oklahoma, as elsewhere in the world, such contacts are the means by which local cultures are sustained (Barth 1987; Jackson 1999; Jackson and Levine 1999). The story of cultural performance elsewhere in the Woodlands retells this tale – maintenance of local ceremonialism in places where multitribal ritual communities were preserved (modern Iroquoia, the late-nineteenth-century Gulf Coast) and its abandonment in places where small tribal groups were isolated in a sea of non-Natives (as evidenced among the Catawba, Mashpee, and Powhatan).

RITUAL AND COMMUNITY

Classic social theory, as well as much ethnographic writing, has described ritual as a means by which communities hold themselves together. More recent work has taken an alternative view, emphasizing the opportunities that rituals provide for contestation by individuals and interest groups within a community. Articulating this theme, Simon Harrison writes: "It is true, for instance, that a community staging one of its important ceremonies may, at one level, be expressing its sense of identity and unity. But often this is only outwardly so, and the performance may in fact be preceded by intense power-struggles among its organizers" (1992:225). In describing Yuchi ritual, there is a certain sense in which I have emphasized its integrative function and neglected its capacity for engendering conflict. In part, I see this as a matter of courtesy toward the Yuchi people who have befriended me and shared something of their world with a curious outsider. In another sense, in the domain of Yuchi public life, there really is surprisingly little conflict. Visitors among the Yuchi with experience in other Native communities are quick to perceive this general pattern.

In keeping with what seems now to be a longstanding pattern in Southeastern Indian life, Yuchi individuals today who are at odds with other participants in ceremonial ground life withdraw their involvement, sometimes temporarily, sometimes permanently (cf. Thomas 1961, 1962). This so-called harmony ethic is a culturally appropriate response to conflict that protects individuals from the spiritual and social dangers that accompany interpersonal strife. Social forms adopted by the Yuchi during the twentieth century, such as Methodism, the Native American Church, the powwow, and the gourd dance provide alternative modes of traditional Indian life to some individuals who have become estranged from the ceremonial ground community. Another option, one taken by some Yuchis at various times in modern history, is to abandon active ceremonial ground practice and replace it instead with a form of individualized traditionality. In this mode, family heads left the ceremonial ground and undertook making medicine and conducting other rites for their own families. In reality, though, this has always turned out to be a temporary solution. Such families eventually returned to ceremonial ground life, permanently migrated toward some other Yuchi institution, or dropped out of engagement with the larger Yuchi community. This pattern reflects the view held by many Yuchis that real Yuchiness is located not in genealogy but in engagement with other Yuchi people in public settings.

With respect to ritual generally, the relative degree to which public ceremonies provide opportunities for both integration and fragmentation seems to be a question open for ethnographic study in specific settings at particular times. In the future, ceremonial ground ritual may become a crucial site for contention and debate in the Yuchi community, but this is not the case at present.

Rather, the ceremonial grounds have provided an important focus around which Yuchi culture work has been organized and expanded.

Although some families have dropped out of engagement with the larger Yuchi community, many Yuchi people continue to be committed to maintaining the cultural forms and social institutions that provide expression of Yuchi identity. Sacred ritual, both at the ceremonial grounds and in other settings, is a primary means toward this end. In recent years, the descendants of Yuchi people estranged from their Yuchi heritage have begun to rediscover Yuchi community life. Wanting to learn what being Yuchi means and to reconnect with other people of Yuchi heritage, these newcomers have sought out the places where Yuchi community is most fully given form – the ceremonial grounds and churches. The reincorporation of such individuals will probably continue as Yuchi community activities continue to gain increased notice in eastern Oklahoma.

CEREMONIAL GROUND LIFE

Ceremonial ground ritual provides, in varying degrees, a central life focus for many Yuchi people. In the distant past Yuchi ritual was part and parcel of everyday life, while today it is a choice. It is something that Yuchi people do without any compulsions beyond those imposed in the intimate domain of the family. Even this pressure is not overpowering, as some children of ritual leaders take little interest in Yuchi ritualism, while some active ceremonialists come from families that in the past demonstrated lack of interest. To make the choice to join in the activities of a ceremonial ground is to acknowledge the benefits and costs that this participation brings. As I have tried to indicate, Yuchi ritual life frames a set of obligations that Yuchi ceremonial ground people take seriously.

One aspect of this responsibility involves interaction with other Yuchi people. Such interaction entails a willingness to accept the moral standards that govern community life. As Morris Foster has noted among the Comanche, tribal gatherings "subject one's social self to public sanction" and require individuals to "accept the conventions and values of . . . shared community" (1991:169).

More than just accepting the social norms of community, Yuchi ritual obligates individuals to interact in appropriate ways with a larger, more diverse world. Ceremonial ground life brings the Yuchi into contact with members of other ritual communities with which the Yuchi share a larger social network. These contacts place further obligations of hospitality and reciprocity on each participant. In turn, such interactions help create an Indian social world within which the Yuchi can both remain Yuchi and identify as traditional Indians sharing common experiences and values with other Woodland peoples.

From the point of view of Yuchi belief, obligations to the Creator and to Yuchi ancestors to renew the world each year and to perpetuate Yuchi culture are perhaps the most crucial responsibilities of all. This is where a sense of tradition enters. This layering of obligations, combined with the practical difficulties that ceremonial ground rituals entail, explain why Yuchis use the word *work* to describe their ceremonial life. Explaining this work publicly, elders frequently comment that this life is harder but more rewarding than any other way available to Yuchi people.

TRADITION

I have not discovered or produced a new and refined definition of tradition that is detachable from this context and ready for use in other settings. I have sought in this work to keep the problem of understanding the nature of tradition foregrounded throughout the process of learning about Yuchi ritual and writing this account of it. The cultural forms that I have described here are a large part of the cultural patrimony that Yuchi people point to and identify as Yuchi *tradition*. In this sense, although I have described part of the content of Yuchi tradition, the inventory of subjects that Yuchi elders identify as tradition is only partially cataloged. From the point of view of ceremonial ground life, I have described aspects of the living tradition of Yuchi ritual – highlighting the stories and experiences that have an active social life as action in the present. There is another aspect of the practices-centered view of tradition that Yuchi people talk about – the part that has slipped from reoccurring practice into memory culture. This heritage is manifest now only in publicly circulating talk. Funeral feasts are important to the Yuchi elders who experienced them, but these events are gone now. Without the trained Yuchi medicine men who ran them, funeral feasts are transformed into heritage culture – traditions embodied in stories and ethnography but unretrievable as practice. In keeping memories of such practices alive in stories, Yuchi elders today pass on what they can of such traditions.

Other cultural forms are similarly being transformed into heritage culture, not for the lack of crucial resources such as medicine men, but simply because times change. Yuchi elders tell rich stories of their own experiences working on family farms, preparing foods by drying, playing old-fashioned games, going to boarding schools, and traveling by wagon. Older Yuchi people who experienced this early-twentieth-century life do not propose to abandon cars, convenience foods, or television in the present, but they do wish to make the stories of these pasts known. Old-time practices such as preparing "traditional foods" and learning about herbal medicines have a different life in the present than they had in the past. Yuchi culture camps, children's language classes, story telling sessions, focus group meetings, and staged demonstrations, along with personal memory and everyday conversation, are the places in which these past forms of everyday life have taken on a new life as tradition or heritage.

The way in which Yuchi people convert certain cultural forms into traditions, both those cultural forms ongoing in the present and those remembered from the past, is the process of traditionalization. A focus on traditionalization provides another useful way of thinking about tradition in Yuchi life. These forms of life are traditions because Yuchi people are actively making "connections that link the present with a meaningful past" (Bauman 1992:136). In presenting extended texts in which Yuchi elders reflect, often publicly, on meaning in Yuchi ritual life, I hope to have illustrated the ways in which traditionalization in achieved in discourse. The social action that accompanies discourse, both as ongoing rituals in the present and as memorializations of past Yuchi culture, such as heritage culture programs like culture camps for Yuchi children, reinforces the process of traditionalization in public discourse.

Not every aspect of Yuchi experience is traditionalized; hence not all Yuchi culture is tradition. Incorporation into tradition is a selective process, and a great deal of cultural change in Yuchi life goes by without extended comment. Even in the ritual sphere, some changes do not warrant traditionalization. The ceremonial grounds now are all connected to municipal water supplies. This means that families do not need to haul many barrels of water from wells up to the ceremonial ground before each gathering. This is a change for the better, and recounting tales of backbreaking work and rusty water are the stuff of "well, when I was a kid . . ." stories, not of tradition making. From the point of view of the Yuchi elders who lived it, this work was not an essential feature of Yuchi lifestyle, it was just life.

As numerous observers have noted, tradition and modernity are not opposites. Canning vegetables was a thoroughly modern process in early-twentieth-century American life. In some Native communities, home economists traveled rural roads giving demonstrations to Indian housewives in canning techniques as a means of bringing Indian people into the modern world. Today, canning produce is the subject of elaborate stories in which it is presented as a key aspect of traditional, old-time Yuchi life. The subtext in these stories is about Yuchi pride in family self-sufficiency. Possessing little money, Yuchi farm families before the Second World War also possessed plenty and were well prepared to support themselves and their community life. Today, Yuchi people are open to putting new technologies into service in the name of preserving traditional culture. For many summers in a row I have videotaped the Green Corn Ceremonies at the Duck Creek Ceremonial Ground. These films tell the story of the reintroduction of the full traditional Yuchi ceremony to that ground. Made at the request of Chief Simon Harry, the tapes have already been a resource facilitating the learning of dance songs by younger men. Independent of the work of outside researchers, Yuchi people are engaged in a community-wide ethnographic project in self-documentation. Photography, audio recordings, computer files, videotapes, computer-based language materials, self-published tribal histories, and an array of other media are being deployed in this effort to capture the stories and knowledge of Yuchi language and culture. Such thoroughly modern approaches to heritage and tradition and culture were becoming worldwide practices at the end of the twentieth century.

In a focus group meeting in 1997, Mr. Littlebear raised a question, unprompted by me, that left me a bit shocked. Referring to my work and to that of Pamela Wallace, another anthropologist working among the Yuchi, Mr. Littlebear suggested that we, as professionals, might be able to explain to the group exactly what the words tradition and culture meant. My sense of dread at not having my tape recorder running at this moment was combined with a feeling of disorientation. Somehow I avoided answering. I have tried to be more interested in what Yuchi people think tradition is than working it out for myself. What I think they mean by tradition is "culture that matters." Yuchis are fully modern Americans and thus share a great deal with countless varieties of non-Yuchi people. Both Yuchi tradition and Yuchi culture are what enable Yuchi people to stand apart from this mass and continue to declare that they are a people with their own meaningful ways of being human.

In exploring the nature of traditionalization, I do commit myself to a certain analytical perspective on tradition. These reflections on tradition reveal that I am skeptical of external definitions of tradition that conceive of it as an inherent quality of pastness contained within inherited cultural forms. Instead, whatever else it is, tradition is a symbol (a meaning, a feeling, a construction) that people form in the present about the nature of themselves and their beliefs in light of a particular understanding of a significant past.

ELDERS AND ABSENCES

In this work I have relied on explanations of Yuchi ritual gathered from Yuchi elders. These are the same people who, at present, have taken on the responsibility for leading the cultural life of their community. While this reliance on elders has been standard anthropological practice for much study in Native American communities, it also represents a bias that I acknowledge here. The perspectives of younger ceremonial ground people, as well as of Yuchis unconcerned with ceremonial ground life, are not accurately represented here. Nor, in any systematic way, are the viewpoints of Yuchi women elders foregrounded, although I have tried to present Yuchi ceremonialism in the round by acknowledging the various contributions that young and old, male and female, make to ongoing ritual life. Other voices, stories, perspectives, and understandings remain to be articulated. In relying on the words and examples of the Yuchi men who take responsibility for Yuchi ritual, I have followed the lead of the Yuchi community itself, but Yuchi people recognize the diversity of their community and go to great lengths not to claim to speak for one another. As in the ceremonial ground business meetings that take place at the end of each ritual season, all participants, no matter what their age or gender or level of involvement, have the right to stand and speak and explain themselves as they see fit. In putting down here the understandings that I have come to through study with Yuchi elders, I have no wish to curtail this ongoing dialogue in Yuchi community life.

More broadly, my account is incomplete in its exclusion of particular kinds of Yuchi perspectives – voices of dissent, voices of youth, voices of women, voices of non-Yuchis participating in Yuchi life. If these limitations have been partially overcome in my synthesis of Yuchi belief and practice, it is because my ties of friendship are much more widely distributed than my reliance here on the teachings of elders would suggest. Between the summer of 1995 and the present, I have participated actively and continuously in Yuchi community life, building what I think are close relationships of friendship and affection with many Yuchi people, young and old, and many Yuchi families. These ties extend beyond the ceremonial ground community to include Yuchi church leaders and beyond the Yuchi community to encompass ceremonial ground people from many tribes. As the structure of Yuchi grammar attests, such relationships lack the power to make a Yuchi of me (although this is a regular joke that follows me). They have had the power to transform my life irrevocably. They quite unexpectedly first turned me into an Oklahoman, and now they have made me into an (Indian) football player, a storyteller, a stomp dance singer, a pallbearer, an adopted brother, and a greatly enriched person.

Another bias to be acknowledged is my lack of consideration of Yuchi relationships with non-Native Oklahomans and their engagement with what they refer to as "everyday life." The last thing that I want a reader to believe is that Yuchi people live completely in a world of age-old ritual isolated from the day-to-day world of turn-of-the-century America. Much more than Native American communities located in remote areas or isolated on tribal reservations or reserves, Yuchi community life is superimposed upon a familiar North American social world politically controlled by non-Natives in which private ownership of land, the daily grind of eight-to-five wage labor, an unending flood of media and consumer goods, and widespread social ills (from bad roads to substance abuse) are experienced daily.

Within this world, Yuchi relations with non-Natives are complex. Yuchi elders can narrate profound experiences confronting racism in their own lives, but they can also idealize a shared rural culture in which neighbors – Indian, White, and Black – worked and played together. Yuchi students today have opportunities unthinkable to earlier generations of Yuchi people, but they can also testify to the ways in which structures of power within their own public schools systematically discriminate against them. With admiration, Yuchi people can tell stories about African Americans, some enrolled as Creek Freedman and some not, who could speak Yuchi or lead stomp dances, or who practiced traditional medicine. Yuchi people can also fall into American habits of stereotyping and denigrating other groups. I lacked the ability to explore such issues here, despite their value. My hope is to have contributed to an understanding of Yuchi ceremonial ground life within a framework that does acknowledge the wider social world of neighboring ceremonial ground communities, but this is clearly not the only social world that matters in Yuchi life.

I hope that acknowledgment of these limitations refines the lens through which readers will view this work. Remaining to be addressed is the extent to which I have evoked an idealization of Yuchi culture rather than presented a picture of Yuchi society as a real, organic whole. To this question, I respond by acknowledging that this study represents an idealization, but I have endeavored to make it one of a particular kind. As my comments above have suggested, Yuchi people, particularly elders and ceremonial ground leaders, are very busy with publicly articulating idealizations of Yuchi culture. These idealizations are important and are doing significant social work in the real life of the Yuchi community. This links my interest (and theirs) in traditionalization with a discourse-centered approach to culture. In such a view, study of the actual ways in which idealizations circulate publicly (in ritual oratory, for instance) deflates the criticism that such study misses what is really going on in a community. In this way, and in the more general sense encompassed by the traditional methods of participant-observation fieldwork, I have sought to reflect both the reality of Yuchi ritual practice and the ways in which Yuchi ritual specialists recast it in ideal terms. Finally, as revealed in my discussion of conformity versus conflict in Yuchi ritual settings, there is the double fact that, on the one hand, exposure of the gaps separating ideal and real is not behavior that one emphasizes when one is a guest, while, on the other, in my experience among the Yuchi, the size of the actual gap has been quite small.

These issues about which I am acknowledging incompleteness pale in comparison to one that I take more seriously. While there is a certain sense in which the goal of writing this study provided a charter for my going and spending time in the Yuchi world, the whole undertaking – note taking, tape recording, photographing, writing – somehow seems secondary now that it is, in a sense, complete. Several hundred pages of text describing Yuchi ritual are no substitute for the rich experience of participating in Yuchi community celebrations, whether by a Yuchi or an odd outsider turned marginal insider. The tastes, smells, fears, sounds, emotions, and excitements, the exhaustion, sadness, and joy, the awareness of the sacred, the amusement at the profane, and the splendor of the absurd – all of the abundant materials out of which life and memory are really made – are absent here. I am fortunate beyond belief to have experienced such things in the company of Yuchi people. For Yuchi people too, these intangibles are also the stuff of Yuchi ceremonial ground life. For now at least, in my own life, they remain subjects for conversation and memory rather than publication. I lack the gifts and the delicacy to share them in words.

Falling short of capturing lived experience, this account is really about something else. It is part of a search for patterns and partial evocations of something sacred and human and important that Yuchi people shared with me. If it has a life of value in some Yuchi future and does no harm in the Yuchi present, then I will be satisfied. If a future reader, Yuchi or not, finds something here worthy of notice, or at least recognizes the depth of my feeling for Yuchi people and the sophistication of Yuchi culture, then I will feel even more grateful.

Afterword

The request to add an afterword to this paperback edition of *Yuchi Ceremonial Life* was a welcome but challenging opportunity. The temptation either to rewrite the book or to begin writing a new one was great, but these impulses obviously had to be suppressed. Afterwords of this sort often offer new information on an older story, but the span of time separating the initial publication of the book and the release of a paperback edition was not so great as to demand an elaborate updating of the basic facts it presents. As in the period evoked in this book, the Yuchi community in 2005 is as active and as vital as ever.

Some things do change, though. As is always the case in stories such as this, some dear friends and teachers have made the final journey home, joining the company of their ancestors. It is comforting to know that Yuchi teachings about the life that follows this one describe it as beautiful—abundantly filled with singing, dancing, games, jokes, and other things that, in smaller quantities, also help make this life worth living. It is similarly encouraging to recall that Yuchi ceremonial life provides an opportunity for those in the spirit world and those in this earthly world to reunite in fellowship each year inside the big houses. Among those Yuchi teachers whose passing occurred during or after the publication of this book, I will especially miss Mose Cahwee and Julia Winningham, each of whom invested considerable time and showed great patience in instructing me in matters of Yuchi custom.

Any author looking back on a published work will have anxieties and regrets, but I have only one reservation worth noting here. I wish that I had not attempted as detailed a survey of Yuchi history as I ventured to present in chapter 2. This is not to say that an account of Yuchi history is superfluous. Rather, I should have been more forceful in articulating how much a serious study of Yuchi history is needed and even more circumspect in describing how provisional and sketchy current knowledge of the subject is. As for the actual narrative offered in chapter 2, I fear I have contributed, in a small way, to reinforcing the false sense that Yuchi history during the colonial and removal periods is adequately known. The good news is that work on preremoval Yuchi history is being taken up by a talented new generation of historians. Their current efforts promise to clarify matters that have long been uncertain, particularly concerning Yuchi relationships through time with their Native neighbors and with the English and Spanish.

A specific correction to the information presented in this volume should be acknowledged as well. The historical discussion provided in chapter 2 relies heavily on the analysis of Yuchi history developed by John Swanton in his *Early History of the Creek Indians and Their Neighbors* (Washington DC: Bureau of American Ethnology, 1922). As discussed on pages 293–94 (note 8), new scholarship examining the linkage of the Yuchis with the contact-era Chisca people was a pressing need when the cloth edition of this book was being finalized. Since then, John Worth has undertaken research on Chisca history. His work has undermined the Chisca and Yuchi linkage upon which my discussion of early Yuchi history was based. For a current assessment of this topic, readers should consult Worth's essay "Chisca" in the *Handbook of North American Indians*, vol. 14 (Washington DC: Smithsonian Institution, 2004) as well as my own chapter on the Yuchis appearing in the same volume.

A number of new works relevant to the study of Yuchi language, culture, and history have appeared since 2003. It is beyond the scope of this afterword to review these sources, but readers of this volume may wish to know that the University of Nebraska Press has reprinted Frank G. Speck's *Ethnology of the Yuchi Indians* (Lincoln: University of Nebraska Press, 2004). The edition makes Speck's book readily available for the first time and includes an introduction that seeks to place Speck and his work among the Yuchis in a historical context.

My Yuchi friends and I are extremely grateful that the University of Nebraska Press has decided to publish this paperback edition of *Yuchi Ceremonial Life*. We are gratified that the book has been well received and that its publisher recognizes an audience for a paper edition. This more modestly priced edition of the book is an especially welcome development for me personally because it will make the book more accessible to the Yuchi people who made it possible. It will also generate some modest royalties, which, as noted on the dedication page, will go toward the collective use of the Yuchi ceremonial grounds.

APPENDIX A

Scheduling of Yuchi Ceremonial Ground Events and Visitations, Summer 1996

The football games, which begin in March and do not involve coordinated scheduling across the Yuchi grounds, are excluded. I do not have information on non-Yuchi dances attended by the members of the Sand Creek Ceremonial Ground. Unless scheduled at the same time (see 5-11), all Yuchi-hosted events were attended by the other two Yuchi communities, as well as visitors from other groups.

4-27	1st Duck Creek Dance
5-4	Open Weekend
5-11	2nd Duck Creek Dance
	1st Polecat Dance
5-18	1st Sand Creek Dance
5-24	2nd Polecat Dance
5-25	3rd Duck Creek Dance
5-26	Duck Creek Visits Tallahassee
6-1	3rd Polecat Dance
6-8	Funeral Postpones Dances
6-15	Duck Creek Men Cut Wood on Sunday for their Ground
6-22	Duck Creek Arbor (4th) Dance
6-28	(Friday) Duck Creek Green Corn
6-29	(Saturday) Duck Creek Green Corn
7-5	Polecat Arbor (4th) Dance
7-6	Duck Creek Visits Tallahassee Wvkokaye
7-12	(Friday) Polecat Green Corn
7-13	(Saturday) Polecat Green Corn
7-20	(Friday) Polecat Soup Dance
7-21	(Saturday) Polecat Soup Dance

7-27	(Friday) Duck Creek and Polecat Visit Arbeka Green Corn
7-28	(Saturday) Duck Creek and Polecat Visit Arbeka Green Corn
8-3	(Friday) Sand Creek Green Corn
8-4	(Saturday) Sand Creek Green Corn
8-10	(Friday) Duck Creek and Polecat Visit Little Axe (N) War Dance
8-11	(Saturday) Duck Creek and Polecat Visit Little Axe (N) War Dance
8-17	Duck Creek Visits Muddy Waters Green Corn
8-17	Polecat Visits Greenleaf Green Corn
8-23	(Friday) Duck Creek Soup Dance
8-24	(Saturday) Duck Creek Soup Dance
8-31	Duck Creek Visits Hickory Ground
8-31	Polecat Visits Fish Pond
9-1	Polecat and Duck Creek Visit Stoke Smith Labor Day Dance
9-8	Duck Creek and Polecat Visit Nuyaka Last Dance Ballgame
9-14	Sand Creek Soup Dance
9-14	Duck Creek Visits Okfuskee Last Dance and Ballgame
9-21	Duck Creek Fall Dance (An extra dance added to this year's schedule)
9-28	Duck Creek Visits Arbeka Last Dance and Ballgame
10-5	(Some) Duck Creek Members visit Alabama Last Dance and Ballgame
10-12	Duck Creek and Polecat Visit Greenleaf Last Dance and Ballgame
10-19	Duck Creek and Polecat Visit Ottawa Stomp Dance
10-19	Little Axe (N and S) Hold their Bread Dances [North ground's dance attended by some Yuchi]

APPENDIX B

Yuchi Green Corn Ceremonial Activities

The following outline includes only major activities that include all participants. The list thus excludes ritual preparations made by the chief, poleboys, and other officials. Exact times vary somewhat within each year's performance. The schedules are rough guides prepared to illustrate the common features and the differences existing among the three Yuchi grounds. The schedules correspond with actual activities at Polecat (1995–1997), Duck Creek (1996–1997), and Sand Creek (1995).

	POLECAT	DUCK CREEK	SAND CREEK
Friday Morning	Earth Mound Constructed		
Friday Afternoon	Men Feast on Ground		
	Ribbon Dancer's Feast		
	Poleboys Selected		
Friday Evening	Evening Lizard Dance	Ribbon Dance	Ribbon Dance
		Four Stomp Dances	Four Stomp Dances
Friday Night	½ Night Dance	½ Night Dance	½ Night Dance
	Picking Feathermen/Whoopers	Picking Feathermen/Whoopers	
	Fasting Begins	Fasting Begins	Fasting Begins
Saturday Morning	Preparation of New Fire	Preparation of New Fire	Preparation of New Fire
	Preparation of Medicine	Preparation of Medicine	Preparation of Medicine
	Preparation of Feather Sticks	Preparation of Feather Sticks	
	American Flag Raised		American Flag Raised
	Scratching Ritual (between dances)	Scratching Ritual (between dances)	Scratching Ritual
	1st Feather Dance	1st Feather Dance	
	2nd Feather Dance	2nd Feather Dance	
	3rd Feather Dance	3rd Feather Dance	

	4th Feather (Bead) Dance	4th Feather (Bead) Dance	
	5th Feather Dance	5th Feather Dance	
	Jumping the Hill Dance		
Saturday Midday	Redroot Medicine Ritual (between dances)	Redroot Medicine Ritual (between dances)	Redroot Medicine Ritual
	6th Feather Dance	6th Feather Dance	
	7th Feather Dance	7th Feather Dance	
	Jumping the Hill Dance		
	Afternoon Lizard Dance	Afternoon Lizard Dance	
		Corn Medicine Ritual	Feeding of Fire Ritual
		Ritual Washing	Ritual Washing
	Fasting Ends	Fasting Ends	Fasting Ends
		Family Meal	Family Meal
Saturday Evening	Ribbon Dance	Old Folks Dance	Creek Buffalo Dance
	Buffalo Dance	Buffalo Dance	Old Folks Dance
		Four Stomp Dances	
	Family and Guest Feasts	Family and Guest Feasts	Family and Guest Feasts
Saturday Night	Starting Song	Starting Song	Starting Song
Sunday Morning	Nighttime Stomps	Nighttime Stomps	Nighttime Stomps
	Closing the Door Dance	Closing the Door Dance	Closing the Door Dance

NOTES

1. INTRODUCTION

1. For readers interested in the larger set of research projects and the literature that it is producing, I note some of it here. Mary S. Linn has undertaken documentation of the Yuchi language in collaboration with many of the language's remaining fluent speakers. This work has produced a grammar of the language (2001) and articles on language structure and use (1997; Jackson and Linn 2000). Pamela Wallace has completed two studies of Yuchi demographic (1993) and social history (1998; forthcoming) based on archival and ethnographic research. Morris Foster has collaborated with the Yuchi community on a study of values related to health care. Donna Myers is presently undertaking a project exploring the interrelation of women's lives and traditional foodways. Each of these projects has been initiated by and conducted in collaboration with the Euchee (Yuchi) Tribe of Indians.

2. My reading of Glassie's essay focuses on its polyvalent, poetic, and thought-provoking qualities. Barry McDonald (1997), treating the same essay as an attempt at a firm position statement rather than, as I think it was intended, an evocative contemplation, has offered a critical assessment that also deserves consideration.

3. This does not mean that I subscribe to a view that a collection of texts constitutes an ethnography, what Clifford Geertz calls "text positivism" (1988:145). Both ethnographic descriptions and transcribed texts are both literary genres attempting to represent some aspect of experience. My hope here is that the two genres are in useful dialogue (Briggs and Bauman 1992).

2. YUCHI HISTORY, CULTURE, AND SOCIETY

1. In his summary *Cultural and Natural Areas of Native North America*, Alfred Kroeber recognized the fuzziness of the Southeastern-Woodland distinction. Describing the Southeast as a sub-area within the broader eastern area, he noted: "It cannot be regarded as marked off by abrupt transitions of either cultural content or cultural satu-

ration such as one encounters in passing out of the Northwest Coast or Pueblo areas" (1947:62). The basic regional summaries for the Native Southeast are John Swanton's (1946) *The Indians of the Southeastern United States* and Charles Hudson's (1976) *The Southeastern Indians.* For the Northeastern groups, like the Sauk, with whom the Yuchi have had contact, the current standard summary is volume 15 (Northeast) of the *Handbook of North American Indians* (Trigger 1978).

2. Another recent critic of Swanton's assumptions of homogeneity is Patricia Galloway (1995). Unlike Galloway, I would shift blame from Swanton, whose industry in collecting Southeastern data remains unmatched, to his successors in Southeastern Indian studies. In a pattern common to American anthropology since World War II, scholars reacted to the volume of Swanton's output as if it signaled that little was left to do (DeMallie 1994). As Galloway's valuable work on the Choctaw reveals, much remained to be done following Swanton's initial spadework. Recent ethnohistorical and archaeological work is producing valuable results, but linguistics and ethnography are only now overcoming the false assumption that little of value can be learned in contemporary Southeastern communities.

The view that nothing of interest remains to be learned from fieldwork with contemporary Southeastern Indian communities is perhaps stated most forcefully in the work of Charles Hudson, one of the leading students of Southeastern Indian studies during the last several decades. In one example from his writings, a discussion of ritual vomiting, he comments, "What remains to be explained, particularly to those who, like myself have always hated to vomit, is why they did it at all. The custom is still practiced to a limited extent by contemporary Southeastern Indians in Oklahoma, but they only retain vestiges of the old Southeastern belief system, and their explanation of why they practice the custom today would not be a reliable guide to aboriginal belief and practice" (1975:95).

As I intend to illustrate in the chapters that follow, contemporary Southeastern communities retain cultural continuity with the earlier periods of interest to Hudson and his ethnohistorical colleagues. In the case of ritual vomiting, attendance at a Yuchi or Creek Green Corn or a conversation of any substance with a practicing Southeastern medicine man reveals that many of the patterns and beliefs that Hudson identifies in the ethnohistorical record exist also among contemporary people.

3. Historian Joshua Piker (1998) and anthropologists Pamela Innis (1997), Jack Schultz (1999), and Pamela Wallace (1998) have initiated important studies in this direction yet much work remains to be done. Deserving particular attention are: the historical and contemporary situation of other enclaved groups within the Creek and Cherokee social systems, such as the Shawnee, Natchez, and Alabama; the social status of those Creeks who settled among the Cherokee after removal; the current life of lower Creek towns; the articulation of old town organizations with modern chartered communities

sponsored by the Creek Nation; the nature of Creek-Seminole social interaction; and the social life and interactional networks of the Creek Christian congregations. Speck (1907a) remains the only ethnographic study of a single Creek town. As William Sturtevant (p.c. 1995) has suggested, deaggregating John Swanton's published and unpublished materials by local town group would greatly assist efforts at understanding cultural diversity among the Creek peoples.

4. The earliest accounts date from around 1880 and more recent versions retain the same basic form to the present (Gatschet 1893; Tuggle 1973:173).

5. Swanton's singling out of a bullsnake art motif as a distinctly Yuchi cultural trait derives from Speck's Yuchi monograph (1909:54). Speck's fieldwork was conducted with support from the American Museum of Natural History as well as the Bureau of American Ethnology. Speck was provided with funds to make a collection of Yuchi material culture for the American Museum. In conjunction with this aspect of his work, he was expected to obtain as much information as possible on decorative symbolism. A common design motif in the fingerwoven textiles produced by the Yuchi and other Woodland peoples in the nineteenth century is the diamond, one of a small number of designs the technique will allow. When questioned, Speck's consultants associated these diamonds with the appearance of a bullsnake. Diamond designs are widespread in nineteenth- and twentieth-century items of Native manufacture, and the same vague association appears among the Seminole and other Southeastern peoples. The recognition of the bullsnake motif as uniquely Yuchi seems to be more an artifact of the interest that Speck and his peers in the Columbia University-American Museum program shared in design symbolism, than of actual Yuchi culture.

6. Recent anthropological histories by Marvin Smith (1987) for the contact period, Brent Weisman (1989) for the Seminoles, Patricia Galloway (1995) for the Choctaw, and Anthony Wallace (1993) for removal have begun to remedy this deficiency. Also noteworthy is Claudio Saunt's (1999b) recent history of Creek social change in the period 1733–1819.

7. A classic anthropological source is Barth's (1969) edited volume *Ethnic Groups and Boundaries*. His recent monographic studies (Barth 1987) continue this line of development. My summary of Yuchi history is derived from secondary sources, especially Swanton (1922) and the research of Pamela Wallace (1996, forthcoming).

8. The identification of the Chisca as a Yuchi group was put forward by John Swanton (1922), and while it has been generally accepted, it remains open to question. Students familiar with the difficult study of Southeastern Indian synonymy will know that Swanton and historian Verner Crane prominently debated Yuchi associations with other contact-era ethnonyms. They disagreed regarding the linkage of the Yuchi with the group known in documents as the Westo, but Crane supported Swanton's linkage of Yuchi and Chisca. On the basis of this concurrence, I am proceeding in this narrative as if

the Chisca were a group of Yuchi-speaking people ancestral to the contemporary Yuchi. Further historical research may overturn this assumption, but I have not yet found evidence that would require abandoning it (Crane 1918, 1919; Swanton 1919, 1922).

9. The late Joseph B. Mahan was the leading figure in pseudo-scientific research bearing on the place of the Yuchi in ancient world history, but his work has inspired the epigraphic interests of assorted others whose questionable research is worthy of a full-scale cultural and critical analysis. The conference discussed by Grounds (1996:66) was a gathering of such persons, more interested in imagining speculative Yuchi pasts than engaging with the Yuchi people in their midst. For other hyperdiffusionist and epigraphic considerations of the Yuchi and other groups, see Farley (1994) and Covey (1993). Mahan's theories have also affected (and hindered) more mainstream attempts at anthropological interpretation of Yuchi culture and history, as illustrated by Matern (1996). Many assertions made in this later study are not supported by historical and anthropological evidence or by widespread agreement in the Yuchi community of today. (A simple example that provides a broader warning is Matern's identification of Coweta as a Yuchi tribal name [1996:17]).

10. Although I am attempting to treat the cowhide tale from a Yuchi point of view, Swanton, who collected similar "cowhide purchase" tales among the Creek, noted that the motif has a wide Old-World distribution (1928d:76).

11. Slave raiding by "Creek" and Yuchi groups into Florida continued during the later 1700s, when raids extended into far southern Florida, decimating the local populations. Documents bearing on the effect of Yuchi raids on the peoples of the Keys and far southeast Florida are presented in Sturtevant (1978).

12. The Yuchi appear always to have been a cultural and linguistic minority among the Seminole in Florida. Yuchi identity is no longer preserved among the Seminole in Oklahoma or Florida. Ethnic or town identities were preserved in Florida until at least 1850, when a census noted such divisions. The census was amended to show that the last Yuchi-Seminole man (or family) emigrated from Florida to Indian Territory in 1852 (Sturtevant 1988:124). In Florida, Seminole ethnic heterogeneity is preserved in the present by the use of two Native languages – Creek and Mikasuki.

13. Describing one of the Yuchi villages, "In-tuch-cul-gau," Hawkins noted: "They have fourteen families in the village; their industry is increasing; they built a square in 1798, which serves for their town house; they have a few cattle, hogs, and horses" (quoted in Swanton 1922:310). I have found no evidence to suggest that the Yuchi built townhouses in Oklahoma, as some Creek towns continued to do after removal in the nineteenth century. The village that Hawkins described resembles present-day Yuchi town communities and their ceremonial grounds both demographically and structurally.

14. For detailed studies of texts as historically constituted and reconstituted cultural objects, see the collection *Natural Histories of Discourse*, edited by Michael Silverstein and Greg Urban (1996).

15. Perhaps the best study of this period and the social dynamics of Indian-European relations in the east is Richard White's (1991) *The Middle Ground*. For the emergence of intertribal resistance to colonization, see Gregory Evans Dowd's (1992) *A Spirted Resistance*. For the social and economic dimensions of the Southeastern frontier viewed as a multicultural borderland, see Daniel Usner's (1998) *American Indians in the Lower Mississippi Valley.*

16. A biographical sketch of one such Yuchi "chief" is presented in Russell (1959).

17. The standard sources for Creek history in Oklahoma are Angie Debo's (1941) *The Road to Disappearance* and Grant Foreman's (1934) *The Five Civilized Tribes*. For the legal history of Creek-U.S. relations after removal, see Harring (1994:57–99).

18. Identification with a tribal town (Creek *italwa*) was, and is, a question of degree. For conservative Creeks and Yuchis it was much greater than for Creek politicians. As previously noted, town identity has been preserved most strongly among the former Upper Creek towns, particularly among ceremonial ground participants.

19. The perspective of the métis leadership during and after the war is well expressed in the autobiography of a principal figure, Chief George Washington Grayson (Grayson 1988). Grayson was also a primary collaborator with John Swanton in his Creek fieldwork. The Grayson family is the subject of current work by Claudio Saunt (1999a), and George Washington Grayson is the subject of a recent biography by Mary Warde (1999).

20. In his monograph, Speck indicates that the practice of "sweating" horses "will be described later" (1909:11). I am not aware of a published account by Speck of a practice with this name, but it is likely that he was referring to the visiting ceremony known as "smoking ponies," which he had already described briefly in his paper on Osage ethnology. "Smoking ponies," which was known among the Osage, Delaware, Sauk and Fox, Shawnee, Quapaw, Caddo, Wichita, Pawnee, and other tribes in Northeastern and Central Oklahoma, was a potlatch-like institution in which tribal delegations visited neighboring groups and were presented horses as gifts. Pipes were smoked to ratify the gift and, at a later date, recipients were expected to reciprocate with horse gifts of increased value. Such public displays of generosity and contempt for wealth are today expressed in the modern Pan-Indian giveaway ceremony. Recalling early-twentieth-century practice, Mose Cahwee described gift giving as accompanying Yuchi family ceremonies, such as baby namings (Roark-Calnek 1977:129; Speck 1907b:170–71).

21. The Yuchi have, in general, been spared the high unemployment rate experienced by Creek people living in the rural, southern half of the nation. Today, the Yuchi settlements have, as a practical matter, become suburbanized regions around metropolitan Tulsa.

3. CEREMONIAL LIFE

1. This understanding is found in the ritual ideology of other Woodland communities; for example, the site for Delaware ritual was also known as a "big house" (Speck

1931). The theology underpinning these ideas was noted in a study of Cayuga ritual by Frank Speck.

> And this brings us to a subject of some importance in the future study of religious concepts of the Indians of the East and Southeast (Delaware, Yuchi, Creek). In the latter cultures we find that the ceremonial grounds, whether in the open or enclosed, represent a deeply significant allegory, a phase of the sky-world on earth within which humans are carrying on actions in ceremonial form, the counterpart of those of the spirits above, the latter being invisibly present during the performances accompanying their living kinsfolk (1995:18).

This view is manifest in Yuchi thought throughout their rituals in the attention paid to the spiritual participation of heavenly ancestors in the ceremonies held on earth. This general view is also expressed today, particularly by Creek ritualists, in a formulation that asserts that the arbors of ceremonial grounds support the weight of the heavens. If all of the ceremonial grounds were abandoned, the sky would collapse, bringing catastrophe to earth.

2. Speck attributed a preference for endogamy to the Yuchi societies, particularly to the chief society. (1909:77).

3. Construction, repair, and improvements on the family camps are prohibited until after the communal work of Arbor Dance. Major construction may be undertaken after the ceremonial season, but before the New (calendar) Year. This belief noticeably differentiates the Yuchi from their Creek neighbors, who do not possess this rule and who today use their own family camps with greater regularity, sometimes independently of any particular ceremonial ground event.

4. The use of three assistant chiefs at Polecat matches the practice that Speck described for the Yuchi (1909:81). It also brings the total number of chiefs to four, the Yuchi ritual pattern number. The use of a single assistant chief at Duck Creek and Sand Creek today appears to be a borrowing from the Creek, although the use of a four-person committee at all three grounds replicates the earlier pattern.

5. I was able to participate in some of the activities of the Sand Creek ground during 1993 and 1995 as a guest of the late James Brown, Sr. and his family, but my familiarity with this community is less than for the other two Yuchi grounds. During the summer of 1996, Sand Creek was adjusting to changes in leadership and participation, and therefore my attention focused on the other Yuchi grounds. In 1993 and 1995, Wade Bucktrot, Jr., the former Sand Creek Chief, was generous in allowing me to participate in the ground's activities.

6. For a useful approach to reoccurring ritual themes, see Vogt (1992).

7. This discussion of sand refers to the lines of white sand running from the fire to each of the three arbors during the Green Corn Ceremony. They symbolize rays of sunlight.

8. Mr. Littlebear's reference to the *Tsoyaha* as the "full Yuchi" reflects the belief that "full blood" Yuchi people formed a special class, more closely related to the Sun and Moon than most modern Yuchi people who are intermixed with other tribes. The modern understanding of kinship, tribal membership, and Indian identity in terms of "blood," while a partial artifact of colonial governmental policies such as tribal enrollment and exposure to Euro-American beliefs about kinship, is complicated by the rich set of beliefs about blood expressed in Yuchi creation narratives (DeMallie 2001; Schneider 1980).

9. Some of my consultants criticized the recent practice among some women at the Green Corn "who do not know any better" of painting "crow's feet" or other powwow-inspired paint designs rather than the red circles expected. Both the use of inappropriate designs and the use of paint outside of the two Yuchi ritual contexts were considered troubling, but there is no community forum in which such deviations from the expected norm can be addressed by female elders. The divergence between talk about paint designs and the practice of wearing paint is reminiscent of Greg Urban's thoughtful discussion of paint designs in lowland South America (1996: chapter 5). The red circle design that I have described as the Yuchi norm was observed by Frank Speck during his fieldwork at Sand Creek, but he illustrates not only red circles at the cheekbones, but one on the forehead as well (1909:plate 10).

10. In the literature on the Yuchi and other Woodland groups, the land of spirits is often situated, by consultants, in the west, yet sometimes in the east. Locating heaven in the west is the logical conclusion of the life-course symbolism already outlined, while as Freeman has noted, situating heaven in the east connects it with the positive associations attached to that direction (1961:29). In contrast to my own information, Speck located the Yuchi "haven of souls" in the east and stated that at burial the "head is always placed at the west, causing the face to be directed toward the east, the direction the departed spirit journeys" (1909:98). Today, bodies laid to rest are oriented in this way, but the practice is differently interpreted. Reflecting Christian belief, I have been told that this is in preparation for a second coming of Christ from the east. The practice of firing shots westward, and of maintaining a fire at the west end of the grave, are interpreted as showing the spirit of the deceased the westward path to heaven. All of the available information on the subject from among the Yuchi and neighboring peoples indicates that heaven is not firmly or conclusively located in either direction, but that the east-west path is symbolically significant. In mythological accounts of journeys by the living to the spirit world, adventurers often travel great lengths east or west and overcome various obstacles, often including a dangerous moving cloud located at the point where earth and sky meet. When visiting this realm, the voyagers often discover that they are located in a skyworld directly above their earthly homes. These myths reveal that the expectations of spiritual and actual geography do not need to concur. Sources for this subject include:

Miccosukee (Freeman 1961); Alabama (Swanton 1929:142); Shawnee (Howard 1981; Voegelin 1936); Creek (Swanton 1928b); Cherokee (Witthoft 1983); and Chitimacha (Swanton 1907).

11. As among the Creek, the greatest fear surrounding the violation of this taboo is that the menstrual flow of a women who breaks it will fail to stop, and she will bleed to death. I was told several stories of near-death experiences caused in this way and averted by Yuchi doctors. Lacking their own Native doctors today and recognizing the ongoing danger that this problem presents provokes anxiety among contemporary ritual leaders. As evident from their account of creation, Yuchi people have powerful ideas about blood, menstruation, and the creative power of women. For a detailed analysis of Creek views, see Bell (1990); for the Cherokee, see Fogelson (1977, 1980, 1990).

4. SPEAKING IN THE BIG HOUSE

1. The speech community of which Yuchi is a part resembles the multilingual situation described by Moore (1993) for Wasco. Into the twentieth century, a considerable variety of languages were spoken by distinct peoples politically labeled Creek. As with Wasco, Yuchi was widely regarded as the most difficult of the local languages to learn. Similarly to the Wasco case, Yuchi speakers learned other Native languages, but the reverse was not generally true for speakers of Creek, Natchez, Cherokee, Shawnee, and other languages of eastern Oklahoma. The parallel to Moore's Wasco findings continues into the present era, where Yuchi has become a prestige variety and the stature that once solely accrued to speakers now is afforded to semi-speakers and language learners capable of deploying Yuchi words and memorized phrases in appropriate contexts. For the concept of "tip" see the work of Nancy Dorian (1989).

2. In speaking words attributed to the chief, the Yuchi speaker's role is similar to that of Chinookian orators, the example of which served to complicate linguistic notions of speaker-hearer in the programmatic writings on the ethnography of speaking (Hymes 1962:25). For a recent African case study see Yankah (1995).

3. I use *function* here in the sense proposed by Urban (1993:241). While he uses the term *cultural function*, some of the purposes that I identify here relate directly to the management of social interaction and might be termed "social functions." These use of *function* emerge from discussion of the relationship between discourse and sociocultural context and are not framed explicitly as functionalist interpretations of social life.

4. Geoffrey Kimball (1991:574, 611–12) discusses Koasati oratory, apparently obsolete, on the basis of oratory-like passages occurring in other narrative genres. He finds that oratory appears to rely on parallelism, poetic repetition, staccato production, and increased stress – features typical of Creek and Yuchi oratory.

5. In her corpus of Creek oratory studies, Bell presents and discusses only a single text, so it is difficult to judge the degree to which her account represents the norm for Creek

oratory. Her own analysis presents this text as a seamless, ideal-type for Creek speech making. She provides rich context in terms of cultural background needed to understand the text, but little by way of situational context that might shed light on the relationship between the text analyzed and the specific context of its performance. The text itself is wonderfully rich, and, as Bell (1984:348) herself suggests, it is deserving of further study. Mr. Spencer Frank delivered the text analyzed by Bell in July of 1981. Mr. Frank was widely regarded as a leading Creek orator, and Yuchi chiefs and speakers regarded him as a respected friend.

6. Concurrent with my own work among the Yuchi, Pamela Innis has undertaken study of discourse practices associated with the Creek ceremonial grounds. She contends that Creek oratory is directed at a range of cultural functions similar to those that I have outlined for Yuchi practice (p.c. 1996). She and I both suggest that Bell's account overemphasizes the alliance-building function in Creek oratory to the exclusion of other concerns.

7. There are two Absentee Shawnee ceremonial grounds named Little Axe near the town of the same name. The group that regularly visits the Yuchi is known as the north or new ground. James Howard refers to this community as the Little River ground (1981:228). During the year 2000, a third ceremonial ground was established in the Little Axe area as a result of social changes internal to the Absentee Shawnee ceremonialist community.

8. This ideal is usually manifest in actual practice, although the amount of support reciprocally extended by the Yuchi grounds to each other has varied through time, and temporary conflicts occasionally emerge.

9. Richard Parmentier (1994a) has provided a useful account of the use of such historical frames for addressing present-day concerns in ritual oratory.

10. Until recently, use of the Yuchi language itself was the most notable key of performance. The description that follows is based on current, English-language practice. In a number of contemporary Oklahoma communities, public performance in ritual contexts is the last situation in which Native languages are used publicly. For monolingual English-speaking audiences, these performances (prayers, speeches, namings, etc.) gain much of their power from the use of a venerated tribal language, yet this speech, perfectly intelligible to the speaker, has no practical referential capacity at all for most and sometimes all of the listeners.

11. The works of Mikhail Bakhtin (1984), V. N. Vološinov (1986), and Erving Goffman (1981) have greatly influenced my thinking about "voices" and participants in Yuchi oratory speech events, as has the work of colleagues who have incorporated the thinking of these scholars into current research in folklore and linguistic anthropology.

12. For students of Iroquois oratory, Mr. Littlebear's recitation of valued natural forces should be of interest for the degree to which it corresponds to the hierarchy addressed in longhouse Thanksgiving rituals.

13. The use of direct reported speech is uncommon in Mr. Littlebear's oratories, although it appears in a variety of other Yuchi genres such as myths, folktales, legends, and personal narrative.

5. INDIAN FOOTBALL

1. Games are sometimes, because of time constraints, shortened to six or four points, similarly divided into three or two points marked, then erased.

2. This cane pole is one of those used by the "stickmen" during nighttime dances at the ceremonial ground. It is used as a symbol of authority throughout Yuchi ceremonial events.

3. This scoring procedure differs from that found in the Shawnee football game and in other Woodland games where score pegs are placed in the ground to tally points (Howard 1981:264–65).

4. The pattern of allowing young boys to compete along with the women is repeated in the single-pole stickball game played today by the Yuchi, Seminole, Creek, and Cherokee.

5. At all three Yuchi grounds, the football field is oriented north to south and is located to the east of the square ground. At the Duck Creek ground, the women defend the south goal. At Polecat and Sand Creek grounds, the women defend the north goal.

6. During the first game at the Duck Creek ground, an additional ritual step is taken after the washing and before the game. The Chief, assisted by the poleboys (the four young men who are responsible for many of the ritual tasks on the square ground) build a small fire on the fireplace at the center of the square. According to Simon Harry, the ground's current chief, the building of this fire signals that the ground is open and that the home members are not to dance elsewhere until Duck Creek's own dances begin.

7. Following Raymond Fogelson's treatment of the Cherokee stickball game, I am here viewing the Yuchi football game as a cultural performance, that is, an event featuring an "organized program of activity, a set of performers, an audience, and a place and occasion of performance" (Singer 1991:29). Key to Fogelson's stickball studies is the view that such cultural performances encapsulate local understandings of the sociocultural universe and reveal the "dynamic interaction of personality, social, and cultural systems" (1971:327).

8. It is unclear to me whether the Yuchi, during Speck's visits, understood the Sun as a separate deity or if, as now, they saw the Sun as a manifestation of the Creator, who is today understood in monotheistic terms.

9. Raymond Fogelson (p.c. 1997) notes that this may be another case of Yuchi affinity with the Northeast in contrast to the Southeast, where the ritual begging-beseeching pattern seems reduced or absent.

10. The matchball or men's stickball game in the Southeast has been widely discussed. As the Southeastern version of the more familiar lacrosse, stickball is most often a form

of institutionalized warfare between the men of rival communities. The game is surrounded by a host of important cultural forms and social practices. The Yuchi abandoned matchball in the early twentieth century, but it remains ritually important among their Creek neighbors, who have transformed it into a community-internal male contest. A summary of the major aspects of the game can be found in Vennum (1994). The best available ethnographic account is Fogelson's (1962) dissertation study of the Cherokee game.

11. It is also worth noting, with respect to the symbolism reflecting themes of renewal and rebirth, that games at each ceremonial ground are usually held on Easter Sunday. A further linking of the two events takes place at the Duck Creek ground. For several years, the women of that ground have organized a children's Easter egg hunt preceding the football game. The egg hunt, with prizes for each age group, takes place in and around the camps on the ground's periphery.

12. In searching the ethnographic accounts of Woodland football, I have set aside the many scattered pre-twentieth-century historical references that attest to the game's presence throughout the Northeast. Jim Rementer's (1993) study of the Delaware game collects many of these references to show that the game has considerable historical depth among coastal Algonkian groups. Although the historic accounts cover several hundred years and are rather sketchy about details, the range of cultural variation parallels that attested in the modern ethnography.

13. This women's version of the game was pictured by the young Seneca artist Jessie Cornplanter (1903).

14. The Seneca-Cayuga Sun Dance should not be confused with the unrelated Sun Dance rituals found among Plains peoples.

15. In another paper on the Seneca-Cayuga, Howard reports the surprising fact that "the men always win. If they do not, another game is played until they do" (1970:8).

16. Football is played today at the Absentee Shawnee ceremonial grounds (two during the period of this research, three since summer 2000) and at the one Loyal Shawnee ground. It is played both by the Delaware living near Anadarko in western Oklahoma and by those settled near Dewey in the east.

17. It is unfortunate that Speck, a relentless fieldworker, never had the opportunity to undertake fully the "study of the religious concepts of the Indians of the East and Southeast" to which his many ethnographic projects were leading (1995:18). In his Delaware study he incorrectly wrote: "There seem to be no closely analogous ceremonies in the eastern area with which to compare this interesting rite outside of the Shawnee analogue, unless they be found in Iroquois, and no specific reference to it in the early Delaware narratives which might serve as a help in determining its former history before the removal west" (1937:74). In his earlier work with the Yuchi (1909), Speck arrived in Oklahoma too late in the year to witness the football game and his account provides only a minimal description. Following his Delaware work, he did document the Cherokee

(Speck and Broom 1983) and Cayuga (1995) game, but he never attempted the comparison toward which he seemed to be moving.

18. Since the game in its secular form is found among the Chickasaw, it would be surprising if it were not similarly found among the Choctaw, with whom they share so much common culture and history. Nonetheless, I have not discovered any references to the game among them. A possible exception to this is David Bushnell's description of a ball game among the Choctaw of Bayou Lacomb, Louisiana in 1909. He interpreted this game as a modification of the stickball game, played without racquets (1909:20).

6. STOMP DANCE

1. My interests here are similar in many ways to those of Amelia Bell, who examined Creek ceremonial ground life during the 1980s. While our interpretations do not contradict each other, she presents her Creek material from a more abstract and analytic point of view than I have attempted here. To the extent that I am more concerned with the interaction order governing stomp dance events, my approach is more like that of Sue Roark-Calnek, who examined Delaware ceremonialism during the 1970s.

2. The success of Oklahoma communities contrasts with the many small, isolated remnant communities located in the Southeast and elsewhere in the East. Lacking Indian neighbors with a similar way of life, groups such as the Catawba and Powhatan were less able to perpetuate elaborate corporate rituals. At the middle of this continuum is the now-abandoned intertribal ritual network of Louisiana tribes described by Victoria Levine (1991). Outside Oklahoma, the other major contemporary intertribal ritual network in the East is among the Iroquois of New York and Canada.

3. This is a general pattern common to all Oklahoma Indian cultural performances, including powwows and peyote meetings. The use of prominent individuals in key positions mobilizes the assistance of such a person's supporters, increasing overall participation (Roark-Calnek 1977).

4. In the Creek area, secular indoor stomp dances take place after the ceremonial grounds close in the fall. All Yuchi grounds and most Creek grounds participate in those dances. Some ceremonial ground people feel that those dances are inappropriate because of the sacred nature of ceremonial ground ritual performances, including dances.

5. Swanton assigned the Yuchi to the white side in his ethnographic present account and provided a footnote to an ethnohistorical source that has Chiaha (red) defeating the Yuchi in 1722. For Swanton this confirms the Yuchi's ancient place on the white side, but Haas's and Spoehr's information suggests otherwise. Swanton was apparently unaware of the switching principle that they discovered (1928d:254–55).

6. The games described by Haas and other previous authors took place at neutral sites, whereas the current games take place at the ceremonial ground of the host. Thus the transformation works at both the symbolic and literal levels that have been well de-

scribed by Fogelson (1962), Bell (1984) and others. The boundaries of Southeastern towns and modern ceremonial grounds symbolize and contain expressions of safety, peace, kinship, and domesticity, while the regions beyond the town are undomesticated, dangerous, alien, and unpredictable.

7. Conflict between grounds today is not particularly strong. Grounds that oppose one another simply seek to avoid and ignore each other. Extreme conflicts are occasionally indexed in informal discourse through witchcraft accusations, but those and other open expressions of hostility are rare. Among ceremonial ground people, hostile feelings are more often today directed outward at politicians and others who criticize or hinder their efforts at preserving customary practices.

8. As noted elsewhere in this study, a third Absentee Shawnee ceremonial ground was established near the town of Little Axe during 2000.

9. Only during the most crowded of events, such as a Green Corn ceremony in which many visitors have shown up, will the intervention of the hosts be required, primarily to ensure that cars are parked in such a way as to prevent stomp ground gridlock.

10. At a regular Yuchi stomp dance, one camp will be used for the ground's potluck meal, for feeding visitors, and for providing coffee breaks. At the Green Corn Ceremony and the Soup Dance, when many visitors are present, those tasks are distributed among the family camps, all of which would be open, with food prepared by their residents.

11. I am extremely appreciative of Mary Linn's efforts in transcribing and translating this text and of the E.U.C.H.E.E. organization and the family of Chief Brown for allowing us to study it. Our hope is that in presenting it, we further Chief Brown's goal of making it available as an example for future use by Yuchi community members. This text presents an interesting parallel with the texts discussed in chapter four in the way it illustrates, in a different ritual speech genre, how the chief is the acknowledged author of the message presented publicly by a ceremonial ground orator (see Jackson and Linn 2000).

12. When I began attending Yuchi dances, this huddle was a feature only at Duck Creek. At the other grounds, the fourth call was followed directly by the men positioning themselves for the starting dance. At Duck Creek, this practice was instituted after the reorganization of the ground at its current site. In recent years (1999–2000), the practice began to be followed at the Polecat ground as well.

13. At Sand Creek and Polecat grounds, the starting songs are sung at the east edge of the square, due east of the fireplace. At Duck Creek ground, the men line up in the southeast corner of the square.

14. The Yuchi Starting Dance songs are similar in melody and vocable texts to the Friendship Dance that is performed by the Creek and Cherokee, but their choreography, symbolism, and use are distinct.

15. Some very energetic visitors will leave one dance in order to attend another during

the same night. This practice is most common among groups of young men who are establishing reputations as singers and building social relationships throughout the stomp dance network.

7. ARBOR DANCE

1. With the encouragement of Simon Harry, the Duck Creek chief, I videotaped that ground's Arbor Dance preparations in 1996. That record, together with additional participation in that event in 1993, 1995, and the years 1997–2000, serves as the basis for my description. Those experiences are supplemented by participation in arbor fixing at the Polecat ground during the years 1996–2000 and by various interviews and public discussions.

2. When leading the men around the fire with their brush, the Polecat chief makes four whoops, which are answered by the men. These whoops were omitted at Duck Creek during the period of my participation. Otherwise, the procedures at the grounds are similar in outline.

3. The word *busk*, used here by Mr. Littlebear, is a common name for the Green Corn Ceremony in the Southeast. It is derived from the Muskogee (Creek) word *posketv* (lit., "to fast"), especially in association with the new corn crop (Martin and Mauldin 2000:100).

4. The use of flint and steel was reinstituted at the Duck Creek ground during the 1997 Green Corn Ceremony. Throughout Oklahoma, a "rock fire" is viewed as more powerful than a fire made by modern means.

5. The swept-yard aesthetic seems to have been retained among Southeastern peoples since preremoval times. Ethnohistorical and archaeological evidence suggests that in the old Southeastern town configuration, household structure mirrored that of the town square, with household buildings bordering a cleared square. Visiting the North Carolina Cherokee ritual leader Will West Long in 1946, William Fenton recorded in his notes: "Will's dooryard was swept clean with a broom when we returned Thursday A.M. (12/5), all the refuse went over the brink of a stone terrace, to form a midden of corn cobs, chips from wood chopping, and wood working. Idea struck me of Southeastern square ground swept clear for dances" (1946:5).

8. GREEN CORN CEREMONY

1. For other Yuchi versions of this story, consult the works of W. O. Tuggle (1973:174), Albert Gatschet (1893:281), and Günter Wagner (1931:107, 238).

2. Linguist Mary Linn provided this transcription of the Lizard Dance call based on audio recordings that I provided. She notes: "There are seven beats/syllables. Each syllable has primary stress. The first three [e] have falling-rising tone. The bottom of the falling tone turns into the glide [y] by the fourth syllable and is continued until the end of the call. With the fourth syllable, the drop in tone becomes rapid. For some dancers, the

initial syllable onset may be a glottal stop rather than [w]. The number of syllables used varies, but seven is the typical number. The vowel combined with [y] at the end of the call may vary. The call is more musical than language, more regular than most dance whoops, and less language-like than vocable songs" (p.c. 1997).

3. The story, for Mr. Skeeter, also helped explain the Jumping the Hill Dance conducted during the Saturday ceremonial at Polecat. In it the dancers leap over a earthen hill representing the hill of earth built by the medicine man in the story in preparation for defeating the lizard.

4. This story is referred to, but not told in full, in an essay by Gary White Deer (1995:11).

5. The furthest reaches of oral history in the Duck Creek community recalls performance of the Feather Dances at their ceremonial ground when it was located on Euchee Creek, west of Hectorville. This period was probably the last decades of the nineteenth century. During Frank Speck's visits to the Yuchi at Sand Creek in 1904 and 1905, they also performed the Feather Dances.

6. The Green Corn Ceremony takes place in the summer, when the sun is at its closest to the earth. The men drink medicine as close to noon as possible, as this is when the sun is the brightest and warmest, and hence most powerful. Both Speck and I have recorded narratives that assert that the Creator, in the form of the sun, takes special note to see if the Yuchi are performing their annual Green Corn Ceremony. If the sun discovers that it has been omitted, then world-changing events will ensue (Speck 1909:106–7).

7. For mention of a Creek variation on this story, see Swanton (1928b:609).

8. In Newman Littlebear's account of the origin of fire, two boys who are off playing by themselves discover, to their amusement, that banging flint rocks together produces sparks. When they show this trick to their grandfather, he recognizes its potential benefit for the people. As a new fire ceremonial, the fire started on the Saturday of the Green Corn Ceremony is made in "Indian" fashion with a flint and steel. As discussed in chapter 7, such a "rock" fire is more powerful than a fire started by modern means. Replicating ancient Southeastern Indian practice, some camps carry coals from this new fire to their camps, renewing their household fires as well. As discussed in chapters 3 and 7, this presents certain difficulties with respect to women not observing menstrual restrictions.

9. For a full consideration of such tradition-making strategies in oral narrative, see Bauman (1992).

10. The full ceremonial includes seven Feather Dances, the fourth of which is also called the Bead Dance. The two Jumping the Hill Dances are also classified as Feather Dances because the feather wands carried in the Feather Dances are also carried during them. The tenth daytime dance is a variation of the Friday evening Lizard Dance using the same song, but differing in choreography. The Saturday version lacks the gunmen, washing, and sweeping found in the Friday afternoon dance. The Feather Dance wands are not carried during this dance.

11. There may have once been other tribes, beyond the Yuchi, Creek, and Seminole, who practiced a form of the Feather Dance. There is ethnohistorical evidence for such a dance among the Cherokee, and potentially the Catawba. The Feather Dance also appears to be related to the Eagle Dance, discussed comparatively by William Fenton (1953). See Capron (1953) for the Florida Seminole, Timberlake (1765) for the Cherokee, and Speck (1939) for the Catawba.

12. Amelia Bell's (1990) detailed analysis of female symbolism in Creek culture explores the resonances of this story in detail.

13. Jim Rementer (p.c. 1997) graciously provided a transcript of the full narrative, which is deposited at the National Anthropological Archives. The author of the account was Lula Gilliland, a Lenape Delaware from eastern Oklahoma. Rementer, who has spent most of his life in close association with Delaware religious leaders, suggests that the reference to Jesus is probably a substitution for the Creator in "the original Lenape version of the story."

14. James Howard reports that a Shawnee consultant, Cody Mack, remembered a Shawnee Lizard Dance that became obsolete in the 1930s, but he provided no details about it (1981:340).

15. A related group of stories found among all of these groups concerns encounters with horned snakes, typically residing under or near water. In these, individuals may acquire power from the snakes, but none of these stories explain the acquisition of collective medicine power.

9. SOUP DANCE

1. During this process, the stickmen begin their visiting with the chief's own camp and then circulate counter-clockwise, as is the pattern throughout Yuchi ritual. This pattern holds throughout all Yuchi ritual activity whenever they are sent around as heralds to the camps. The only exception is prior to the Ribbon Dance, when they begin their visitations at the head dancer's camp.

2. The formal contribution of wood by the men after the feast has been omitted in recent years at Duck Creek, although it is acknowledged as the traditional procedure.

3. Acknowledging that my description of Yuchi ritual life has emphasized an ideal moral order at the expense of focusing on actual cases of interpersonal conflict, the subject of these meetings provides an opportunity to address the latter briefly but directly. If intra-community conflict is to emerge in a public ceremonial ground context, it would emerge during these meetings. That said, the format is a dangerous one in which to raise disagreements, because it provides disputants an immediate and open opportunity for rebuttal. The sacred character of the setting also mitigates what might otherwise become overly frank discussions. In making contentious points, speakers seek to frame their criticisms or arguments as positions rooted in a desire to observe traditional custom and outlooks. In my experience, issues of conflict may be aired in such meetings but are never

resolved there. Resolution takes place in the context of informal discussions among individual participants and through decisions reached by the chief and his committee.

4. Recall that water is both a witness and a medicine. W. L. Ballard reports a variation on this naming ritual: "If the baby is named in the traditional fashion, it is taken at four days of age, preferably by an older child of the family, around a body of water (such as a creek, pond, or well) four times, the older child repeating the name on each round, and then a necklace of white beads is put on the child. He wears this until it is too small for him" (1971:6). None of my consultants have reported this exact ritual, but the existence of family variations is highly likely.

5. An account of historical and contemporary Yuchi funeral practices would be a complicated task, one that I postpone for the time being. The many Yuchi elders with whom I worked have demonstrated a strong interest in documenting and interpreting these rituals, something that I hope to continue in the future. As with other aspects of their culture, Yuchi funerals are closest, as Yuchi people frequently comment, to Shawnee funerals, but they also appear to possess several unique features that make them distinctively Yuchi. For Shawnee practices, see Voegelin (1944) and Howard (1981).

6. For the Yuchi, pork has become the standard substitute for wild game. This was also the case for the Delaware. Among the Loyal Shawnee, beef has likewise become the accepted substitute for game in their Bread Dance. Among the Creek, Seminole, and Absentee Shawnee, squirrels are now substituted in rituals where deer was once preferred. For the Yuchi, the adoption of pork took place long ago, and as the Yuchi Soup Dance does not place emphasis on male hunting, the switch is not remembered as having a particular significance.

7. Howard also failed to note that a less formal squirrel feast is held during the opening events at Creek, and probably Oklahoma Seminole, ceremonial grounds during the early spring (Robbins 1976:129).

8. A feature of the Creek-Seminole dance variously called the Horned Owl, Snake, or Hunting Dance is a serpentine dance in which the participants hold hands and are led in spiraling patterns around the ground by the leader. The dance or dances associated with the fall ceremonial (Swanton identifies both a Snake Dance and a Horned Owl Dance) appeared to have been unique stand-alone dance forms with their own music. As noted in chapter 6, a variation of the standard stomp dance is now known today as the Snake Dance. In it, the stomp dance leader first prompts the dancers to hold hands and then leads them in a spiraling dance away from the fire. Both forms share the same dance technique and the older form may have contributed to the development of the modern form. The Oklahoma Cherokee are often credited with popularizing the modern snake dance form and Cherokee singers have the most developed song repertoire for leading this dance. The basic form involves leaving the fire and forming a moving spiral away from it. Some leaders have further elaborated the dance by introducing additional figures, including having the dance line pass through itself under the raised arms of a cou-

ple and circling the fire in one giant circle, then leading the dancers in a charge toward it, followed by a retreat. Some of these figures also appear in the "two-step" danced at southern Plains powwows. The decision to dance the modern snake dance is made by the leader while he is leading. It is not grouped with other named social dances such as the Garfish, Bean, Duck, or Guinea dances. Thus, among the Yuchi, leaders may instigate a Snake Dance at any time, whereas nighttime social dances are postponed until after the Green Corn.

9. The Yuchi Turtle Dance is unique, but dances featuring one of its songs are found among other Woodland tribes. I hope to explore the culture history of this dance at a future date. Yuchi ceremonial ground elders have enjoyed comparative musicology in the form of listening to my tapes of other tribal dance songs. Their observations and those of singers from other tribes provide a rich source of information on Woodland music and dance. I should also note that the Bean Dance has been learned and performed by a Yuchi singer, meaning that it might properly be added to the social dance songs in the Yuchi repertoire, despite its lack of a recent history of performance.

10. No special social dances were performed during the Soup Dance at Sand Creek in 1997. The Yuchi Old Folks Dance (listed in table 5 as the first social dance of the evening at Polecat in 1997) is a daytime dance at Duck Creek, performed following the Buffalo Dance on Saturday evening of Green Corn. At Polecat, where the dance does not appear on the daytime Green Corn program, it can be used as an alternative to the starting song to begin the nighttime dance. This practice was reestablished at the Polecat Soup Dance in 1997 after a lapse of several years. During discussions prior to the 1997 Soup Dance, elders recalled how this dance used to be danced to begin the evening dancing very early in the evening at Polecat, around sundown. The dancing would then continue straight through until daylight. In 1997, Duck Creek Chief Simon Harry led the dance to start off the Polecat evening dance at the normal time of about 11:00 P.M. The Yuchi Old Folks Dance is cognate with the Long Dance of the Oklahoma Creek, Seminole, and Natchez-Cherokee (Howard and Lena 1984; Heth 1975). The dance is used as a closing dance in the morning after an all-night dance by the Cherokee at the Stoke Smith Ceremonial Ground.

11. The Drunk (Drunken) Dance, also called the Morning Dance, has been a subject of considerable recent interest among the Yuchi ritualists with whom I have worked. Several songs have been sung for recordings by elder ritualists and several younger men have begun to learn them. The Drunk Dance may be revived in coming years.

12. For related patterns among the Cherokee, see Fogelson (1977).

13. As I hope to have shown, a concern with summer-winter, agriculture-hunting transitions is also found in the Soup Dance and cognate rituals. I feel that in present practice, this aspect of the ritual and belief system is less pronounced.

REFERENCES

Abramson, David

1997 Traditionalizing Modernities and Modernizing Traditions: The Forming and Reforming of Ideology in Post-Soviet Uzbekistan. Manuscript in the author's possession.

Anderson, Benedict

1991 Imagined Communities: Reflections on the Origin and Spread of Nationalism. Revised ed. New York: Verso.

Bakhtin, Mikhail

1984 Problems of Dostoevsky's Poetics. Translated by Caryl Emerson. Minneapolis: University of Minnesota Press.

Ballard, W. L.

1971 Yuchi Ethnographic Fieldnotes. Copies in the author's possession.

1978 The Yuchi Green Corn Ceremonial: Form and Meaning. Los Angeles: American Indian Studies Center, University of California.

Barth, Fredrick

1969 Introduction. *In* Ethnic Groups and Boundaries: The Social Organization of Culture Difference, edited by Fredrick Barth, 9–38. Boston: Little, Brown and Co.

1987 Cosmologies in the Making: A Generative Approach to Cultural Variation in Inner New Guinea. New York: Cambridge University Press.

Bartram, William

1955 Travels of William Bartram. New York: Dover.

Basso, Ellen B.

1981 A "Musical View of the Universe": Kalapalo Myth and Ritual as Religious Performance. Journal of American Folklore 94:273–91.

1990 Introduction: Discourse as an Integrating Concept in Anthropology and Folklore Research. *In* Native Latin American Cultures through Their Discourse, edited by Ellen Basso, 3–10. Bloomington: Indiana University Folklore Institute.

1995 The Last Cannibals: A South American Oral History. Austin: University of Texas.

Basso, Keith H.

1990 Western Apache Language and Culture. Tucson: University of Arizona Press.

Bauman, Richard

1986 Story, Performance and Event: Contextual Studies of Oral Narrative. New York: Cambridge University Press.

1992 Contextualization, Tradition, and the Dialogue of Genres: Icelandic Legends of the *Kraftaskáld*. *In* Rethinking Context: Language as an Interactive Phenomenon, edited by Alessandro Duranti and Charles Goodwin, 125–45. New York: Cambridge University Press.

1993 Disclaimers of Performance. *In* Responsibility and Evidence in Oral Discourse, edited by Jane H. Hill and Judith T. Irvine, 182–96. New York: Cambridge University Press.

Bauxar, J. Joseph

1957a Yuchi Ethnoarchaeology, Part I: Some Yuchi Identifications Reconsidered. Ethnohistory 4:279–301.

1957b Yuchi Ethnoarchaeology: Parts II–V. Ethnohistory 4:369–464.

1995 Ethnohistorical Reconstructions. *In* Thomas M. N. Lewis and Madeline D. Kneberg-Lewis, The Prehistory of the Chickamauga Basin in Tennessee, edited by Lynne P. Sullivan, 1:241–64. Knoxville: University of Tennessee Press.

Bell, Amelia R.

1983 Performative Effectiveness of Textual Cohesive Structures in Creek Long Talks. *In* 1982 Mid-America Linguistics Conference Papers, edited by Frances Ingemann, 335–48. Lawrence: Department of Linguistics, University of Kansas.

1984 Creek Ritual: The Path to Peace. Ph.D. diss., University of Chicago.

1985a Discourse Parallelisms and Poetics in Creek Formal Language. *In* In Memory of Roman Jakobson: Papers from the 1984 Mid-America Linguistics Conference, edited by Gilbert Youmans and Donald Lance, 323–30. Columbia MO: Linguistics Area Program.

1985b Dialectics of Discourse Parallelism in Creek Oratory. International Journal of American Linguistics 51:344–47.

1990 Separate People: Speaking of Creek Men and Women. American Anthropologist 92:332–45.

Bierhorst, John

1995 Mythology of the Lenape: Guide and Texts. Tucson: University of Arizona Press.

Blankenship, Roy, ed.

1991 The Life and Times of Frank Speck, 1881–1950. Philadelphia: Department of Anthropology, University of Pennsylvania.

Blu, Karen I.

1980 The Lumbee Problem. New York: Cambridge University Press.

Boas, Franz

1915 Mythology and Folk-Tales of the North American Indians. *In* Anthropology in North America, by Franz Boas, Roland B. Dixon, Pliny E. Goddard, A. A. Goldenweiser, A. Hrdlička, William H. Holmes, Robert H. Lowie, Paul Radin, John R. Swanton, and Clark Wissler, 306–49. New York: G. E. Stechert and Co.

1916 Tsimshian Mythology. Thirty-First Annual Report of the Bureau of American Ethnology, 29–1037. Washington DC.

1966 Kwakiutl Ethnography. Edited by Helen Codere. Chicago: University of Chicago Press.

Booker, Karen M., Charles M. Hudson, and Robert L. Rankin

1992 Place Name Identification and Multilingualism in the Sixteenth-Century Southeast. Ethnohistory 39:399–451.

Boon, James

1982 Other Tribes, Other Scribes: Symbolic Anthropology in the Comparative Study of Cultures, Histories, Religions, and Texts. New York: Cambridge University Press.

Bourdieu, Pierre

1991 Language and Symbolic Power. Cambridge: Harvard University Press.

Briggs, Charles, and Richard Bauman

1992 Genre, Intertextuality, and Social Power. Journal of Linguistic Anthropology 2:131–72.

1999 The Foundation for All Future Researches: Franz Boas, George Hunt, Native American Texts and the Construction of Modernity. American Quarterly. 51:479–528.

Brown, Cynthia

1993 The Vanished Native Americans. Nation 257:384–89.

Bureau of Indian Affairs, Department of the Interior

1999 Final Determination Against Federal Acknowledgment of the Yuchi Tribal Organization. Federal Register 64(245):71814–16.

Bushnell, David I.

1909 The Choctaw of Bayou Lacomb, St. Tammany Parish, Louisiana. Bureau of American Ethnology Bulletin 48. Washington DC.

Caffrey, Margaret

2000 Complementary Power: Men and Women of the Lenni Lenape. American Indian Quarterly. 24:44–63.

Callender, Charles

1994 Central Algonkian Moieties. *In* North American Indian Anthropology: Essays on Society and Culture, edited by Raymond J. DeMallie and Alfonso Ortiz, 108–24. Norman: University of Oklahoma Press.

Cannadine, David

1983 The Context, Performance and Meaning of Ritual: The British Monarchy and the 'Invention of Tradition,' c. 1820–1977. *In* The Invention of Tradition, edited by Eric Hobsbawm and Terence Ranger, 101–64. New York: Cambridge University Press.

Capron, Louis

1953 The Medicine Bundles of the Florida Seminole and the Green Corn Dance. Bureau of American Ethnology Anthropological Paper No. 35. Washington DC.

1956 Notes on the Hunting Dance of the Cow Creek Seminole. Florida Anthropologist 9:67–78.

Chafe, Wallace

1993 Seneca Speaking Styles and the Location of Authority. *In* Responsibility and Evidence in Oral Discourse, edited by Jane H. Hill and Judith T. Irvine, 72–87. New York: Cambridge University Press.

Clifford, James

1988 Identity in Mashpee. *In* The Predicament of Culture, 277–346. Cambridge: Harvard University Press.

Comaroff, John, and Jean Comaroff

1992 Ethnography and the Historical Imagination. Boulder CO: Westview Press.

Cornplanter, Jesse

1903 Iroquois Indian Games and Dances Drawn by Jesse Cornplanter, Seneca Indian Boy. Pamphlet, publisher and place of publication unknown. Copy held by Gilcrease Museum, Tulsa, Oklahoma.

Covey, Cyclone
1993 The Yuchi/Yuki Nonplus. Columbus GA: ISAC Press.

Craig, Alan K., and Christopher Peebles
1974 Ethnoecological Change Among the Seminoles, 1740–1840. Geoscience and Man 5:83–96.

Crane, Verner
1918 An Historical Note on the Westo Indians. American Anthropologist 20:331–37.
1919 Westo and Chisca. American Anthropologist 21:463–65.

Curtain, Jeremiah
1884 Yutci Myths. Manuscript no. 1293, National Anthropological Archives, Smithsonian Institution. Washington DC.
1948 Jeremiah Curtain in Indian Territory. Edited by Carolyn Thomas Foreman. Chronicles of Oklahoma 26:345–56.

Darnell, Regna
1989 Correlates of Cree Narrative Performance. *In* Explorations in the Ethnography of Speaking. 2d ed., edited by Richard Bauman and Joel Sherzer, 315–36. New York: Cambridge University Press.

Debo, Angie
1941 The Road to Disappearance. Norman: University of Oklahoma Press.

DeMallie, Raymond J.
1988 Lakota Traditionalism: History and Symbol. *In* Native North American Interaction Patterns. Mercury Series 112, edited by Regna Darnell and Michael K. Foster, 2–21. Hull, Quebec: Canadian Museum of Civilization.
1993 "These Have No Ears": Narrative and the Ethnohistorical Method. Ethnohistory 40:515–38.
1994 Introduction: Fred Eggan and American Indian Anthropology. *In* North American Indian Anthropology: Essays on Society and Culture, edited by Raymond J. DeMallie and Alfonso Ortiz, 3–22. Norman: University of Oklahoma Press.
1999 "George Sword Wrote These": Lakota Culture as Lakota Text. In Theorizing the Americanist Tradition, edited by Lisa Philips Valentine and Regna Darnell, 245–58. Toronto: University of Toronto Press.
2001 Procrustes and the Sioux: David Schneider and the Study of Sioux Kinship. *In* The Cultural Analysis of Kinship: The Legacy of David Schneider, edited by Martin Ottenheimer and Richard Feinberg, 46–56. Champaign: University of Illinois Press.

Dillingham, Betty Ann Wilder

1963 Oklahoma Kickapoo. Ph.D. diss., University of Michigan.

Dinwoodie, David W.

1999 Textuality and the "Voices" of Informants: The Case of Edward Sapir's 1929 Navajo Field School. Anthropological Linguistics 41:165–92.

Dorian, Nancy C., ed.

1989 Investigating Obsolescence: Studies in Language Contraction and Death. New York: Cambridge University Press.

Dowd, Gregory Evans

1992 A Spirited Resistance: The North American Indian Struggle for Unity, 1745–1815. Baltimore: Johns Hopkins University Press.

Driver, Harold

1961 Indians of North America. Chicago: University of Chicago Press.

DuBois, John W.

1986 Self-Evidence and Ritual Speech. *In* Evidentiality: The Linguistic Coding of Epistemology, edited by Wallace Chafe and Johanna Nichols, 313–36. Norwood NJ: Ablex.

Dundes, Alan

1980 Interpreting Folklore. Bloomington: Indiana University Press.

1984 Introduction. *In* Sacred Narrative: Readings in the Theory of Myth, edited by Alan Dundes, 1–3. Berkeley: University of California Press.

Duranti, Alessandro

1992 Oratory. *In* Folklore, Cultural Performances, and Popular Entertainments, edited by Richard Bauman, 154–58. New York: Oxford University Press.

Duranti, Alessandro, and Charles Goodwin, eds.

1992 Rethinking Context: Language as an Interactive Phenomenon. New York: Cambridge University Press.

Eggan, Fred

1937 Historical Changes in the Choctaw Kinship System. American Anthropologist 39:34–52.

1966 The American Indian: Perspectives for the Study of Social Change. Chicago: Aldine.

1975 Essays in Social Anthropology and Ethnology. Chicago: Department of Anthropology, University of Chicago.

Euchees United Cultural, Historical, and Educational Efforts

1997 Euchees Past and Present. Sapulpa OK: E.U.C.H.E.E.

Fairbanks, Charles H.

1978 The Ethno-Archeology of the Florida Seminole. *In* Tacachale: Essays on the Indians of Florida and Southeastern Georgia during the Historic Period, edited by Jerald Milanich and Samuel Proctor, 163–93. Gainesville: University Presses of Florida.

Farley, Gloria

1994 In Plain Sight: Old World Records in Ancient America. Columbus GA: ISAC Press.

Farnell, Brenda

1995 Do You See What I Mean? Plains Indian Sign Talk and the Embodiment of Action. Austin: University of Texas Press.

Feld, Steven

1990 Sound and Sentiment: Birds, Weeping, Poetics, and Song in Kaluli Expression. 2d ed. Philadelphia: University of Pennsylvania Press.

Fenton, William N.

1936 An Outline of Seneca Ceremonies at the Coldspring Longhouse. Yale University Publications in Anthropology 9. New Haven CT: Yale University Press.

1946 Notes on Cherokee Masks and the Eagle Dance Made at Cherokee, North Carolina, 4–5 December 1946. Manuscript held by Gilcrease Museum, Tulsa, Oklahoma.

1951 Introduction: The Concept of Locality and the Program of Iroquois Research. *In* Symposium on Local Diversity in Iroquois Culture, edited by William N. Fenton, Bureau of American Ethnology Bulletin 149, 3–12. Washington DC.

1953 The Iroquois Eagle Dance: An Offshoot of the Calumet Dance. Bureau of American Ethnology Bulletin 156. Washington DC.

1978 Cherokee and Iroquois Connections Revisited. Journal of Cherokee Studies. 3:239–46.

1995 Introduction to *Midwinter Rites of the Cayuga Longhouse*, by Frank Speck. Bison Book ed. Lincoln: University of Nebraska Press.

Fenton, William N., and Gertrude P. Kurath

1951 Feast of the Dead, or Ghost Dance, at Six Nations Reserve, Canada. *In* Symposium on Local Diversity in Iroquois Culture, edited by William N. Fenton, Bureau of American Ethnology Bulletin 149, 143–65. Washington DC.

Fogelson, Raymond D.

1962 The Cherokee Ball Game: A Study in Southeastern Ethnology. Ph.D. diss., University of Pennsylvania.

1971 The Cherokee Ballgame Cycle: An Ethnographer's View. Ethnomusicology 15:327–38.

1977 Cherokee Notions of Power. *In* The Anthropology of Power, edited

by Raymond D. Fogelson and Richard N. Adams, 185–94. New York: Academic Press.
1980 Windigo Goes South: Stoneclad among the Cherokees. *In* Manlike Monsters on Trial, edited by Marjorie M. Halpin and Michael M. Ames, 130–51. Vancouver: University of British Columbia Press.
1984 Who were the Aní-Kutánî? An Excursion into Cherokee Historical Thought. Ethnohistory 31:255–63.
1989 The Ethnohistory of Events and Nonevents. Ethnohistory 36:133–47.
1990 On the "Pettycoat Government" of the Eighteenth-Century Cherokee. *In* Personality and the Cultural Construction of Society: Papers in Honor of Melford E. Spiro, edited by David K. Jordan and Marc J. Swartz, 161–81. Tuscaloosa: University of Alabama Press.
1998 Bringing Home the Fire: Bob Thomas and Cherokee Studies. *In* A Good Cherokee, a Good Anthropologist: Papers in Honor of Robert K. Thomas, edited by Steve Pavlik, 105–18. Los Angeles: American Indian Studies Center, University of California.

Foreman, Grant
1934 The Five Civilized Tribes. Norman: University of Oklahoma Press.

Foster, Michael K.
1974 From the Earth to Beyond the Sky: An Ethnographic Approach to Four Longhouse Speech Events. National Museum of Man, Mercury Series, Canadian Ethnology Service Paper No. 20. Ottawa: National Museums of Canada.
1989 When Words Become Deeds: An Analysis of Three Iroquois Longhouse Speech Events. *In* Explorations in the Ethnography of Speaking. 2d ed., edited by Richard Bauman and Joel Sherzer, 354–67. New York: Cambridge University Press.

Foster, Morris
1991 Being Comanche: A Social History of an American Indian Community. Tucson: University of Arizona Press.

Foster, Morris, Pamela Innes, Pamela Wallace, Jason Baird Jackson, and Tracy Abla, eds.
1995 The Yuchi Petition for Federal Acknowledgment: A Research Report. Unpublished report submitted to the Branch of Acknowledgment and Recognition, Bureau of Indian Affairs, Washington DC.

Fowler, Loretta
1987 Shared Symbols, Contested Meanings: Gros Ventre Culture and History, 1778–1984. Ithaca: Cornell University Press.

Freeman, Ethel Cutler
1961 The Happy Life in the City of Ghosts. Florida Anthropologist 14:23–33.

Galloway, Patricia

1995 Choctaw Genesis 1500–1700. Lincoln: University of Nebraska Press.

Gatschet, Albert S.

1893 Some Mythic Stories of the Yuchi Indians. American Anthropologist 6:279–82.

Gearing, Fred

1962 Priests and Warriors: Social Structures for Cherokee Politics in the 18th Century. American Anthropological Association Memoir 93. Menasha, Wisconsin.

Geertz, Clifford

1973 The Interpretation of Cultures. New York: Basic Books.

1988 Works and Lives: The Anthropologist as Author. Stanford: Stanford University Press.

Gilbert, William Harlen, Jr.

1943 The Eastern Cherokees. Bureau of American Ethnology Anthropological Paper No. 23. Washington DC.

Glassie, Henry

1982 Passing the Time in Ballymenone. Philadelphia: University of Pennsylvania Press.

1994 The Practice and Purpose of History. Journal of American History. 81:961–68.

1995 Tradition. Journal of American Folklore 108:395–412.

Goffman, Erving

1963 Behavior in Public Places: Notes on the Social Organization of Gatherings. New York: The Free Press.

1981 Forms of Talk. Philadelphia: University of Pennsylvania Press.

Grayson, George Washington

1988 A Creek Warrior for the Confederacy: The Autobiography of Chief G. W. Grayson. Edited by W. David Baird. Norman: University of Oklahoma Press.

Green, Michael D.

1982 The Politics of Indian Removal: Creek Government and Society in Crisis. Lincoln: University of Nebraska Press.

Grounds, Richard A.

1996 The Yuchi Community and the Human Genome Diversity Project: Historic and Contemporary Ironies. Cultural Survival Quarterly 20(2):64–68.

Haas, Mary R.

1940 Creek Inter-Town Relations. American Anthropologist 42:479–89.

1974 Multilingualism in the Southeast. Manuscript in the possession of Raymond D. Fogelson.

Hagan, William T.
1961 American Indians. Chicago: University of Chicago Press.

Hamill, James
2000 Being Indian in Northeast Oklahoma. Plains Anthropologist 45:291–303.

Handler, Richard, and Jocelyn Linnekin
1984 Tradition, Genuine or Spurious. Journal of American Folklore 97:273–90.

Harkin, Michael
1997 The Heiltsuks: Dialogues of Culture and History on the Northwest Coast. Lincoln: University of Nebraska Press.

Harring, Sydney L.
1994 Crow Dog's Case: American Indian Sovereignty, Tribal Law, and United States Law in the Nineteenth Century. New York: Cambridge University Press.

Harrison, Simon
1992 Ritual as Intellectual Property. Man 27:225–44.

Henri, Florette
1986 The Southern Indians and Benjamin Hawkins, 1796–1816. Norman: University of Oklahoma Press.

Heth, Charlotte
1975 The Stomp Dance Music of the Oklahoma Cherokee: A Study of Contemporary Practice with Special Reference to the Illinois District Council Ground. Ph.D. diss., University of California, Los Angeles.

Hill, Jane H.
1999 The Meaning of Writing and Text in a Changing Americanist Tradition. *In* Theorizing the Americanist Tradition, edited by Lisa Philips Valentine and Regna Darnell, 181–94. Toronto: University of Toronto Press.

Hill, Jane H., and Judith T. Irvine, eds.
1993 Responsibility and Evidence in Oral Discourse. New York: Cambridge University Press.

Hitchcock, Ethan Allan
1930 A Traveler in Indian Territory: The Journal of Ethan Allen Hitchcock, Late Major-General in the United States Army. Edited by Grant Foreman. Cedar Rapids IA: The Torch Press.

Hobsbawm, Eric, and Terence Ranger, eds.
1983 The Invention of Tradition. New York: Cambridge University Press.

Honko, Lauri

1984 The Problem of Defining Myth. *In* Sacred Narrative: Readings in the Theory of Myth, edited by Alan Dundes, 41–52. Berkeley: University of California Press.

Howard, James H.

1955 Pan-Indian Culture of Oklahoma. Scientific Monthly. 81:215–20.

1961 Cultural Persistence and Cultural Change as Reflected in Oklahoma Seneca-Cayuga Ceremonialism. Plains Anthropologist 6(11):21–30.

1970 Environment and Culture: The Case of the Oklahoma Seneca-Cayuga (Part 2). Oklahoma Anthropological Society Newsletter 18(7):5–21.

1975 The Culture-Area Concept: Does it Diffract Anthropological Light? Indian Historian 8(1):22–26.

1980 Discussion: Social Context of Late Nineteenth and Early Twentieth Century Delaware Religion. Papers in Anthropology 21:153–61.

1981 Shawnee! The Ceremonialism of a Native Indian Tribe and Its Cultural Background. Athens: Ohio University Press.

Howard, James H., and Willie Lena

1984 Oklahoma Seminoles: Medicines, Magic, and Religion. Norman: University of Oklahoma Press.

Hudson, Charles

1975 Vomiting for Purity: Ritual Emesis in the Aboriginal Southeastern United States. *In* Symbols and Society: Essays on Belief Systems in Action, Southern Anthropological Society Proceedings 9, edited by Carol Hill, 93–102. Athens: University of Georgia Press.

1976 The Southeastern Indians. Knoxville: University of Tennessee Press.

1978 Uktena: A Cherokee Anomalous Monster. Journal of Cherokee Studies 3:62–75.

1990 The Juan Pardo Expeditions: Exploration of the Carolinas and Tennessee, 1566–1568. Washington DC: Smithsonian Institution Press.

1997 Knights of Spain, Warriors of the Sun: Hernando de Soto and the South's Ancient Chiefdoms. Athens: University of Georgia Press.

Hymes, Dell

1962 The Ethnography of Speaking. *In* Anthropology and Human Behavior, edited by Thomas Gladwin and William C. Sturtevant, 13–53. Washington DC: The Anthropological Society of Washington.

1968 Foreword to *The Rites of Modernization: Symbolic and Social Aspects of Indonesian Proletarian Drama*, by James Peacock, xi–xvii. Chicago: University of Chicago Press.

1975 Folklore's Nature and the Sun's Myth. Journal of American Folklore 88:345–69.

Innes, Pamela Joan

1997 From One to Many, From Many to One: Speech Communities in the Muskogee Stompdance Population. Ph.D. diss., University of Oklahoma.

Jackson, Jason Baird

1995 Five Documents on the History and Significance of the Native American Church among the Yuchi. *In* The Yuchi Petition for Federal Acknowledgment: A Research Report. Morris Foster, et. al., eds. Report submitted to the Branch of Acknowledgment and Recognition, Bureau of Indian Affairs, Washington DC.

1996a "Everybody Has a Part; Even the Little Bitty Ones": Notes on the Social Organization of Yuchi Ceremonialism. Florida Anthropologist 49:121–30.

1996b Yuchi Custom Ways: Expressions of Tradition in a Southeastern American Indian Society. M.A. Thesis, Indiana University, Bloomington.

1997 The Work of Tradition in Yuchi Oratory. Florida Anthropologist 50:197–202.

1998a Architecture and Hospitality: Ceremonial Ground Camps and Foodways of the Yuchi Indians. Chronicles of Oklahoma 76:172–89.

1998b Dressing for the Dance: Yuchi Ceremonial Clothing. American Indian Art Magazine. 23(3):32–41.

1999 Indian Territory as a Model of Woodland Social History. Paper presented at the American Society for Ethnohistory Meetings, 21 October, Mashantucket, Connecticut.

2000a Customary Uses of Ironweed (*Vernonia fasciculata*) by the Yuchi in Eastern Oklahoma. Economic Botany 54:401–3.

2000b Signaling the Creator: Indian Football as Ritual Performance among the Yuchi and Their Neighbors. Southern Folklore 57:33–64.

2002 Gender Reciprocity and Ritual Speech among the Yuchi. *In* Southern Indians and Anthropologists: Culture, Politics, and Identity, edited by Lisa J. Lefler and Frederic W. Gleach 89–106. Athens: University of Georgia Press.

Jackson, Jason Baird, and Victoria Lindsay Levine

1999 What Garfish Like to Listen to: Music and Social Organization in Eastern Oklahoma. Paper presented at the American Anthropological Association Meetings, 18 November, Chicago.

Jackson, Jason Baird, and Mary S. Linn

2000 Calling in the Members: Linguistic Form and Cultural Context in a Yuchi Ritual Speech Genre. Anthropological Linguistics 42:61–80.

Jackson, Jean

1995 Preserving Indian Culture: Shaman Schools and Ethno-Education in the Vaupés, Columbia. Cultural Anthropology 10:302–29.

Jorgensen, Joseph G.

1972 The Sun Dance Religion: Power for the Powerless. Chicago: University of Chicago Press.

Kilpatrick, Jack F.

1964 Folk Formulas of the Oklahoma Cherokee. Journal of the Folklore Institute 1:214–19.

Kilpatrick, Jack F., and Anna G. Kilpatrick

1964 Friends of Thunder: Folktales of the Oklahoma Cherokees. Dallas: Southern Methodist University Press.

Kimball, Geoffrey D.

1991 Koasati Grammar. Lincoln: University of Nebraska Press.

Kluckhohn, Clyde

1941 Patterning as Exemplified in Navaho Culture. *In* Language, Culture, and Personality: Essays in Memory of Edward Sapir, edited by Leslie Spier, A. Irving Hallowell, and Stanley S. Newman, 109–30. Menasha WI: The Sapir Memorial Publication Fund.

Knoke, David, and James H. Kuklinski

1982 Network Analysis. Sage University Paper Series on Quantitative Applications in the Social Sciences No. 07–028. Beverly Hills CA: Sage.

Kroeber, A. L.

1947 Cultural and Natural Areas of Native North America. University of California Publications in American Archaeology and Ethnology 38. Berkeley: University of California Press.

Kroeber, Karl

1992 American Indian Persistence and Resurgence. boundary 2 19(3):2–25.

Kurath, Gertrude Prokosch

1981 Tutelo Rituals on Six Nations Reserve, Ontario. Special Series No. 5. Ann Arbor: The Society for Ethnomusicology.

Lankford, George

1987 Native American Legends. Little Rock AR: August House.

Latorre, Felipe A., and Dolores L. Latorre

1976 The Mexican Kickapoo Indians. Austin: University of Texas Press.

Lee, Danya Bowker, ed.
1995 Remaining Ourselves: Music and Tribal Memory. Oklahoma City: The State Arts Council of Oklahoma.

Levine, Victoria Lindsay
1991 Arzelie Langley and a Lost Pantribal Tradition. *In* Ethnomusicology and Modern Music History, edited by Stephen Blum, Philip C. Bohlman, and Daniel M. Neuman, 190–206. Urbana: University of Illinois Press.

Lévi-Strauss, Claude
1969 The Elementary Structures of Kinship. Translated by James Harle Bell and John Richard von Sturmer and edited by Rodney Needham. Boston: Beacon Press.
1987 Introduction to the Work of Marcel Mauss. Translated by Felicity Baker. London: Routledge and Kegan Paul.

Lewis, Thomas M. N., and Madeline Kneberg
1949 Hiwassee Island: An Archaeological Account of Four Tennessee Indian Peoples. Knoxville: University of Tennessee Press.

Linn, Mary S.
1996 Positionals in Yuchi/Euchee. *In* 1994 Mid-American Linguistics Conference Papers, vol. 2, edited by Frances Ingemann, 576–85. Lawrence: Department of Linguistics, University of Kansas.
1997 Yuchi and Non-Yuchi: A Living Classification. Florida Anthropologist. 50(4):189–96.
2001 A Grammar of Euchee (Yuchi). Ph.D. diss., University of Kansas, Lawrence.

Mahan, Joseph B.
1992 North American Sun Kings: Keepers of the Flame. Columbus GA: Institute for the Study of American Cultures Press.

Malinowski, Bronislaw
1961 Argonauts of the Western Pacific. New York: E. P. Dutton.

Martin, Jack B., and Margaret McKane Mauldin
2000 A Dictionary of Creek/Muskogee. Lincoln: University of Nebraska Press.

Martin, Joel W.
1991 Sacred Revolt: The Muskogees' Struggle for a New World. Boston: Beacon Press.

Matern, Dorothy Ann
1996 Native American Culture Change: History of the Yuchi Nation. M.A. Thesis, California State University, Stanislaus.

Mauss, Marcel

1990 The Gift: The Form and Reason for Exchange in Archaic Societies. Translated by W. D. Halls. New York: W. W. Norton.

McDonald, Barry

1997 Tradition as Personal Relationship. Journal of American Folklore 110:47–67.

McDowell, John H.

1990 The Community-Building Mission of Kamsá Ritual Language. *In* Native Latin American Cultures through Their Discourse, edited by Ellen B. Basso, 67–84. Bloomington: Indiana University Folklore Institute.

Medford, Claude

1970 Songs of the Muskogee Creek, Part 2. Recording with liner notes. Indian House 3002.

Miller, Jay

1980 A Structuralist Analysis of the Delaware Big House Rite. Papers in Anthropology 21:107–33.

1997 Old Religion Among the Delawares: The Gamwing (Big House Rite). Ethnohistory 44:113–34.

Mithun, Marianne

1989 The Incipient Obsolescence of Polysynthesis: Cayuga in Ontario and Oklahoma. *In* Investigating Obsolescence: Studies in Language Contraction and Death, edited by Nancy Dorian, 243–57. Cambridge: Cambridge University Press.

de Montellano, Bernard Ortiz, Gabriel Haslip-Viera, and Warren Barbour

1997 They Were NOT Here before Columbus: Afrocentric Hyperdiffusionism in the 1990s. Ethnohistory 44:199–234.

Mooney, James

1890 Cherokee Theory and Practice of Medicine. Journal of American Folk-Lore 3:44–50.

1900 Myths of the Cherokee. Nineteenth Annual Report of the Bureau of American Ethnology, 11–576. Washington DC.

Moore, Robert E.

1993 Performance Form and the Voices of Characters in Five Versions of the Wasco Coyote Cycle. *In* Reflexive Language: Reported Speech and Metapragmatics, edited by John Lucy, 213–40. New York: Cambridge University Press.

Nettl, Bruno

1954 North American Indian Musical Styles. Memoirs of the American Folklore Society 45. Philadelphia: American Folklore Society.

Newcomb, W. W.
1955 A Note on Cherokee-Delaware Pan-Indianism. American Anthropologist 57:1041–45.

Olbrechts, Frans M.
1927 Cherokee Games. Manuscript no. 4600, National Anthropological Archives, Smithsonian Institution. Washington DC.

Opler, Morris
1952 The Creek "Town" and the Problem of Creek Indian Political Reorganization. *In* Human Problems in Technological Change: A Casebook, edited by Edward H. Spicer, 165–80. New York: Russell Sage Foundation.
1972 The Creek Indian Towns in 1937. Papers in Anthropology 13:1–116.

Ortiz, Alfonso
1989 Some Cultural Meanings of Corn in Aboriginal North America. Northeast Indian Quarterly, Spring/Summer:64–73.

Paredes, Anthony J.
1992 Federal Recognition and the Poarch Creek Indians. *In* Indians of the Southeastern United States in the Late 20th Century, edited by J. Anthony Paredes, 120–39. Tuscaloosa: University of Alabama Press.

Parmentier, Richard
1994a The Political Function of Reported Speech. *In* Signs in Society: Studies in Semiotic Anthropology, 70–97. Bloomington: Indiana University Press.
1994b Transactional Symbolism in Belaun Mortuary Rites. *In* Signs in Society: Studies in Semiotic Anthropology, 47–69. Bloomington: Indiana University Press.

Piker, Joshua Aaron
1998 "Peculiarly Connected": The Creek Town of Oakfuskee and the Study of Colonial American Communities, 1708–1785. Ph.D. Diss., Cornell University.

Rementer, Jim
1993 Pahsaheman – The Lenape Indian Football Game. Bulletin of the Archaeological Society of New Jersey 48:52–55.

Roark, Sue N.
1978 Delaware Moral Economy: Transaction and Transformation in Ritual Exchange. Acts of the Forty-First International Congress of Americanists 5:327-33.

Roark-Calnek, Sue N.
1977 Indian Way in Oklahoma: Transactions in Honor and Legitimacy. Ph.D. diss., Bryn Mawr College.

Robbins, Lester E.

1976 The Persistence of Traditional Religious Practices Among Creek Indians. Ph.D. diss., Southern Methodist University.

Russell, Orpha B.

1959 Notes on Samuel William Brown, Jr., Yuchi Chief. Chronicles of Oklahoma 37:497–501.

Sahlins, Marshall

1993 Goodbye to Triste Tropes: Ethnography in the Context of Modern World History. University of Chicago Record 27(3):2–7.

1995 How "Natives" Think: About Captain Cook, for Example. Chicago: University of Chicago Press.

Sapir, Edward

1985 Cultural Anthropology and Psychiatry. *In* Selected Writings in Language, Culture, and Personality, edited by David Mandelbaum, 509–22. Berkeley: University of California Press.

Sattler, Richard

1996 Remnants, Renegades, and Runaways: Seminole Ethnogenesis Reconsidered. *In* History, Power, and Identity: Ethnogenesis in the Americas, 1492–1992, edited by Jonathan D. Hill, 36–69. Iowa City: University of Iowa Press.

Saunt, Claudio

1999a An American Family: The Graysons of the Creek Nation and the Legacy of Race. Paper presented at the 1999 American Society for Ethnohistory Meetings, 21 October, Mashantucket, Connecticut.

1999b A New Order of Things: Property, Power, and the Transformation of the Creek Indians, 1733–1816. New York: Cambridge University Press.

Schieffelin, Edward L., and Robert Crittenden (with Bryant Allen, Stephen Frankel, Paul Sillitoe, Lisette Josephides, and Marc Schlitz)

1991 Like People You See in a Dream: First Contact in Six Papuan Societies. Stanford: Stanford University Press.

Schneider, David M.

1980 American Kinship. 2d ed. Chicago: University of Chicago Press.

Schultz, Jack M.

1999 The Seminole Baptist Churches of Oklahoma: Maintaining a Traditional Community. Norman: University of Oklahoma Press.

Schupman, Edwin, Jr.

1984 Current Musical Practices of the Creek Indians as Examined through the Green Corn Ceremonies of the Tulsa Cedar River and Fish Pond Stomp Grounds. M. M. thesis, Miami University, Oxford, Ohio.

Schutz, Noel William, Jr.

1975 The Study of Shawnee Myth in Ethnographic and Ethnohistorical Perspective. Ph.D. diss., Indiana University, Bloomington.

Sherzer, Joel

1983 Kuna Ways of Speaking. Austin: University of Texas Press.

Shimony, Annemarie Anrod

1994 Conservativism Among the Iroquois at the Six Nations Reserve. Syracuse NY: Syracuse University Press.

Silverstein, Michael

1993 Review of *Language and Symbolic Power*, by Pierre Bourdieu. American Ethnologist 20:648–49.

1996 Encountering Language and Languages of Encounter in North American Ethnohistory. Journal of Linguistic Anthropology 6:126–44.

Silverstein, Michael, and Greg Urban

1996 The Natural History of Discourse. *In* Natural Histories of Discourse, edited by Michael Silverstein and Greg Urban, 1–17. Chicago: University of Chicago Press.

Singer, Milton

1991 Semiotics of Cities, Selves, and Cultures: Explorations in Semiotic Anthropology. New York: Mouton de Gruyter.

Smith, Hale G., and Mark Gottlob

1978 Spanish-Indian Relationships: Synoptic History and Archeological Evidence, 1500–1763. *In* Tacachale: Essays on the Indians of Florida and Southeastern Georgia during the Historic Period, edited by Jerald Milanich and Samuel Proctor, 1–18. Gainesville: University Presses of Florida.

Smith, Marvin T.

1987 Archaeology of Aboriginal Culture Change in the Interior Southeast: Depopulation during the Early Historic Period. Gainesville: University Press of Florida.

Smith, Marvin T., and David J. Hally

1992 Chiefly Behavior: Evidence from Sixteenth Century Spanish Accounts. *In* Lords of the Southeast: Social Inequality and the Native Elites of Southeastern North America, Archeological Papers of the American Anthropological Association 3, edited by Alex W. Barker and Timothy R. Pauketat, 99–109. Washington DC: American Anthropological Association.

Speck, Frank G.

1905 A Comparative Study of the Native Mythology of the South-Eastern United States. M.A. thesis, Columbia University.

1907a The Creek Indians of Taskigi Town. Memoirs of the American Anthropological Association 2(2). Washington DC.

1907b Notes on the Ethnology of the Osage Indians. Transactions of the Museum of Science and Art, University of Pennsylvania 2:159–71. Philadelphia.

1909 Ethnology of the Yuchi Indians. Anthropological Publications of the University Museum, University of Pennsylvania 1(1). Philadelphia.

1911 Ceremonial Songs of the Creek and Yuchi Indians. Anthropological Publications of the University Museum, University of Pennsylvania 1(2). Philadelphia.

1931 A Study of the Delaware Bighouse Ceremony. Harrisburg: Pennsylvania Historical Commission.

1937 Oklahoma Delaware Ceremonies, Feasts and Dances. Memoirs of the American Philosophical Society 7. Philadelphia.

1939 Catawba Religious Beliefs, Mortuary Customs, and Dances. Primitive Man 12:21–57.

1942 The Tutelo Spirit Adoption Ceremony: Reclothing the Living in the Name of the Dead. Harrisburg: Pennsylvania Historical Commission.

1995 Midwinter Rites of the Cayuga Long House. Lincoln: University of Nebraska Press.

Speck, Frank G., and Leonard Broom (in collaboration with Will West Long)

1983 Cherokee Dance and Drama. Norman: University of Oklahoma Press.

Spicer, Edward

1971 Persistent Cultural Systems: A Comparative Study of Identity Systems That Can Adapt to Contrasting Environments. Science 174:795–800.

1992 Nations of a State. boundary 2 19(3):26–48.

Spoehr, Alexander

1938 Fieldnotes on Southeastern Indian Social Organization. Department of Anthropology Archives, Field Museum of Natural History, Chicago.

1941 Creek Inter-Town Relations. American Anthropologist 43:132–33.

Stewart, Omer C.

1987 Peyote Religion: A History. Norman: University of Oklahoma Press.

Sturtevant, William C.

1955 The Mikasuki Seminole: Medical Beliefs and Practices. Ph.D. diss., Yale University.

1978 The Last of the South Florida Aborigines. *In* Tacachale: Essays on the Indians of Florida and Southeastern Georgia during the Historic Period, edited by Jerald Milanich and Samuel Proctor, 141–62. Gainesville: University Presses of Florida.

1988 Creek into Seminole. *In* North American Indians in Historical Perspective, edited by Eleanor Burke Leacock and Nancy Oestreich Lurie, 92–128. Prospect Heights IL: Waveland.

Swanton, John R.

1907 Mythology of the Indians of Louisiana and the Texas Coast. Journal of American Folklore 20:285–89.

1912 A Foreword on the Social Organization of the Creek Indians. American Anthropologist 14:593–99.

1919 Identity of the Westo Indians. American Anthropologist 21:213–16.

1922 Early History of the Creek Indians and Their Neighbors. Bureau of American Ethnology Bulletin 73. Washington DC.

1928a Aboriginal Culture of the Southeast. Forty-Second Annual Report of the Bureau of American Ethnology, 673–726. Washington DC.

1928b Religious Beliefs and Medical Practices of the Creek Indians. Forty-Second Annual Report of the Bureau of American Ethnology, 473–672. Washington DC.

1928c Social and Religious Beliefs and Usages of the Chickasaw Indians. Forty-Fourth Annual Report of the Bureau of American Ethnology, 169–273. Washington DC.

1928d Social Organization and Social Usages of the Indians of the Creek Confederacy. Forty-Second Annual Report of the Bureau of American Ethnology, 23–472. Washington DC.

1929 Myths and Tales of the Southeastern Indians. Bureau of American Ethnology Bulletin 88. Washington DC.

1946 The Indians of the Southeastern United States. Bureau of American Ethnology Bulletin 137. Washington DC.

Taylor, Lyda Averill

n.d. Manuscript on Koasati Town. Frank G. Speck Papers, Box 15, American Philosophical Society, Philadelphia.

1940 Plants Used as Curatives by Certain Southeastern Tribes. Cambridge: Botanical Museum of Harvard University.

Tedlock, Dennis

1983 The Spoken Word and the Work of Interpretation. Philadelphia: University of Pennsylvania Press.

1992 Ethnopoetics. *In* Folklore, Cultural Performances, and Popular Entertainments: A Communications-Centered Handbook, edited by Richard Bauman, 81–85. New York: Oxford University Press.

Thomas, Cyrus

1907 Timpoochee Barnard. *In* Handbook of American Indians North of Mexico, edited by Frederick Webb Hodge, Bureau of American Ethnology Bulletin 30, part 2, 752. Washington DC.

Thomas, Robert

1961 The Redbird Smith Movement. *In* Symposium on Cherokee and Iroquois Culture, edited by William N. Fenton and John Gulick, Bureau of American Ethnology Bulletin 180, 161–66. Washington DC.

1962 Cherokee Values and World View. Manuscript in the author's possession.

1990 Audiotape Notes on Cherokee Ethnography. Recording and transcript in the possession of Raymond D. Fogelson.

Timberlake, Henry

1765 The Memoirs of Lieutenant Henry Timberlake. London: Privately printed.

Trigger, Bruce G., ed.

1978 Northeast. Handbook of North American Indians Volume 15. William C. Sturtevant, gen. ed. Washington: Smithsonian Institution.

Tuggle, W. O.

1973 Shem, Ham, and Japheth: The Papers of W. O. Tuggle, Comprising his Indian Diary, Sketches, and Observations, Myths and Washington Journal in the Territory and at the Capital, 1879–1882. Edited by Eugene Current-Garcia and Dorothy B. Hatfield. Athens: University of Georgia Press.

Turner, Victor

1975 Ritual as Communication and Potency: A Ndembu Case Study. *In* Symbols and Society: Essays on Belief Systems in Action, Southern Anthropological Society Proceedings 9, edited by Carole E. Hill, 58–81. Athens: University of Georgia Press.

Urban, Greg

1981 Agent- and Patient-Centricity in Myth. Journal of American Folklore 94:323–44.

1991 A Discourse-Centered Approach to Culture: Native South American Myths and Rituals. Austin: University of Texas Press.

1993 The Represented Functions of Speech in Shokleng Myth. *In* Reflexive Language: Reported Speech and Metapragmatics, edited by John A. Lucy, 241–59. New York: Cambridge University Press.

1994 The Social Organizations of the Southeast. *In* North American Indian Anthropology: Essays on Society and Culture, edited by Raymond J. DeMallie and Alfonso Ortiz, 172–93. Norman: University of Oklahoma Press.

1996 Metaphysical Community: The Interplay of the Senses and the Intellect. Austin: University of Texas Press.

Usner, Daniel H.

1998 American Indians in the Lower Mississippi Valley: Social and Economic Histories. Lincoln: University of Nebraska Press.

Valentine, Lisa Phillips

1995 Making It Their Own: Severn Ojibwe Communicative Practices. Toronto: University of Toronto Press.

Vennum, Thomas, Jr.

1994 American Indian Lacrosse: Little Brother of War. Washington DC: Smithsonian Institution Press.

Voegelin, C. F.

1936 The Shawnee Female Deity. Yale University Publications in Anthropology 10. New Haven CT: Yale University Press.

Voegelin, C. F., and Erminie W. Voegelin

1935 Shawnee Name Groups. American Anthropologist 37:617–35.

Voegelin, Erminie Wheeler

1944 Mortuary Customs of the Shawnee and Other Eastern Tribes. Prehistory Research Series 2(4):226–444. Indianapolis: Indiana Historical Society.

Vogt, Evon

1992 Tortillas for the Gods: A Symbolic Analysis of Zinacanteco Rituals. Norman: University of Oklahoma Press.

Vološinov, V. N.

1986 Marxism and the Philosophy of Language. Translated by Ladislav Matejka and I. R. Titunik. Cambridge: Harvard University Press.

von Reck, Philip Georg Friedrich

1990 Von Reck's Voyage: Drawings and Journal of Philip Georg Friedrich von Reck. Edited by Kristian Hvidt. Savannah GA: Beehive Press.

Wagner, Günter

1931 Yuchi Tales. Publications of the American Ethnological Society 13. New York: G. E. Stechert and Co.

1932 Entwicklung and Verbreitung des Peyote-Kultes. Baessler-Archiv 15:59–139.

Wahrhaftig, Albert
1968 The Tribal Cherokee Population in Eastern Oklahoma. Current Anthropology 9:510–18.

Walker, Amelia Bell
1981 Tribal Towns, Stomp Grounds, and Land: Oklahoma Creeks After Removal. Chicago Anthropology Exchange 14:50–69.

Walker, Willard
1981 Cherokee Curing and Conjuring, Identity, and the Southeastern Co-Tradition. *In* Persistent Peoples: Cultural Enclaves in Perspective, edited by George Pierre Castille and Gilbert Kushner, 86–105. Tucson: University of Arizona Press.

Wallace, Anthony F. C.
1970 Culture and Personality. 2d ed. New York: Random House.
1993 The Long, Bitter Trail: Andrew Jackson and the Indians. New York: Hill and Wang.

Wallace, Pamela
1993 The 1898 Creek Census Cards: A Demographic/Social Structure Analysis of the Yuchi Indians. M. A. Thesis, University of Oklahoma.
1995 Yuchi Intermediaries: 19th and 20th Century. *In* The Yuchi Petition for Federal Acknowledgment: A Research Report. Edited by Morris Foster, et. al. Submitted to the Branch of Acknowledgment and Recognition, Bureau of Indian Affairs.
1996 Yuchi History through 1800. Manuscript in the author's possession.
1998 Yuchi Social History Since World War II: Political Symbolism in Ethnic Identity. Ph.D. Diss., University of Oklahoma.
forthcoming Indian Claims Commission: Political Complexity and Contrasting Concepts of Identity. Ethnohistory.

Warde, Mary Jane
1999 George Washington Grayson and the Creek Nation, 1843–1920. Norman: University of Oklahoma Press.

Wax, Murray L.
1982 Research Reciprocity Rather Than Informed Consent in Fieldwork. *In* The Ethics of Social Research: Fieldwork, Regulation, and Publication, edited by Joan E. Saber, 33–48. New York: Springer-Verlag.

Weisman, Brent Richards
1989 Like Beads on a String: A Culture History of the Seminole Indians in North Peninsular Florida. Tuscaloosa: University of Alabama Press.

White, Richard

1991 The Middle Ground: Indians, Empires, and the Republics in the Great Lakes Region, 1650–1815. New York: Cambridge University Press.

White Deer, Gary

1995 Pretty Shellshaker. *In* Remaining Ourselves: Music and Tribal Memory, edited by Danya Bowker Lee, 10–12. Oklahoma City: The State Arts Council of Oklahoma.

Wilson, David, ed.

2000 OIMC Membership and Average Attendance Increases. Advocate 14(3). [An archived version of this print publication was consulted online at *www.gbgm-umc.org/oimc/news.htm* on 13 January 2001.]

Wissler, Clark, and D. C. Duvall

1908 Mythology of the Blackfoot. Anthropological Papers of the American Museum of Natural History 2(1). New York: American Museum of Natural History.

Witthoft, John

1949 Green Corn Ceremonialism in the Eastern Woodlands. Occasional Contributions from the Museum of Anthropology of the University of Michigan 13. Ann Arbor: University of Michigan Press.

1983 Cherokee Beliefs Concerning Death. Journal of Cherokee Studies 8(2):68–72.

Wolf, Eric

1994 Facing Power: Old Insights, New Questions. *In* Assessing Cultural Anthropology, edited by Robert Borofsky, 218–28. New York: McGraw-Hill.

Yankah, Kwesi

1995 Speaking for the Chief. Bloomington: Indiana University Press.

INDEX

IN *STUDIES IN THE ANTHROPOLOGY OF NORTH AMERICAN INDIANS*

The Four Hills of Life: Northern Arapaho Knowledge and Life Movement
By Jeffrey D. Anderson

One Hundred Years of Old Man Sage: An Arapaho Life
By Jeffrey D. Anderson

The Semantics of Time: Aspectual Categorization in Koyukon Athabaskan
By Melissa Axelrod

Lushootseed Texts: An Introduction to Puget Salish Narrative Aesthetics
Edited by Crisca Bierwert

People of The Dalles: The Indians of Wascopam Mission
By Robert Boyd

The Lakota Ritual of the Sweat Lodge: History and Contemporary Practice
By Raymond A. Bucko

From the Sands to the Mountain: Change and Persistence in a Southern Paiute Community
By Pamela A. Bunte and Robert J. Franklin

A Grammar of Comanche
By Jean Ormsbee Charney

Reserve Memories: The Power of the Past in a Chilcotin Community
By David W. Dinwoodie

Haida Syntax (2 vols.)
By John Enrico

Northern Haida Songs
By John Enrico and Wendy Bross Stuart

Powhatan's World and Colonial Virginia: A Conflict of Cultures
By Frederic W. Gleach

Native Languages of the Southeastern United States
Edited by Heather K. Hardy and Janine Scancarelli

The Heiltsuks: Dialogues of Culture and History on the Northwest Coast
By Michael E. Harkin

Prophecy and Power among the Dogrib Indians
By June Helm

Corbett Mack: The Life of a Northern Paiute
As told by Michael Hittman

The Canadian Sioux
By James H. Howard

Yuchi Ceremonial Life: Performance, Meaning, and Tradition in a Contemporary American Indian Community
By Jason Baird Jackson

The Comanches: A History, 1706–1875
By Thomas W. Kavanagh

Koasati Dictionary
By Geoffrey D. Kimball with the assistance of Bel Abbey, Martha John, and Ruth Poncho

Koasati Grammar
By Geoffrey D. Kimball with the assistance of Bel Abbey, Nora Abbey, Martha John, Ed John, and Ruth Poncho

The Salish Language Family: Reconstructing Syntax
By Paul D. Kroeber

The Medicine Men: Oglala Sioux Ceremony and Healing
By Thomas H. Lewis

A Dictionary of Creek / Muskogee
By Jack B. Martin and Margaret McKane Mauldin

Wolverine Myths and Visions: Dene Traditions from Northern Alberta
Edited by Patrick Moore and Angela Wheelock

Ceremonies of the Pawnee
By James R. Murie
Edited by Douglas R. Parks

Archaeology and Ethnohistory of the Omaha Indians: The Big Village Site
By John M. O'Shea and John Ludwickson

Traditional Narratives of the Arikara Indians (4 vols.)
By Douglas R. Parks

Osage Grammar
By Carolyn Quintero

They Treated Us Just Like Indians: The Worlds of Bennett County, South Dakota
By Paula L. Wagoner

A Grammar of Kiowa
By Laurel J. Watkins with the assistance of Parker McKenzie

Native Languages and Language Families of North America
(folded study map and wall display map)
Compiled by Ives Goddard